The Global Environment of Business

Frederick Guy

OXFORD

UNIVERSITY PRESS

OXFORD

UNIVERSITY PRESS

Great Clarendon Street, Oxford ox2 6DP
Oxford University Press is a department of the University of Oxford.
It furthers the University's objective of excellence in research, scholarship,
and education by publishing worldwide in

Oxford New York

Auckland Cape Town Dar es Salaam Hong Kong Karachi
Kuala Lumpur Madrid Melbourne Mexico City Nairobi
New Delhi Shanghai Taipei Toronto

With offices in Argentina Austria Brazil Chile Czech Republic France Greece
Guatemala Hungary Italy Japan Poland Portugal Singapore
South Korea Switzerland Thailand Turkey Ukraine Vietnam

Oxford is a registered trade mark of Oxford University Press
in the UK and in certain other countries

Published in the United States
by Oxford University Press Inc., New York

© Frederick Guy 2009

British Library Cataloguing in Publication Data

Data available

Library of Congress Cataloging in Publication Data

Data available

Typeset by SPI Publisher Services Ltd, Pondicherry, India
Printed in Great Britain
on acid-free paper by
CPI Antony Rowe, Chippenham, Wiltshire

ISBN 978-0-19-920662-9 (Hbk.)   978-0-19-920663-6 (Pbk.)

1 3 5 7 9 10 8 6 4 2

For
George Alden Guy (1916–2006)
Ann Dexter Jencks Guy (1925–2008)
and
Leonardo Guy (2006–)

⌐ ACKNOWLEDGMENTS

The tracks of my teachers both at the University of California at Berkeley and the University of Massachusetts, Amherst, will be plain throughout this book. More immediately, the book originated in a course I teach to Masters' students in the Department of Management at Birkbeck College in London. Their observations both in the classroom and in term papers have often led me to material I hadn't known about, and much of that is here. In recent years, discussions with many friends and colleagues, in particular Suma Athreye, Michel Goyer, and Soo Hee Lee have contributed a great deal to both my teaching and this book. My wife, Simona Iammarino, has similarly contributed both ideas and scholarship, and so many other things as well. David Musson and Matthew Derbyshire at Oxford University Press have been extremely patient. So much help, all I have left to claim is the errors!

CONTENTS

LIST OF FIGURES

LIST OF TABLES

1 Introduction

This book aims to help the reader understand the economic, political, and technological context in which international business operates. That is a lot to bite off when reading (or writing) one book. In order to make the material manageable, I have approached it from three different angles, progressing from one to the next; we can call them "global," "historical," and "comparative."

The first, or global, part of the book (Chapters 2–6), deals with the multinational corporation and with the politics and economics of international business. I ask why it is that many businesses, in both manufacturing and services, now operate so freely across international borders: why do they make everyday products out of parts from several different countries, enter into joint ventures with companies on the other side of the world, and outsource customer services to people who will never meet their customers? Easy answers to this would be "because they can" or "because it is profitable": improved transport and communication have effectively reduced distances. That does not tell us, however, why national governments have chosen to allow it. It was in the late nineteenth and early twentieth centuries that advancing technology made it possible and profitable for manufacturing companies to operate internationally; in that case, far from opening up, the international system closed down, restricting international trade and investment. Today, international transport and communication are even better, but that is a matter of degree, not of kind. Why has the response of national governments been different? Chapter 2 offers one set of answers to this question, focusing on technological change and the multinational corporation. In addition to improved transport and communications, we see that the *pace* of technological change, the difficulty of transferring technological knowledge from one place to another, and changes in the way production systems are organized, all have effects on the motivation for corporations to organize internationally, and on the willingness of national governments to cooperate.

Should we call these processes "globalization"? We might, but the word has already assumed wider connotations: it includes, in some definitions, almost everything that is happening today. In Chapter 3, I argue that such an umbrella term cannot help us understand what is happening in the world, or what different paths are plausible in the near future, or how we – "we" as individuals, as corporations, as states, or as human society – can affect the course of events. Putting all of today's developments under a single umbrella term like "globalization" invariably encourages us to regard them as a single composite phenomenon, and to view that phenomenon as part of an inexorable process. I therefore recommend avoiding that term, and using more narrowly drawn, and analytically useful, terms instead.

Chapter 4 reviews some basic concepts in international trade theory, and in that part of the economic theory of production called "increasing returns." All of these concepts are employed in various different chapters of the book, but not in a technically demanding manner.

Chapter 5 returns to the question of how the rules of international trade and investment are determined. Compared with Chapter 2, this chapter does not deal with the multinational corporation in as much detail, but focuses more on the power of the nation-state. I address the role of hegemonic states, of political coalitions within states, and of changes in transport costs and commodity prices. Chapter 6 continues this discussion but focuses on the question of why states sometimes acquire empires. Both Chapters 5 and 6 deal with political theory, and historical cases ranging from the mid-nineteenth century to the present day are illustrated. This gives us a range from a flowering of free trade within Europe (mid-nineteenth century); to rising tariff barriers and expanding empires (late nineteenth century); to a new rise in international trade and investment, followed by the catastrophic collapse of the international economic system (early twentieth century); to the gradual re-liberalization of the world economy, accompanied by the amalgamation of nation-states into regional blocs, and wars to control the oil supply (late twentieth century and present).

The second section (Chapters 7–10) shifts the focus from the international system to national business systems in a historical perspective. Chapter 7 deals with the period from the first industrial revolution in Britain in the late eighteenth century to the second industrial revolution in Britain, the US, and Germany in the late nineteenth century. The first of these was dominated by cotton textile manufacturing, saw the introduction of factories and rapid urbanization, and was tied up with colonies and slavery (to supply both cotton and sugar) and the exploitation of coal. The second was marked by the invention of methods for producing steel cheaply and in large quantities, and by the emergence of large industrial corporations. This chapter also introduces theories of technologically driven long waves (Kondratiefs).

Chapter 8 traces the development of large corporations in the late nineteenth and early twentieth centuries: the production technologies they used, their role in system-atizing and processing information, and their efforts to both stabilize and monopolize markets. It considers different explanations for the rapid rise of large corporations in the nineteenth century; it also examines how heavy investment in special-purpose equip-ment accentuated the problem of stabilizing the economy.

Chapter 9 deals with the mass production economy of the mid-twentieth century, in particular the American "Fordist" institutions of economic management. It follows this story up to the crisis of Fordism – slow productivity growth, inflation, and social conflict – in the 1970s.

Chapters 10–14 are comparative: they deal with different business systems in the world today. The focus is on the interplay between business organization and national political and legal institutions. Chapter 10 deals with the much different responses in Japan and the US to the crisis of mass production. It considers Japan's flexible mass production system as well as America's form of post-Fordism. The latter sees a polarization of the economy between knowledge- and information-intensive industries on the one hand, and low-wage services on the other; it has also brought "financialization," which entails an active market for corporate control, a rhetorical priority to shareholder value over all other corporate objectives, and elevated pay for both corporate executives and financial market operators.

Chapter 11 compares the business and political systems of the leading industrial countries. This includes differences in labor markets (broadly construed to include such topics as job training, employment, and social insurance); capital markets and corporate governance; and relationships between companies, both vertically along the supply chain and horizontally among competitors in an industry. The analytical framework of the chapter is that of "varieties of capitalism," which sees national institutional differences as underpinning comparative advantage in particular kinds of production processes and hence particular kinds of products.

Chapter 12 adds a local geographical dimension to the comparative framework. It looks at how companies located in specialized clusters work together – or fail to do so.

Chapter 13 turns from the richer and longer established industrial countries to newly industrialized ones such as South Korea and Taiwan, and now India and China. It has not been easy for any country to join the exclusive club of rich industrial nations. We are interested in how countries such as South Korea and Taiwan managed to do so in the late twentieth century, and also in the challenges facing countries such as India and China today. Chapter 14 examines some "poverty traps" that can stifle a country's development. In both these chapters, we ask whether there are simple policies a country can adopt to improve its economic fortunes; whether deeper institutional changes are needed, and if so how these can come about; and what a country's fortunes today may owe to its history – in which case, change becomes problematic indeed.

The concluding chapter (Chapter 15) returns to the causes of international economic integration, raised in Chapters 2–5. Its focus, however, is the future: what balance will be found between global and regional integration, and the likely effects on this balance of efforts to halt or mitigate global warming.

While my personal biases will probably be apparent to readers, I think that I have managed to maintain sufficient analytical detachment that some who share my biases will be frustrated by, say, treatment of imperial expansion as a rational business decision from the standpoint of the imperial power. On that particular point, my interests here are, first, to explain the choice rather than judge it and, second, to understand the lasting effects may be on the colony's economic development. Hunger, inequality, global warming...they're all here somewhere, but you'll have to bring your own anger. My aims here are to comprehend some large patterns in the development of the world's business systems, to understand rival explanations for these patterns, and to practice the use of some analytical tools that can be used to study the social world.

Part I
Causes of International Economic Integration

2 Technological Change and International Production

In recent decades, the international economy has rapidly become more integrated. Trade in goods and services, cross-border investment, and the organization of production networks across borders, all have blossomed. This chapter explores the nature of these developments. It also considers some explanations for what has *caused* the rise in international economic integration. But there's no simple answer to the causation question (or perhaps it would be better to say that there are too many simple answers, several of which have something to add to our understanding of events), and some pieces of the puzzle will have to wait for later chapters. Here I will focus on the effects of technological change.

2.1. Cars: From national to international markets

Let us begin by considering the changes in one important industry. Between the end of World War II and the 1980s, it seemed as if every country wanted its own automobile industry. Almost all of the cars made or sold in Japan, France, or Italy were the products of companies based in those countries; so were most of the parts from which the cars were made. Most of the cars sold in the US and Canada were produced by American companies, with negotiated shares of production taking place on each side of the border. In Britain and West (as it then was) Germany, the markets were shared between domestic and foreign companies, but even the cars sold by the leading foreign companies – Ford and General Motors – were made by their local divisions, mostly from locally made parts, and even designed and engineered separately for European markets.

National markets were kept separate by high tariff barriers, along with transportation costs, and political non-tariff barriers such as incompatible safety regulations. The protected markets kept the car companies and their suppliers profitable; they also maintained stable industrial jobs in assembly, in the manufacture of parts, and in many of the industries supplying the parts makers, like steel, electrical components, glass, and plastic.

This pattern was not restricted to the automobile industry. There was a good deal of international trade, but in comparison with today it was concentrated in raw materials, agricultural commodities, and in manufactured goods aimed at smaller markets – capital goods and luxury goods.

Poorer countries, and smaller ones, were importing many manufactured consumer goods. They saw in the large industrial countries a model of industrialization, prosperity, and a greater degree of self-reliance. Following World War II, poor countries around the world adopted policies of import substitution industrialization (ISI). The name tells the story: it is an industrialization strategy based on making domestically products that you have been importing.

In mass production processes, the final stage of manufacture consists of the assembly of parts. As a strategy, ISI for automobiles began with assembly plants, with the aim of working backwards up the supply chain to make more and more the parts domestically as well. But where was the assembly plant to come from? Where would the designs, technologies, parts, and the management needed to make it all function, be obtained?

In each and every case or ISI in the automobile industry, the answer to these questions involved a major role for an existing multinational car company. Some countries invited multinational automobile companies to come and set up the entire business. Companies such as Volkswagen, Ford, General Motors, Renault, and Fiat made deals to assemble cars in Mexico, Argentina, Brazil, Spain, Australia, Poland – and also in much smaller markets, such as Venezuela, Israel, and Egypt. Often, the local operation was in the name of a company with substantial domestic ownership – 51 per cent of the shares in Volkswagen de Mexico were owned by Mexican nationals, 49 per cent by Volkswagen AB. Despite the domestic majority interest, the company functioned as a subsidiary of the multinational parent.

In other cases, governments were more intent on developing domestic car companies. Sometimes they took the state ownership route, sometimes the private. Proton in Malaysia, Lada in the former Soviet Union, Yugo in what was then Yugoslavia, Trabant in East Germany, SEAT in Spain, Skoda in the then Czechoslovakia, the automotive operations of Hyundai, Daewoo, and Kia in South Korea, and so on. Even in these cases, however, the technologies and designs were licensed from one multinational car company or another. More often than not, the assembly plants themselves were built by the same companies that were providing the designs and technologies: Italy's Fiat, in particular, made a good business of building such factories, and clones of its cars could be found in many countries under as many different names.

Suddenly, in the space of a few years around 1980, something changed. Multinational car companies became reluctant to operate assembly plants which served only national markets, or to purchase parts from local suppliers that could not compete internationally.

2.2. **The global, the regional, the corporation, and the state**

"International" does not necessarily mean "global." The auto industry is dominated by MNCs that might be said to operate globally – selling almost everywhere, assembling cars in many different countries around the world. The efforts at creating smaller car companies to serve national markets have almost all folded, as have many of the stand-alone assembly operations run by the multinationals. The first tier of car parts suppliers – the companies that deal directly with the big car companies – is increasingly dominated by a handful of large multinationals, as big as the car companies themselves. All of this might look like a familiar picture of "globalization."

A more careful look shows a more complicated picture. True, some of the big manufacturers operate globally; true, national borders are becoming less important. Yet, the production and sale of cars is not so much global as regional. In the old days of ISI, Fiat was one of two car companies sharing a small but cozy Polish market; now, its Polish assembly plant produces one Fiat model for the large and fiercely competitive European market; similar story can be told of SEAT, once owned by the Spanish government and now a subsidiary of Volkswagen. When Toyota locates a pick-up truck factory in Thailand, it is to serve not just the Thai but the ASEAN market (ASEAN – the Association of South-East Asian Nations – being, among other things, a trade bloc). Several Japanese and American car companies have set up production in Mexico for the combination of cheap labor and tariff-free access to the US and Canadian markets, thanks to NAFTA. What once took place within national borders now takes place within regional blocs such as the European Union (EU), NAFTA, Mercosur, and ASEAN – or within China or India, each of which has a larger population than any bloc.

Hence, while international trade generally has grown, international trade within regional blocs has grown even faster (Mansfield and Milner 1999). Figure 2.1a shows global trends for international trade and foreign direct investment (FDI) relative to total output. Figures 2.1(b)–(d) chart the ratio of international trade within the region to trade with the rest of the world.

In explaining the growing international integration of car markets, then, we actually have two things to explain: Why are car markets now regional instead of national? And why, when the markets are regional, are the corporations that make the cars global?

To answer these questions, we need to account for choices made by two sets of actors – corporations and nation-states. I assume, following Strange (1992), that corporations and states interact strategically, each with their own objectives, and taking into account the other's behavior.

Now, to attempt accounting for the choices of these is to open a can of worms: within any corporation there are many actors with different opinions and different interests at stake; the same is true of states, except that within states the actors are more numerous and the differences in viewpoint and interest are far, far greater than within a corporation. In later chapters, we will consider the nature of such internal differences, and how they are resolved. For now, however, we will treat both corporations and states as unitary actors, with fairly simple interests, as follows. Corporations want profits. States want to increase national income, and do so by adopting policies that aim to capture high

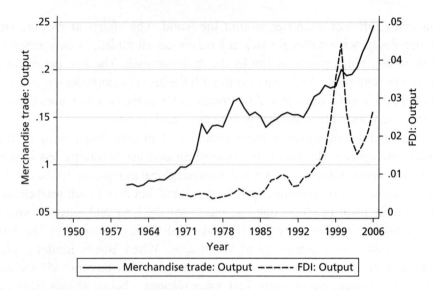

(*a*) International trade and FDI relative to world output

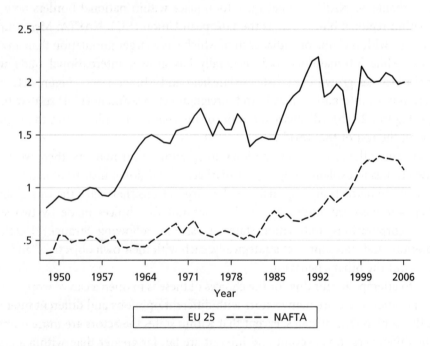

(*b*) EU and NAFTA: internal vs. external international

Figure 2.1 Regional trade and world trade, 1948–2003: International trade as a whole has grown faster than GDP (Figure 2.1a), which some would call "globalization." Yet international trade within regions has been growing faster than international trade overall – often without the benefit of a regional trade bloc (Figures 2.1b–d)

Sources: UNCTAD, World Bank.

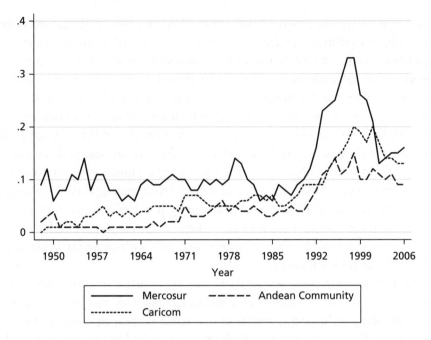

(c) South American and Caribbean blocs – internal: external trade

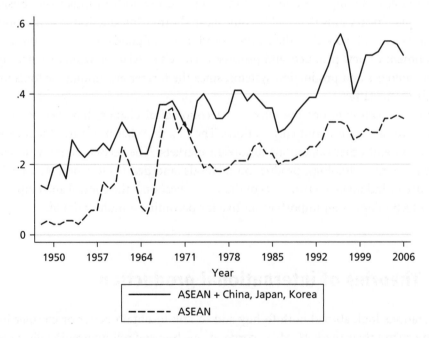

(d) East Asia – internal: external trade

value-added industries or processes (the *value-added* in a particular business is the sum of that business's payments to factors of production – wages, salaries, pensions, and such to labor, profit, and interest to capital). Assuming that increased value-added is the objective for states allows us to ignore for the moment such questions as how the value-added is distributed between labor and capital, between low wage and high wage workers, or between industries that are helped by trade and industries that are hurt. I'll return to these questions in later chapters. For the purposes of this chapter, I will also assume that the choices corporations and states make are rational policies that can be expected to further these objectives. This is not always a justifiable assumption, and if you argued that many of the state policies I describe were making their countries poorer rather than richer, you would have a lot of company. It is useful to start out by assuming that both the states and corporations have these simple objectives and pursue them rationally, because it provides a simple framework within which we can begin to analyze the effects of technological change.

The technological changes we need to consider can be divided into two broad categories: what we can call distance-shrinking technologies and production systems. Distance-shrinking technologies are those that make it cheaper, easier, or faster to do business over a distance; they include both information and communications technologies (ICTs) and transportation technologies. Production systems are technologies in a broad sense, including not only machines but also methods of organizing businesses and people. For reasons that will become clear shortly, "production systems" includes not only what is involved in the routine production of goods or services, but also the development of new products and processes. There's overlap between distance-shrinking technologies and production systems, since the former are among the tools used in organizing the latter.

Before we can consider the effects of technological change, however, we need to answer two questions about corporations. The first is: What motivates them to set up production and other operations in foreign markets? The second is: How do corporations put new technology, production methods, and designs to work? As we will see, these often wind up being two parts of the same question – the control and employment of new technology is an important motive for becoming a multinational.

2.3. **Theories of international production**

Corporations look abroad both to buy and to sell: to obtain better or cheaper inputs, and to expand their markets. Many corporations buy and sell internationally, however, without becoming multinationals: they import, they export, but they don't establish foreign operations.

Trade barriers provide one motive for establishing foreign operations, as we have seen in the case of the automobile industry: a car company, instead of exporting cars to a protected market, would set up an assembly plant there. There was also a third strategy: license the technology and designs to a local company within the protected market.

Theories of the multinational corporation are largely answers to this question: "Why engage in international production, rather than either simply trading goods *or* licensing the intellectual property (IP) required to produce the goods?" Since this book is about the environment in which multinationals operate, rather than the corporations themselves, I'll restrict myself to a brief answer to that question. For a more thorough discussion, see John Dunning (1993) or Grazia Ietto-Gillies (2005).

International production has its costs: coordination and control, are more difficult at a distance; it is neither easy nor cheap to adapt to operation within a foreign culture and an unknown institutional setting; lack of local knowledge and political connections can expose the company to large and unknown risks.

The process of incorporating functions within a corporation, rather than entrusting them to market transactions, is sometimes called *internalization*. International production thus entails international, or cross-border, internalization. There are two broad ways of answering the question of why corporations decide to bear the costs of international internalization rather than simply trading or licensing. The first argues that international production occurs when it provides a way of minimizing the total cost of getting certain goods or services made and marketed – otherwise, it wouldn't be done. The second says it results from strategic choices by corporations aiming to build and maintain market power. (These same approaches are used to explain why big corporations exist in the first place, never mind multinationals; we'll return to them in more detail in Chapter 8.)

2.3.1. COST-MINIMIZATION THEORIES OF INTERNATIONAL PRODUCTION

The cost-minimization argument rests on the proposition that, in competitive markets, only the cost-minimizing structure will survive. This is an evolutionary argument, one of competitive selection (Alchian 1950; see also Penrose 1952, 1953; Alchian 1953). If we accept that competition works this way, and if we also believe that the markets we're interested in are sufficiently competitive, then the market structure and corporate behavior we observe must be cost-minimizing. But *why* should it be cost-minimizing to operate a corporation in many countries?

There are two distinct theories of cost minimization to consider: transactions costs, and capabilities. The transaction cost theory concerns costs which result from transactions between firms. If these costs are higher than the costs of internalization, the cost minimizing strategy is to eliminate some transaction costs by internalizing (Buckley and Casson 1976; internalization, for the purposes of this chapter, means undertaking international production in place of international trade in goods or IP). The capabilities theory starts with the assumption that much of what a corporation knows is a sort of collective *tacit knowledge*, which cannot be fully communicated to those outside of the organization and therefore cannot be sold: the only way to make full use of such organizational capabilities (sometimes called "competencies") in a foreign market is for the firm to go there itself. This explanation is favored by Bruce Kogut and Udo Zander (1993).

2.3.1.1. Transaction cost theories

Two reasons why the market for IP might fail are standard ones from the economic theory of incomplete contracts: adverse selection (Akerlof 1970), and the risks associated with transaction-specific investment and lock-in (Williamson 1987). A high cost of capital at the customer's end can have the same effect. Since we're dealing here with cases in which productive knowledge can be bought and sold, we'll call it "intellecutal property."

The adverse selection reasoning follows from, and works like this: licensees are less well informed about the value of technologies offered than licensors. Knowing that they know less, the licensees might fear that the licensor is trying to sell an inferior technology – as DuPont unloaded the rights to its failed synthetic leather, Corfam, on an unfortunate state-owned enterprise in Poland in 1971. Apprehension on the part of the buyers drives down the price they're willing to pay for IP. This apprehension can become self-fulfilling – because if the buyers expect to be cheated and so require low prices, the better technologies will be withdrawn from the licensing market.

The lock-in problem facing a customer (licensee) is this: say it starts using a company's (the licensor's) IP. It knows that it may need to make later deals with the same supplier, since the supplier will be developing the technology further, or producing complementary technologies, designs, etc. Since the customer has already invested in the technology, perhaps shaping its product line or production system around it, the supplier has the customer over a barrel when the time comes to negotiate the next deal.

The adverse selection and lock-in problems are also likely to be greater when the potential market is a poor country, because the potential licensors are then more likely to lack the technological sophistication needed either to judge the product or to work around the lock-in. In poor countries, the potential licensor is also likely to face a very high cost of capital, due to poorly developed financial markets.

Adverse selection, hold-up, and the customer's high cost of capital all have the same effect: the IP will be worth less to the customer, and this provides the seller with a reason to internalize rather than sell.

2.3.1.2. Capabilities

Toyota has certain technologies and designs, and certain procedures governing production and quality management. If you and I persuaded a foolish bank to lend us the money to set up a company, bought a turnkey plant from Toyota-approved contractors, paid for a license to use all of Toyota's technologies, designs, and procedures, and perhaps paid for a few training sessions in the bargain, would we be able to make cars that are as good as Toyota's? Not likely. What would we lack? Call it know-how, something that the large team of people we call "Toyota," and its affiliated and partner companies, can do but can't write down as a set of instructions. Toyota can license the part of its knowledge that can be written down, but that explicit knowledge is more valuable when combined with Toyota's tacit know-how; using the latter outside of Japan requires that Toyota undertake foreign operations. Another way of looking at it is that for our company to learn to make cars as good as Toyota's – to replace Toyota's know-how by something just as good – would require a large expenditure over a long period; it would cost far less for Toyota just to do it itself.

Take a closer look at the story I've just told. You and I may not be the best qualified buyers for Toyota's technology. We wouldn't really know how to make the best use of it. Wesley Cohen and Daniel Levinthal (1990) would say we would lack the *absorptive capacity* to make good use of Toyota's tacit knowledge. If we were already operating a pretty good car company, our absorptive capacity would be much higher. Tacit knowledge sometimes gets defined as knowledge that can't be communicated, but that's too simple: it's usually a matter of degree, how much of one's knowledge can be communicated, how quickly, at what cost, with the answers depending on the absorptive capacity of the one listening.

Notice, also, that in most industries companies with good absorptive capacity are more likely to be found in rich countries. This has various implications that we'll see as we go along.

2.3.2. MARKET POWER AND INTERNATIONAL PRODUCTION

The market power approach sees the choice between licensing and internalization as shaped by the aim of forestalling or controlling competition. Here we can distinguish between cases of investment from one rich country or bloc to another, and cases of investment from rich countries to poor ones. In the former, the MNC is typically moving into the home market of one or more of its international competitors, and the formal analysis is that of strategic interaction within an oligopoly (a market shared by a few large companies) that operates in both countries (Knickerbocker 1973). In the latter, we see the MNC extending market power to a new country, without actual or threatened reciprocal investment by competitors from that country (Hymer 1971, 1976). The basic issues in the two cases are the same, however; I will focus on the latter, which is simpler.

Hymer's essential point is that the licensing route undermines a company's market power by helping to establish future competitors, while the internalization route extends that market power into new markets. We may combine this observation with more recent analysis of the difficulties of markets for knowledge, paralleling the cost-minimization theory related above. To make use of licensed technologies and designs, the licensee must develop certain capabilities. While the cost-minimization approach would see the presence or absence of these capabilities as something that affects the cost of using the market (no capabilities means no absorptive capacity in the buyer, so the IP owner internalizes instead of selling), the market power approach sees the buyer's investment in capabilities as something that may come back to bite the seller: the buyer may develop the ability to compete with the seller, eventually developing technologies and designs on its own.

2.3.3. MULTINATIONALS AND CROSS-BORDER NETWORKS

The theory of the MNC started with economic theories that assumed a sharp distinction between firms (or organizations) and markets. Firms were subject to central control, and markets were places where fully independent actors engaged in self-interested, arm's length transactions. Although a lot of that theoretical apparatus remains, we would now recognize a whole realm of situations intermediate between firms and markets: networks and quasi-market relationships of various kinds. This is an important aspect to international production. Just as much international trade is intra-firm (i.e., it is trade between countries as far as customs officials are concerned, but for the firm's purpose it is an internal transfer), much of the trade that is *not* internal to a single firm is nonetheless internal to an organized production chain or network. Cross-border production networks raise most of the same questions – and fit many of the same answers – as do MNCs.

2.4. **Technological change and the internationalization of production**

With these theoretical tools at hand, we can ask how recent changes in technology may have changed the picture. How have they affected the relative payoffs for corporations from licensing versus foreign operations? How have they affected the policies adopted by states with regard to foreign trade and foreign investment, whether global or regional? I have explored these questions previously (Guy, 2007).

2.4.1. INFORMATION AND COMMUNICATIONS TECHNOLOGIES AND GLOBAL FINANCIAL MARKETS

The most obvious and ubiquitous technological changes of the past thirty years are in ICT – digitization of information, computers, the Internet, and other forms of tele-communications. These are among the distance-shrinking technologies, increasing the speed at which great volumes of information can be transmitted between distant points. The changes in ICT have been so dramatic that it is perhaps too easy to attribute to them great, globalizing power. Anthony Giddens (1999, p. 9) tells us:

In the new global electronic economy, fund managers, banks, corporations, as well as millions of individual investors, can transfer vast amounts of capital from one side of the world to another at the click of a mouse. As they do so, they can destabilize what might have seem rock-solid economies – as happened in the events in Asia.

Attributing such power to mouse clicks ignores the simple fact that rapid global movements of financial assets have been technologically possible, and quite widespread, since the first transatlantic telegraph cable was laid in 1866. Money and debt are just entries on balance sheets, numbers that can be passed around the world with electronic communications of the narrowest of bandwidths: a few taps of a telegraph key work just as well, and almost as fast, as a click of a mouse. Subsequent improvements to electronic communications have done little to increase the speed of transmission. Bandwidth has increased, so that more information can flow down one line; connections of the communications systems to data entry, processing, and storage complete the picture. These are important developments for many purposes, but they are not critical to the rapid international movement of large amounts of money. Already in 1910, interest rates in one country responded, within hours, to changes in another (Hirst and Thompson 1999).

Giddens' statement, published in 1999, should probably be put down to the contagion of technology fetishism that claimed many fine minds during the dot com boom. The constraints on international capital movements are *not* found in the ICTs at the disposal of the financial markets. Some of the constraints are political. For instance, foreign exchange controls, which were common between 1914 and 1980, are now uncommon, but they have not been banished by electronics – as the government of Malaysia showed when it brought them back after the Asian financial crisis of the late 1990s. Other constraints are organizational – a company may be able to move money to another country, but how does a company based in Germany manage its investment in Brazil? Improved ICTs have affected international investment flows largely by helping solve the latter problem: facilitating the coordination and control of far-flung corporate divisions and of inter-company production networks. Communications which are not only high speed, but also high bandwidth, are important for the coordination and control of cross-border production networks.

2.4.2. SPEED

And what of improved transport? We need to think here about the transport of both goods and people, and about both speed and cost. Paul Krugman is among those attributing globalization to lower transportation costs, and others have tried to show that this is so (Evenett et al. 1998; Baier and Bergstrand 1998; Rose 1991, Krugman 1995). But a more recent and thorough examination of the evidence by David Hummels (2006) has shown ocean shipping costs have not declined much since World War II. Air freight costs have fallen, but there was hardly any air freight before 1970, and since air freight remains substantially more expensive than ocean or rail freight, the growing use of air freight represents an *increased* cost of shipping.

What has changed is speed. Due to the containerization of most non-bulk ocean shipping (for instance, the shipping of most manufactured goods), the door-to-door speed of a freight shipment that includes an ocean voyage, has fallen considerably. Containerization began in the late 1960s, and by 1980 accounted for most of the non-bulk cargoes between East Asia, Europe, and North America; since then it has become increasingly prevalent in other parts of the world, as well. Non-container ships carrying similar cargoes have to spend between half and two thirds of their lives in port. Reduced time spent in port does reduce the cost of shipping, but this is included in Hummels' estimates of the total shipping cost. The important change, for both the shipper and the recipient of the goods, has been the elimination of the delay that time in port, loading, and unloading, represents. The growth of air freight, similarly, represents improvement is in speed, not in cost.

Speed is more important for some kinds of trade than for others. For some products, long distance trade is impossible without high speed – shipments of fresh vegetables or cut flowers, for instance. For others, trade does not require great speed, but slow transport leaves local producers with a large advantage. Clothing comes into this category, since styles change and the precise styles, colors, and sizes that will sell are all hard to predict. Without high-speed international transport, nearby producers have the advantage of being able to replenish stock as needed. For these reasons, it is plausible that increased transport speed has been a factor in creating many international, and even global, markets.

2.4.3. TRANSPORT SPEED, MODULAR PRODUCTION, AND REGIONAL NETWORKS

The ability to replenish stock quickly becomes particularly important in the trade of intermediate goods. Historically, most international trade has been in one of two categories: in what we might call commodities – raw or semi-processed materials or foodstuffs – or in finished manufactured goods. But from the beginning of the era of the mass production of machines – roughly, the early twentieth century – there has been a growing trade in intermediate goods – goods such as machine parts, electrical components, or pieces of cloth that have been cut for particular garments but not yet sewn together. The shipment of intermediate goods of this sort is part of a planned production process – you don't ship large numbers of automobile transmissions to another country to satisfy some general demand for transmissions, but because there is a particular factory there that needs so many transmissions of a particular type at a particular time.

The shipment of intermediate goods as part of a planned production process occurs when production has been *modularized*: part of the production process is done in one place, part of it in another. Modular production can occur within one company – that is to say, under conditions of vertical integration – or it can be done by two or more companies working together. We can call the latter *modular organization*, or *network organization*.

We don't have figures for these things, but it is commonly agreed that both modular production and modular organization have become more prevalent since the 1970s. In the early and mid-twentieth centuries, different stages of production were more likely to be gathered together at a single site, and it was more common to incorporate as many stages as feasible within one company.

Increased modularity of production may be a necessary condition for a large increase in long-distance trade in intermediate products, but it is not sufficient. As we will see in later chapters, the methods of modular production were pioneered at much closer quarters, in places like Toyota City, Japan, or clusters of small- and medium-sized companies in small cities in central Italy. In those circumstances, the new methods of production and organization benefited not only from short delivery times, but also from face-to-face contact between the people working at different stages of production. As the modules in a production process are now often not across towns but across borders, mountain ranges, or oceans, some of this face to face contact is inevitably sacrificed. To some extent, it is replaced by electronically mediated communications: the gamut from phone to fax to e-mail to websites to video hook-up. These media are used not only for person-to-person communication, but also for the transmission of masses of technical information connected with, say, computer-assisted design and manufacturing (CAD/CAM). Modern ICTs are thus essential to the operation of far-flung production networks. Yet we must again, as in the case of ICTs and finance, take care not to overstate their power. While necessary for the great expansion of modular production at a distance, modern ICTs are not sufficient: production networks that cross oceans still rely heavily on face-to-face contact. To take one out of thousands of possible examples, the electronics companies of Taiwan have close business relationships with companies in many other countries. Some of these are relatively close to Taiwan: mainland China, Japan, South Korea, Singapore, and so on. But many others are in the US, and a large number of people in that industry spend a great deal of their life in the air between Taipei and San Francisco (for the Silicon Valley): they have come to be called "astronauts" (Saxenian 1999).

Because face-to-face meeting has a certain value in business relationships, the relative ease of traveling long distances today has made all forms of international business more travel-intensive than they were a few decades ago. This applies even to cases of simple commodity trade. I spoke recently with a man who buys coal for the principal electric utility in Italy. Like the Taiwanese astronauts, he travels constantly – to South America, to Australia... This surprised me; I had thought of coal as a generic commodity, traded on international exchanges. The astronauts might need to meet about technical specifications, IP, product design, marketing – any number of things. But why, I asked, should the power generator in one country go to the expense of maintaining ongoing personal contact with mining companies around the world? Reliability of supply was his answer: there are fluctuations in supply and demand, and in case of a temporary shortage the personal relationship is important in maintaining a steady flow of coal. How was this managed in, say, 1970, when flights were less frequent and more expensive? Specialist brokers did the work then, effectively handling the buying for a number of different customers. The reduction in travel costs has made it possible – and, in a competitive world, necessary – to eliminate these intermediaries and establish personal relationships with remote suppliers. The low cost of flights, then, brings new face-to-face contact to old trade arrangements, as well as playing a role in new production networks. This makes it impossible to know when the face-to-face contact is indispensable to the networks, and when it is used just because it is affordable.

There is, however, growing evidence of the importance of face-to-face contact in networks. And, even with the speed and frequency of long-haul flights today, the costs of maintaining face-to-face contact across oceans is considerable: greater than the monetary costs of the flights are those of having highly skilled employees spend so much time sitting on planes, away from their work groups, and of employees' reluctance to live on the road, away from friends and family. Hence, even in businesses adapted to long-distance networking, there is a preference for networks which do not stretch quite so far. The denser international networks tend to be regional. Tomokazu Arita and Philip McCann (2000) find that companies in California's Silicon Valley are more likely to participate in networks with companies located in cities that can be reached in a same-day round trip, including time for a meeting: San Diego, Tijuana, Seattle, Vancouver, and Salt Lake City fit in this category; Austin, Tokyo, and Tapei do not. Regions defined in this way seldom coincide with the politically defined regional blocs discussed earlier, although they often exist *within* such blocs: that identified by Arita and McCann is one such within NAFTA; others would include the region that would run along the US–Mexican border, with *maquiladora* assembly plants along the Mexican side, higher-value-added operations and executives' residences along the American (Kenney and Florida 1994; Shaiken 1994); another would be around the Great Lakes, from Chicago to Toronto, on both sides of the US–Canadian border. Michael Dunford and Grigorio Kafkalas (1992) identify what they call "Europe's major growth axis," a band running from London to Milan and Genoa, by way of the Netherlands, Belgium, the cities of the Rhine and southern Germany, and Switzerland. This axis includes or overlaps with several smaller dynamic regions: an English Channel/North Sea grouping which includes the northern tail of the axis plus Paris; southern Germany; and northern Italy. Yeung and Lo (1996) identify a number of large "economic zones" in East Asia, including a Pan-Japan Sea zone (Japan and Korea), a Pan-Yellow Sea Zone (Korea and northeast China), and so on.

The creation of such regional production networks is distinct from the political process of creating regional blocs. Kenichi Ohmae (1993) goes so far as to treat network-defined regions as "natural," and regards almost any state action – whether by one nation-state or a bloc of them – as unfortunate interference. Yet whether or not we like states and blocs, or regard them as less (or more) natural than corporate networks, it is clear that the two kinds of regionalization are not entirely independent of each other. The fact that production networks are regionalizing is a consideration for policy makers in the creation of blocs, and the borders of both nation-states and blocs help guide the location of many production networks.

2.4.4. STATES AND CORPORATIONS

Our story so far: improved electronic communications, faster transport for goods, and faster, more frequent and cheaper air travel, have made it *possible* to organize production and supply networks over long distances. This effect is particularly strong within under about two hours' flying time from a company's headquarters. We should not leap from this to the conclusion that such distance-shrinking technologies make the internationalization of production, or any other form of international economic integration, *inevitable.* Great improvements to international transport and communications have occurred before. In the late nineteenth century, the arrival of the steamship, the trans-oceanic telegraph, and steel (as opposed to iron) rails for trains made *possible* a great increase in trade, the further integration of international financial markets, and the beginnings of the modern multinational corporation. Yet, they were soon followed by rising trade barriers and a *reduction* in many forms of international economic integration; as we will see in later chapters, there is a case to be made that the very technologies that made greater integration possible also contributed to the collapse of the liberal international economic system of which had prevailed in Europe in the mid-1800s.

We need to ask, then, why, in recent decades, states have chosen to adopt policies that amplify the integrating effect of technology, rather than treating it as a problem to compensate for. As we have already seen, some of that amplification is regional and some is global, and just where the balance is struck between regionalization and globalization is a question we'll return to. The more general question, however, is why the choice for nation-states (except, perhaps, the very largest ones) is between these two different approaches to internationalization, rather than between internationalization and going it alone.

Susan Strange (1992) argues that states' decisions to facilitate international economic integration are a consequence of "structural change." The structural changes she names include the various distance-shrinking technologies discussed above, and also a faster pace of technological change in production and in products. The faster pace of change is reflected in rising research and development (R&D) expenditures. Her argument actually hinges not on the absolute level of R&D expenditures, but the level of R&D relative to the marginal cost of producing goods or services after the development has taken place. Viewed over the life cycle of a product, R&D is a fixed cost (i.e., a certain expenditure on R&D is necessary for the product to exist at all, whatever the volume of production). If R&D costs rise, or marginal production costs fall, or both, the result is greater returns to scale. A state that has aimed to develop industries oriented primarily toward domestic markets therefore becomes poorer, in relative terms, because it must spread the higher fixed costs over the same limited national market. It can achieve lower average costs by exporting; under these circumstances, the pressure from citizens for improved standards of living puts pressure on states to reduce barriers to international trade and investment.

Strange also sees improved distance-shrinking technologies as contributing to political pressure for improved living standards: satellite television, she argues, shows people in poor countries how well those in rich countries are living, and makes them demand changes in economic policy. Such an effect of television on demand can occur within rich countries as well, and does not necessarily have much to do with how well real people anywhere in the world are living. What we see on television is a largely imaginary world – soap opera characters, excepting those of the anomalous working-class soaps broadcast in the UK, lead lives of bizarre extravagance. Juliet Schor (1998) has shown that Americans who watch a lot of television spend more and save less than Americans who watch less, even after controlling for such factors as income and education. It is an open question whether TV's effect on our perceptions of living standards has the sort of political effect Strange claims.

Whether for the reasons Strange gives or for some other, a state may desire to benefit from economies of scale by increasing exports of goods and services produced within its borders. It often needs help in accomplishing this. It needs to find customers for its products in the big, rich markets – Europe, North America, and Japan. Its industries need capital in order to grow, and so require access to financial markets – again in Europe, North America, and Japan. The path to both consumer and financial markets is often mediated by established multinational corporations – based in Europe, North America, or Japan. By putting states in greater need of access to world markets, Strange argues, a faster pace of technological change puts bargaining power in the hands of MNCs. Strange argues that bargaining between MNCs and states should be regarded as a form of diplomacy, just like bargaining between state and state. Policies which emerge from an imperative to increase trade are thus also shaped by the demands of corporations, including reduced barriers to foreign direct investment, to capital flows including the repatriation of profits, and to the free flow of intermediate goods to the end of further modularization of international production.

2.4.5. COLLABORATIVE PRODUCTION AND THE REDUCTION OF BARRIERS TO TRADE AND INVESTMENT

Strange's theory is a good starting point in understanding why states have decided to reduce the barriers both to trade and to investment by MNCs. Yet it rests on too simple a picture of technological change and its place in the production system. In particular, it rests on the unstated assumption that the fixed cost of R&D are fixed, not only in the financial accounts of the corporation, but also in place, either geographically or organizationally. Strange does not address this point explicitly, but in order for her argument to make sense we must assume either that R&D always occurs in the same place (or at least in the same country) as production, or that R&D and production occur in the same company. If the fruits of R&D can travel across borders by being sold, licensed, imitated, or stolen, then how would a rise in R&D costs create pressure for increased international trade in goods, or for greater FDI? This brings us back to the theory of the MNC, and the problems of trading, transferring, and controlling productive knowledge.

Productive knowledge is often transferred between companies without trade in goods, and without foreign investment. Pharmaceutical companies, for instance, license the formulae for their drugs to various manufacturers around the world. The same applies to our auto manufacturing example: consider Fiat's construction of turnkey plants and licensing of designs. The country that was then Yugoslavia built something of an auto industry in the 1970s. That was *not* because R&D costs were so low in the 1970s that the Yugoslav market, either on its own or even with the added scale afforded by the export of the late, unlamented Yugo car, could sustain the costs of developing the next generation of automobile technology. It was because the Yugoslav state set up a company that licensed technology and product designs from Fiat: Fiat did the R&D, and Yugo bought the results. Or, to take a more successful example from the same period, Korea's Hyundai licensed (and continues to license) technology from Japan's Mitsubishi. It is hard to see how rising R&D costs would have made such deals so much more difficult.

There are, however, plenty of cases in which productive knowledge has a high tacit component, and so is either difficult or costly to transfer in this way. There are also cases in which a company controlling productive knowledge doesn't *want* to license or sell it, preferring to keep knowledge in-house. Strange's argument about R&D costs forcing down barriers to trade and barriers to FDI would still hold if either the feasibility of transferring knowledge, or the willingness of companies to transfer it, had declined in recent decades. And there is good reason to believe that changes in the organization of production *have* made simple, arm's length knowledge transfer of productive knowledge between companies more difficult, at least in the case of our automobile industry example.

Since the 1970s, production methods in the auto industry have changed dramatically, as have relationships between customers and suppliers along the supply chain of materials and parts. Many of the changes in question are associated with the production techniques pioneered by Toyota, starting in the 1950s, and with the sort of inter-firm relationships typical of Japanese manufacturing. The practices of Japanese manufacturers such as Toyota gave birth to such concepts as "lean production," "just-in-time delivery," and "total quality management," which will be known to many readers. When referring to these practices as a package, I will call them "flexible mass production." Both flexible mass production, and the classical mass production it has replaced, will be examined in more detail in Chapters 9 and 10. For now, we need to consider briefly how this change has affected the development and transfer of productive knowledge.

Until the 1970s, the Detroit-style classical mass production was a standard to which industries around the world aspired. The Detroit system was Taylorist. Taylorism, or scientific management, involves giving each production worker very precise instructions about what to do and how to do it. These instructions are formulated by the company's managers and engineers after systematic study – hence the label "scientific." Production workers themselves have little, if any, involvement in the study of methods or formulation of instructions.

The Taylorist separation of conception (by managers) and execution (by workers) was paralleled, under mass production, in the relationship between the lead company – be it Ford, Fiat, Renault, Nissan, or some other – and its suppliers of parts. The design and engineering departments of the lead company would design a car, including most of the parts. Some parts would then be made by the lead company, and others purchased from suppliers. Would-be suppliers would bid for the work of making parts on the basis of full technical specifications, spelled out on paper blueprints (today it would be CAD/CAM files) provided by the lead company. Companies supplying parts needed some technical capabilities, of course – they needed to be able to make production decisions. Moreover, for reasons that will be explored in later chapters, relations between mass producers and their suppliers tended to be adversarial; when suppliers did have production problems, they worked them out on their own. They were not, however, expected to contribute to product design.

The hierarchical separation of conception and execution in the mass production process made both *spatial* and *organizational* separation of production activities relatively simple. It is easy to miss this point because both spatial and organizational separation are more prevalent in today's production systems than they were under mass production – then it was common to integrate many stages of production in one building under one ownership, and today we have modular organization and ocean-spanning production networks. Even so, significant spatial and organizational segmentation of production did occur under mass production, and when they did the requirements for interaction between the different production units – the flow of information, instructions, and products – were much less exacting than they are today. A mass production assembly plant, with its special purpose machines and detailed instructions, could be located almost anywhere, provided there was a supply of parts, and a small number of managers and engineers trained in the company's methods. Most of the employees in such factories were semi-skilled, and required little special training either in their trades or in the company's particular methods. Companies supplying parts needed the appropriate production capabilities, plus the blueprints.

The flexible mass production methods used in the auto industry today make much greater use of the knowledge of both production workers and suppliers. Within the lead company, they emphasize involvement of a skilled workforce in the continuous improvement of the manufacturing processes they use. Production workers are expected to identify problems and opportunities for improvement, and to participate in developing solutions. This requires ongoing two-way communication and cooperation between production workers and the management/engineering teams. Because these methods are considered important for both the maintenance of quality and the ongoing reduction of costs, the lead companies expect their suppliers to follow similar practices.

Flexible mass production companies often expect a supplier to design the parts it will be supplying. This is sometimes called "black box design": if we imagine the lead company's schematic sketch of the mechanical systems for a new car, certain parts and sub-assemblies might not be shown in detail, but represented by simple boxes. The lead company's designers know what the part represented by the box needs to *do*, but they do not know how this will be achieved. Details – the contents of the proverbial black box – will be worked out later, in a collaborative process involving both the lead company and the supplier.

Black box design requires – and makes use of – distributed design capabilities. It is particularly useful in circumstances where technology is changing rapidly; under such circumstances, the distribution of design capabilities both makes it possible to keep product design up to date and ensures that suppliers have the technological capacity to adapt their production systems to the fast-changing technologies. Clearly, however, black box design demands more of the suppliers. Small suppliers that were capable of making parts from blueprints were not necessarily able to collaborate on the development of new parts; even if they were, the lead company may need just one fuel injection system for a particular model of car, so if suppliers are to be involved in design, the lead company will want just one supplier for this product. For these reasons, the transition to black box design has been accompanied by a move to fewer, and larger, first-tier suppliers (first-tier refers to the suppliers that deal directly with the lead company; the first-tier suppliers, of course, have suppliers of their own, and so on).

The upshot of these changes in the way cars are designed and made is that knowledge about how to assemble a car or to make parts for it, has become more difficult simply to buy on the market. This is not to say that such knowledge is no longer bought and sold – companies today buy and sell technology and design licenses more than they ever have. With technologies and products changing as fast as they now do, however, making use of such licenses in order to build a car calls for greater technological capabilities than it did before. For that reason, small national car companies and stand-alone subsidiaries of multinationals both are obsolete. Small suppliers, without the capability to collaborate on design and to supply an international production network, find themselves in a similar situation. For a detailed discussion in the case of Argentina's car parts manufacturers, see Marcela Miozzo (2000); for a comparison of the cases of Argentina, Spain, Taiwan, and South Korea, see Mauro Guillén (2003).

Thus, in the automobile industry, it has become more difficult for companies serving small national markets to keep up to date on technology, design, and production methods. The reason is not, as Strange supposed, the rise in R&D costs (though that has occurred), but changes in the way products are designed, the "continuous improvement" approach to refining production processes, and the consequent changes in relations between companies up and down the supply chain.

2.4.6. OTHER INDUSTRIES, OTHER PATTERNS

The auto industry provides us with a good illustrative example because it is an important industry, with backward linkages to numerous others (metals, machine tools, plastics, composite materials, glass, rubber, electronics). Yet in having these properties it is somewhat peculiar, and in many ways unrepresentative. To what extent can we generalize from this example? Let us, briefly, consider some other industries.

2.4.6.1. Civil aircraft

Like making cars, making large planes is the manufacture of complex machines, requiring inputs from numerous industries. As in the auto industry, production in the aircraft industry has become more modular and more collaborative; product life cycles have shortened. The industries differ in that large aircraft are far more complex and expensive than cars, and are produced in much lower volumes. Here, not surprisingly, the number of producers is smaller and the market is global, rather than regional. Nation-states and regional blocs do come into play, as the US and the EU search for ways to continue subsidizing their respective champions – Boeing and Airbus – while challenging the legitimacy of the other's subsidies. In large markets such as Japan and China, the state has enough influence over the purchase of aircraft, and an eye on entering aircraft manufacturing, that Boeing and Airbus both find it prudent to source some systems or components there; indeed, each also sources many components in the other's home market. So here we have an actual global market for the product, but with regional blocs and large nation-states jockeying for a share of the high value-added work. Despite the cross-sourcing, the US and the EU each has an interest in keeping its respective company healthy, for three reasons. First, having two companies maintains competition in this market; if the world had only one supplier of large civil aircraft, that company would reap monopoly profits. This would impose a cost on users of aircraft everywhere, but those costs would look bigger from outside the monopolist's home country. Second, part of the motive for cross-sourcing parts is that it helps Boeing and Airbus to sell aircraft in one another's home markets – just as sourcing parts in Japan and China helps them there. Without competition, the motive for foreign sourcing would be weaker, which would likely mean a reconcentration of supply in the remaining company's home market: if your country (or bloc) loses its final assembler, it also loses leverage in getting contracts to make parts and to design sub-systems. Third, the airframes used for large civil aircraft are also used for military transport purposes, so being a commercial producer of such planes provides a country with a military asset.

2.4.6.2. General-purpose software

Some products consist entirely of codified knowledge. We call these *information products*. An example of this is general-purpose software, also called shrink-wrapped software (because it is sold as a complete product, requiring little or no customization), such as that made by Microsoft or Oracle. Here, as with aircraft, the market is global, but global for different reasons. Although the replacement of blueprints with digitized systems has reduced the marginal cost of assembling aircraft (Sabbagh 1995), the organization and the physical plant required to do that job in a satisfactory way are still considerable. That is one reason why the world has only two manufacturers of large civil aircraft. The global market for personal computer operating systems and standard office applications is even more concentrated than the market for large civil aircraft: one important producer, Microsoft, dominates both markets. Yet, the organization and physical plant required to make additional copies are trivial – you can do it on your PC. Moreover, multiple competing versions of the software code required for a good personal computer or server operating system are widely available, many of them based on open source code and available at very low prices. The reason there is not a competitive market with large numbers of suppliers of both operating systems and standard office software is only that governments have thus far permitted Microsoft to use proprietary document formats and interface protocols. Software has strong network externalities: I will not use a word processor that can't make perfect conversions to and from the Microsoft Word documents produced on most other machines. Similar considerations apply to application program interfaces (APIs), which enable different programs and different machines (computers and peripherals, personal computers and servers) to work together.

If document formats and APIs were made transparent, then the market structure of the software industry would change abruptly. It would cease to be one in which a particular type of software application can be dominated by a single multinational, worldwide. It would likely become one in which many competing vendors worked to augment, customize, and service a common body of open source and public domain software. Much of this work would likely continue to be traded internationally – software work is done easily at a distance – but the shift in focus to customization and service would mean a bigger role for local and regional players (Stallman, 1985; Benkler, 2006). There are two reasons to be interested in this possibility. One is that regulators in Europe, South Korea, and elsewhere have been pushing the market in exactly this direction. The other is that – unlike the market for large civil aircraft, or automobiles – the structure of the market for general purpose software is in no sense determined by the production technology: it can tip one way or another, from monopolistic to ultra-competitive, on the basis of small changes in the competition policies of a few governments. Consequently, the politics of the global market in general-purpose software are entirely different than those of the global market for aircraft. In the aircraft case, governments accept that there will be a very small number of final manufacturers, and compete for shares of the jobs and profits. In the case of general-purpose software, the main contest is over the rules governing interface and format standards, and the circumstances (if any) under which software is covered by patents in addition to copyrights. In the case of aircraft, the fact of a concentrated and global market is technologically determined, while in general-purpose software the continuation of a global near-monopoly hinges on political choices.

2.4.6.3. Pharmaceuticals

A fourth kind of case is offered by the pharmaceutical industry. Here we have high product development costs and relatively low, but not trivial, marginal costs of production. In pharmaceuticals, unlike modern auto and aircraft manufacture, the product development and production stages – discovering and testing a new drug in the first case, and making it in a factory in the second – are quite separable. These technical characteristics of the development and production processes, together with the political sensitivity of medicine supplies and prices, have led many national governments to favor domestic pharmaceutical manufacture. It is common for companies which develop new drugs – which is to say, mostly the large multinational pharmaceutical companies – to manufacture them for sale in some national markets, and to license manufacturing rights in others. In both the separability of development and production and the mix of own-manufacture and licensing by multinationals, the pharmaceutical industry today resembles the auto industry of the mass production era. It differs in that it has a much higher ratio of R&D to marginal production cost than the auto industry ever had, and also in the international political contest over the scope of patent rights in pharmaceuticals (Sell and May, 2001; Matthews, 2004; Oliviera et al., 2004).

In both pharmaceuticals and in general-purpose software, rapid technological change and high R&D costs are important determinants of the range of possible international market structures; in both cases, however, the actual structure in place is highly sensitive to political choices by national governments and, increasingly, by the governments of regional blocs.

2.4.6.4. Clothing and textiles

Gary Gereffi (1999) makes a distinction between two kinds of international commodity chain: between buyer-driven and supplier-driven chains (in later work he adopts Michael Porter's (1985) term value chain; both are more or less synonyms for value-added chain and for supply chain). All of the cases we have considered above are supplier-driven chains; such chains are organized by companies whose position in the market is secured by their product development or manufacturing capabilities. Gereffi's study focuses instead on the clothing industry, which is buyer-driven. The value chains of the industry are controlled, not by manufacturers, but by branders like Levi's or retailers like Wal-Mart.

Coordination of the various stages of a buyer-driven value chain may be handled by the brander or retailer, or may be passed on to a full-package supplier (known in other industries as an original equipment manufacturer, or OEM). Full-package suppliers are often multinationals, and often based in middle-income countries such as Taiwan or Turkey; since they put others' brands on their goods, full-package suppliers are generally unknown outside of their own industries.

In recent decades, tariffs on clothing and textile products have fallen, and the international system of quotas called the Multi-Fibre Agreement (MFA) has been phased out. Together with the improvements to communication and transport discussed above, this has made it profitable to stretch many value chains across several countries, with cutting done in one country, sewing in another, perhaps dyeing in a third.

Proximity of manufacture to the final market remains important for the most fashion-sensitive goods, where the selling price is high but the demand for particular items is unpredictable; hence, the continuation of some garment manufacture in New York, Los Angeles, and certain cities in Europe and Japan. For much of the clothing market, however, the organizers of supply chains face somewhat less exacting timetables. Modern transport systems allow fast delivery from hundreds of cities, in countries around the world; retailers and OEMs can shop the world for a cost-minimizing combination of skills, infrastructure, and labor cost, after taking into consideration any remaining tariffs or quotas. Because of the low cost of entry in garment manufacturing, the work moves easily from one country to another and is very sensitive to changes in trade barriers. For instance, the phase-out of the MFA together with the formation of NAFTA shifted the sources of America's clothes from a number of smaller countries which had benefited either from generous MFA quotas or from the US's older Caribbean Basin Initiative, to China (which had only a small MFA quota) and Mexico (which is in NAFTA). Turkey and Morocco, which have special trade agreements as neighbors of the EU, are major sources of clothing for European markets, along with China and the other big East and South Asian suppliers. Thus, while most clothing manufacture has left the rich countries, just where this work goes remains up for grabs, and the global and regional dimensions of the market grow in parallel. The politics of the market revolve around labor costs – low labor costs can bring a country business, but mean, of course, low wages – tariffs, and, to a small but increasing extent, consumer concern about the wages and working conditions of the manufacturing workers in other countries.

2.4.6.5. Weight-gaining products and local services

So far, we have considered industries where MNCs are facilitators of trade in goods and organizers of supply chains which cross borders; even when an MNC sets up manufacturing operations aimed purely at serving demand in a particular state or bloc, this will usually result in considerable international or inter-bloc trade in inputs – parts and materials: that is why intra-firm and intra-industry trade have grown in importance.

Yet multinational, and indeed global, companies also have thrived in a number of industries in which there is very little international trade. Sometimes there is little trade because the companies in question provide goods or services not only locally, but also to other multinationals, and the latter prefer to deal with a small number of suppliers worldwide. We saw examples of this preference in auto parts; it is equally so in auditing, management consultancy, data processing, and temporary personnel services.

Still, if we look further, we find multinationals in industries where neither trade nor serving other multinationals seems to be important. Consider, for example, beer, water, and food retailing.

Brewing beer, like making soft drinks, is what economic geographers call a "weight-gaining process." Making beer adds weight – water and packaging – to the ingredients, and the resulting product is perishable. A thread of economic geography called "location theory" tells us that weight-gaining processes will be carried out on a distributed basis, with plants located near to markets. This prediction is usually borne out – container transport has made long-distance trade in beer feasible, but high-volume "import" brands are often not actually shipped very far: it is cheaper to brew American Budweiser and Japanese Kirin in England for the British market than to ship it from its respective home countries. But, regardless of whether the beer is shipped or made locally, a handful of MNCs such as SAB Miller and Interbrew have steadily been taking over the industry. In this respect beer is following in the footsteps of a similar weight-gaining industry, that for soft drinks; and the beer multinationals' footsteps are marked by multinationals in what must be the ultimate weight-gaining industry, bottled water.

The same may be said of water which is not in bottles, but in pipes: public utilities such as water, electricity, telecommunications, and ports have come increasingly under the ownership and management of multinational corporations. Large retailers in food, clothing, and furniture are increasingly likely to be multinationals as well.

All of these cases call for us to ask why the companies choose to become multinationals. It would be hard to make the case that global operations in these industries are cost-minimizing ways of transferring technology, or necessary for managing collaborative production and value chains. We can look, instead, to four factors: market power in brands and distribution, management methods, protection from political risk, and access to capital markets.

That brands are powerful has gone, in a few years, from being a hypothesis, to an article of faith, to a pervasive metaphor for our identities and personalities. In this context, it is easy to think of the power of brands in sociopsychological terms: we make brands part of our individual and collective identities, we value them. Economists tend not to like this sort of talk, because economic models assume that our desire for products is innate, something we bring to the marketplace rather than something created by the marketplace. To explain why certain brands dominate markets and command a premium price, economists attribute their power to the value of reputation: we are willing to pay more because we know that a company with a powerful brand makes profit by maintaining its quality and reputation. There is, of course, no reason that the psychosocial and economic explanations for brand power cannot both be true: we can believe the economic version (the value of reputation) without believing the formal assumption that consumers and companies are all rational actors whose preferences don't depend on the opinions of others.

Yet neither the psychosocial nor the economic explanations of brand power readily explain why brands go international, even global. One needs extra assumptions. Do global brands have more psychosocial power than local or national ones? It seems obvious that this could go either way. Indeed, in most matters of identity we are told that the local trumps the global, that connections to smaller groups are stronger, that identity is strengthened by having an outsider, an "other," to oppose. So if brands are about identity and social worth, it would be surprising for this to favor Coke against some local brand. As for the power of reputation: how does this power lead to reputable local brands being either gobbled up, or driven out, by global ones?

One explanation that is often used to save both the psychosocial and economic explanations is economies of scale in advertising. Once, this was applied to the development of national brands: many advertising media – television, magazines – are national, so national brands have an advantage over local ones. The argument is extended from national to global brands through the sponsorship: major sporting events and entertainers get global exposure. Advertisements on football (soccer) jerseys or Formula 1 cars are broadcast globally, and this expenditure is wasted if the sponsor does not sell globally. Yet it is not at all clear that the direction of causation does not go the other way, from global markets to global sponsorship. There are plenty of opportunities for national and local sponsorship; both national and global brands are ubiquitous in American football and NASCAR races, although the international reach of these sports is relatively slight.

We do not need economies of scale in advertising and sponsorship, however, to understand the global reach of brands of weight-gaining products – and of the multinationals behind these brands. We need only to take into account these factors: economies of scale and market power in local distribution systems for weight-gaining products; the growth motive of corporations, together with the desire to shut out potential competitors; and the superior access to financial markets enjoyed by multi-nationals. These factors can also help us understand the growth of MNCs in public utilities and in retailing.

2.5. **Summing up**

In all of the industries we have examined in this chapter, the growth of multinationals and international production networks have been facilitated by improved distance-shrinking technologies. In all, there has been increased modularization of production: devolution of tasks within a network to units that are under separate ownership and management, at the same time that coordination within the network is tightened. In all, the development of international production has been encouraged by liberalization in the trade and investment policies of governments.

It is tempting, seeing this, to treat this entire picture as one of "globalization," driven by technological progress and accepted as inevitable by national governments. Techno-logical changes have made international production more appealing to MNCs, and have made national markets small for many purposes. MNCs have rushed to fill the oppor-tunities open to them. It would be rash, however, to assume that this adds up to a technologically pre-ordained and irreversible shift from national to global. In all of the industries considered above, both the extent of internationalization and the particular form it takes are remarkably sensitive to political choices made by nation-states.

In many industries, such as the weight-gaining, public utility, and retail industries discussed above, the cost benefits of international production are not evident. We can see the transfer of management methods, which in previous episodes has proven a short-lived basis for internationalization; we can also see political insurance for private sector purchasers of public utilities; and more generally, we see evidence of the com-bination of corporations that seek growth and market power, together with superior access to international financial markets. Multinationals in these industries are essen-tially riding on a larger wave of policies favoring international production, and their advance could easily be reversed by a combination of policy and the transfer of management knowledge – as has happened in the past.

The location of clothing and textile manufacture, and of many other buyer-driven processes, is highly sensitive both to changes in trade policy and to changes in relative labor costs.

In the case of general-purpose software, the scale economies enjoyed by the dominant multinationals are a reflection of legal and regulatory choices which have, thus far, allowed those companies to use network externalities to create monopolies. The legal and regulatory framework for this industry is hotly contested, and it is likely that the global monopolies will be replaced by a more competitive market structure with a much larger role for local, national, and regional firms.

More complex, high-tech manufacturing – such as the automobile, aircraft, and pharmaceutical cases discussed above – the economics of knowledge development and transfer do create a technological imperative for some form of international production. Even here, however, the geographical scale of the international production unit, and even the choice between internalization and licensing of productive knowledge, is shaped as much by politics as by technology.

3 Globalization?

3.1. What's happening?

Everything I've discussed in the previous chapter — is that what's called globalization?

Too often, it is — and not only what's in the previous chapter, but much more, besides. Anthony Giddens (2000, p. 1) says that "The global spread of the term [globalization] is evidence of the very changes it describes," and that those changes "[are not] just a single set of changes. A number of overlapping trends are involved." He goes on to list "the worldwide communications revolution"; "the knowledge economy," giving financial markets as the leading example; the fall of the Soviet Union; growing equality between men and women; and certain "changes affecting the family and emotional life more generally." In a similar vein, James Mittelman (2000, p. 4) describes globalization as "a syndrome of processes and activities . . . [A] pattern of related characteristics of the human condition or, more specifically, within the global political economy . . . Integral to the globalization syndrome are the interactions among the global division of labor and power, the new regionalism, and resistance politics." In constructing his own definition of globalization, Peter Dicken (2007, p. 8) approvingly cites Mittelman, and also quotes Bob Jessop (1994, pp. 113–14): "globalization is a . . . supercomplex series of multicentric, multiscalar, multitemporal, multiform and multicausal processes."

All of these definitions treat globalization as something new — a phenomenon or "syndrome" of the past few decades — and at the same time something with many, many facets. By defining a phenomenon with so many variables in such a short time frame, they give a name and pride of place to something that cannot be analyzed. What causes globalization? What effects is globalization likely to have? Can anything be done to change globalization's course? When globalization includes both the integration of global markets and regionalist reactions to such integration (as in Mittelman), the fall of the Soviet Union and various changes in family and emotional life (Giddens), all part of "a supercomplex series of multicentric, multiscalar, multitemporal, multiform and multicausal processes" (Jessop), we might as well say "globalization is whatever happens to be happening today," and forget about analysis.

Not all definitions of globalization are so hopeless. Gereffi, like Dicken in his less expansive moments, defines it as the integration of production across borders — a concept that will be familiar from Chapter 2. But we can avoid a lot of confusion by just saying "integration of production across borders," rather than "globalization." Daniele

Archibugi and Jonathan Michie (1995) discuss different ways in which technological development and dissemination can be globalized. But the way in which technological development is globalized, if so it happens to be, can be more clearly discussed without assuming it is part of some all-encompassing process called globalization.

If we wanted to speak of a multifaceted "globalization" as a long-run phenomenon, that would make sense. Over centuries, people in different parts of the world have become more interdependent and more closely connected in many different ways, due to ongoing improvements in distance-shrinking technologies, and to changes in governance, markets, and commercial organization which make use of those technologies. The trouble with using the term to deal with short-term changes – changes on the scale of a few decades – is that in the short run there is no reason to expect the different elements of the globalization package to move forward together. Distance-shrinking technologies and their applications keep moving ahead, but in certain important aspects of connectedness and interdependence – trade and investment, for instance – have been known to shift abruptly into reverse for several decades.

3.2. **Globalization in the long run**

We might speak of the ongoing globalization of human civilization, since Neolithic advances in boat-making, domestication of large animals, and the venerable wheel. To save time and to be a bit more modest in the scope of our inquiry, we can start shortly after 1492. At that point, interdependence and connectedness quickly became global.

This may seem far-fetched, as seen from the world of the Internet and the jumbo jet: if we think of historical maps showing the routes of European explorers and early colonial empires, they might conjure up a picture of a few armed men in little wooden ships landing in the New World, and conquering it almost inadvertently, as town-bred Old World diseases killed off most of the indigenous population. Score one for European expansion, but did the livelihoods and living standards of people living on different continents really become interdependent?

In fact, a global economy came close on the heels of these conquests. Spain was now in possession of the richest silver mines in the world, in Mexico and in what is today Bolivia. But what to do with so much silver? Turning it all into money within Spain would merely have caused tremendous inflation (plenty of which occurred, in any case). Much of it got spent on imports from elsewhere in Europe, but in those days, other European countries did not have so much to sell. As luck would have it, there was tremendous demand for silver in China. In about 1400, at the beginning of the Ming dynasty, China had begun a process of remonetization, ending the previous dynasty's experiments with paper and copper money, and switching to silver. It imported a great deal from mines in Japan, but these were running low in the 1500s; China was large and thriving – it and its immediate neighbors (many of which also used Chinese money) accounted for about 40 per cent of the world's commercial economy, its commerce was growing, and so it needed more money. And China made things Europe wanted, particularly textiles and porcelain. Its Southeast Asian neighbors produced spices, also in demand in Europe. So Spanish ships brought silver across the Pacific to China or (more often) to ports in Southeast Asia where Chinese merchants also traded, and exchanged it for goods. (One of the areas in which Europe did have a technological edge at this point was in making coins, and the silver was often coined before it was sold.) Had the looted silver not serendipitously met the needs of Chinese monetary policy and the ongoing expansion of market activity in East and South Asia generally, the Spanish venture in the Americas might not have amounted to much at all. But it did, and so the surviving indigenous populations of the Spanish colonies were pressed into labor and taxed; the wheels of commerce in Asia were lubricated by a growing money supply; weavers, potters, and farmers in Asia sold products to Europe; and the states of Europe's Atlantic seaboard grew stronger and contended for world power.[1]

We can get another glimpse of the global economy, slightly closer to our industrial present, in the 1700s. Small-scale industrial production was booming in China, India, and Europe; or, to put it more precisely, since each of those is a large and diverse area, it was booming in the lower Yangtze (near today's Shanghai), parts of China's southeast coast, Bengal, England, and a small part of north-west continental Europe. Textiles, in particular, were the focus of intense international competition. One of the markets for textiles was in West Africa, where they were traded for slaves. British slave traders did not necessarily buy with British cloth; the British East India company obtained cloth in India and elsewhere in Asia, and the better quality Asian cloth was more in demand in Africa. Slaves purchased at the coastal prisons of Africa were taken to plantations in the Americas. There, those who had survived the voyage produced crops for export to Europe. In the early years of these ventures, the plantations concentrated on production of a new set of luxury products: sugar, tobacco, and cocoa. Late in the 1700s and onward, cotton production grew as well. The plantation owners traded these crops for textiles (in this case, the lower quality English textiles, to clothe the slaves) and food; England had an advantage over other European colonial powers in that it had an ample source of food in its North American colonies and so did not have to trade food from the home country to get its New World luxuries.

It was in the context of this global economy that the first industrial revolution – which is to say the development of textile *factories*, as opposed to production in households – took place in England in the late 1700s and early 1800s. The factories used more machines, and their machines were driven not by muscle power but by inanimate power sources – first water, later steam. These developments took place under the pressure of intense competition from both China and India. The raw materials for the new factories came from slave plantations in the New World, as did the sugar which was quickly moving on from being a luxury to providing a large share of British food energy. Britain and other countries on Europe's Atlantic seaboard were also feeding their industrial and imperial workforces with large quantities of grain from what are now Poland and Ukraine, and other states around the Baltic Sea; timber came from the same area. Plantations in Southeast Asia supplied a growing appetite for spices.[2]

We could find other examples for any period of time since 1500. Clearly, around the world, livelihoods and lives were shaped by this new global economy. Of course, transport and communications were slower than today, and the global interdependencies were in fewer areas of life. One could say the same thing, however, about connections and interdependencies *within* countries at the time, or even between neighboring towns and villages: a much larger proportion of production of all kinds was household production for one's own use, or traded locally if traded at all; many people never traveled more than a day's walk from the village in which they lived. Even so, the prices of important things that they did make or use, sell or buy, were affected by global markets. And this, today, remains the most important form of global connectedness. Even in our own age of hypermobility, a great many Americans who wear clothes made in China, drive cars made in Japan, and fly on aircraft made in Europe, never leave their own country, and get all their news from sources that don't seem to know the rest of the world exists except when it is perceived as threatening the US: their connection to the rest of the world is primarily through markets.

3.3. **Globalization's retreats**

Throughout the 500 years of the modern world economy, distance-shrinking technologies have improved, and there has been a trend toward greater interdependence and connectedness. Yet, international economic activity has had pronounced ups and downs.

To take a recent and important example, a relatively open and interdependent international economy developed in the mid-nineteenth century, especially among the nations of Europe and the considerable parts of the world those nations then governed. We'll return to the details of this episode in Chapter 5. For now, let us just note that the liberal international economic order of the nineteenth century collapsed. Most readers will be familiar with the dramatic conclusion of that collapse: World War I, followed by two decades of economic instability, revolutions, and increasing isolation of national economies, and finally World War II. By many important measures, the pre-World War I levels of economic integration – trade as a proportion of manufacturing output, international capital flows – were not reached again until the early 1980s. In other words, during the last century, political events set the progress of global economic integration back by seventy years (Hirst and Thompson 1999; Frieden 2006). And, many scholars date the retreat of the nineteenth century international system from three or four decades *before* World War I, making the reversal even longer: after a period of growing free trade within Europe, the 1870s saw a sudden rise in trade barriers, and in the extension of European colonial empires (Krasner 1976).

In the heyday of the liberal international order, its continuation had seemed inevitable. In *The Communist Manifesto*, Karl Marx and Friedrich Engels (1848) wrote:

The bourgeoisie has, through its exploitation of the world market, given a cosmopolitan character to production and consumption in every country. [...] it has drawn from under the feet of industry the national ground on which it stood. All old-established national industries have been destroyed or are daily being destroyed. They are dislodged by new industries, whose introduction becomes a life and death question for all civilized nations, by industries that no longer work up indigenous raw material, but raw material drawn from the remotest zones; industries whose products are consumed, not only at home, but in every quarter of the globe. In place of the old wants, satisfied by the production of the country, we find new wants, requiring for their satisfaction the products of distant lands and climes. In place of the old local and national seclusion and self-sufficiency, we have intercourse in every direction, universal interdependence of nations.

This passage from 1848 could easily be describing the world of 2008 (the one anachronistic note is the use of the term "bourgeoisie" for the class of people owning industrial or commercial capital). Had Marx and Engels spotted one of the great trends of the modern world? For several decades after the publication of the *Manifesto*, it seemed that they had. This was the golden age of free trade in Europe; tariffs fell, trade rose, and liberal economic theory was ascendant.

After World War I, John Maynard Keynes (1920) was singing a different tune. Before the war, he wrote, an inhabitant of London:

... could secure ... cheap and comfortable means of transport to any country or climate without passport or other formality, could dispatch his servant to the neighboring office of a bank for such supply of the precious metals as might seem convenient, and could then proceed abroad to foreign quarters, without knowledge of their religion, language, or customs, bearing coined wealth upon his person, and would consider himself greatly aggrieved and much surprised at the least interference. But most important of all, he regarded this state of affairs as normal, certain, and permanent, except in the direction of further improvement ...

Again, we need to read past some archaic bits – today we would use the Internet rather than sending a servant, and carry plastic rather than precious metals – but on the whole, Keynes describes a situation that would apply to most people in any rich country, and to rich people in poor countries, today. Yet he was writing about the past. Restoration of the conditions he describes did not begin until after World War II. Even then, huge parts of the world – the Soviet Bloc and China – would have been effectively off limits to his London-based tourist; even if traveling to another country in the capitalist West, that traveler could not have been such a carefree spender until Britain's foreign exchange controls ended in 1979.

It would be wrong to dismiss the twentieth century retreat of the global economy as a freak incident. Throughout history we can find cases where trade thrived, only to fade. Trade depends on political systems capable of protecting it from pirates, corrupt officials, and bad roads. Consider, more than 2,000 years ago, what we now call the ancient world. Due to the sailing technologies of the day, we cannot call this global – the ancient Old World was a thing apart. In the third century CE, the temperate core of that world was governed by four great empires – Rome, Persia, the Gupta empire of India, and China. Each of these empires governed, and established connections and interdependencies within, vast areas. A glimpse of one such connection offered by Peter Brown (1971), tells us that, around the year 150 CE,

...it was possible for a young student, Tatian, to pass from the eastern, Syrian, fringe of the Roman empire to Rome, speaking Greek all the way and participating in a uniform Greek philosophical culture...To humbler men, [the Empire] meant wider horizons and unprecedented opportunities for travel; it meant the erosion of local differences through trade and emigration, and the weakening of ancient barriers before new wealth and new criteria of status.

A few hundred years before, Tatian would not have had these opportunities. And, a few hundred years later, the western half of the Roman Empire was gone. Nor was Rome alone in that: the empires of China, Persia, and the Gupta empire in India, all suffered big setbacks at around the same time. The reasons for these collapses were complicated, and are of course disputed by historians. Whatever the reasons, the political stability and the economic connectedness and interdependence that these empires had brought to a large part of the world would be a long time returning.

3.4. More useful ways of talking about changes in international interdependence and connectedness today

In the long run, the connectedness and interdependence of people in different parts of the world increases, and does so in many different aspects. At any given time, however, integration may be increasing in some aspects, and diminishing in others. Nor is it safe to say that such departures from trend are just random deviations, mere noise in the model. The end of the nineteenth century liberal international system can be explained in many ways, but almost any way you do explain, it involves some *reaction* to the consequences of liberalization, and to the effects of improvements in distance-shrinking technology and industrial production: integration in one aspect can actually cause disintegration in others. We'll see more of that in Chapter 5.

Some would bundle both integration and reactions to integration in the world today, General Motors and Al Qaeda, under one concept, "globalization." This doesn't help us understand anything. Perhaps it is comforting to give our era a tidy handle, but we will see more clearly if we leave that choice to historians of the future.

If we want to understand what is different *now*, to understand the forces that shaped the world economy yesterday and will reshape it tomorrow, we need to be analytical, to unpack the big picture a bit. We saw in Chapter 2 that the structure of international production is highly sensitive to political choices by states, varies in particular ways from industry to industry, and is deepening within regional blocs in certain ways and globally in others. These specifics tell us things about what is happening now. If you catch somebody saying "globalization," ask "globalization of *what*?"

4 **Some Economic Concepts**

This chapter consists of brief summaries of some economic tools and theories that are used throughout the book. Specifically, it deals with the standard theory of international trade, increasing returns, and implications of increasing returns for the theory of trade. Those familiar with one or more of these areas should probably just skim the relevant sections. Some readers will prefer just to skip this chapter, and refer back to it if and when that is necessary for understanding the chapters that follow.

4.1. **Standard trade theory**

Standard trade theory holds, in essence, that all countries gain from reducing (or eliminating) barriers to international trade in goods and services. The most common normative application of this body of theory is unqualified support for the global reduction of barriers to international trade (free trade); qualified support for reductions within regional or other supra-national, sub-global blocs (qualified because the increased regional trade may be displacing global trade); and qualified support to the elimination of barriers to captial flows. For a good example of this line of argument, see Jagdish Bhagwati (2002).

The theory has a positive application, as well, in that it provides one way of explaining a reduction in barriers to trade when one does occur. Within any country, there are always many particular interests opposed to a reduction in barriers; seen through the lens of standard trade theory, *support* for reducing trade barriers is not associated with any particular interest, but instead with the common interest, both at the national and the global levels. A reduction in barriers to trade is then understood as a triumph for the common interest. Even if we accept the theory, this is not really a complete explanation for a reduction in trade barriers (nor for a rise in trade barriers, which also occurs), because it does not say how the triumph is achieved.

But what, exactly, does the standard theory of trade consist of?

4.2. **Origins: Smith and Ricardo**

The foundations of trade theory come from Adam Smith (1776) and David Ricardo (1817). Among the many insightful propositions in Smith's *The Wealth of Nations* are two concerning the division of labor. One is that productivity, or output per worker, increases as the division of labor, or specialization, increases. The second is that the extent of specialization is limited by the size of the market. Hence, bigger markets mean more specialization, which means higher productivity. At the time Smith was writing, the issue of free trade was as fraught within countries as it was between them: goods moved freely within Britain and within China, but in many others – France and the states that later became Germany, for instance – they faced many internal tariffs and fees. Britain was much richer, and industrializing more quickly. Smith was arguing that free trade between countries could bring similar benefits to that within them: the bigger the market, the better. Not until a decade after Smith published his book did the US constitution finally guarantee free trade among the thirteen American states. Shortly thereafter, the French revolution put an end to internal tariffs. Through most of the nineteenth century, Britain led the way in promoting the principle (if not always the practice) of free trade *between* countries.

Ricardo's contribution was to observe that two countries can both gain from trade even if one of them produces everything at lower cost than the other: both countries will be better off specializing in what they are *relatively* good at. A country with good, well-watered farmland may require smaller inputs of labor to produce either cattle or rice than a country with poor, dry farmland, but in the country with poor dry land the amount of labor required to produce any rice at all is very high indeed; both countries will be better off if the country with good land specializes in rice and that with poor land in cattle. This is the principle of *comparative advantage*.

4.2.1. COMPARATIVE ADVANTAGE AND FACTOR PROPORTIONS

The modern version of Ricardo's story is found in the Heckscher–Ohlin theorem, which gives us a way to think about the differences in relative cost in rich countries and poor countries. There are two factors of production in the model: labor, and capital. Everything is produced using some combination of labor and capital, but some require more labor and others require more capital. Rich countries are, by definition, those with higher ratios of capital to labor. The Heckscher–Ohlin theorem is a mathematical demonstration that richer countries will specialize in capital-intensive goods, while poorer countries will specialize in labor-intensive goods.

While the Heckscher–Ohlin theorem does show both rich countries and poor countries gaining from trade, this may not be much consolation to the poor countries: the theory says that they are better off with free trade than without, but they have now specialized in labor-intensive, capital-extensive industries, which is to say in being poor. Later developments in trade theory offered help, or at least hope, in this regard. In perfectly competitive markets, like those assumed by these theories, a factor of production is paid according to its marginal product. In poor countries labor is plentiful and capital is scarce, so though wages are low the rate of profit should be higher than in rich countries. A higher rate of profit in a poor country should encourage a higher level of investment. As a theoretical proposition this result can be derived even without international capital movements, because the high rate of profit encourages domestic saving and investment. If international capital flows are allowed, then funds from abroad will be attracted by the high profit rate, and the capital stock in poor countries should grow even faster. In the long run, the theory tells us, more rapid investment in poor countries should lead to factor price equalization – which is to say, wages and rates of profit being the same in different countries.

In practice, it has usually not been true that poor countries enjoyed higher savings rates, higher rates of investment, or large inflows of foreign capital. The theory is certainly correct in assuming that opportunities for profit will bring forth investment; it is also correct in assuming that the marginal product of capital is higher in a capital-poor setting than in a capital-rich one, if the capital is put to its best use. For various reasons, however, the theory is wrong to assume that a poor country's lower ratio of capital to labor indicates that there will be higher rate of profit on new private investments. We will consider some reasons for this later in the book.

At first glance, the standard theory also seems to be wrong in predicting that the poorer a country is, the more it will specialize in labor-intensive products. In fact, relatively poor countries often export capital-intensive goods to rich countries; the export of steel, for instance, has often been associated with growing (but not yet rich) industrial powers: Japan in the 1950s and 1960s, South Korea in the 1980s and 1990s, and India today. This is called a *factor intensity reversal*, and the widespread occurrence of such reversals is known as the *Leontief paradox* (Leontief 1953). It may appear that this paradox contradicts the Heckscher – Ohlin theorem, but in fact what it does is show the limits to reasoning based on one type of "labor" and one type of "capital"; the paradox goes away if we allow for a range of different kinds of investment – human, public, organizational. Steel production requires costly equipment, but compared with many industrial activities it does not require much in the way of highly skilled or educated labor (human capital), infrastructure, or business organization. All of these are forms of capital that rich countries have in abundance, and of which most newly industrializing countries are relatively lacking; if we regard each as a type of capital and extend the Heckscher – Ohlin logic to this more nuanced notion of "capital," steel might not be as capital intensive as, say, manufacturing artificial joints and limbs (now a speciality of Sheffield, once the capital of England's steel industry).

4.2.2. WINNERS AND LOSERS I: CAPITAL VERSUS LABOR, SKILLED VERSUS UNSKILLED

Imagine two "closed" economies: nations which do not trade. Now imagine that they start trading with each other. Let's say that one is richer than the other. In that case, the

Heckscher–Ohlin theorem tells us that the richer country will increase its production of capital-intensive goods, and export some of these to the poorer country; the poorer country will increase its production of labor-intensive goods, and export some of these to the richer country.

With each of the two countries now exploiting its comparative advantage, total income rises in both countries. Does everybody in both countries share in this bonanza? In keeping with the simplifying assumptions of the model, let us say there are two kinds of people, workers and capitalists – owners of the two factors of production, labor and capital. Income for these two classes is represented by the wage rate and the profit rate, respectively.

According to the Stolper–Samuelson theorem, a reduction in trade barriers will mean that in each country the factor which is relatively abundant improves its income relative to the factor which is relatively scarce (Stolper and Samuelson 1941). In the rich country, capital is relatively abundant, and labor is relatively scarce; in the poor country, it's the other way around. Lowering trade barriers will mean that the rich country increases its production of capital-intensive goods and reduces its production of labor-intensive goods; and this raises the rate of profit relative to the wage (we are assuming here that goods and services are traded but that labor and capital stay in their home countries). It is possible that both the rate of profit and the wage in the rich country will rise; on the other hand, the wage *may* actually fall. In either case, in the rich country capital gets a disproportionate share of the gains from trade. In the poor country it's the other way around, with labor getting the disproportionate share.

We can tell the Stolper–Samuelson story in a different way – not in terms of capital and labor, but in terms of two types of labor. Comparing a rich country to a poor one, in the rich country skilled labor is relatively abundant, and unskilled labor is relatively scarce. Following a reduction in trade barriers, skilled labor should receive a disproportionate share of the benefits within the rich country, and unskilled labor a disproportionate share within the poor country; unskilled labor in the rich country, and skilled labor in the poor country, could actually lose in absolute terms.

During the recent decades of trade liberalization, it is certainly the case that the relative earnings of lower skilled workers, within rich countries, have deteriorated, but economists disagree as to how much of this deterioration is due to a reduction in trade barriers (Wood 1994; Leamer 1996). During the same period, the relative incomes of less skilled workers have fallen in many poor countries as well (contrary to the Stolper–Samuelson prediction), so it is clear that there are other factors affecting income distribution during this period.

4.2.3. WINNERS AND LOSERS II: INDUSTRY-SPECIFIC FACTORS

One of the simplifications the Heckscher–Ohlin approach uses is to treat all capital as the same, and all labor (or all labor at a particular level of skill) as the same. A textile factory, however, is not the same as a shopping mall. Both are "capital," but they will be affected differently by falling (or rising) barriers to trade. Textiles are tradeable; a reduction in trade barriers will mean both export opportunities and import competition, which may add up to a windfall or may lead to bankruptcy, depending on the country's comparative advantage (or lack of it) in textile production. The services of the shopping mall can't be exported and are pretty much insulated from import competition; rising national income should be a boon to the owners of the shopping mall.

This problem is addressed, in the usual abstract formulations of economic theorists, in the Ricardo–Viner, or three-factor model. In the Ricardo–Viner model there are again three factors, usually interpreted as labor and two different kinds of capital, for two different industries.[3] Within this framework, it is easy to find cases where the lowering or raising of trade barriers reduces the rate of profit in one industry, while increasing it in the other.

Although the formal models usually assume one kind of labor, in practice labor may be industry-specific as well. That is to say, workers may have skills that would be less valuable (perhaps even worthless) if they had to change industries.

Both the Stolper–Samuelson and the Ricardo–Viner frameworks point to the not-very-surprising conclusion that trade liberalization can produce both winners and losers within any of the trading countries. With Stolper–Samuelson, the winners and losers are what we could call social classes: workers versus capitalists, or unskilled workers versus skilled workers. With Ricardo–Viner, winning or losing depends on which industry you have invested in. The two models therefore have different predictions about the shape of trade politics: who will form a coalition with whom? This difference will become important in later chapters when we see that factor mobility between industries is different in different countries. In more liberal economies, such as the US, both capital and labor are more mobile between industries than in what are sometimes called "coordinated" economies, such as Germany. Peter Hall and Daniel Gingerich (2004) argue that trade policy disputes within the two countries reflect this: class politics in the US, following Stolper–Samuelson, and industry politics in Germany, following Ricardo–Viner. I'll return to this point in Chapter 5.

4.3. **Increasing returns**

In many situations, if you produce more of something, the average cost comes down. We call this "increasing returns." There are various forms of increasing returns, depending on the unit of analysis – is "you" a single factory, a company, a network of companies, a city, a country? There is also a question of whether "more" means a *rate* of output – more per day, for instance – or a cumulative amount of output.

The simplest case, which will be familiar to many from introductory economics, is that of average costs being lower in a large factory than in a small one. (In making this comparison, we are assuming that both factories are producing at their minimum average cost, which means that the larger one is producing much more.) This form of increasing returns is usually called *returns to scale*, or economies of scale.[4] The same term is typically used when a company can reduce average costs by increasing capacity, even if that means producing in several different plants. This is relevant if there are fixed costs not associated with particular plants, which can be spread across two or more of them; one example of such multi-plant overhead would be R&D costs, discussed in Chapter 2.

Returns to scale are increasing returns in the production of a particular product. It may also be possible to spread costs over a number of different products: the R&D lab of a chemical company works on both fertilizers and explosives, McDonalds sells both hamburgers and soft drinks. When producing more of one product brings down the average cost of producing another, we have *economies of scope*.

When we speak of economies of scale or scope, our unit of analysis is usually either a single facility – factory, restaurant, or what have you – or a single company. But increasing returns may also be a geographical feature: a company may have lower costs because it is located close to certain other companies, or to a location within a particular political boundary. There are several reasons this may be so: sharing a common infrastructure and specialized inputs; knowledge spillovers between companies, making it easier to learn how to reduce costs; competitive pressure to reduce costs; enhanced collaborative relationships with other companies – suppliers, customers, and even competitors. These issues will be explored in more depth in Chapter 12.

We can call increasing returns within a particular plant or company *internal*, and those based on proximity to other firms *external*: in the latter case, the firms located near to each other are providing each other with *external benefits*. Of course, they could be creating external costs as well – congestion costs, for instance. If the external costs were to outweigh the external benefits, we would have a situation of external decreasing returns (rising costs due to proximity).

We can think of either internal or external increasing returns in terms of scale or in terms of learning over time. The usual textbook model of internal increasing returns is specifically about scale: bigger plants or companies, higher *rates* of output, and lower average costs. It is also useful to think about unit costs falling as total *cumulative* production rises, over time. This is sometimes called "learning-by-doing," and in simple cases can be represented by a learning curve. Costs will come down with experience. To keep the example simple, assume that a factory keeps making the same product with the same technology. If we measure experience in terms of the amount produced, the "progress ratio" is the percentage decline in average cost for every doubling of the cumulative output. Early studies, from the 1930s and 1940s, put this at about 20 per cent. Later studies found a range of between 16.5 and 25 per cent across different processes. Of course this "steady" decline in costs is nonlinear: each doubling of output involves twice as much output as the previous one, with about the same percentage reduction in cost, so if we plot cost against cumulative output we get a curve – the "learning curve" – that is steep at first, then gradually tapering off but never quite becoming level. For more detail on learning-by-doing, see Debraj Ray (1998, pp. 669–72).

As with returns to scale and scope, learning-by-doing can be external as well as internal; here again, the idea of knowledge spillovers is important.

4.4. **Increasing returns and the theory of international trade**

The standard trade theory discussed earlier in this chapter has a built-in assumption of *constant returns*. That is, the unit cost of making a good or providing a service stays the same, no matter what the volume of your company or country's production, and no matter how long you've been producing: no returns to scale, no learning-by-doing. Without going into the technical details, constant returns is an assumption that gives you a model of a perfectly competitive industry, with lots of small companies operating at the same unit cost, and new competitors freely leaving or entering the industry as demand falls or rises. Obviously, this isn't a complete and realistic descrip-tion of any industry, but in some applications it may be close enough to be a useful model.

In the case of international trade, however, the constant returns assumption is often seriously wrong. The constant returns model assumes that in a country completely lacking in some industry, one small company can start up and immediately compete head-to-head against established rivals in international markets. That doesn't happen. What we see is that companies based in particular countries dominate international markets in many industries, or in particular market segments within industries: Japan-ese companies make most of the better-quality cameras, most surgical scalpels in the world are made in either Germany or Pakistan, and so on. Even when new competitors do try to enter markets against such entrenched competition, they usually don't go head-to-head with the incumbents, but look for a niche they can occupy – and keep. Such patterns are not consistent with constant returns, and are consistent with increas-ing returns – internal and external, scale, scope, and learning-by-doing.

What happens to trade theory in a world of increasing returns? There have been many attempts to answer this question, and the answers provided are different. Institutional economists from Friedrich List (1856) in the nineteenth century to Gunner Myrdal (1968) in the twentieth century have used it as the basis for an argument that free trade won't lead to the development of poorer countries – not, in the language of standard trade theory, to factor price convergence – and that catch-up requires concerted efforts in protected markets. A body of theory called "New Trade Theory" – new because it was new in the 1980s, and hasn't been replaced by anything else yet – introduces increasing returns into the formal mathematical models of standard trade theory, and so models situations in which the cost advantages of incumbents can prevent new countries from jumping into markets (Helpman and Krugman, 1985). Most of them conclude that new competitors will *eventually* be able to enter the increasing returns markets, because as the industry grows congestion or rising input costs will come to cancel out the benefits of increasing returns. The theory cannot tell us when this reversal of fortune will come about, however. Differences in income and wealth, between the richest countries and the poorest, have been growing steadily since European overseas expansion in the 1500s (Pritchett 1997; Pomeranz 2000). If we were to believe that the New Trade Theory offers a general explanation for international differences in income, wealth, and industrialization, we would have to conclude that the convergence force in the models is very weak, and overwhelmed by the advantages increasing returns offer to the already rich. If we do not believe this (and there are other explanations for the divergence – notably power relationships between rich and poor states, and bad institutions in poor states), then we are left asking how much of the picture the New Trade Theory – or any trade theory – does explain.

A less optimistic variant of New Trade Theory is offered by Ralph Gomory and William Baumol (2000). They argue that countries compete to get increasing returns industries that they can keep. Their model works like this. For simplicity, there are only two countries. By assumption, the advantages of increasing returns are such that each industry operates in only one of the two countries. Start with a situation in which one country is rich, and has all the increasing returns industries; the other is poor, and has none. This is obviously a bad situation for the poor country, but the rich country can also do better: since it has all the increasing returns industries and the poor country does not provide much of a market, the rich country will benefit if a few of those industries move to the poor country. That way, the industries remaining in the rich country expand, achieving greater economies of scale, and trade between the two countries grows. Let us say this happens. Both countries are better off than before, enjoying the benefits of trade-based comparative advantage, but the poor country has still not caught up with the rich country in wealth or per capita income. It wants to do so, and so it makes an effort to take some more of the increasing returns industries. If this process continues, it eventually begins to hurt the rich country. The transfer of additional industries to the poor country may still be increasing global income, by expanding markets and making it possible for both countries to achieve even greater economies of scale, but after some point the advantages of this to the rich country are outweighed by the loss in income from the lost industries. At that point, the acquisition of additional increasing returns industries by the poorer country becomes the object of conflict between the two. Thereafter, according to Gomory and Baumol, the rich countries are in a "zone of conflict": one cannot gain without hurting the other.

As for poor countries: think back for a moment to the starting point of the Gomory–Baumol story, where the poor country has no increasing returns industries. At that point, the model says, both the rich country and the poor country will benefit if some industries move to the poor country. But how does this happen? Centuries of experience tell us that it is not easy to establish internationally competitive increasing returns industries in non-industrial countries. We can call the problem of getting onto the industrial ladder in this way the problem of development. What the Gomory–Baumol model suggests is that after a country solves the problem of development, it may soon find itself with another problem – conflict with the longer-established rich countries. Out of the frying pan, into the fire.

Notice that this is a different conflict from those which may arise *within* countries about trade policy: class conflicts (following the Stolper–Samuelson argument) or sectoral ones (following the Ricardo–Viner model). If the US textile industry moves to Mexico it may, in terms of the Gomory–Baumol model, benefit the US; clearly, however, there will be groups in the US who will be hurt, and will organize to oppose this move. If we take those possibilities into account as well, then these simple economic models suggest all sorts of conflicts over trade policy, within and between countries.

5 The Politics of International Trade

In Chapter 2, I outlined an explanation for increased international economic integration, based on changes in technology – transport, information, and in particular production systems and the management of technology within corporations. It is time now to consider some other explanations. These will be clearest if we look back in history to an earlier episode of international market liberalization, and its gradual collapse.

5.1. When the US and Germany were NICs

In 1870, Britain was the unquestioned workshop of the world. Britain was also among the early developers and adopters of the new, steel-based technologies that were leading the latest wave of industrial growth. But steel and related industries grew even faster in several other countries, notably the US, Germany, and Belgium. By the 1860s, the US and Germany were already overtaking Britain's erstwhile rival, France, in important areas of industrial production; although the term was not then in use, they were the NICs (newly industrialized countries) of the day (Figure 5.1).

The age of steel was also the end of a period of free trade in Europe – this at a time when most of the world's industrial output was in Europe, and European powers ruled much of the rest of the world. In the 1850s and 1860s, a veritable contagion of bilateral treaties reduced tariff levels and stimulated trade. Then, policies changed, and tariffs moved up: France raised tariffs in 1872 and 1875, Italy in 1878, and Germany in 1879.

Higher tariffs were not the only new protectionist measures at the time. An international treaty governing patents was adopted in Paris in 1883, and one governing copyrights in Berne in 1886. These remain the basis of international intellectual property law to this day, the foundation upon which the World Trade Organization's (WTO) Trade Related Intellectual Property (TRIPs) agreement was erected in 1995. TRIPs is generally regarded as part of a program of trade liberalization, but in the late 1800s, international protection of intellectual property rights was seen in the opposite light: it was protectionist, an obstacle to the free flow of ideas and technology. As such, it

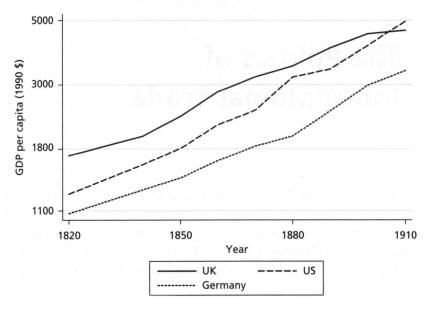

Figure 5.1. Catching up with Britain
Source: Maddison (2007).

was opposed by prominent advocates of free trade such as – then, like now – *The Economist* magazine (Sell and May 2001).

As barriers to trade between national markets were rising, the national markets themselves were being enlarged. The US consolidated its control of the western half of what were to become the forty-nine continental states; in Germany a free trade area known as the Zollverein was consolidated, under Prussian leadership, to form the modern German state; similarly, in the period from 1860 to 1870, Italy was unified to form a single state for the first time since it formed part of the Roman Empire. In these and other states, national markets were integrated through the development of rail networks. Until the railway, water transport had always had both cost and time advantages over land transport, and for many cities this had meant that access to foreign markets was easier than access to domestic ones. With the railway, land transport became faster.

At the same time, the industrialized and industrializing countries went on a new binge of empire building. The earlier phase of empire building, in the sixteenth and seventeenth centuries, had sought gold, spices, places to grow crops such as cocoa and sugar, and natural resources such as timber and fish. Most of the early colonies in the Americas had since gained independence, and the two earliest colonial powers – Spain and Portugal – showed little sign of joining the ranks of industrial countries.

The new imperialism focused on Asia and Africa. European power had continued to grow, for some time, on both continents. Throughout the early nineteenth century, Britain had been consolidating control of India (an area which included not only today's

India, but Pakistan, Bangladesh, and Sri Lanka as well). From 1842, when Britain defeated China in the First Opium War (part of a saga of imperial drug-pushing that is unfortunately outside the scope of this book) Western powers gained, among other things, rights to trade in China, and the control of many coastal cities (treaty ports). After some American gunboats visited Japan in 1854, the US gained trade rights and numerous other concessions, including foreign control of Japanese tariff levels. Russia rounded out its eastward expansion in Siberia and Central Asia.

In the age of steel, however, this new imperialism kicked into high gear. In 1884–5, at the Conference in Berlin, a group of European countries carved up the map of Africa, Portugal, and, Spain, the once-great empires, were allowed to keep some of their claims of earlier centuries; the rest was divided up between the industrial powers, with the exceptions of Ethiopia, and the colonies of repatriated slaves – Liberia and Sierra Leone – which maintained their independence. In 1898, the US took over Hawaii, and also attacked, and acquired, most of Spain's remaining colonies, including Cuba, Puerto Rico and, far larger and more populous, the Philippines (Cuba was soon granted independence, but under a treaty which, among other indignities, allowed the US to invade whenever it saw fit, which turned out to be often; the US also kept a small part of Cuba called Guantanamo Bay).

The proliferation of treaty ports in China picked up pace during this flurry of imperialism, and extended inland up the major rivers. Japan, however, changed roles, from colonized to conqueror. It grabbed Taiwan and a bit of Manchuria from China in 1894–5, following which it managed to repudiate most of its unequal treaties with the West; it did not regain full control of its own tariffs, however, until 1911. In 1904–5 it fought and won a war with Russia, winning effective control of both Korea and Manchuria; it formally annexed Korea in 1910.

Yet, despite the higher tariffs and the carving out of larger markets under national control, the international economy continued to grow: trade as a proportion of output was fairly steady between the late 1870s and 1900, and then rose up until the outbreak of World War I in 1914. Overseas investment rose sharply during the same period. But the great powers of Europe went to war in 1914, producing a great continental cataclysm, and eventually drawing in the US; after that war, trade and foreign investment did not return to prewar levels. Economic instability was the rule, and many countries suffered high unemployment, inflation, and low growth. Then, more war, this time engulfing Asia as well as Europe, in the 1930s and 1940s. After 1945, international financial stability was restored in ways that will be discussed in Chapter 9; by many measures, however, the level of international economic integration – trade, investment – did not return to its 1910 levels until the late 1980s.

Why did it happen? There's more than one question there, really. Why did free trade flower, in the first place, between the late 1840s and late 1870s? Why did it then give way to protected national markets and empire? Why did these national systems which, despite tariffs, were bound together in a thriving international economy, descend into war and revolution, totalitarian dictatorships and mass unemployment, and in some cases into mass starvation or the systematic slaughter of civilians?

One would be ill-advised to seek simple or complete answers to such complex historical questions but, as with international production today, we can make a good case for the role played by changes in production, transport and communication technologies and the organization of industry. And, in working through this case, we can understand how economic forces can work against international integration as well as for it.

5.2. **The rise and decline of free trade**

The defeat of Napoleon in 1815 ended a long conflict between Britain and France, and left the former as Europe's – and thus the world's – preeminent military power. It was also the preeminent industrial power.

Britain's economy was, at the time, heavily protected. In order to protect its cost advantage in textile production, export of its advanced industrial machines was prohibited; so was the emigration of skilled artisans, which is to say people who knew how to use or make the machines (since the machines were actually fairly simple, knowing how to use them and how to make them were close to the same thing). These restrictions had carried over from the previous century. To them had been added protection for agriculture, in the form of the Corn Law. British grain prices had been high during the Napoleonic wars, and this had raised the value of agricultural land in Britain. To prevent a fall in these values, landowners backed legislation to put a floor under the price of grain in Britain by prohibiting imports of grain if the domestic price fell below that floor (in a later, reformed, version of the law, the prohibition was replaced with a tax on imports which kicked in when the price fell below the floor). Before 1832, large landholders effectively controlled the British Parliament, so this protection was not hard to obtain; once in place, it was hard to remove.

Other tariffs served not to protect domestic production, but only to raise revenue for the state: those on coffee and cocoa, for example, commodities with no domestic producers – or even producers of close substitutes – to protect. All of these trade restrictions were controversial within Britain at the time. Adam Smith's *Wealth of Nations* (1776) was, more than anything, an attack on trade restrictions. The doctrine of free trade was not only intellectually respectable, it also had powerful material interests behind it. The broad coalition behind the repeal of the Corn Laws, for instance, included workers seeking a better standard of living; factory owners whose aim was to pay the same workers lower wages (cheaper food was the common means to these apparently conflicting ends); and those who believed it would encourage other countries to specialize in agriculture, leaving industry to Britain (a position sometimes called "free trade imperialism").

Still, the politics of trade were complicated. Tariffs on imported iron protected the iron industry, but hurt machine makers and, through the cost of machines, textile manufacturers. Prohibitions on the emigration of skilled machine makers weren't nearly as effective at preventing their departure as they were at discouraging their return: it was not so hard to leave, but coming back one risked arrest. Prohibitions on the export of machines may have slowed the development of textile production elsewhere, but it also provided a motive for other countries to develop machine-building industries, and was a point of conflict between machine makers who saw a world market for their products, and textile manufacturers who wanted to keep their technical advantage by keeping the machines at home. Through this thicket of interests and arguments, the free trade side of the argument gradually won out, culminating in the repeal of the Corn Laws in 1846. In the 1850s and 1860s, Britain's unilateral liberalization was followed by a series of bilateral trade liberalization agreements between various pairs of European countries.

To understand why most European countries then returned in the late 1870s and early 1880s to the protection of national markets, it may help to have an idea of why the liberalization occurred in the first place.

5.2.1. TRADE BARRIERS AS A COLLECTIVE ACTION PROBLEM IN DOMESTIC POLITICS

One way of explaining why trade barriers exist for some products and not others is what I will call the concentrated interest theory, which sees trade barriers as the result of political mobilization and lobbying by those who benefit from the barriers (and, conversely, a lack of such mobilization by those who are hurt by the barriers). The theory holds that small groups in which each member has a lot at stake are easier to organize. An early version of this was laid out by Vilfredo Pareto, and a later one by Jonathan Pincus (1972). In both cases the logic is the same as Mancur Olsen's (1965) more general theory of collective action. Olsen's theory, in turn, is an application to political problems of the standard economic theory of public goods and the problem of free riding. A public good is one characterized by non-excludability: if it is provided, any member of the public can use it, whether or not they pay for it. Public goods can be either good things or bad things, from the standpoint of the relevant public; public "bads" are more commonly known as negative externalities, with urban air pollution being a simple example. A tariff is a public good for a small group – the Corn Law, for instance, was a public good for the owners of agricultural land in Britain, since by raising the price of grain it raised the rents they could charge their tenants. It was a public bad for a large group, which is to say most of the people in Britain who were not owners of agricultural land, and had to pay high prices for food.

The concentrated interest theory is that, for the members of either group to get their way, they must organize and take action to influence government policy. The principal obstacle to each group's organizing and acting is the problem of free riding. When the benefits of collective action are spread thinly over a large group (as in the majority of Britons who would have benefited from repeal of the Corn Law), it is harder to solve the free riding problem than when the benefits are shared among a small group. Particular trade barriers usually do benefit some small group. Why, then, are there not even more trade barriers than there are? Because, while a trade barrier helps one small group, it may hurt another: protect steelmakers from foreign competition, and you are raising the costs for domestic producers of anything made from steel, reducing their profits, and possibly sending their business to foreign competitors. Companies using steel may be more numerous and diffuse than steel manufacturers, but they are fewer and easier to organize than the broad consuming population.

This theory is intended as explaining policies within representative democracies, and as an explanation of why the majority often don't get their way in democratic systems: representatives respond to pressure from groups that are well organized around particular issues.

5.2.2. GROUP INTERESTS, OR IDEOLOGY?

Charles Kindleberger (1975) provides a good review of the advance of trade liberalization in Europe from 1820 to 1875. His aims are to show that liberalization in that period is *not* well explained by the concentrated interest theory, and that the spread of a liberal economic ideology explains more. The first aim is off to an easy start, since no European country in the early nineteenth century could really be described as a democracy, representative or otherwise: as noted above, big landowners dominated Britain's parliament in 1815; French tariff reductions in the 1850s were put into place by Napolean III, who had no obligation to consult the French Parliament on the matter.

Kindleberger presents various bits of evidence for the proposition that liberalization occurred, in large part, because the *idea* of free trade gained acceptance. In Britain, he argues that some manufacturers who had sought protection for their own products but not for those of others, abandoned their own tariff claims and embraced free trade because they became persuaded of a need for intellectual consistency. In the case of Italy, he shows that Cavour, the first prime minister of Italy, was a free trade ideologue, and persuaded his compatriots to adopt free trade, with the unintended effect of wiping out the nascent manufacturing industries of the country's south.

Evidence for the power of ideas is easy to find, and at the same time it is difficult ever to make this evidence into a convincing case that it is ideas that are the prime movers of events. Certainly, ideas can have force: the world is a complicated and confusing place, and ideas help us to organize our understanding of the world and decide how to act; ideologies and principles can provide focal points for collective action, which help to cut through a web of particular and conflicting interests. Yet, material interests, questions of wealth and power, can shape ideas and can limit the agenda, selecting which ideas become powerful and which remain the province of well-meaning cranks. These issues are well understood, but argument about the roles played by interests and ideas is not likely to be resolved soon. Kindleberger's evidence for the power of ideas is essentially that the pattern of liberalization could not be explained by certain theories of material interest, particularly the concentrated interest theory. Yet, Kindleberger makes no attempt to explain why, if the idea of free trade had become so powerful among European decision makers in the 1850s, 1860s, and early 1870s, it became so weak in the late 1870s. In light of the fifty year process by which the idea purportedly became hegemonic, how did the idea so quickly lose its power?

5.2.3. HEGEMONY AND FREE TRADE

One explanation for the reversal of the free trade tide in the 1870s is that the liberal international system that came before had been maintained by British power. From the 1870s onward, other powers – Germany within Europe, and the US in the wider world – were, if not on an equal footing with Britain, then certainly headed in that direction. Stephen Krasner (1976) says that an international system dominated by a single globally hegemonic power can produce an open trading system, while systems with several large states are unlikely to be open. Sometimes, this is called the "hegemonic leadership" or "hegemonic stability" theory, but that nomenclature causes confusion because a related, but distinct, theory of Kindleberger's deals with leadership (as distinct from hegemony) and stability (of which openness may be a consequence). I will therefore refer to Krasner's theory as the hegemony–openness theory.

Krasner identifies four interests which states seek to further, and which influence trade policy: aggregate national income, social stability, political power, and economic growth. For the purposes of discussing his theory, we can lump economic growth in with aggregate national income.

According to the theory of comparative advantage, an open, or liberal, trading system will maximize expected economic output (income). Krasner accepts that view, but argues that this benefit may be achieved at some cost to social stability, because each country's industries are exposed to the vicissitudes of international markets. The benefits and costs of openness are positively correlated: small states and less developed states need to trade more, and also are more vulnerable to its socially disruptive effects. Despite this trade-off, small countries generally benefit more from trade or, to use Krasner's terminology, their cost of closure is high. To see this, consider that both the US and Sweden are major producers of both heavy trucks and fighter aircraft. The US, with about 300 million inhabitants, vast spaces to drive across, and frequent wars to fight, is also the world's largest market for both types of product. Sweden, with 9 million inhabitants, a much smaller territory, and a long record of not fighting wars, has a much smaller domestic market for both. In the US, these industries could survive and remain up-to-date technologically, without exporting; in Sweden, they could not. Thus, for these industries (and, by the same logic, many other industries), Sweden's *cost of closure* is much higher than America's.

From this taxonomy of state interests, Krasner derives a theory of the relationship between the openness of the trading system and configurations of national power. Briefly, his prediction is this: when there is a large country which is the unquestioned industrial and technological leader, the trading system will tend to be open, both because that state can use its power to keep the system open, and because the other countries gain so much by trading with it. There may be many aspects to such a state's power – military, for instance, and financial – but in terms of Krasner's model, the central issue is that the smaller countries need access to foreign markets and technologies – not least, to the markets and technologies of the leading power – while the leading power is relatively self-sufficient, and so has a good fallback position in bargaining.

When there is no hegemonic leader to keep the global system open, Krasner sees two possible configurations for the international trading system. One is what he calls a regionalized system, the other is a system of small or midsized states. The regionalized system is composed of multiple imperial and/or regional hegemonic systems which are large, but not global: the British and French empires in the interwar period, the Soviet bloc, the Americas under US hegemony in certain periods, the Zollverein under Prussian leadership, prior to the creation of the German state. Such "regional" systems have relatively free trade internally, and relatively high barriers with the rest of the world. Note that when Krasner says "regional" there is no implication of geographical continuity, of something that looks like a region on a map: the sun never set on the British Empire because it was scattered around the globe, but he treats it as a region.

In the case of the collection of small or midsized states, the argument is that openness is likely because the cost of closure is so high for all concerned. Krasner does not discuss enforcement mechanisms within such collections of states; in the absence of a hegemonic leader, the solution to the collective action problems associated with free trade is not obvious. The clearest historical examples are interesting not as clusters of independent nation-states trading, but of clusters in which the benefits of trade have been used as a lever for creating a unified political entity: the EU today, or the US at its transition from confederation to federal system in the 1780s (those with some knowledge

Table 5.1. Hegemonic stability and systemic openness

Period	Systemic openness	Indicators of systemic openness		
		Tariffs	Trade proportions	Regionalization
1820–79	Increasing	Decreasing	Increasing	No data
1879–1900	Decreasing modestly	Increasing	Decreasing	No data
1900–13	Increasing	Little change	Increasing	Decreasing
1918–39	Decreasing	Increasing	Decreasing	Increasing
1945–70	Increasing	Decreasing	Increasing (esp. after 1960)	Decreasing (esp. after 1960)

Sources: Krasner (1976), Tables I–III; Thompson and Vescera (1992), Table 1.

of US history or law will know that much of the power of the federal government in the US derives from generous judicial interpretations of a single clause in the US Constitution – the one giving the federal government authority over all matters of interstate commerce). Notice, incidentally, that these are regional systems, in a more usual sense of that term than some of the imperial/hegemonic systems in Krasner's regional category (Table 5.1).

For Krasner, regionalism is something that happens when global openness is absent. Yet since his paper was published, we have seen increasing global economic openness, and also of increasing regionalism, side by side.

5.2.3.1. Problems of timing

Krasner's theory of hegemony and openness does not, by his own admission, do a terrific job of explaining the time of the rise and fall of trade barriers. It does offer an explanation for the renewal of tariffs and other trade barriers in the 1870s; as we will see below, however, there are plenty of other good explanations for that. It does not explain why Britain's promotion of free trade was halfhearted between 1815 and 1846, despite its unquestioned dominance during this period; nor can it account for why the US didn't pick up the hegemonic role sometime before 1945, though it seemed to have the means to do so. Krasner treats the period of 1945–70 – the years of steady, stable growth after World War II – as a period of openness. His measure of openness is the level of tariffs. Timothy McKeown (1991) shows that when openness is measured not by tariffs but by actual imports, the leading industrial economies were less open in the post-World War II period (US hegemony) than they had been in the years before World War I (which was after British hegemony had passed, in Krasner's reckoning).

In Britain in the early nineteenth century, despite its preeminence in industry, agricultural interests retained the power to protect their markets; in US in the early twentieth century, the political mechanisms which had facilitated protection for its young industries (trade policy made in congressional committees) continued to protect them in maturity. It was only after some shock to the system (revolutions across Europe in 1848; depression and war in the 1930s and 1940s) that new leaders and renewed institutions led these countries to assume fully their hegemonic roles.

One resolution to Krasner's problems of timing is offered by William Thompson and Lawrence Vescera (Thompson 1990; Thompson and Vescera 1992), who combine Krasner's theory with the neo-Schumpeterian theory of economic long waves. I'll return to that in Chapter 7.

5.2.3.2. Hegemony, or leadership?

Krasner's theory is about hegemony – one state exercising power over others, and setting out and enforcing rules which, while they may be mutually beneficial, best serve the interests of the hegemon. Kindleberger provides a different answer (Kindleberger 1973, 1981, and 1986). He sees the international economic system as a public good, which is likely to be underprovided due to free riding. Such functions as providing some coordination of national monetary policies, managing foreign exchange rates, and providing a rediscount mechanism so that liquidity is maintained even during a financial panic, are not filled automatically. A large state has a sufficiently large interest in maintaining the international economic system that it may decide not to free ride, and may simply step forward to provide the good. While it may also be in a position to encourage other states to contribute, the leader bears a disproportionate share of the cost. In this respect, the leadership theory borrows from the game-theoretic theory of military alliances (Schelling 1960).

Notice that Kindleberger's point is not about free trade *per se*, but about the management of the international financial system. This is actually a more fundamental issue than that of trade barriers: trade can go on despite tariffs, but it cannot go on if there's no way to finance it; in response to instability, states tend to raise trade barriers.

5.2.3.3. Finance, production, and periods between hegemons

Kindleberger's emphasis on finance is in contrast to Krasner's emphasis on industrial, technological and political power. This raises a question of what sort of power is required to be the hegemonic power. Kindleberger came to this topic while studying the Great Depression of the 1930s. At that time, the US appeared to have the power in production – technology, manufacturing, and modern agriculture – to play the role. Yet, long after Britain had ceased to be the leading country in production, it remained a leader in international finance. Krasner assumes that the US *could* have exercised hegemonic power at any point after 1918, if it had chosen to exercise the same. Was this so?

In Krasner's paper, you get the feeling that he thinks of hegemony as the normal state of affairs; the great puzzle for him is why it took the US so long to take the torch Britain was trying to pass on. Immanuel Wallerstein (1983), in contrast, thinks hegemonic episodes are rare. His theory provides a useful way of understanding the period between British and American hegemonies.

Wallerstein is a proponent of world systems theory, and as its name would suggest the proponents of that theory take a particularly long and broad view of things – the world, as a system, from about 1500 to the present. He believes that up to about 1980, there had been three instances of hegemony in the capitalist world economy. The first was under the Dutch between 1625 and 1672; the second, under the British between 1815 and 1873; the third, under the Americans between 1945 and 1967.

According to Wallerstein, hegemony is achieved when a single country is the leader in three areas at once: agricultural and industrial production, commerce, and finance. Each of the hegemonic powers achieved its advantage in production before that in commerce, and that in commerce before that in finance; the advantage in each area was lost to rivals in the same sequence. The period of hegemony begins when a country, already the leader in production and commerce, gains leadership in finance as well; it ends when the country loses its edge in production, even though it may remain the leader in commerce and finance for some time. So, while a country might be a leader in one or two of these areas for a long time, its period of leadership in all three is relatively short. The date of 1967 that Wallerstein gives as an endpoint to US hegemony tells us something about the context, and limitations, of much of this analysis. In the 1970s and early 1980s, it appeared to many that America had lost its edge in production to Japan and western Europe. I'll return to the reasons for this belief in Chapter 9; it is of interest because the corporate and political responses to the crisis of the 1970s gave us the management theories and institutions we have today. For now, let us just say that if there is such a thing as American hegemony, it had (or has) a longer life than Wallerstein was giving it.

5.2.3.4. Are states unitary, self-interested actors?

Earlier, we considered the concentrated interests theory, which sees trade barriers as the product of a state's internal politics, with different interest groups or classes pitted against one another. You may have noticed that in Krasner's hegemony-openness theory, there is no mention of such conflicting interests within states. Instead, he treats nation-states as unitary entities with well-defined *national interests*. This way of thinking about states comes from the field of international relations – people who study relations between states. Ignoring the political processes and conflicting interests within states obviously means missing a lot of what is going on. Any theory, of course, makes simplifying assumptions. In addition, however, to being an assumption used in analysis, the idea that each nation-state serves its national interest has a political purpose and a foundation in international law. Since the Treaty of Westphalia in 1688, the theory (if not the practice) of the international system has been one of sovereign states with equal rights. When a national government expresses its policy, it is a good diplomatic form to accept that policy as a representation of its national interest; to do otherwise would be seen as meddling in another country's internal affairs. That diplomatic fiction also became part of the language of the scholars who advise, and study, diplomats.

Today, the assumption of a unitary state with well-defined interests is associated with the "realist" school of international relations, which treats states as self-interested actors, much as standard economic theory treats individuals as self-interested utility maximizers. Even in its own terms, Krasner's theory shows some of the limits of this approach: he gives the state four different objectives (income, growth, stability, and political power), but doesn't say how the state chooses the right balance between these. Unless the state comes equipped with a predefined utility function to settle the trade-offs, its priorities will have to be determined by some domestic political process.

It is difficult to tell, really, whether Krasner is a doctrinaire realist (or, technically, neorealist, but let us not delve into that distinction), or more eclectic. The opening sentence of his paper extols the virtues of a simple model of the state, without internal contradictions. His model linking hegemony and openness appears outright mechanistic. But then he gets into trouble; he cannot explain why British hegemony took so long to produce free trade, and why America waited so long to take up its hegemonic responsibilities. He faces up to this trouble and, by the end of his paper, we are in a whole different world, analytically speaking. He has let in all sorts of actors: farmers and industrialists, financiers oriented toward the domestic market and other financiers oriented toward foreign investment, believers in free trade and believers in protection; he is taking into account the leading country's domestic political institutions, the forces which shaped them, and the way the form of the inherited institutions empowers certain groups and shapes policy. Notice his analytic strategy, because it is very common in the social sciences: he starts with his favored theory, explains what he can with it, and then brings in other theories to explain what is left over. This is as good a method of investigating the world as any, but for proponents of other theories it does of course raise the question: "Why did he start with *his* theory, explain what he could, and then use *my* theory just to patch the holes?"

5.3. Cheap grain

Actually, despite his realist bluster, Krasner tips his hand early on in his paper, when he says "*the* event that precipitated higher tariff levels (from the late 1870s onwards) was the availability of inexpensive grain from the American Midwest" (Krasner 1976, p. 337). This has nothing to do with hegemony. It is, however, commonly acknowledged as a factor, and there's nothing Krasner could do to avoid it.

Why did the price of wheat fall? And why would a response to the price of wheat lead to tariffs on steel and textiles and electrical goods?

The price of wheat fell because new supplies were available from the US; soon Argentina, Australia, and Canada became players in this market as well. US grain exports had grown gradually as settlers drove native Americans from the Midwest, and as first canals and then railroads made it practical to bring grain to river and sea ports. This trade had been interrupted, from 1862–5, by the US Civil War. After the Civil War, supplies were restored. In the same period, newly abundant steel brought more and better railroads, and bigger and faster ships; moreover, products which became widely available in the age of steel – mechanical reapers, chemical fertilizers – gave a bigger boost to productivity in the newly settled lands where labor was relatively scarce, than in the traditional grain exporting countries where the ratio of labor to land was higher.

For several hundred years before this, the relatively rich countries of Europe's Atlantic seaboard had imported grain from the Baltic, particularly from states which were to become the northeastern part of Germany (Prussia, Mecklenberg, and Pomerania), and what was then Poland (which included, in the periods when it was an independent state and not part of Russia or some other large neighbor, much of what is now Ukraine and Lithuania). Denmark's kings had grown rich collecting tolls from the grain-laden ships passing the straits guarded by a castle better known to us in fictional form, as the location of Shakespeare's *Hamlet*. Low-priced grain from America put an end to this trade. It also put European farmers everywhere into a price squeeze.

Different European countries responded differently to this problem. In Italy, and much of central and eastern Europe, marginal farms were abandoned and a wave of emigrants headed for the New World; this despite new tariffs which protected the farmers who remained. Denmark (which had exported grain in addition to collecting tolls) managed to move into higher value-added products, exporting cheese, eggs, and bacon. Germany and France protected their agriculture with tariffs. European settler colonies with ample agricultural land – Argentina, Australia, Canada, the US – left their agricultural tariffs low. Peter Alexis Gourevitch (1977) summarizes the outcomes for both agriculture and industry in both major European countries and major wheat exporters (Table 5.2).

Table 5.2. Tariff levels in industry and agriculture (late nineteenth century)

		Industrial tariffs	
		High	Low
Agricultural tariffs	High	France, Germany, Italy	Austria, Hungary
	Low	Australia, Canada, US	Argentina, Great Britain

Source: Gourevtich (1977), Table 1.

The way in which these new agricultural tariffs contributed to new industrial tariffs is well illustrated by the German case. The big German grain farms were estates owned by the Junkers, the aristocratic class of Prussia. The Junkers also dominated the German army and civil service, and were disproportionately represented in the parliament. Before the arrival of cheap American grain, they had supported free trade. Now, they wanted a tariff on grain imports. Despite their considerable political influence, however, they were not powerful enough to get such a tariff on their own. The laborers on the Junkers' estates would have benefited from such a tariff, but they were not a political force, nor did the Junkers want them to be. Almost everybody else stood to be hurt by such a tariff: the owners of smaller, family-run farms in the south and west of the country would have been better off following the Danish model; industrialists and industrial workers would be hurt by higher grain prices; the professional and commercial classes generally favored freer trade.

There were, however, some industries which keenly wanted tariffs on products competing with their own: heavy industry, particularly iron, steel, chemicals, and textiles. Here again, though, almost everybody else in the country would be hurt by such a tariff: the manufacturers of other products which used heavy industry outputs as their inputs; the consumers of these products, including the big farms of Prussia.

The outcome was a deal, brokered by the Chancellor, Otto von Bismark. The deal has come to be known as "the marriage of iron and rye" (Gerschenkron 1966): agriculture and industry both got their tariffs. Gourevitch shows the interests, and outcome, in this way (Table 5.3):

A glance at the table will suggest that a different deal was quite possible. Although the marriage of iron and rye was good for heavy industry and the grain farmers, each had to live with the other's tariff, which they would rather have been without. Others would have preferred to be without both tariffs. Why was the outcome high-high, not low-low? After studying the outcomes in France, Britain and the US, as well as Germany, Gourevitch comes to this conclusion:

Table 5.3. Interest groups and tariffs (late nineteenth century Germany)

		Industrial tariffs	
		High	Low
Agricultural tariffs	High	Actual outcome – "the marriage of iron and rye"	Best outcome for both capitalists and workers in heavy industry ("iron")
	Low	Best outcome for Junkers (agricultural landlords in the east – "rye")	Best outcome for both capitalists and workers in light (finished) manufacturing

Source: Gourevtich (1977), Table 3.

There is a striking similarity in the identities of the victors and losers from country to country: producers over consumers, heavy industrialists over finished manufacturers, big farmers over small, and property owners over laborers. In each case, a coalition of producers' interests defined by large scale basic industry and substantial landowners defeated its opponent. *It is probable, therefore, that different types of groups from country to country are systematically not equal in political resources.* (pp. 307–8; emphasis added)

Quelle surprise.

5.3.1. WHY DID HEAVY INDUSTRY PREVAIL ON TARIFFS?

Gourevitch's understated conclusion about differences in political resources does not quite do justice to the evidence of his cases: in almost all cases, heavy industry got what it wanted. (The only case where it wanted low industrial tariffs was Britain, which still had a head start in many industries; by the 1920s, even British industry was protected, under the rubric of "imperial preference.") But this had not always been so. At the start of the 1870s, both France and Germany had growing heavy industry, and low industrial tariffs. So, either these industries didn't always *want* tariff protection, or didn't always get what they wanted. What changed?

One thing that changed, in Europe, was that cheap grain on world markets meant possibility of an alliance with agriculture, along the lines of the marriage of iron and rye. Yet this doesn't explain why grain exporting countries like Australia, Canada, and the US protected their industry – as, with the spread of industry, did others.

The other thing that had changed was that there was now a lot more heavy industry, both because there was more industry, and because a greater proportion of it was heavy. Partly that was due to the growth of such basic industries as steel and chemicals. It would be a mistake, however, to conflate "heavy" and "basic." By "heavy industry" we mean *capital-intensive* industry; the manufacture of silicon chips is heavy industry, just as much as steel. Heavy industry at the time required big investments in special-purpose equipment. These industries were capable of achieving low average costs when a high level of output was maintained. When there are many competitors and excess capacity in such an industry, however, it can be an arena of ruinous competition, with prices cut so low that all companies in the industry are losing money. As we will see in Chapter 8, companies within each country solved this problem either by merging or by forming cartels. Such a solution *within* countries is futile, however, under conditions of free trade. For this reason, Michael Piore and Charles Sabel (1984) attribute the renewed protection of national markets to the growth of heavy industry.

Notice that if industrial trade barriers were, among other things, a means of stabilizing markets in emerging capital-intensive industries, we need to be cautious about understanding the political economy of tariffs simply in terms of interest groups or classes. While the owners and workers in a particular industry may be the only ones to gain unambiguously from a tariff protecting that industry, it is arguable that everybody in a country has an interest in economic stability (and recall that stability was one of the four objectives Krasner attributed to nation-states). It is possible, if you accept this line of argument, to put the rising tariffs of the late 1870s into a national interest framework, like that of the neorealist school of international relations.

5.3.2. CLASSES AND INTEREST GROUPS: A NOTE ON TRADE THEORY AND TRADE POLITICS

When we do want to account for the way domestic politics affect trade policy, we should bear in mind some different ways of classifying groups of interested parties. Specifically, we can make a distinction between classes (which can be very large) and interest groups (which tend to be smaller).

In the early 1990s, the governments of the US, Mexico, and Canada were negotiating the North American Free Trade Agreement (NAFTA). NAFTA is an unusual trade bloc in that it straddles the line between the first and third worlds, the rich and the poor. Most labor unions in the US opposed NAFTA, while business interests largely supported the agreement. The principal argument in opposition to NAFTA was that US workers would be put in direct competition with workers in Mexico, where wages are lower, and where environmental and workplace health and safety standards are more lax. This would lead, the argument went, both to a loss of jobs in the US, and to a reduction in wages and a deterioration of working conditions. Labor lost the argument, and NAFTA was ratified. Whether or not NAFTA deserves a share of the blame for the continued decline of the relative earnings of lower-paid workers within the US, is too complicated a question to answer right now. The important thing is simply this: labor (to the extent we can say that the positions taken by US unions reflect the interests or views of US workers) thought that it would be hurt by NAFTA, while capital thought that it would be helped.

The views of the unions and the capitalists in the US were consistent with standard trade theory. As we saw in Chapter 4, the Stolper–Samuelson theorem holds that when trade barriers between two countries are lowered, the gains go disproportionately to the more abundant factor in each country (that being capital in the US, labor in Mexico); in each country, the scarcer factor is the relative loser, and may even lose in absolute terms. The Stolper–Samuelson theorem is within the standard Heckscher–Ohlin framework of trade theory. As such, it sees a country's comparative advantage as resulting from its capital–labor ratio: rich countries have high ratios and specialize in capital-intensive goods, while poor countries have low ratios and specialize in labor-intensive goods. In the US, capital expected to gain from NAFTA and labor expected to lose. (I'll consider the Mexican side of the bargain in later chapters.) That divides one large country into two groups, identified with two factors of production. Marx would have called these *social classes*.

Compare this with the case of Germany in the 1870s, and the marriage of iron and rye. There, the owners of heavy industry and large farms supported tariffs, those of light industry and small farms opposed them. Workers were similarly divided. This situation, too, has a place in standard trade theory. The Ricardo–Viner model helps to understand what happens when capital can't be moved from one industry to another: spindles and looms can't be used to make silicon chips. In this case, we divide capital into two or more *industry-specific factors*. Now, when trade barriers are lowered (or raised), some industries win, and others lose. But now the groups of winners and losers are *interest groups,* much smaller and more numerous than social classes.

The concentrated interests theory is about interest groups: concentrated interests are more likely to organize and to exercise influence. Is that the best way to understand the politics of trade? Kindleberger, you will recall, thought not, and argued that ideology played a large role. The NAFTA case raises a different question about the interest group model: when does political organization go beyond interest groups to something broader, such as class?

The answer suggested by the difference between the Heckscher–Ohlin and Ricardo–Viner models of trade, is that it depends on the degree of factor specificity within a country. Hall and Gingerich (2004) tell us that the political response to international production today has been different in the US than it has in Germany, and argue that this is because both labor and capital move more easily between industries in the US. I will discuss the reasons for this difference in mobility in Chapter 11. For now, just notice that in the NAFTA case we are in a Heckscher–Ohlin world, where labor and capital move easily between industries. In such a world all workers within a country are in one boat, and all owners of capital in that country are in a different one; the politics of trade are then class politics. In the marriage of iron and rye (and, Gingerich and Hall argue, in Germany today) capital and labor are both industry specific, and trade politics are interest group politics.

Another way of understanding differences in trade policy between countries and over time is that when there are both low barriers to trade and high international capital mobility, the industry-specific nature of capital may not matter as much: many manu-facturers in the US are threatened by imports from low-wage countries, but NAFTA made it easier for the companies to buy or build factories in Mexico; while this strategy requires some scrapping of their established capital stock in the US, this is not nearly so great a sacrifice as that required to move their capital to another industry altogether. In that case, the problems addressed in the Ricardo–Viner model disappear, as does any common interest between capital and labor in particular industries.

6 Empire

The previous chapter concerned ways in which states interact to shape the international trading system. In the history of the international system, however, it has often been the case that certain states have chosen not to interact diplomatically with others, but to simply conquer them. Krasner uses the heading of "regionalization" to cover anything that brings two or more states together in a single market. This category includes regional blocs like the EU; systems of regional hegemony, such as once exercised by the US in the western hemisphere (those schooled in American history may know it by the anodyne title of the Monroe Doctrine); and the formation of empires through outright conquest. For Krasner, this serves a useful analytical purpose, because he's concerned with the formation of large "regional" markets as an alternative to global liberalization – it doesn't matter if they are voluntary unions or empires.

The difference does matter though, in more ways than one. I will not dwell here on the injustices of empire; readers with an interest might find a good starting place in Mike Davis's *Late Victorian Holocausts* (2001). With reference to Krasner's argument, however, we need to recognize that while empires can serve as large protected markets, many colonies simply do not have much purchasing power, and it is hard to attribute this kind of empire to Krasner's motive of creating protected markets. The late nineteenth century European colonial expansion in Africa and Southeast Asia was primarily about access to raw materials – rubber, tin, copper, and so on.

The growth of new industries and high-volume production in the late nineteenth century had increased the appetite, in all industrial countries, for such previously minor materials. Yet on the face of it, empire was an odd procurement strategy. The new imperialists of that era had been schooled on the principles of free trade. Nowhere is the concept of comparative advantage more clear-cut than with raw materials – different parts of the world have natural comparative advantages in the form of endowments of certain minerals, or climates and soils suitable for growing certain crops. Why, then, not simply buy the raw materials?

A simple answer is that it is sometimes cheaper to steal than to buy. This, certainly, has been the motive for empire more often than not. North Africa was the granary of the Roman empire. Prior to conquest by Rome, grain had been traded across the Mediterranean, now it was seized. The relationship between Rome and its colonies was, in fact, just a blown-up version of the relationship between the Roman cities and the countryside. Peter Brown (1971, p. 12) quotes the Roman physician Galen, who was writing about famine in the countryside:

The city dwellers, as was their practice, collected and stored enough corn for all the coming year immediately after the harvest. They carried off all the wheat, the barley, the beans and the lentils and left what remained to the country folk.

Not a pretty picture, if you lived in the countryside, which almost everybody did in those times. The parallel between empire and colonies, city and countryside, is reflected in one set of twentieth century terms for the rich industrial countries, and the others: metropolis, and periphery.

The early centuries of modern European expansion can certainly be cast in similar terms: the seizure, first, of gold, silver – what Marx called "primitive accumulation" – and land; then of people, in the use of slaves on plantations and in mines. All of these were unadorned theft. The question is whether this is also a good way of understanding the renewed imperialism of the late nineteenth century.

6.1. **Natural resources, transaction costs, and colonial control**

An alternative interpretation, provided by Jeffry Frieden (1994), uses Oliver Williamson's (1979) transaction cost theory. Before explaining that theory, it is best to offer an example.

Suppose a company in Paris in the late 1800s is deciding whether to invest in a rubber plantation in Vietnam. This requires an investment in obtaining and clearing land, planting trees, establishing whatever local processing and transport infrastructure is required, and training local staff. In deciding to make this investment, the company has certain expectations about its property rights, local tax rates, labor market institutions, and so on. But will these expectations be fulfilled? What happens if, after the investment is made, the government of Vietnam decides to change the rules of the game, raising taxes, permitting plantation workers to form unions, or even expropriating the plantation altogether? In that case, the value of the company's investment – or, to be precise, the investment's value *to the company* – is reduced, or even lost altogether.

With this kind of risk in mind, Friedman suggests, the investment is unlikely to happen unless the Paris company expects the French state to guarantee that the Vietnamese state will not take actions that reduce the value of the assets. There are many such actions that the Vietnamese government might take, many of them within the ordinary scope of a state's authority, so even though the French state is much more powerful than the

Vietnamese state, such a guarantee is not easy to fulfill. One way of providing the guarantee is to build an empire – the French state simply takes over the Vietnamese state.

To put this in the language of transaction cost economics, the relationship between the investor and the host country is a *transaction*. The value the assets have for the investor is *transaction specific*. That is to say, if the transaction goes sour, the value of the assets to the investor falls (or is lost altogether). This situation makes the investor vulnerable to *opportunistic behavior* on the part of the host country. The investment will not be made unless there is a governance structure in place which protects the investor from such behavior.

Williamson developed this framework to explain vertical integration – that is, why one company takes over another, either upstream (a supplier) or downstream (a customer). Frieden is employing it to explain why one country takes over another. We will see transaction costs again, used in the original way, in Chapter 8.

Notice that the host country's vulnerability is different than the firm's because what is being produced is a generic commodity, rubber. Assuming that there is an open international market for rubber, the value of the assets of the rubber plantation and associated infrastructure is *not* transaction specific for the Vietnamese state: whoever operates the plantation and however much profit they make, the rubber will be produced and exported, the government will collect taxes, and a certain number of Vietnamese will be employed.

Compare this with an investment in a manufacturing plant which is part of an international supply network, such as Intel's semiconductor plants in Malaysia and Costa Rica. Intel does not invest in the local infrastructure – it expects the host governments to provide this. The most valuable equipment in the factory could, if necessary, be moved by Intel to another country. So, while Intel has some exposure, its entire investment is not at risk. Moreover, the value of the factory to the host government is transaction specific. Intel provides new designs, technology, and training on an ongoing basis; it also provides the worldwide market for the chips. Without the relationship with Intel, such a factory would lose almost all of its value; for this reason, Intel has little to fear from the governments of host countries.

6.2. **Control without colonies**

Notice, too, that while Friedman's paper is about why industrial states established colonies, the essence of the argument is not territorial empire *per se*, but control more generally. Friedman is saying that a country like France had a motive to take over a country like Vietnam, because that was a way to guarantee the investments French companies wanted to make in primary sector industries there. There are other ways of providing such a guarantee.

By the time the European powers and Japan renewed their colonial expansion in the late nineteenth century, the US had nearly finished its straightforward territorial acquisition. It did conquer formerly independent Hawaii; it also grabbed the choicer remaining bits of the Spanish empire, but soon released Cuba and the Philippines into states of quasi-independence, keeping only Puerto Rico under direct rule. But from then on, it exercised control over countries in which its companies established mines, plantations, or oil wells, not by conquest but with the threat of overthrowing the government.

Between the 1920s and 1966, the US sent small invasion or occupation forces to many countries. Most of those were small countries in Latin America and the Caribbean. In addition, numerous governments were toppled (or elections annulled) by the domestic military, with US backing (Kinzer, 2006). The countries whose governments were changed in these ways were principally primary sector exporters, with substantial primary sector investment by foreign companies.

The US was not the only practitioner of this form of control. In 1953, the newly elected government of Iran nationalized the oil industry, previously controlled by a British company, Anglo-Iranian Oil. Britain attempted to organize the overthrow of the Iranian government. In this case, Britain failed. Britain approached the US for help, and the Iranian government was successfully replaced – this began the reign of the Shah, which ended with the revolution of 1978.

In 1954, the newly elected government of Guatemala nationalized the unused land connected with the plantations of the US-based United Fruit Company (Chiquita bananas). The nationalization was part of an ambitious land reform, aimed at converting a countryside of large estates into one of small family farms. Such reforms have been attempted in many countries; they played an important role in the development of South Korea and Taiwan, but more often they have encountered insuperable domestic political opposition, a subject I will return to in later chapters. For now, we are concerned not with domestic, but with foreign, opposition to reforms. The Guatemalan government compensated United Fruit, but based its compensation payment on the ludicrously low value the company had itself given for the property on its tax forms. This might seem just desserts for a corporate tax cheat, but in the transaction cost framework of Frieden's model we would describe it, with a bit more clinical detachment, as opportunistic behavior by the host government. Soon, the US government had engineered a coup which overthrew the Guatemalan government. The land reform was immediately reversed; the country's subsequent history of slaughter is beyond the scope of this book.

In both cases, historians argue about why the coups took place: was it to protect investments, or was it geopolitical, part of the Cold War? Britain had a clear interest in protecting the investment of Anglo-Iranian, but when it turned to the US for help it told its ally a story (not, as it happened, a true one) about communist influence in the Iranian government. United Fruit was an American company – one, in fact, in which the families of US Secretary of State John Foster Dulles and his brother, CIA director Allen Dulles, owned shares – but it is also true that Washington did not like the fact that one member of the governing coalition in Guatemala was the country's communist party – a party which, while small, had played a key role in organizing the rural poor in favor of the government and the land reform.

In 1960, the CIA backed the coup which installed the kleptocrat Mobutu Sese Seko as president of the resource-rich Congo (known for most of his rule as Zaire). Mobutu ruled from 1965 to 1997, benefiting from a steady stream of military and economic assistance from the US and France, until he died, with his country in impoverished shambles and his personal foreign bank accounts bulging. Mobutu made life easy for foreign investors, but there were also geopolitical stakes – the Soviet Union had its own ideas about who should be president. So it would be reckless to conclude that these interventions were carried out solely for the protection of the investments of companies in the primary sector. Let us just say that American geopolitical interests seemed to coincide with the interest of Western companies in a great many cases. For a readable and well-documented overview, see Stephen Kinzer's *Overthrow* (2006).

The efficacy of small invasions and coups for protecting investments can be seen as an index of hegemonic power. Recall our discussion, in Chapter 5, of the 1970s as a period in which US hegemony had faded: US military power was stretched thin in Vietnam, its economic superiority threatened by Japan and western Europe, its strategic dominance challenged by Soviet missiles. Thus weakened, threats of gunboat diplomacy and *coups d'etat* were somewhat reduced in credibility (not to say that they stopped altogether). It was in this period that numerous countries suddenly nationalized their oil fields, and OPEC went from a talking shop to a powerful cartel. How different from the outcome in Iran, less than twenty years earlier; how different from Iraq, after the American victory in the Cold War. Hegemony can be seen as an alternative mechanism to accomplish the purpose Frieden attributes to empire – protecting investments in the primary sector.

Oil, while it fits Frieden's reasoning, is such an important strategic resource that it could be seen as a special case: steady prices and volumes of supply would be seen as important by the governments of the industrial countries, whether or not they felt a need to protect the investments of particular companies. Yet, microprocessors are also of strategic importance, while bananas are not. And while bananas have invited US-sponsored regime change in Honduras and Guatemala, it is unlikely that a government will ever be toppled to protect Intel's investment in its factory in nearby Costa Rica. The dependence of these factories on Intel's technologies and its marketing network protects the company's investment, without the assistance of the CIA or the US Marine Corps.

6.3. **Explaining decolonization**

Can we explain, within this theoretical framework, why decolonization occurred so quickly after World War II? The industrial countries' appetite for raw materials continued to grow, but colonialism almost vanished in less than twenty years.

Sometimes, empire's retreat was a direct result of the war: foreign concessions in China, barring Hong Kong and Macao, ended in 1943; Japan lost Korea and Taiwan at the end of the war, and the US gave up the Philippines. But then India gained independence in 1947, and in the late 1950s and early 1960s, most of Africa and Southeast Asia – countries where empire had been oriented almost purely toward resource extraction, not market creation – achieved independence from Britain, France, the Netherlands, and Belgium. We must be careful, of course, not to make this sound easier than it was. Although colonial rule usually ended with a ceremonial handover of power that made the whole thing look planned, the imperial powers were putting a good face on a bad situation. France fought – and lost – long wars in Indochina and Algeria; Britain fought to keep Kenya, Cyprus, and Malaya; Belgium's exit from the Congo was hardly peaceful; and Portugal (a relatively small and poor European power which, improbably, kept its African colonies long after anyone else) fought to keep Angola, Mozambique, and Guinea-Bissau. Yet, peacefully or not, the colonial powers did leave. What had changed that these empires, all advancing around the turn of the century, were in headlong retreat fifty years later?

Part of the answer may lie in the facts that the advance of both nationalist and communist ideologies, and resistance organized around these, had made imperialism more expensive; that most of the countries with overseas empires were now economically and militarily weak, if not defeated altogether; and that the defeat of the imperial designs of the Axis powers delegitimated empire. Still, there had always been resistance to empire, with one ideology or another; the modern armies of the European powers still had advantages over most of their ill-equipped challengers; and the legitimation of empire has often proved robust in the face of cognitive dissonance – from the Monroe Doctrine of 1820 through the Spanish-American war of 1898, for instance, Americans were indignant about European imperialism, yet conquered ever more territory themselves, and came at times to speak of themselves as an empire (van Alstyne 1960). So, while there may be something in these answers, they are not entirely satisfactory.

What about Frieden's theory? It would seem to fail in face of the fact that the industrial economies needed more resources than ever in this period of rapid growth, and yet gave up control of their colonies. There are two considerations we need to add. First, as these countries achieved independence, they typically launched programs of import substitution industrialization (ISI). ISI is often thought of as cutting a country off from world markets, but as we saw in Chapter 2, it actually requires the ongoing transfer of technology, equipment, parts, and in many cases investment, from rich countries to poor ones; moreover, if the developing country has aspirations to export industrial goods, it must reckon with the fact that most industrial exports are not generic, but require access to particular markets. Therefore, much of the investment in ISI was, from the developing country's standpoint, transaction specific: its value depended on continuing business relationships with particular companies or countries. If a developing country's policies toward the primary sector could not be kept entirely separate from its policies toward the emerging industrial sector – separate *both* in the country's own practice and in the foreign investors' expectations of the developing country's behavior – then the effort to industrialize made it more costly for developing countries to treat foreign primary sector investors opportunistically.

6.4. **The consequences of designing institutions for resource extraction**

Transaction cost theory provides a powerful framework for analyzing imperial motivations, but a hazard of using it is that "guaranteeing the value of transaction-specific investments" has human costs, which become invisible in this analysis. The examples of Guatemala and Congo/Zaire, above, begin to make this clear. The latter country also provides one of the most vivid examples of the depredations of simple colonial rule. From 1908 to 1960, it was the Belgian Congo that was regarded as a personal property of the King of Belgium. The Belgians established rubber plantations and mines. Africans were forced to work in these, in fear of having their hands cut off if they refused. Very little education was available for Africans in the Congo, and there was little infrastructure investment beyond that required to get supplies in and raw materials out.

Given this legacy of colonial hell, the postcolonial hell of Congo/Zaire is not surprising. Nor, sadly, is it unique. Recent research by Daron Acemoglu, Simon Johnson, and James Robinson (2001) examines the relative economic development of the world's ex-colonies. It turns out that the countries that have fared worst are those where the imperial power sought simply to extract resources, and not to settle. Countries with colonial pasts as simple providers of natural resources, it seems, have postcolonial histories of being places where investment is relatively unsafe from expropriation or other arbitrary government action; this insecurity reduces investment and retards economic growth. Acemoglu et al.'s interpretation of this is that institutions established under colonial rule helped shape post-colonial institutions, and that institutions established for the purpose of resource extraction by colonial powers were not designed to protect the property rights of local businesses. This brings an ironic closure to Frieden's transaction cost story: systems set up to protect foreign investors from "opportunistic" behavior by local authorities, fostered regimes that did not offer this protection to a wider range of entrepreneurs. We will return to this problem in Chapter 14.

Part II
The Rise of Big Business

7 Changing Technology, Changing Industry

Liberal trade regimes come, and they go. So do empires. Technology, on the other hand, keeps accumulating. Yet the application of new technologies does not happen at a steady pace. New technological applications are always changing the economy and society, but in some periods they do it more than others.

7.1. Industrial revolutions

It is conventional to speak of two industrial revolutions, the first and the second. The first occurred primarily in Britain in the late eighteenth and early nineteenth centuries – an approximate starting date is 1760. Its distinguishing features were the emergence of the factory system and the development of labor saving production equipment that used inanimate power sources (water at first, coal-generated steam later on). The second industrial revolution occurred in the late nineteenth century, its beginnings marked by the discovery, in the 1860s and 1870s, of ways to make steel cheaply. Important uses of the now-plentiful steel included the development, from the 1870s onwards, of a staggering array of manufacturing equipment, mechanizing the production of everything from oatmeal for porridge to cigarettes. By 1900, applications of electric power were becoming widespread, and we can mark the end of the second industrial revolution with that development. A good account of the technological and industrial developments during both of these periods – and the time between – can be found in David Landes' *The Unbound Prometheus* (1969), although his coverage is restricted to western Europe.

This demarcation of industrial revolutions has become controversial, among economic historians, in recent decades (see, for instance, Jones 1988). Both the idea that the first industrial revolution was a great turning point and the primacy accorded Britain are challenged by those who claim a gradual development of "proto-industry" in much of Europe over the preceding centuries. And the claim of special status for the second industrial revolution must face the fact that between the first and the second, industrial progress was considerable: railways were invented and built, water power replaced by steam, iron production expanded thanks to the expanding supply of coal, and so on.

Claims of sharp historical demarcations can always be faulted, but the first and second industrial revolutions do mark watersheds that are important for our understanding of the world today. In 1750, Britain and the other early-industrializing areas of Europe were on a par, in terms of manufacturing output and standard of living, with comparable parts of China and Japan; parts of India were comparable in terms of manufacturing, if not the general standard of living. The first industrial revolution marked the beginning of what Kenneth Pomeranz (2000) calls "the great divergence," in which the economies of Britain, parts of Europe, and certain colonies of European settlers took off, leaving the rest of the world increasingly far behind for over two hundred years. The second industrial revolution saw the birth of big business, the corporation with shareholders and professional managers, and the methods of organization which have made multi-national companies the power they are today.

7.1.1. COTTON AND THE FIRST INDUSTRIAL REVOLUTION

In the third quarter of the eighteenth century, most textiles produced in England and elsewhere in Europe were of wool. Taken in aggregate, the production of wool textiles was big business, but there were no big companies involved in textile manufacturing. In fact, there was nothing we would recognize as a textile factory. Entrepreneurs would buy raw materials, and then arrange to have different stages of production – spinning, weaving, fulling, dying, and the rest – done in small batches at different locations, usually in the cottage of somebody contracted to do a bit of the work. This was called the "putting out" system. Putting out was, in effect, a way for cloth merchants to outsource production to the low-wage, unregulated environment of the countryside, away from the traditional textile production centres in towns. It was easier to do this in England than in most of continental Europe because, on the continent, craft guilds and town authorities had the political power to keep production in the towns.

The tools used by the cottage producers were simple. English wool textile production grew, and in the mid-eighteenth century growth was causing costs to rise. Relationships between the cottage producers and the entrepreneurs were deteriorating; wages were rising, as was the cost of transporting materials further and further to reach the workers where they lived. Together, these considerations led to rising demand for machines to mechanize some of the steps in fabric production. The first such machines were developed with wool in mind, but wool is harder to work by machine than cotton.

Cotton production took off. Machine after machine was invented for one aspect or another of transforming raw cotton into cloth. Machines were brought together in dedicated buildings which had the benefit of water power and the presence – whether this was a benefit or not depends on your point of view – of a supervisor's discipline (Marglin 1974; Landes 1986; Clark 1994). Instead of materials going to cottagers who fit that work in alongside farming and other pursuits, workers moved to factories and the work became full time.

Cotton does not grow in England, but England could import cotton from colonies such as Georgia and South Carolina, and from other producers such as Egypt. The invention of the cotton gin, a machine for separating the cotton fibre from the rest of the plant, soon made it practical to use short-staple upland cotton, which grew in environments not friendly to the better quality long-staple sea-island cotton. So the supply of cotton grew, as cotton plantations and slavery spread across what was now the southern US, from the Atlantic coast to Texas.

Cotton textiles may seem a narrow base for something so sweeping that it can be called the industrial revolution. We need to bear in mind the relative economic importance of textiles in the eighteenth century. Cloth was a major factor in consumer budgets; because it was relatively easy to transport, it was an even bigger factor in international trade. We also need to bear in mind the considerable spin-offs from expanded textile production. The demand for more and better machinery to equip factories stimulated the machine building industries, so that England became the world's leading producer not only of textiles but also of manufacturing equipment. Similarly, the demand for dyes spurred growth and innovation in the chemical industry.

7.1.2. PROPERTY RIGHTS AND THE RISE OF THE WEST

Why did this happen in England in the late eighteenth century? Why did China, despite the advanced state of its textile manufacturing, not make the move to factories and inanimate power sources? How did England's move to factories come to mark the start of a period of sustained economic growth in Europe and its settler colonies that has lasted until the present day? Answers to such questions, as always, must be treated with caution: since the events are unique and the possible causes are many, there is limited scope for testing theories. It will be useful, however, for us to consider two important explanations. In addition to helping us to understand the historical puzzles of the industrial revolution and the great divergence, these two explanations will help us later on when we study differences today in the economic institutions of various countries, and also the problems of economic development today.

The first explanation sees the first industrial revolution not as a break with western Europe's past, but as a natural development given its institutional framework. But what were the important features of that framework, and where did they come from? The basic sources here are Douglass North and Robert Thomas (1973), and Eric Jones (1981).

Since the collapse of the western half of the Roman Empire, there has been no single dominant state in Europe. The result was over a thousand years of intense military competition between states. War is expensive, and to succeed in this competition states needed to be able to raise revenues and also to borrow money. This, the story goes, led European states to develop systems of property rights which encouraged investment and economic growth – so that there would be sufficient economic activity to tax, and thus sufficient revenues to fund wars. Similarly, this competition led to the development of financial institutions capable of raising even greater sums in the short term – with repayments assured from the ongoing stream of taxes. The countries which became dominant in Europe were those with tax revenue streams in which bankers had confidence – those governments were able to finance wars at lower rates of interest (Brewer 1990; Macdonald 2003).

The North/Thomas/Jones argument is that a competitive environment (competition here being manifested in warfare between states) selects for efficient institutions. This particular style of evolutionary argument is typical of the New Institutional Economics, which uses the notion of optimal or efficient institutions emerging from competition. As a theoretical proposition, the idea that competition will select the most efficient, or optimal, institutions would have to be classed as extremely naïve societal Darwinism (which should not be confused with the theory of Darwin). A more careful application of evolutionary theory to institutions might argue that competitive selection will favor institutions which are more fit for the particular environment in which the selection occurs, subject to whatever constraints they have inherited. An environment of interstate military competition will select for institutions that are fit for war. The New Institutional argument rests on the claim that, in the case of western Europe, these same institutions were good for the growth of commerce and eventually industry.

There are actually two distinct phases of western European expansion that need to be explained by such a theory. One is the conquest of large parts of the world, and domination of the seas and international trade, from 1500 onwards. The other is the first industrial revolution, from 1750 onwards. Kenneth Pomeranz (2000) argues that the crucial institutional differences which explain the second of these, the industrial revolution, were *not* property rights, competitive markets, or the ability of industry to tap financial markets. None of the countries in question, whether in Europe or in Asia, had markets for land and labor that were as liberal as we might expect today; Pomeranz – a specialist in Chinese history – makes a case that such markets, in many respects, functioned better in China and Japan than in most of western Europe. He argues that two things made the difference for northwestern Europe – and England in particular. One was the location of good coal deposits near to existing industry – in England, and in Flanders and northern France. The other was the supply of sugar and cotton, produced by slaves in overseas colonies.

Throughout human history, new technologies have facilitated economic growth. Another way of thinking about this is that improved technologies allowed people to get more out of the same endowment of natural resources. This increased income has typically been used to support a larger population, perhaps at a somewhat better standard of living. Through most of history, however, technology has changed slowly and provision for investment has been uncertain; a rising population would soon eat away at whatever productivity gains technology had brought. In Europe between 1400 and 1700, agricultural technologies improved considerably, but the population grew, and by 1700 most people were eating less well than they had been in 1400 (Braudel 1981). In short, human societies have usually pushed against what we call the "Malthusian constraints," which are based on the theory of Thomas Malthus (1798).

Pomeranz maintains that in the mid-1700s, both western Europe and China were pressing up against Malthusian constraints. This was not simply a matter of population growth outrunning the food supply. Expanding textile production was competing with food production for land: wool, flax, and cotton all required land that could have been used for food crops. Fuel and building materials both came from forests, which again competed for land. Two factors enabled England, and then other countries in north-western Europe, to grow quickly while China and Japan did not. One was coal. The other was the products grown by slaves on colonial plantations – most significantly, sugar and cotton. Together, Pomeranz argues, these allowed Europe to leapfrog past the Malthusian constraints: coal relieved pressure on wood supplies; sugar (which became a major source of food energy in England during the early nineteenth century: see Sidney Mintz, 1985) and cotton relieved the constraints on agricultural uses of land. Investment in science and new technology then made the break-through self-sustaining.

China lacked overseas colonies, and produced both sugar and cotton at home. Sugar remained a luxury product in China, rather than a major source of calories, while cotton competed for land with both food crops and wood. In the absence of the conditions that kick-started sustained growth in Europe, China did what human societies have usually done – productive capacity and population grew in parallel, close to the limits of what the land could sustain.

The coal half of Pomeranz's story is not about institutions but about luck – coal deposits in England happened to be located near to existing industry, and thus to mechanics and investors with the ability and motivation to work out better ways getting it out of the ground; Chinese coal deposits were far from industry. Coal mining in England couldn't go far without a way to pump water out of mines, and the technology developed for doing this was the steam engine. That steam could provide power had been known in antiquity, and was known in early modern China. Converting this principle into a practical engine was not easy, however. Early steam engines were dangerous and tremendously inefficient. The challenge of getting water out of coal mines provided incentives to compensate for the danger. The ready source of fuel from the mine itself meant that, in that one particular application, the inefficiency of the early steam engines was not a problem. And, since there were coal deposits located near to established centres of machinery manufacture in England, there was a ready supply of mechanics to set their minds to this problem. So, coal was mined, supplementing wood as a fuel, and in the process of mining the crude early steam engines were refined into what would become a widely applicable technology.

The plantation half of Pomeranz's story is about institutions, but not about liberal institutions. European states had conquered much of the world, established the Atlantic slave trade, and now enjoyed an industrial revolution because of institutions which had allowed them to take control of much of the world. European public finance depended heavily on states chartering private monopolies, and the sale of such monopolies was an important part not only of raising revenue for overseas expansion but for organizing the expansion itself. Armed corporations were granted monopolies on trade and quasi-governmental powers over parts of the non-European world (the British and Dutch East India companies are two of the best known examples). This was in marked contrast to China, which expected its overseas merchants simply to trade.

Thus Pomeranz, like North, Thomas, and Jones, attributes the rise of the West to institutions borne of interstate military competition. In Pomeranz's version, however, the European advantage was in institutions of monopoly, conquest, colonization, and slavery – not those of private property and free markets. There is no doubt that European institutions exhibited both sets of features.

7.1.3. STEEL AND THE SECOND INDUSTRIAL REVOLUTION

People have used iron for about 14,000 years. The principal limitations on its use have been access to good quality ore and fuel for processing the ore into iron (lower quality ore requires more fuel). The development of coal mines, discussed above, relaxed the fuel constraint, and made possible a rapid rise in the production of iron in Europe and North America during the early nineteenth century.

Steel, however, remained scarce and expensive. Steel is iron with a carbon content of between 0.1 and 2 per cent. Carbon above 2 per cent gives you pig iron, which is harder and too brittle to work, though it can be cast – hence, cast iron. Carbon below 0.1 per cent gives you wrought iron, which is softer; it can be easily shaped, but is not as strong as steel, and will not hold a cutting edge for long.

Getting the right amount of carbon, doing so predictably, and getting rid of crippling impurities such as phosphorous, were no small problems. Prior to the invention of the Bessemer process in the 1850s and the competing Siemens-Martin process in the 1860s, steel production required both arduous labor and huge amounts of fuel; it was expensive and used mostly for small, expensive tools, cutting edges, and some weapons.

Following adoption of the Bessemer and Siemens-Martin processes, steel outputs rose and prices fell in Europe (Britain, Germany, France, Belgium, and Sweden being the significant producers) and in the US from the late 1860s onwards. From 1879, the Thomas process solved the problem of phosphorous residues, making possible the use of cheaper ores; the rise in production and the fall in price continued.

The sudden availability of relatively cheap steel had a revolutionary effect. Steel is much better than other forms of iron for making mechanical devices, and the availability of steel made possible a vast array of machines for manufacturing and information processing (typewriters, tabulating machines).

Steel also greatly improved the performance of railways, because steel rails lasted about six times longer than iron ones. It made possible both the structures and the elevators (which you really wouldn't want to use without steel cables) for tall buildings. It led to great improvements in interchangeable parts, and thus made possible the mass production of complex machines, in particular the automobile. This collection of innovations transformed the way people live and move in the space around them – horizontally by rail or auto, vertically by elevator.

As we will see in the next chapter, the products of steel provided the impetus for the development of the large, professionally managed corporation, and also provided an important motivation for the retreat from free trade in the late nineteenth century.

7.2. **Socioeconomic paradigms**

Steel, or rather the cheap and plentiful steel of the post-Bessemer era, can be called a "universal and cheap key factor": an input to production, the use of which created widespread opportunities for new inventions; which led to high levels of investment in a new generation of capital goods using those inventions; and which made large parts of the existing capital stock suddenly obsolete.

Steel can be seen as one of five "universal and cheap key factors" (UCKFs) in the history of industrial society. Cotton was the first, in the late eighteenth century; coal and iron in the early-mid nineteenth century; then steel, as we have seen, in the late nineteenth century, followed in the early-mid twentieth century by petroleum and plastics; and finally, in the late twentieth century, microelectronics and networked computing (see Table 7.1).

Long waves (also called Kondratief waves, or simply Kondratiefs) are, according to the theory, alternating periods of faster (the "upswing") and slower economic growth (the "downswing"). Each wave, including both upswing and downswing, lasts in the neighborhood of fifty years. The first wave started with the first industrial revolution, in the 1880s; the fifth, and current, wave started with the widespread application of microelectronics and networked computing, in the 1990s.

Table 7.1. Successive waves of technological change

Long waves or cycles			Key features of dominant infrastructure		
Approx. timing	Kondratief waves	Science technology education and training	Transport communication	Energy systems	Universal and cheap key factors
First 1780s–1840s	Industrial revolution: factory production for textiles	Apprenticeship, learning-by-doing, dissenting academies, scientific societies	Canals, carriage roads	Water power	Cotton
Second 1840s–90s	Age of steam power and railways	Professional, mechanical, and civil engineers, institutes of technology, mass primary education	Railways (iron), telegraph	Steam power	Coal, iron
Third 1890s–1940s	Age of electricity and steel	Industrial R&D labs, chemicals and electrical, national laboratories, standards laboratories	Railways (steel), telephone	Electricity	Steel
Fourth 1940s–90s	Age of mass production ("Fordism") of automobiles and synthetic materials	Large-scale industrial and government R&D, mass higher education	Motor highways, radio and TV, airlines	Oil	Oil, plastics
Fifth 1990s–?	Age of microelectronics and computer networks	Data networks, R&D global networks, lifetime education and training	Information highways, digital networks	Gas/oil	Microelectronics

Source: Freeman and Soete (1997), Table 1.3. Reproduced by permission of the authors.

There are various versions of the long wave theory current today; for a brief review, see Thompson (1990). The variant followed here is the neo-Schumpeterian version (Perez 1983, 1985; Freeman and Perez 1988; Freeman and Soete 1997). This theory sees the economic growth wave and the associated technology as creating, and then being embedded in, what they call a "techno-economic paradigm." This paradigm can be understood in terms of four characteristics. One of these, and the most important for defining a wave, is a small set of UCKFs. For the first Kondratief, the UCKF was cotton. For the second, it included iron and coal; for the third, steel; for the fourth, oil and plastics; and for the fifth, microelectronics.

The other defining characteristics of the techno-economic paradigms are the dominant energy systems of the period; the methods of transport and communication; and the systems of science, technology, education, and training. In the neo-Schumpeterian view these various characteristics form a package, a complementary set of technologies and institutions, which defines an era.

Cycles of slower and faster growth have been discerned by many in the data, but others don't find them: there are a lot of data series to choose from, and many ways of analyzing them. Again, see Thompson (1990) for an overview (he, of course, says that *he* finds good empirical evidence for the waves, using yet another means of analyzing the data.)

So the empirics are contentious. What of the theory? Why should we expect alternating periods of fast and slow growth, and why should any two such periods be of about the same length? The answer to the first of these questions is not hard. Occasionally, a new "UCKF" appears. These factors, the story goes, open the way for a large number of new inventions and applications, and hence investment opportunities; old capital is scrapped in favor of new, and since the new capital represents a step change in productivity, there is a period of rapid growth.

Over time, it becomes harder to find new applications and investment opportunities associated with the universal cheap key factor; this is the familiar principle of diminishing returns. There may be potential new cheap key factors waiting in the wings, but investment does not switch to them automatically. Nobody knows in advance what the next big thing will be, and in any case the society's ways of doing business, its systems of education and training, its institutions of economic regulation – in short, the whole techno-economic paradigm – are built around the use of the old UCKF. But when diminishing returns have finally reduced the profit opportunities in the old system sufficiently, the demand for new UCKFs and associated technologies builds, and eventually a new techno-economic paradigm emerges.

The neo-Schumpeterians use the term "paradigm" advisedly. The word was brought into common use by Thomas Kuhn (1962), in his study of revolutions in scientific theory. He argued that really big changes in scientific theory – the shift from Copernican to Ptolmeic astronomy, or Newtonian to Einsteinian physics – don't happen because the new theory is just obviously better. For one thing, those whose careers were made working with the old theory seldom convert to the new one – the victory of the new is not complete until that generation have left the scene. For another, the new theory is usually *not* unambiguously better. Especially at first, there will be things the old one can do or explain, better than the new one. The revolution doesn't occur until enough anomalies and unanswered questions have piled up that the old theory is a real mess, *and* an attractive alternative is proposed. Victory for that alternative means scrapping much of the knowledge of the older generation, and building on a new foundation. It may be a real advance, but it comes at considerable cost, and doesn't happen often.

The idea of a techno-economic paradigm is similar, except that it is not just one scientific community that is involved, but the whole economy. The logic is clear, but the idea that the paradigms should show any wave-like regularity (something not observed with scientific paradigms) is difficult for many to accept.

7.3. **Long waves and hegemonic power**

If you don't find long waves *too* hard to swallow, then you might be interested in the work of William Thompson and Lawrence Vescera (1992; see also Thompson 1990). They use the neo-Schumpeterian theory of long waves to explain the coming and going of hegemonic power. Specifically, they offer it as a way to explain the anomalies in Krasner's theory of hegemony and openness, discussed in Chapter 5.

Consider the process of diffusion of the technologies and forms of social organization which make up the techno-economic paradigm associated with the long wave. At the beginning, the new technologies are disproportionately concentrated in a handful of countries: Britain for the first Kondratief (cotton) and the second (iron and coal); the US for the third (steel), fourth (oil/plastic), and fifth (microelectronics).

Thompson and Vescera observe that in some Kondratiefs, the leading country grows faster than its rivals, ending the wave in an even stronger position than it started, while in others the rivals are catching up. Within the limited sample of five waves, these "ascent waves" and "catch-up waves" alternate: the first Kondratief (i.e., the first industrial revolution) propelled Britain to dominance, the second (iron and steam) saw France, Germany, the US, and others narrow the gap; the third Kondratief (steel, electricity) saw the US rise to overwhelming dominance, while the fourth (petroleum, plastics) saw Europe and Japan catch up again. How the fifth (microelectronics) will end, it is too soon to say. For what it's worth, however this scheme gives us a sort of two-phase wave, made up of two Kondratiefs – one ascent and one catch-up (or diffusion).

Thompson and Vescera tell us that trade policies and international politics are different in the ascent wave than they are in the catch-up wave. The upswing of the catch-up wave is characterized by diffusion of technology, and freer trade. This leads to intense international competition and the development of surplus production capacity. It followed, in the downswing of the catch-up wave, by what Thompson and Vescera call "defensive protectionism": relatively mild trade barriers to protect established industries. This, they say, was the story from the late 1870s to about 1900, and again in the 1970s and 1980s.

In the upswing of the ascent wave – the late 1700s for Britain, the beginning of the 1900s for the US, and today for the US, again – the leader's advantage in the leading industries is great. The powers that would like to catch up respond with what Thompson and Vescera call "offensive protectionism." This entails high trade barriers and a concerted, state-led effort to catch up with the leading power. In both the first Kondratief and the third, the conflicts entailed in the catch-up effort led to global war, and in both cases the leading power won. So, France's coalition was defeated by Britain's in the early nineteenth century; Germany's and Japan's were defeated by the Soviet Union, the US, and their allies in the mid-twentieth century. We can ignore the fact that the Soviet Union, at least as much as Germany and Japan, evidenced offensive protectionism as part of a concerted effort to catch up: the point is that the US, leading at the start of the global war (which may be dated either from 1914 or from sometime in the late 1930s), ended it with an even greater advantage, just as had been the case between Britain and France 130 years earlier (Table 7.2).

Conflict between nations can take many forms, and can be resolved in many ways. Thompson and Vescera don't say they are predicting a new global war. Their reading of the history of the past two centuries does, however, make one pause for thought. With the widespread application of microelectronics and computers in the 1980s and 1990s, the economy was transformed as fundamentally as it had been by the application of steel in the 1870s, 1880s, and 1890s. The technological capabilities which brought this about are overwhelmingly concentrated in one country. Rivals, such as China, are naturally making concerted efforts to catch up. Will this lead to conflict? Will the conflict become war?

Table 7.2. Long waves and hegemonic leadership

Wave	Universal and cheap key factors	Type of wave	System leader
First	Cotton	Ascent	Britain
Second	Coal, iron	Catch-up	Britain
Third	Steel	Ascent	US
Fourth	Oil, plastics	Catch-up	US

Sources: Thompson and Vescera (1992), Table 4; Freeman and Soete (1997), Table 1.3.

Note: Each wave has an upswing (a period of faster growth), followed by a downswing (slower growth). The upswing of the ascent waves sees the rise of a system leader; the downswing sees global war and "offensive protectionism," as others challenge the leader. The upswing of the catch-up waves sees greater international diffusion of technology, catch-up by some of the leader's rivals, and freer trade. The downswing of the catch-up waves sees intensified competition and "defensive protectionism."

We'll leave that question for you to sleep on. The next chapter will deal, instead, with how the second industrial revolution – the age of steel – brought with it the invention of the modern business corporation.

8 The Origins of the Modern Corporation in the Age of Steel

Before the mid-nineteenth century, there were few companies run by managers who worked for salaries. Almost all business enterprises everywhere were small, and managed by members of the families that owned them. Organizationally, we would hardly recognize them. They did not have departments or divisions, and seldom operated at more than one location. The thousands of manufacturing companies that emerged from the first industrial revolution, in England and then elsewhere, were mostly self-financed from retained profits; few had anything to do with stock markets.

There were a few, famous, exceptions. The most important were the great trading-cum-government companies – such instruments of empire as the British East India, Dutch East India, and Hudson Bay companies – and the railroads. Both types of exceptions were involved in businesses that required the coordination and control of staff in widely separated locales, and in response to this need these companies developed the beginnings of modern managerial hierarchies and administrative methods. Manufacturing companies getting their products to market, or retailers searching for products to sell, all remained small: they stuck to one function, and depended on market intermediaries to handle transactions that required travel.

For purposes of clarity, it is useful to divide the emergence of big companies after 1870s into four stages. First, in the US, in the 1870s and 1880s, a great many relatively large companies were using new, high-volume mechanized processes to produce homogenous products – flour, chemicals, and steel – in high volumes. These companies were bigger than their predecessors not only because they produced more, but because they undertook a degree of vertical integration, internalizing various functions previously carried out by other manufacturers or by market specialists. Second, from the 1880s until the early 1900s, some industries saw the horizontal consolidation of these companies, forming giant companies many of which continue as multinationals today. Third, from 1908 onward, the management methods that had been used to produce flour on a continuous basis were combined with the manufacture of interchangeable parts, and the mass production of machines – most notably, of automobiles – began. Fourth, from 1920 onward, the larger of the companies that had emerged from the three stages just described, began to adopt multidivisional structures. I will address the first three stages here, but not the fourth. The classic source on the fourth is Chandler's *Strategy and Structure* (1962).

8.1. **How big machines led to big companies**

Following Alfred Chandler (1977), the leading chronicler of big business in America, we attribute the sudden emergence of large companies to two factors. One is that improvements in transportation and communications had made it easier for a manufacturer to serve a large market. The other was the explosive growth of very productive, and costly, special-purpose machines in manufacturing. Both of these developments owed a great deal to the new availability of cheap steel, discussed in the previous chapter.

Improved transport made it easier for one company to ship products to a large market, and the combination of improved transport and communication made it possible to coordinate and control activities over a distance. Before the 1870s, however, most manufacturing processes did not enjoy sufficient economies of scales to make wide distribution attractive. Suddenly that changed, due to the arrival of the machines just mentioned. Let us begin with an overview of the changes, and then turn to competing explanations for *why* the changes happened.

In 1881, an American named Bonsack patented a machine for making cigarettes. The machine was capable of producing 70,000 cigarettes per day, and within few years had been improved to the point that it could produce upwards of 120,000. Before Bonsack's machine, a cigarette factory had consisted of a room full of people, seated at workbenches, making cigarettes by hand; the best cigarette makers could produce 3,000 per day by hand. So, the one machine did the work of forty skilled workers. Few people, anywhere, smoked cigarettes in those days. Many American men did smoke tobacco, in pipes or in the form of cigars. Under those circumstances, just three of Bonsack's machines could satisfy the entire demand for readymade cigarettes in the US at that time.

If you were so rash as to invest in such a machine, you would be faced by a string of problems.

First, inputs: in order to produce its unprecedented volume of cigarettes, the machine required a steady supply of inputs, mainly tobacco and paper. This involved procurement, and some preliminary processing.

Second, operation: the company's entire output now depended on a small number of machines – maybe just *one* machine. A few skilled workers were required, who knew how to operate and maintain it.

Third, what to do with the output? As noted, the cigarette market was small. But the problem was greater than that, because there was no "US market" for cigarettes: cigarette factories were small, and served local or regional markets within the US; there were no nationally known *brands* of cigarettes, no distribution system. As in most industries at that time, many small cigarette manufacturers produced unbranded products which were sold in bulk to wholesale merchants, who in turn sold them on to retailers. After investments had been made in costly special-purpose production machinery, this passive approach to marketing and distribution was no longer adequate.

Bear in mind, too, that the example of a single machine for making cigarettes understates the size of the problem. Few products are processed in a single step; a high-volume machine for one step would beget the need for additional high-volume machines for others. A flow chart for Washburn's experimental flour mill, built in Minneapolis in 1879, shows 32 different machine processing stages to make one input – wheat – into a few different grades of flour, plus by-products. This does not include machines for packaging, or for moving either raw materials or finished products (Storck and Teague 1952, p. 250, reproduced in Chandler, 1977, p. 252).

The organizational problems created by mechanization were not entirely new, of course. The cotton mills of the first industrial revolution had dealt with unprecedented volumes of inputs and outputs. They, and the numerous other manufacturing concerns that had grown up since, relied on brokers and wholesalers and jobbers for both: their firms stuck to manufacturing, and did not have specialized staff responsible for such functions as purchasing, marketing, or distribution – other, specialist, firms did that. But the new generation of machines had suddenly made it more problematic to rely on the market for either the flow of inputs or the disposition of outputs. The response by business was twofold: first, vertical integration; then, horizontal growth.

Vertical integration means that the companies internalized certain functions which would previously have been left to the market. Relying less on brokers and jobbers, a company would now have a purchasing department, to ensure a steady flow of inputs. Similarly, at the sales end, the company would no longer sell unbranded products in bulk at the factory door, but undertook packaging, labeling, branding, and shipping; it developed a sales force that covered a wide territory. Controlling such an operation required a separate accounting function, and if the company turned to financial markets for funds it might add a treasury function as well. With all of these new departments added, production – which had once defined the company – became another department. This was the birth of the functionally departmentalized, or U-form, organization. A discussion of this form of organization can be found in any management textbook.

One important aspect of integrating forward (downstream), into marketing and distribution, was the spread of branding. There were already some branded products at the time, but they tended to be durable, complicated, expensive things: Singer's sewing machines, McCormick's reapers, Colt's revolvers. Manufacturers of sewing machines and harvesting equipment had also been the first, starting in the late 1850s, to establish in-house sales forces, so that they could provide technical support and credit to customers. From the late 1870s, we suddenly have brands and sales forces not only for complicated and costly machines, but also for consumer products which are produced and consumed in volume: cigarettes, flour (Pillsbury gets its start here), oatmeal (Quaker, often regarded as the first consumer brand; Kellogg and its breakfast cereals came soon after), soap (Unilever and Procter & Gamble, both were started as soap companies in this period), and many others.

A few years after the formation of these new companies, consolidation began in a different direction: firms combined horizontally, joining with competitors by various means – mergers, takeovers, and cartels. In many industries, the resulting oligopolistic market structure has lasted until the present day, and many of today's large corporations trace their origins to this period.

This story leaves us with three questions. One is why there was an explosion in the mechanization of manufacturing at this particular time. The second is to understand better why big, costly machines led so quickly to big companies. The third is to understand the role that big machines and big companies had in the return of protected national markets from the 1870s onward. The first of these questions we can answer quickly: a combination of large markets – offered, in particular, by improved and expanding railroads – and the availability of steel as a material. The importance of steel, both for the construction of manufacturing equipment and as a factor in the improvement of railroads, has been addressed in Chapter 7.

There are three different theories we need to consider in response to the question of why big machines led to big companies, and that is what we will do in the next section. After that, I will offer some observations on how big companies with high fixed costs were a factor encouraging political barriers to international trade.

8.2. Why did big machines produce big companies? Three theories

Chandler explains the emergence of big companies in terms of the efficiency benefits of administrative coordination, especially in achieving what he calls "economies of speed." I will also discuss James Beniger's variant of this theory, which puts it in terms of information processing and a general problem of control. Next comes Williamson's transaction cost theory, which sees costly special-purpose equipment as a transaction-specific asset, and vertical integration as the form of governance that minimizes the costs associated with opportunism. Finally, I will consider Naomi Lamoreaux's argument that monopoly power and market stabilization were the motives – and the results – of the horizontal mergers of 1890–1904.

We have actually seen these theories before, in Chapter 2, when considering why companies become multinational. The question of why a company becomes large is not so different. Chandler and Williamson represent two versions of the cost-minimization theory: Chandler the perspective of organizational capabilities, Williamson that of transaction costs. (We also saw Williamson's theory applied to the motives of states building empires, in Chapter 6.) Lamoreaux's theory follows logic similar to Hymer's. What is different in the present case is the particular place of costly, special-purpose machinery. This will continue to be important when we study twentieth century mass production, in Chapter 9.

8.2.1. CHANDLER'S VISIBLE HAND

Alfred Chandler (1977) attributes the emergence of big companies to the benefits of administrative coordination. Profitable operation of costly special-purpose machines required keeping the machines busy, and also selling the product. To begin with, that meant having the right quantities of inputs in the right place at the right time. The cigarette supply chain was a simple one, but even if we imagine a simplified version of that simple chain, we can see that it required having the right kind of tobacco leaf on hand, shredding it, having the papers on hand, making the cigarettes, having the packaging and labels on hand, doing the packaging, moving the packaged cigarettes on to the warehouse, shipping as orders were received – and we haven't even looked at the advertising and sales functions required to bring the orders in. All of this required having not only the materials, but also people who knew what they were doing, in the right place at the right time. In a world with such machines, argues Chandler, success came to those who kept the product flowing, who achieved what he calls *economies of speed*. Economies of speed were better achieved with administrative coordination than by the caprices of the market. His title, *The Visible Hand*, makes a strong claim, pitting his administrative hierarchies against the invisible hand of the market; Adam Smith (1776) had made the case for the latter almost exactly two hundred years before Chandler's book appeared.

Chandler's advocacy of administrative coordination of supply chains can be understood as a claim about the power of organizational *capacities,* or *competencies.* The idea of competencies is that organizations, with their rules and records and routines, and ongoing team of personnel, can get good at doing particular things, and at solving particular kinds of problems; more to the point, they get *better* at doing that than *ad hoc* collections of actors, meeting in the market, would be likely to be. Chandler's work was going against the flow, since he was making this argument at a time when large administrative hierarchies in business were not doing well. Companies such as General Motors (which Chandler had studied in his earlier work, *Strategy and Structure* (1962)), were losing ground to companies like Toyota, which outsourced much more of its work (see Womack, Jones, and Roos 1990).

In recent years, the idea of organizational competencies has taken two directions. The most highly visible is represented by the term *core competencies*, which often reduces to identifying what your organization is uniquely good at (or, alternatively, where it makes its money), and outsourcing almost everything else (see, e.g., Prahalad and Hamel

1990). The competencies of Chandler's administrative hierarchies sit uneasily with the core competencies approach, since they are competencies of integration, of running the whole show. A related line of management theory, however, deals with organizational capacities in a way entirely consistent with Chandler. This body of theory derives from Edith Penrose's (1959) *Theory of the Growth of the Firm*, and from Carnegie School's behavioral theories of the firm (Simon 1957, 1991) (Cyert and March, 1963). Applications to the multinational corporation include (Kogut and Zander 1993), discussed in Chapter 2.

8.2.1.1. Visible and invisible hands as information processors

James Beniger (1986) frames Chandler's account of the emergence of large companies in terms of information processing requirements. He sees not only administrative systems but also markets from this perspective, and sees information processing as a means of control.

Beniger argues that by the mid-nineteenth century, the growth of industrial and commercial society had created requirements of information processing which the methods of the time could not meet. This brought about what he calls a "crisis of control." He construes "control" very broadly. One familiar meaning is that of command and control within organizations. But he also includes the institutions and business arrangements that provide structure for what might appear to be the spontaneous organization of markets, and also the policies and institutions used to stabilize markets at both the industry and macroeconomic levels. For Beniger, the problems caused by special-purpose machines were just part of a larger crisis, and the creation of big companies with administrative hierarchies was just part of the solution.

To understand Beniger's argument, recall Adam Smith's two fundamental propositions about the division of labor: first, that productivity rises as the division of labor rises; second, that the extent of the division of labor is limited by the extent of the market. I discussed these propositions in Chapter 4, with reference to the theory of international trade.

Smith gives two examples to illustrate the power of the division of labor. One (Smith, p. 5) is a pin factory, in which the process of making a pin with hand tools has been broken down into eighteen operations, with each of ten workers doing one, two, or three operations over and over; the result, by Smith's estimate, is that the productivity of each worker was at least 240 times what it would have been if they worked as individuals, each making pins entire. Producing lots of pins at a low average cost is not much use, however, unless there is a market for such a quantity of pins: hence Smith's second proposition.

Smith's other example is of remote parts of the Highlands of Scotland in Smith's time, where the farmer "must be butcher, baker, and brewer for his own family," and the people are very poor (p. 16). In this case, geographical isolation, and the consequent difficulty of using markets, leads to a lack of specialization and poverty.

Why, exactly, should specialization raise productivity? Smith gives three reasons. The first is improved dexterity. When you specialize in something, you get better at it: the same manual operation, for instance, can be done faster and more reliably. The second is that if you repeat the same task many times rather than changing from one task to another, you save time that would be wasted while changing tasks. The third is that when complex jobs are broken down into small, simple tasks, it often becomes possible to develop specialized tools, and even to figure out how to make a machine to do the task. An increased division of manual labor can thus be a step toward labor-saving mechanization.

The drawbacks of working in a place like Smith's pin factory, and its eerie foreshadowing of the Taylorized factories of mass production, are well known. They were obvious even to Smith, who believed that working in repetitive, specialized jobs like those he described would make a person "as stupid and ignorant as it is possible for a human creature to become." At this point, then, we need to step back from Smith's famous example, and recognize that a highly developed division of labor does not necessarily mean that people have simple jobs like putting heads on pins all day; Smith's own reasoning has it that jobs like that would be early candidates for mechanization, as indeed proved to be the case. An alternative picture of a pin-factory worker, after the division of labor had proceeded even further than in Smith's example, is a skilled maintainer of automatic pin-making equipment. What remains from Smith's example is that such a worker inhabits a very narrow specialization, and is very productive, provided there is a large enough market to absorb all those pins.

Smith tells us that the activities of so many specialist workers will be coordinated by the market, "as if by an invisible hand." He ignores coordination within firms. We might ask: "Were the workers within his pin factory coordinated by an invisible hand, or by their boss?" Chandler offers a corrective to that. Smith also ignores the problem of information. Yet the division of labor creates a need for information, and for information processing. The Scottish farm family Smith tells of may have been poor, but they never needed to learn the price of beef – they raised and butchered their own. The more elaborate the division of labor, the greater the information requirements.

As the economy develops and information requirements grow, how does that information work get done? Think back to our discussion in Chapter 2, of the difference between tacit and explicit knowledge; the latter we can also call "information." Even if all knowledge were explicit, the complexity of the modern economy would make it difficult to classify, process, and use. The fact that much knowledge is tacit adds a dimension to this problem.

There are those who assume that markets spontaneously do the necessary translation from tacit to explicit, and communicate the resulting information without cost. The classic statement of this view is from Friedrich Hayek (1945). He argued that nobody knows everything that is going on in a market economy, but that this lack of knowledge doesn't matter. Everybody makes economic decisions based on a combination of prices (which he assumes are explicit and known to all who need to know them), and their own local knowledge (Hayek uses the term "local" rather than "tacit," as the latter usage had not yet been coined). For instance, if I have a large garden which I know is unusually well suited to growing lemons, I will grow lemons, and sell them. By using my local knowledge in this way, I have a small effect on the price of lemons; other such contributions are made by thousands of other gardeners and farmers, in the form of decisions whether, where, and when to grow lemons. There is no need to communicate, to the consumers of lemons, any of the local knowledge that goes into these decisions – the price of lemons tells them all they need to know about lemon production. By this mechanism, the interaction of individuals in the marketplace distills a vast collection of local knowledge held by different individuals into a simple set of numbers – prices.

If we were to put Hayek's argument in today's language, we would say that the market codifies, makes explicit, or converts into information, that which is relevant to us in the tacit knowledge of millions of other people. Any codification results in a loss of knowledge, and the codification done by the market is extreme, throwing away almost all of the knowledge – everything about growing lemons is reduced to a single number, the price. It is as if the answer to the secret of life, the universe, and everything were 42 (Adams 1979).

Would that it were so simple! Many decisions we make in the marketplace use information beyond the combination of prices and our own local knowledge. An interest rate (which is a price of capital) together with a merchant's local knowledge may be woefully inadequate in decision about whether to advance credit to a customer, which is why we have credit rating agencies. Similarly, the heavy expenditure on various forms of consumer information, such as advertising, technical standards, and independent product evaluations, is testimony to the fact that the combination of price and local knowledge does not finish the job.

This insight, that an increased division of labor brings increased information processing demands, is due to Fritz Machlup (1962). As economies grow, he said, an increasing proportion of the workforce is engaged in information work. Some information work involves coordination and control functions within organizations – supervision of employees, cost accounting – while other involves the informational aspects of market relationships – sales, advertising, credit reporting, financial accounting (which is to say, accounting done for the benefit of shareholders and creditors, which is reckoned as a financial market function).

Figure 8.1 shows the proportions of US private sector workers doing four different types of work, from 1800 to 1980. The four types are agriculture, manufacturing, services, and information. Traditionally, we speak of three *sectors* of the economy: primary (agriculture, mining, forestry, fishing), secondary (manufacturing), and tertiary (services). Information work is not a sector, and may occur in any of the three

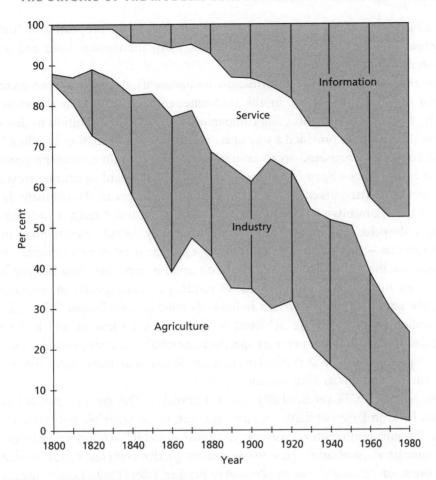

Figure 8.1. US Civilian labor force by four sectors, 1800–1980
Reprinted by permission of the publisher from *The Control Revolution: Technological and Economic Origins of the Information Society,* by James R. Beniger, p. 23, Cambridge, Mass.: Harvard University Press, Copyright © 1986 by the President and Fellows of Harvard College.

sectors (cost accountants in manufacturing companies, for instance). The sectoral employment figures reported in Figure 8.1 have had the information workers in those sectors netted out, with information occupations in all sectors reported together as a fourth group. As we can see, the proportion of information workers does increase steadily. Charles Jonscher (1994) shows that the proportion of information workers tracks the growth of US per capita GDP quite closely. This is consistent with Machlup's reading of Smith: productivity (proxied by GDP per capita) reflects an increased division of labor, which in turn requires more information work. Jonscher uses census data that is collected every ten years; starting with the 1980 census, he found it impossible to use official statistics to produce estimates of the proportion of information work: with the microeconomics revolution, many information tasks had become integrated with production tasks.

Beniger's view is that the information requirements imposed by the increasing division of labor grew faster, in the mid-nineteenth century, than the economy's capacity to handle information. Big companies were part of the solution to that crisis, because their routines provided a way of economizing on information handling.

Like computer programs, organizations economize on information processing by *pre-processing*. The company's routines – its budgets, standard operating procedures, rules, and customary practices – tell the various employees of the company how to respond to certain bits of new information, such as an order from a customer or a change in the price of an input. The response dictated by the rules may not be – indeed, might *never* be – the best possible response to a particular bit of new information, but the rules save the cost of figuring out the best response each time. Even individuals use routines for this purpose, but the value of routines is much greater in organizations, where the activity of many different individuals must be coordinated. What Chandler calls economies of speed are achieved by knowing the times at which particular quantities of many different precisely specified raw materials, semi-processed materials, parts, or products will be at particular locations. Speed in systems of this sort requires predictability, and that is what routines provide.

With primitive ICTs, predictability meant inflexibility. This gives us insight into why we look back on large twentieth century organizations as inflexible bureaucratic behemoths. The nineteenth century crisis of control passed, and ICTs continued to develop, but at the same time organizations grew in size and complexity, ever creating further demands for information processing. See, in addition to Beniger, Yates (1989), Lamoreaux and Raff (1995), and Cortada (1993).

Not until the 1970s did the microprocessor and associated technologies allow information systems finally to improve more quickly than the ever-increasing demands of the increasing division of labor, and thus to reduce dependence on routine (Jonscher 1994).

Finally, we should note a parallel between Hayek's treatment of the price system and Beniger's understanding of organizations (and markets) as information systems. Both are about how information that we can use is extracted from large complex systems that we cannot fully comprehend. In Hayek's case this means that local knowledge held by individuals throughout the economy is boiled down, through the operation of the market, into simple numbers called prices; in Beniger's case it means that the countless possible actions an employee might take in a particular situation are reduced to a manageable number by the organization's routines. Both are arguments about how order is created in complex systems. Hayek's is rooted in a belief that markets organize such systems spontaneously, while Beniger's is about how organizations and institutions create such order.

8.2.2. WILLIAMSON AND ASSET SPECIFICITY

Oliver Williamson (1979) offers a different explanation for the emergence of large corporations. If you invest in an expensive special-purpose machine, but fail to secure control of the rest of the supply chain, both upstream and down, others may be in a position to take advantage of you. And if they can, they will.

Williamson's theory rests on three pillars: incomplete contracts, opportunism, and transaction-specific assets. Williamson picks up the concept of incomplete contracts from Ronald Coase's (1937) earlier transaction cost theory. Coase's question was, in essence, "If markets are so wonderful, why do we have companies at all? Why aren't we all working as independent contractors?" His answer was: for most jobs, it is simply not practical to write a contract which specifies exactly what a worker would do, and for what compensation, in every foreseeable circumstance. Does the contract specify what each worker will do when demand shifts from one product to another, when it rains, when there's a sudden queue of customers, or when the computer system breaks down? Rather than trying to write a contract which specifies what we'll do in every circumstance, we enter into employment relationships in which the boss has some authority over the worker. Thus, for Coase, the high cost of writing complete contracts gives us incomplete contracts, and hierarchical organizations.

Williamson begins by applying Coase's scheme not to the employment relationship, but to the vertical integration (make-or-buy) decision (I say "begins" because Williamson's ambitions for his theory are not modest: he seeks to explain all economic institutions within capitalism, at least, and perhaps in other systems and eras as well. We'll use him for what he's best at, which is the vertical integration decision). So we're not talking about boss and worker, but about two production operations in a supply chain. Will they be part of the same company, or will they be two separate companies, doing business with each other in the market? Williamson assumes that contracts will be incomplete. He motivates this assumption differently than Coase does, however. Where Coase says it would be too costly to write a complete contract, Williamson doesn't mention costs. Instead, he argues that the human brain can't work out all the possible future situations that we would need to write down in a complete contract. Williamson calls this "bounded rationality," after the theory of Herbert Simon (1957).

For many applications of Williamson's theory it wouldn't matter if he used Coase's rationale for incompleteness (high cost), instead of cognitive and epistemic limits (bounded rationality). It could be tempting to say that Simon's theory appears as part of Williamson's only because Simon was one of Williamson's teachers. But, for the application of Williamson's theory to vertical integration, Simon's foundation is better than Coase's. Choices about vertical integration versus outsourcing are big corporate decisions where there's a lot of money involved, so Coase's reasoning encounters the objection that it might well be worth spending the time and money to write an extraordinarily detailed contract (and, indeed, modern outsourcing contracts can look a bit like telephone directories for small cities: the lawyers are eating well!); bounded rationality is not subject to that objection, since it is specific to those cases where no amount of money will solve the problem of incompleteness.

What Williamson calls "opportunism" could be seen as just the assumption, standard for economists, that economic actors (such as corporations, or the people who run them) are self-interested and willing to take advantage of others to further their own interests. Williamson needed to state this explicitly because, at the time he first proposed his theory, most economists didn't consider how the assumption of self-interested behavior could undermine the smooth functioning of market transactions. Williamson defined opportunism as "self-interest with guile"; today, that formulation sounds a bit melodramatic, since it's identical to the assumption of self-interest in noncooperative game theory, which now provides the foundation for most standard economic theory.

Transaction specific assets are assets whose value is greater if the transaction goes ahead as planned, than if it does not. Say that the first people to invest in Bonsack's machines did not try to build their own cigarette brands, marketing, and distribution, but to contract with somebody else to provide those services – call that somebody else "the marketing company." The machine owner would face the risk that the marketing company, having developed its brand and distribution network, could threaten to change cigarette suppliers; since the Bonsack machine was good only for making cigarettes, the value of machine to the investor is transaction specific. Since both production technology and the cigarette market will change in unpredictable ways, the contract between our investor and the marketing company will be incomplete, and the former will be vulnerable to opportunistic behavior by the latter: as circumstances unforeseen in the contract arose, the marketing company might be able to *hold up* the investor, squeezing her profits. Reasonable people would be unwilling to make large investments in special-purpose equipment under such circumstances. The cost-minimizing solution, according to Williamson, is the creation of a vertically integrated company.

8.2.3. LAMOREAUX: STABILIZATION AND MONOPOLY

A third explanation for the growth of big business in the late 1900s is that the high fixed costs entailed in the new special-purpose equipment created both a powerful incentive, and a means, for reducing competition in product markets. Naomi Lamoreaux (1985) provides a good account of this. In the new production processes, high fixed costs went together with low marginal costs: Bonsack's machine wasn't cheap, but it could replace several factories full of skilled cigarette makers. When the factory was operating at capacity, the average cost of making a cigarette was much lower than it had been without the machine. As we saw before, the production capacity of such machines could be very large relative to a national market, even in a large country such as the US.

This kind of cost structure can pose a problem in a market with many competitors. If enough companies in the same industry have invested in special-purpose machines to make similar products, they will have created excess capacity. Then, if each company is making its production and pricing decisions independently, prices will fall. Even if all the companies are covering their marginal costs, they may be failing to cover their cost of capital, or to provide for replacement of their equipment. This in fact happened in the American, German, and British manufacturing sectors during the 1870s and 1880s: prices and profits fell, even as output grew.

To restore profitability under these conditions required restricting production (in order to raise prices), and reducing excess capacity. This, the theory goes, provided a motive for mergers and cartels. Consolidation of mass production industries occurred in each of the manufacturing countries of the day, but took a different form in each depending on the county's institutions. In Germany, cartels were legal (which meant, among other things, that price-fixing contracts could be enforced in court), so companies stayed relatively small. In the US, cartels (more generally, "combinations in restraint of trade") were prohibited by the Sherman Anti-Trust Act in 1890. This made it impossible to maintain price discipline in industries with large numbers of firms. In an industry dominated by a few large firms, however, it was usually possible for those firms to find ways to avoid intense price competition without being prosecuted. For this reason, US competition policies had the paradoxical effect of encouraging large companies. Wall Street interests financed the takeover and consolidation of small manufacturing companies in one industry after another; typically, the families controlling the small firms would be bought out entirely, and would leave the business. In Great Britain, small companies in an industry would often combine to become large ones in a legal sense, but the founding families would stay on to manage their old firms as divisions of the new. These differences are detailed in Chandler and Herman Daems (1980), and Chandler (1990).

Competitors can be foreign companies as well as domestic ones. For this reason, the creation of a tight oligopoly or cartel within a country would often have been insufficient to stabilize the market in an industry, if barriers to international trade were too low. Thus, as noted in Chapter 5, heavy industry was an important political force behind the sharp rise in manufacturing tariffs in the 1870s. Recall that "heavy" in this context means "capital intensive" – the introduction of big expensive machines in the age of steel, and not least in the steel industry itself, meant that more industry was now heavy industry, demanding protection.

8.2.4. VISIBLE HAND, TRANSACTION COSTS, OR MARKET CONTROL?

Both Chandler and Williamson tell us that large companies were created because they minimize costs, but they give very different reasons for this purported efficiency.

According to Chandler, administrative coordination was better than the market at achieving economies of speed: the visible hand was more dextrous than the invisible one. Williamson offers no opinions on the relative abilities of markets and organizations to coordinate and control; he comes from a tradition in economics that assumes markets to be superior for these purposes unless there are specific reasons to the contrary, but he is not really interested in coordination and control, which are questions of ongoing operation of the system. His focus, instead, is on investment; for him, large organizations can, under certain conditions, produce more efficient results by encouraging investment in more productive special-purpose assets. He sees vertical integration as an answer, under certain market conditions, to the question "What institutional structure is best at encouraging productive investment?" This is the same question that motivates some of the lines of inquiry we have seen in previous chapters: Frieden's application of Williamson's theory to the connection between empire and investment in natural resource extraction; Acemoglu et al.'s finding that institutions designed for colonial natural resource extraction in the past lead to poor environments for investment today; and the contention of North, Thomas, and Jones that western Europe rose to world power because interstate competition produced institutions that encouraged investment. It is a theme to which we will return from time to time.

Lamoreaux's theory is not about efficiency, but about companies seeking to control markets for the purpose of keeping prices high and stable. There is no difference between Lamoreaux on the one hand, and Chandler and Williamson on the other, with regard to the companies' motives: all three authors assume that companies are motivated by profit. Chandler and Williamson reject the market control explanation on the grounds that, if large companies were put together simply to control markets, it is unlikely that they would also be producing at the lowest possible cost; high profits in the industry would attract smaller, lower-cost producers, and the market power of the large firms would be lost. This, in fact, happened in many industries, from footwear to furniture, where fixed costs are relatively low; Chandler offers that as an argument for his efficiency argument, but it really proves nothing. All three authors are seeking to explain, not the patterns in industries like footwear or furniture, but in industries with much higher fixed costs, like newsprint or electrical equipment.

Lamoreaux's theory is strongest for explaining horizontal consolidation. Chandler and Williamson both start out with powerful explanations for vertical integration – up and down the supply chain. Chandler addresses the horizontal consolidation question in later work, in terms of economies of scale and scope (Chandler 1990).

The reader should note that, while the three theories above offer different explanations and have different implications, they are in no sense mutually exclusive. All three – or any two – might be part of the true account of how costly special-purpose manufacturing machines contributed to the formation of big business.

8.3. **Mass production of machines**

Our focus so far in this chapter has been big manufacturing companies that used machines to make large quantities of uniform products which require only a small number of inputs: steel, cigarettes, kerosene, breakfast cereal, flour, canned foods, soap, paper – there are many such products. The ideal for production processes in this period was continuous flow – products which kept moving as they were transformed, untouched by human hands. In order to keep production flowing, organizations were designed to keep inputs and finished products flowing as well.

Not all manufacturing conformed to this model. Among the giant companies started in this period were electrical equipment producers like General Electric, Westinghouse, and Siemens. The manufacture of electrical equipment, and of machines of all kinds, was not itself mechanized. The mass production of machines, however, was soon to come.

There are two distinct definitions of "mass production" in widespread use. One applies the term to all cases of large scale production of uniform goods at a low average cost. That definition includes the sort of continuous flow processes with small numbers of inputs and outputs, discussed previously. Another definition starts with that one, but applies it only to the mass production of more complicated things – machines, electrical equipment, and so on. The first, and most important, example of such mass production is the production of automobiles – Henry Ford's factories, Charlie Chaplin in *Modern Times*. It is not until mass production has been extended to the production of machines, that we refer to the economy as a mass production economy.

As with cigarettes, flour, or soap, the mass production of machines employed the principle of flow and made heavy use of special-purpose machines. Several things had changed, however. To begin with, the mass production of machines required far more inputs, so the management of their flow was more difficult, and the investment in special-purpose machines was much greater. Mass production of machines also required interchangeable parts. And, because the production of machines is more difficult to mechanize than the production of simpler products, the mass production of a machine required a large workforce, including a great many unskilled or semi-skilled workers. Management of mass production systems lent itself to Taylorism, also known as Scientific Management.

8.3.1. INTERCHANGEABLE PARTS

Cars are put together from interchangeable parts. As a partially assembled car moves down the assembly line, a succession of workers attach parts which have been made in other workshops or factories; the line keeps moving, and if a part doesn't fit there is no time to grind it, file it, drill it or hammer it until it does. Assembly line workers expect parts to fit the first time. As do all of us. Your new DVD player connects to the television using cables with standard plugs; if it didn't do so, you would consider it defective.

Automobiles powered by internal combustion engines were being produced for sale in Germany, France, and the US by the early 1890s. It was not until 1908, however, that Ford first made cars from interchangeable parts. Before that, cars were assembled one at a time, and each part had to be made to fit the parts which had been made before it. Each car, then, was unique; replacement parts would also need to be custom fitted. This method of manufacturing required a great deal of skilled labor, and is often referred to as *craft production*.

In 1913, five years after making the first Model T from interchangeable parts, Ford opened the world's first moving assembly line. The assembly line has become emblematic of mass production, but it was really the icing on the cake. Interchangeable parts, and an organization that could achieve the synchronized delivery of thousands of such parts, were the critical steps.

The habit of speaking of important technological developments as revolutionary can mask a new technology's long, difficult, and quite deliberate gestation. The progress of interchangeable parts from conception to use in automobiles took well over 100 years. The best source on this is David Hounshell's *From the American System to Mass Production, 1800–1932* (1984).

The principle of interchangeability had been proposed in 1765 by General Jean-Baptiste de Gribeauval. He sought to apply this principle to the manufacture of weapons for the French military. The General was interested in interchangeability because it would make it easier to repair guns, which would be a source of military advantage: repair in the field would be quick, and an army could reduce the number of fitters and mechanics who had to travel in its wake to keep the guns working.

Making interchangeable parts, however, was easier said than done; it says much for the power of the idea that it became a durable part of French military doctrine long before anyone had succeeded in putting it into practice. In 1800, guns were still being made as cars were made in 1900, one at a time, each one unique. The quest for interchangeability was taken up by the US War Department, which in its early years was much influenced by French advisors. For the first half of the nineteenth century, the federal armories in Springfield, Massachusetts and Harper's Ferry, Virginia, strove to make guns with interchangeable parts. The US government offered rewards for the successful production of a gun with interchangeable parts – leading to some fraudulent demonstrations of interchangeability, including one by Eli Whitney, renowned inventor of the cotton gin.

Actually making parts that could be interchanged required a substantial investment in – and the invention of – special-purpose machines. There are many cutting, grinding, and boring operations required to make a gun, and dedicated machines – machines that would do just one operation over and over – were one of the ways uniformity was achieved. The armories also established procedures for getting consistent measurements of machine settings and parts. This meant requiring skilled gunsmiths to give up a degree of autonomy and follow the procedures prescribed by managers – not something they always appreciated.

Armory practices spread to the armories' subcontractors – as in modern quality management systems, adoption of the practices was a condition of getting the business (Best 1990). By mid-century, guns made with interchangeable parts were in commercial production, notably by Samuel Colt's company. Even then, it was not altogether clear that this was a better way of making guns – or of making anything. With the materials and techniques available at the time, parts made with the expectation of interchangeability did not fit as well as parts finished by hand, so any saving on repair cost came at some sacrifice of quality. In the 1850s, Britain was still pondering whether to adopt the practice for its own army's guns, and much of what we know about the relative merits of different manufacturing practices at that time comes from the records of a British Parliamentary commission established to investigate the question.

After 1850 armory practices spread, gradually, mostly within American manufacturing; as sewing machines, agricultural implements such as reapers, and, late in the nineteenth century, bicycles went into production, the methods pioneered in the federal armories were spread by mechanics trained there. Yet even in these industries, where the advantages of interchangeability might seem obvious, the leading companies were usually not the first to adopt the system. International Harvester and Singer, the leading companies in reapers and sewing machines, led through marketing and reputations for quality; they moved to interchangeable parts relatively late, and then only because production bottlenecks forced them to do so.

It is a measure of the organizational and technical obstacles to the adoption of interchangeable parts, that when the automobile industry was starting up in Germany, France, and the US in the 1890s, interchangeable parts did not play an important role. In 1906, the Ford Motor Company's factory was an ill-equipped workshop; its cars were cheap, and far from the best; like all other car manufacturers at the time, it used craft methods. Ford recruited a good team of mechanics, one or two of whom had experience in other industries with interchangeable parts and with the construction of special-purpose machine tools to make such parts. Benefiting from the concept's development over the previous century, from improved steel, and from Henry Ford's personal determination to build a car in that way, they were able to make it work.

8.3.2. SPECIAL-PURPOSE MACHINES, BUT MORE SO

Mass production made heavy use of special-purpose equipment. This was a continuation of a trend that began with the factory system of the first industrial revolution of the 1760s onward – buildings full of spindles or looms. From the 1870s onward, mechanized high volume production brought even higher levels of special purpose equipment to a large number of industries. The tools which the US armories were using in the 1840s to make interchangeable parts for guns extended the use of special purpose equipment into the manufacture of machines themselves; it was not until 1908, however, that interchangeable parts really came into their own, in the system we know as mass production. In each of these stages, the proportion of the economy dependent on special-purpose machines grew, both because it was used in more industries and because the value of such machines devoted to particular products grew.

A mass-produced car required a large number of special-purpose machines. A car has a great many parts, and most parts required several different operations to make. Most of those operations were done by machines dedicated to that particular purpose, for two reasons. One was that, given the technologies of the day, there was a trade-off between flexibility and precision. The other was that mass production companies employed mostly unskilled and semi-skilled workers. This was a cost-minimizing strategy for the companies, and at the same time a reflection of the poor supply in the US of workers with industrial craft skills; the latter problem is one I'll return to in Chapters 10 and 11. For now, let us just note that workers with few skills made good operators for machines that did just one thing, while more versatile machines required operators with more skill. One of Ford's early machine builders spoke proudly of his "farm-boy machines," with which work previously accomplished by a skilled machinist could be done by somebody with no industrial training, straight off the farm.

With each of the many cutting, boring, casting, planing, or stamping operations using a different machine, factories were huge and produced very large numbers of identical products. They were huge because they had to be in order to accommodate so much equipment and the people operating it; they produced large numbers of cars because that was the only way to get good use out of the equipment when each machine was devoted to a particular operation; they produced a narrow range of fairly uniform cars because the equipment was inflexible and the workforce was not very skilled. The River Rouge factory near Detroit, successor to mass production's birthplace in Highland Park, had over 1.5 square kilometers of floor space and, in the 1930s, employed over 100,000 people. Between 1927 and 1942, River Rouge production averaged a million cars per year.

8.3.3. TAYLORISM

The production of parts that were interchangeable required uniformity of practice. This requirement, together with the heavy use of less skilled labor, favored the use of Taylorist management techniques. These are named after Frederick Taylor, a management consultant of the late nineteenth and early twentieth centuries (Taylor 1967; for a good account of Taylor's life and work, see Kanigel, 1997). Taylor advocated a system he called "scientific management." Managers were to study jobs systematically, and determine the best way – the *one* best way was the expression Taylor favored, with great confidence in his system's ability to find that unique optimum – of performing each task. After managers had made this determination, workers were expected to carry out their instructions: Taylorism entails a sharp division between conception and execution.

While Ford's methods were Taylorist, they were a particular type of Taylorism. Job procedures in Ford's factories were tightly prescribed on the basis of careful study by management; to a large extent, however, the prescriptions were not given to the workers in the form of instructions, but built into machines. This is an example of what Richard Edwards (1979) calls mechanical control.

The place of Taylorist practices in mass production is undeniable. Unfortunately, one of the best-written and most provocative analyses of twentieth century business goes overboard on this point. Harry Braverman's *Labor and Monopoly Capital* (1974) treats Taylorism and the ever-increasing use of unskilled labor (de-skilling) as a universal law within industrial capitalist economies. We will see as we go along, that one of the most interesting things about the industrial systems of different countries is the extent to which the development and use of skill *varies*.

8.3.4. VERTICAL INTEGRATION, AGAIN

Earlier in this chapter, we saw how even a single costly piece of special-purpose manufacturing equipment could set off a chain of decisions that resulted in the internalization of both supply and marketing functions (vertical integration), and before long to the creation of a large corporation. The mass production of machines presented the same issues, but on a larger scale. Ford responded to the challenge by taking mass production to extremes: its huge River Rouge plant had coal and iron ore coming in at one end, and finished cars going out at the other; the company owned iron mines and rubber plantations; when it came to add radios to its cars, it made them as well. The early Ford Motor Company, and its River Rouge plant in particular, were extreme cases. Even so, vertical integration was a distinguishing characteristic of early- and mid-twentieth century companies.

9 Fordism, or the Golden Age of Mass Production

9.1. The triumph of mass production

Hitler once said that he never would have attacked the Soviet Union had he known it had so many tanks. That it did have so many may surprise us today as much as it surprised Hitler. Pre-Soviet Russia had been an industrializing country, but it was not a great industrial power. Its experience in World War I was costly, and that was followed by years of civil war. After the civil war, the road to establishing a centrally planned system of industry was excruciating: forced collectivization of agriculture leading to reduced food output, further civil strife, and many deaths in the famine of the early 1930s; an industrial system which is now generally regarded as having been terribly inefficient; to say nothing of a leader who killed off most of his top officers just before the war.[5] Germany attacked, inflicted huge casualties, and occupied most of the Soviet Union's industrial heartland. Yet, new tanks (and planes, trucks, guns, tractors . . .) kept coming. How?

Part of the answer is that supplies arrived from the US; by the end of the war, two thirds of the trucks used by the Red Army were American. Another part of it is that the centrally planned Soviet economy, though wasteful of resources in many ways, was good at concentrating those resources in a particular sector chosen by the planners. But a third, and critical, part of the answer lies in the mass production nature of Soviet industry.

Mass production factories that stood in the path of the advancing German armies were packed up and moved, by rail, to Siberia, far from the front lines; there the factories were reassembled, and production resumed. To understand the feasibility of this colossal undertaking, recall some of the features of Taylorism and mass production, discussed in Chapter 8. Like Ford's factories in the early days of the assembly line, vertical integration of Soviet heavy industry was extreme, with motor vehicle factories producing their own steel, and even their own machine tools (a vertical step too far even for Ford). The system was Taylorist, with production planning and engineering in the hands of a relatively small group; most of the workers were semiskilled, and easily replaced. Thus, the whole system for producing a tank or a gun from raw materials – the machines, the managers, and a few skilled workers – could be loaded onto a few freight trains and taken east of the Urals.

For the same reasons that Soviet factories could be shipped to Siberia, mass production systems are easily scaled up. The Taylorist approach to production organization means that each product is fully specified, like the recipe in a cookbook: following this template, a few managers and engineers with the right equipment can put thousands of semi-skilled workers to work. Once the product has been designed and the machine tools made, inexperienced workers can produce large numbers of machines quite quickly. Additional factories can be built on the same template. We saw in Chapter 2 how this feature made it possible to set up turnkey mass production factories in countries undertaking import substitution industrialization. The same capability underlay the US' ability to supply its various allies, and its own forces, in Europe, Asia, and the Pacific. My father and his comrades were ferried between islands in the Pacific in ships they derisively called Kaiser Coffins. The Kaiser in question was not a German monarch, but an American industrialist who had responded to wartime demand by setting up a shipyard in California. Those traveling in these mass-produced ships did not regard them as well made or safe, but there were plenty of them.

The German production system, as we will see in Chapter 11, relied more on networks of smaller companies, with the companies dependent in turn on a local population of skilled workers. That system could often produce better products, but it was more difficult to scale such operations up. Japan's now-famous flexible mass production capabilities were developed only after the war.

Mass production was the characteristic method of production in what Eric Hobsbawm (1995) called the "short twentieth century," the period from the outbreak of World War I in 1914 to the fall of the Berlin Wall in 1989. Not all countries used mass production as extensively or did it equally well, but it was the standard to which all aspired, the latest and the best (Piore and Sabel 1984).

9.2. **Stabilizing mass production**

To move beyond the limitations of mass production, and the forms of corporate organization associated with it, has been a preoccupation of government policy-makers and corporate managers around the world since the late 1970s. We'll come to that toward the end of this chapter, and in the next. Yet, even in its heyday, the mass production system was not without serious weaknesses. It may have been the quartermaster of victory in World War II, but it was also the system of idle factories and soup kitchens in the world's richest country during the 1930s. We saw in Chapter 8 how the growth of heavy industry in the late 1800s led to problems of market instability. Those problems were mitigated both by mergers or cartels in the industries affected, and by raising tariffs to protect national markets. Despite these measures, however, economies remained susceptible to extremes of boom and bust. And, as the mass production system spread, the stabilization problem became greater. There were ever larger concentrations of investment in equipment to make some particular product. These concentrations of capital now came along with equally large concentration of workers who had no other livelihood. Moreover, unlike the food, fertilizer, fuel, and soap characteristic of the new high-volume producers in the late nineteenth century, the new mass-produced machines were durable goods – automobiles, office machines, farm implements, and household appliances. The demand for these products was highly cyclical. This meant that price stabilization at the industry level was insufficient, and new methods of macro-economic stabilization were needed.

During the interwar period, as mass production spread in both the US and Europe, instability was pronounced. Profits, jobs or the value of a currency could vanish overnight; national political systems could turn from Jekyll to Hyde; the international trading system could, and did, collapse. How much of this was due to the problems with mass production that I have just noted, how much was inherent in the move from farm to factory, and how much was due to political errors, international competition, and class conflict within countries, we cannot say. What we can say is that by the 1930s there was general awareness that the problem of stabilizing industrial economies was not going away on its own.[6]

The system of regulation that prevailed in the US from the 1940s until the 1970s has come to be known as *Fordism*. *Regulation* here refers to the whole system by which a country's economy is managed. This includes not only the way markets are stabilized, but also the methods by which conflicting claims among different classes and interest groups are resolved, and the way long-term economic growth is provided for.

During its Fordist period, the US was the dominant industrial country. Among capitalist countries, it was also the one in which mass production became the most pervasive. The systems of regulation in other rich capitalist countries in that period were like American Fordism in some ways, but whether they should be called "Fordist" is disputed. I will focus here on American Fordism. Later in this chapter, we will see how Fordism, in America and elsewhere, became dysfunctional in the late 1960s and about 1980; how Japan seemed, for a time, to offer a vision of the post-Fordist world; and how post-Fordism actually worked out in the US. For the most part, comparison with other countries today will be left to Part III.

An exhaustive analysis of the economics of mass production economies is beyond the scope of this book. I will focus here on the problem of maintaining consumer demand. There are two elements to this problem: first, the levels of wages and employment; second, what provisions are made for the incomes of people who are, for one reason or another, not employed.

9.2.1. INCOME DISTRIBUTION AND DEMAND

To sell a large quantity of uniform, inexpensive consumer goods you need a lot of customers with moderate disposable incomes. As it happens, the Fordist era in the US had such a market. Compared to the period before 1940 or after 1981, the distribution of income became more even, with many manual workers joining the middle class and with middle class incomes growing much faster than those of the rich.

Figure 9.1, constructed by Thomas Piketty and Emanuel Saez (2003), uses data from US federal tax returns to show the real (inflation adjusted) incomes of the top 1 per cent and bottom 99 per cent. Notice that the two lines are measured on different scales: the bottom 99 per cent on the left-hand scale, with average incomes ranging up to US$35,000, the top 1 per cent on the right-hand scale, with average incomes ranging up to just over US $700,000, all at 2000 prices. Tracing the real incomes of these two groups from 1917, we see that between 1917 and 1940 they track each other quite closely, going down with the onset of depressions (1917–21 and 1929–33), and up again as the economy recovers. After 1940, the two lines diverge sharply. The period from 1941 to 1968 shows sustained and substantial growth in the real incomes of the bottom 99 per cent, and only slight growth in the real incomes of the top 1 per cent. Between 1968 and 1981, the real incomes of both groups stagnate. From 1981 to 2000, the bottom 99 per cent stagnates and the top 1 per cent gains strongly. (The losses for the top 1 per cent in 2001 and 2002 are, like their setback between 1992 and 1995, due to dips in the stock market, which disproportionately affect those with high incomes.)

This figure encapsulates the story of the triumph, decline, and fall of Fordism. The astonishing rise of real incomes for most of the population between 1940 and 1973 is what some have called the Golden Age of Capitalism (Marglin and Schor 1990). Capitalism is a most adaptable organism, and seems to have many golden ages, so let us give the period the more modest label of the Golden Age of Mass Production.

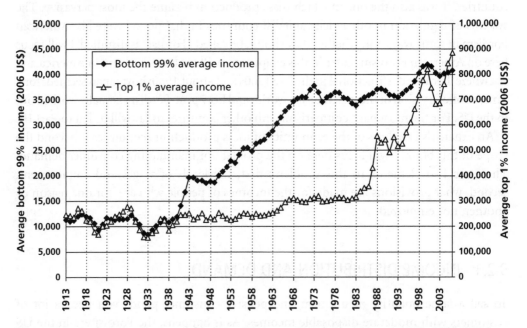

Figure 9.1. Average real income of bottom 99 per cent and top 1 per cent: US, 1913–2006

Source: Piketty and Saez (2003), figure updated 2008. Reproduced by permission of the authors.

The period between 1968 and 1981 was a period of crisis for American capitalism, and for mass production economies generally. Some students of the era would date the crisis from earlier: in 1966, when the average rates of profit and of productivity growth – in the US, and also in the OECD as a whole – began to fall. (If we are to view this as a general crisis of mass production economies, rather than Fordism in particular, it is worth noting that the mid-1960s timing accords with Emmanuel Todd's (1976) on the beginning of the Soviet collapse.)

The period from 1981 to present can be called post-Fordist. Here we see a resumption of productivity growth, but with the benefits going disproportionately to those with the highest incomes. Note that 1981 was also the year in which Ronald Reagan took office as president of the US. I'll discuss the post-Fordism period in the next chapter.

The reduction in income inequality during the Fordist era may have helped maintain stable demand for mass produced goods, but how did this redistribution come about?

9.2.2. WAGES I: FORD'S FIVE-DOLLAR DAY

The term "Fordist" comes from two things: first, mass production, which was of course Ford's system; second, that the wages of production workers were sufficient to afford mass produced consumer goods.[7] The Ford Motor company came to be associated with good wages in 1914, the assembly line's second year of operation. The company decided to pay assembly line workers US$5 per day. That was more than double the company's previous rate, and well more than other Detroit employers were paying unskilled workers. Henry Ford's public explanation for paying such a high wage was that his workers should be able to afford his cars. That story has been seized on as an easy way to understand "Fordism," with mass production companies *choosing* to pay their workers enough that they could buy mass produced goods.

We would be prudent, however, not to accept Ford's public statements as a true statement of his motives, much less as an explanation of how wages were set in mass production companies generally. Ford's explanation does not make sense from the standpoint of a profit-seeking business making the wage decision on its own. Perhaps the Ford Motor Company did pay high wages out of Henry Ford's altruism or pride, but if that were so we would not expect the typical mass producing corporation to follow its lead. Maintaining consumer demand in a mass production economy is a collective action problem for employers: the manufacturer of washing machines wants the manufacturer of cars to pay well so that the car workers can buy washing machines, and *vice versa*; each manufacturer also wants to minimize its own labor cost, however (Kalecki 1968).

Ford *needed* to raise wages in 1914 because he couldn't get people to show up for work in his factory on a reliable basis. When an employer pays a wage above that required to get qualified workers to take the job, in order to reduce turnover or to encourage punctuality or to elicit greater effort, economists call it an "efficiency wage" (Akerlof and Yellen 1986). There is good reason to believe that Ford was following an efficiency wage strategy (Raff and Summers 1987). Ford's annual turnover rate for workers in 1913 was 380 per cent (Sward 1972, cited in Hounshell 1984, p. 275). This would be shockingly high for any big business today, but in American manufacturing in the early twentieth century, it was not so anomalous. High turnover was a serious cost for manufacturers, one which many struggled to get under control by various means (Fairris 1997). Ford, however, had made absenteeism and high turnover into a more serious problem than it was for other manufacturers, by synchronizing the various stages and branches of production. His production system was a dazzling dance of parts and processes, tightly choreographed, everything needing to be in the right place at the right time. Before mass production, if somebody didn't show up to work, one person's job didn't get done that day. With the assembly line, unless enough workers showed up, on time and sober, the whole elaborate mechanism slowed down. Making the assembly line jobs well paid gave the workers something they didn't want to lose, and so ensured their punctual and sober presence. Ford raised wages, but by doing so raised productivity, and profits, even more.

If all jobs were like Ford's assembly line jobs and all employers had followed the same logic, then perhaps everybody would have been paid decent wages, and demand for consumer products would have been both high and steady. There are three problems with this story. One is that most jobs did not have the same strategic importance that led assembly line jobs to be relatively well paid. Second, even if they did, the same efficiency wage theory that explains the five-dollar day tells us that, in a competitive market, some people *must* always either be stuck in bad, low paid jobs or unemployed (Shapiro and Stiglitz 1984; Bowles 1985; Gintis and Ishikawa 1987). The reason Ford's five-dollar day got workers to show up for boring and unpleasant jobs, day after day, is that the immediate alternative was either unemployment or a job that paid much less. That particular incentive doesn't function if everybody gets the same deal. Finally, our efficiency wage explanation does not tell us how macroeconomic stability was achieved. So, however it was that Ford's five-dollar day came about, we need something more to explain both the redistribution of income, and the relative macroeconomic stability, of the Fordist period.

9.2.3. WAGES II: UNIONS

In the late 1930s, American labor unions succeeded in organizing workers in many mass production companies, and secured significant wage increases. Unions gained strength outside of the mass production industries, as well, with the proportion of US private sector workers represented by unions growing from 13% in 1930 to 39% in 1958. During the 1930s and the first years after World War II, conflict between unions and management was intense and sometimes violent. A new pattern for resolving conflicts was set in 1948, with the contract between General Motors (GM) and the United Automobile Workers (UAW). This agreement was based on two key understandings between the company and the union. One was that, over time, wages would increase in line with labor productivity. The other was that the company had a right to manage its operations. The latter might seem obvious to many readers today, but it was a significant development. It established that the union would not block the adoption of new labor-saving technology, or Taylorist practices in which managers assumed the right to specify exactly how tasks should be carried out.

The pattern set by the 1948 GM–UAW contract has been called the "postwar capital–labor accord." It affected not only the automobile industry, but most heavy industry and other unionized sectors in the US and Canada. Yet while the accord was a widely accepted principle, it was just a broad principle. The devil remained in the details of wages, benefits, working conditions, job security and so on, and in the US there was no national forum for resolving these disputes. While settlements now came more easily, they still occurred under the threat of strike action from the employees, and of plant closure and relocation from the management. For reasons that will be explored in Chapters 10 and 11, this made it impossible for the US to reduce unemployment as far as countries with more centralized systems of resolving labor–capital conflict, such as Sweden, Germany, and Japan all had in the postwar period.

The bargaining power of unions was a factor in the Fordist redistribution of income. But what was the source of this power? Before the late 1930s, American unions had had significant bargaining power only in a few industries and occupations.

It might be seen as the workers' response to the dire economic conditions of the Great Depression. Such an explanation would be contrary to standard game-theoretic theories of bargaining, which tell us that in conditions of high unemployment the workers' bargaining position should become weaker, not stronger. On the other hand, severe economic conditions may affect workers' understanding of their condition, and their willingness to organize and act collectively. John Kelly (1998) takes the latter view in his analysis of British industrial relations, and his arguments fit the US case as well.[8]

In the 1930s there were three important changes in the environment within which American labor unions were organized. These were the spread of the mass production system itself; the adoption of the National Labor Relations Act (NLRA); and a leap forward in the managerial (as opposed to shareholder) control of corporations.

9.2.3.1. Mass production, bureaucratic organization, and bargaining power

We saw above that Ford's five-dollar day owed much to the fact that each position on the assembly line needs to be staffed on time. Twenty-two years after the five-dollar day, workers in the factories of Ford's competitor, General Motors, secured further increases in pay and improved working conditions (little things like the right to talk to each other during the lunch break) by sitting down at their workplaces and doing nothing for forty-four days. They soon affected not only the factories in which the sit-downs occurred, but also others up and down General Motors' supply chains. The same vulnerability to disruption that had made it profitable to provide a powerful individual financial incentive for reliability also made it possible for organized workers to shut down the company. Moreover, when the workers were organized, the vulnerability was as great in the supply of parts as it was on the assembly line itself.

Flows of information were also vulnerable to disruption by employees. With everything written on paper, each bit of information followed a particular physical path, so that the flow of information within large companies was smooth.

Neither craft production systems like those that preceded mass production, nor the flexible network systems that have succeeded it, are so vulnerable to disruption by organized groups of employees. Craft production lacks the synchronized flow of specialized parts, while under flexible networked production it is more often feasible to change sources of parts. Information systems under craft production were less well developed than in the paper-based bureaucracies of mid-twentieth century corporations; today, information systems are no longer tied to paper, and in many cases information work can be directed down any of several alternate paths, reducing opportunities to hold up the flow (Guy and Skott, 2009).

9.2.3.2. The National Labor Relations Act

For those of us who have grown up in times and places where unions are an established part of the economic landscape, and a declining and somewhat dreary part of it at that, it may be difficult to picture situations in which their presence arouses passion in workers and employers alike. In both England and the US, union activity had been treated as criminal conspiracy through much of the nineteenth century; many of the basic rights now associated with union organization in most countries today were not firmly established until the 1930s. In the US case, the National Labor Relations Act (NLRA) made the non-management workers in most workplaces – specifically, non-agricultural private sector ones – into a kind of electorate: they could choose, by majority vote, whether or not to be represented by a particular union. If they opted for representation, management was obligated to bargain in good faith over issues like wages and working conditions. Management retaliation for union membership or activity was prohibited. The NLRA became law in 1935, and came to be widely enforced after it was upheld by the US Supreme Court in 1937. While it was weakened by further legislation in 1947, it still provided a legal foundation for worker representation and bargaining.

Like any action by a state, however, the adoption of the NLRA raises a new question for each one it answers. The new question is *why* the US government chose to empower unions at the time it did. The same question will need to be answered with regard to other policy changes, made in the same period, which established the beginnings of the American version of the welfare state. Rather than answering the question twice, I will do so after considering the roles of the managerial corporation and the welfare state in Fordism.

9.2.3.3. The managerial corporation

Up to a certain point, a company may raise wages in order to increase productivity, and thus profit. That is the idea of efficiency wage theory, discussed above with reference to Ford's five-dollar day. Higher wages can also boost productivity if they allow the company to hire more skilled workers. But, at some point, further increases in wages will come at the expense of profit. If a company's shareholders have the simple objective of increasing their own wealth, as most economic models assume, then once that point has been reached they will refuse any further increase in wages.

Shareholders, however, do not always control corporations. Often, these are controlled instead by managers – specifically, by the top executives. When the company's stock is owned by thousands of relatively small shareholders, none has the means to control management, or even the financial incentive to spend resources monitoring management. Recall that the first wave of large industrial corporations in the US was the result of mergers that occurred during the 1890s; we saw in Chapter 7 that these mergers often ended with a controlling interest in the hands of a Wall Street investment bank, such as that controlled by J P Morgan. Over time, the investment banks tended to sell shares off to the public. When this process went far enough, the managers were effectively left in charge of the company. Adolph Berle and Gardiner Means, in *The Modern Corporation and Private Property* (1967), argued that this "separation of ownership and control" had become common in American corporations by the late 1920s. A good discussion of the phenomenon is provided by Mary O'Sullivan (2001, pp. 70–104).

The separation of ownership and control grew greater during the 1930s. In addition to continuing dispersion of what had once been controlling blocs of shares, there were changes in the law that limited the role of banks in American corporate governance (Herman 1981). Although shareholdings of many companies had become widely dispersed by the late 1920s, individual share accounts were often managed by banks. Taken together, the shares managed by a bank could be sufficient that the bank would have a considerable influence over other companies, especially if it also provided credit to that company. Following the stock market crash of 1929 and the wave of bank failures of 1932, Congress passed the Glass–Steagall act in 1933. This law created various barriers between the provision of banking services and activities involving dealing in shares or managing share portfolios. The intention was to prevent banks from gambling in the stock market. The law had the further effect of reducing banks' role as trustees of their customers' shares, and using this role to oversee corporate management.

The second change was the 1938 Chandler Act, which protects the rights of small creditors. If a large creditor (such as a bank that has lent a company a large sum) intervenes in the management of a company, and the company subsequently becomes bankrupt, the bankruptcy court is likely to make the large creditor's claims subordinate to those of other, smaller creditors (suppliers who have advanced goods on credit, for instance): in effect, the court would be saying that forceful intervention by a large creditor means that the creditor is running the company, so any claim by that creditor should be treated as equity, not as debt (Frankel and Montgomery 1991).

Taken together, these changes in the regulation of American banking reduced share-holders' already weak control of American corporations, ushering in the age of managerial capitalism. Executives' attitudes toward the trade-off between wages and profits can be much different than that of shareholders. Unless executives have such huge ownership stakes or incentive packages that they give the wealth of shareholders priority over everything else (a fair assumption in most mid-twentieth century American corporations), they will care about profits to the extent that profits help them meet certain objectives. One such objective is likely to be the maintenance of managerial control; another is making the company appear successful relative to its peers, not least through growth. Profits need to be sufficient that the company can grow without recourse to financial markets, because depending on financial markets for new capital would threaten managerial control. Profitability requires, among other things, that the company's costs not be much higher than those of its competitors. Managerial control did not mean the complete absence of market discipline, but it did leave the executives without a strong motivation to squeeze every last penny out of the workforce. Moreover, the executives of companies paying high wages were, themselves, better paid (Roberts 1956; Simon 1957).

9.2.4. THE WELFARE STATE

States, throughout history, have often taken a role in supporting the indigent – transferring food from one region to another in case of crop failure, for instance. The industrial revolution, the factory system, and urbanization bring a new type of indigence, however, in the form of mass unemployment. Recall from Chapter 7 that, before there were factories, many households in the English countryside manufactured yarn and cloth for the market. "In the countryside" is crucial here: those households were diversified enterprises, their members participating not only in manufacturing but also in commercial agriculture (whether as hired laborers, tenant farmers, or yeomen), and also engaging in what would today look like extremely high levels of household production.

A fall in demand for yarn might leave the family without much spinning income for a year, but agriculture and household production remained, and the family could get by.

Move the same family to a town where everybody is employed in yarn factories: a slump in the yarn market now raises the question of how the family will avoid starvation. This vulnerability to changes in the market is a feature of the very division of labor that, as Adam Smith told us, enhances productivity. Industrialization and the growing division of labor have meant that households and communities both have become more specialized (the specialization has occurred in the countryside as well as the city: farms have become steadily more specialized in their output, and also more dependent on the market for their inputs). How to provide for people when the job market turns against them or they live beyond their working age is, for all modern states, a problem of central importance. In Chapter 11, we will consider the variety of ways in which different industrial countries have answered this question. When we do that, we will see that the US, like other English-speaking industrial countries, has generally opted for minimalist "safety net" approaches to social insurance (Esping-Andersen 1990).

In the job market as on the trapeze, however, a good safety net is not to be sneezed at. It is a safety net not only for the individuals receiving payments, but for the economy as a whole. Unemployment insurance and means-tested benefit payments are what economists call "automatic stabilizers" for the economy: when employment falls, so does consumer demand – but automatic stabilizers make up some of the difference. State-mandated pensions like the US Social Security system, medical insurance, and disability insurance, all provide security for individuals; in so doing they help smooth out spending on consumption. The welfare state thus forms part of a larger package of Keynesian stabilization policies, along with discretionary spending and monetary policy.

But, social insurance – and, indeed, many elements of the Keynesian policy package – were at odds with America's laissez faire traditions, and opposed by most business interests. As with the NLRA, we need to ask why, starting in the depression of the 1930s and continuing through the Fordist era, the US government chose to establish this social safety net. Answering this question will give us some tools for answering other questions, in later chapters, about why governments do what they do.

9.2.5. WHO BROUGHT THE GOLDEN AGE?

One way of summarizing the arguments made above is that legislation granting union representation rights to workers and social insurance, and Keynesian macroeconomic policies were all *functional* for an economy based on mass production: they contributed to a reduction in income inequality and to the smoothing out of business cycles, thus ensuring steady demand for mass produced consumer goods. We should not, however, fall into the trap of accepting functionality as an explanation. Not everybody liked these policies. Look back at Figure 9.1, and consider those in the top 1 per cent of the income distribution, whose relative position deteriorated throughout the "golden age"; those in the top 0.1 per cent fared even worse (Piketty and Saez, 2004). We're talking about small numbers, but very powerful people. In some countries in this period, the rich allied themselves with right-wing authoritarian, or fascist, leaders, who rather than granting unions rights either outlawed them, or subjected them to state or party control. How, then, did the US go down the path it did during the golden age of mass production, half way between liberal markets and social democracy?

This is not a question we can expect to answer definitively, but we should be aware of a few different plausible answers. One is that the US democratic system was sufficiently robust that the response to prolonged depression was the triumph not of fascism, but the New Deal coalition.

A robust democratic system in response to hard times does not complete the story, however, Great Britain, Sweden, and the US were all in that situation at the same time, and the results were much different. In Britain, social insurance and Keynesian policies had to wait, until after the war; in Sweden, a more sweeping social democratic program was adopted; the US case was the bold but eclectic experiments in the New Deal, followed by a partial rollback of union rights but the gradual expansion of social insurance after the war. We could say that different electoral systems produce different results; for instance, Sweden's proportional representation system could produce the kind of intergenerational bargain implied in some forms of social insurance, while the majoritarian systems of the US and UK could not. Thus, "robust democracy" is not a sufficiently detailed description: different constitutions, different outcomes. I will return to this line of argument in Chapter 11.

Another explanation starts from the assumption that policies are made, not through democratic processes, but by capitalist elites. Jill Quadagno (1984), for instance, argues that Social Security – the US public pension system – was favored by big business as a necessary cost of achieving economic and political stability; implicit in her argument is that such a policy would not have been adopted without big business' support. Although the income distribution numbers suggest that the relative position of American capitalist elites suffered during the Golden Age, it is possible either that they misjudged their policy choices – not knowing what the outcomes would actually be – or that they correctly identified the functional need for a prosperous working- and middle-class in an economy based on mass production. Since the US shifted to mass production earlier than the UK, the capitalist elites of the two countries would have had different interests.

One important strain of elite leadership theory takes a different tack, asking to what extent the elites in the state are autonomous, as opposed to being dominated by capitalists or other powerful non-state actors. Margaret Weir and Theda Skocpol (1985) argue that the different receptions of Keynesian economic policy in Sweden, the UK, and the US were due to the ideologies dominant in the particular parts of the state apparatus that was shaping economic policy. Similar arguments are made about social insurance and other policies of the era (see, for instance Skocpol and Finegold 1982; Skocpol and Ikenberry 1983). The questions of elite power and state autonomy will return in Chapters 13 and 14.

9.2.6. INTERNATIONAL FORDISM

The postwar Fordist bargain in the US was made easier by the country's overwhelming military and industrial dominance at the end of World War II. As discussed in Chapter 6, the US was able to intervene in the Third World as it saw fit, to ensure the steady supply of cheap raw materials. The other major industrial powers were rebuilding after wartime devastation, and so were not important competitors during the 1950s and most of the 1960s.

A set of institutions established following an agreement at the Bretton Woods conference of 1944 ensured international financial stability, on terms largely favorable to the US. These included the eponymous Bretton Woods exchange rate system, the International Monetary Fund (IMF), and the International Bank for Reconstruction and Development (World Bank). The General Agreement on Tariffs and Trade (GATT), another outgrowth of the Bretton Woods deliberations, was established in 1947.

Under the Bretton Woods system, exchange rates were fixed with the reference point of a strong US dollar. This part of the system lasted until 1971, when the US was not able to sustain the strong dollar and let the rate float. The IMF was designed to provide member states with credit when a shortfall in demand for their currency within the fixed exchange rate framework left them unable to pay their bills until a negotiated change in rates or some other remedy could be found. After rates floated in 1971, this problem took care of itself and the IMF was an agency in need of a mission; it found the latter in forcing poor countries that had borrowed too much money from banks to adopt neoliberal economic policies as a condition for financial rescue. The BIS clears payments between banks of different countries. The GATT was a forum for negotiating the reduction in trade barriers; it was replaced by the World Trade Organization (WTO) in 1995. The World Bank was established for purposes of postwar reconstruction, morphed into an institution for general development finance, and has been home to some of the same policy enthusiasms as the IMF.

9.3. **The end of the Golden Age**

If we exclude World War II, the Golden Age of mass production lasted twenty or twenty-five years, from the late 1940s until the late 1960s or early 1970s. In the mid-1960s,

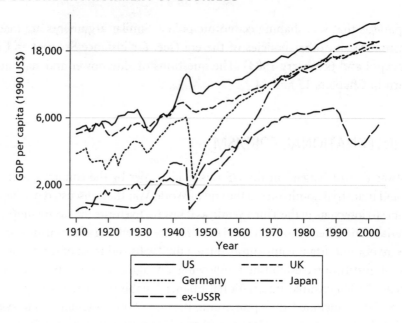

Figure 9.2. Rich industrial countries in the twentieth century: Instability and war followed by rapid growth

Source: Maddison (2007).

as I noted above, something began to go wrong. In addition to low rates of profit and of productivity growth, the 1970s saw high rates of inflation and unemployment in many of the world's industrial economies. Figure 9.2 shows this period of steady growth in several industrial countries. Compare the turbulent decades before the Golden Age, and the somewhat slower growth afterwards.

The international institutions of Fordism also suffered setbacks in this period. With the US encountering competition from other industrial countries at the same time it was spending large amounts to fight a war in Vietnam, the strong dollar became an overvalued dollar. In 1971 the US abruptly abandoned the Bretton Woods fixed exchange rate mechanism. Oil exporters saw the weakness of the US; the Organization of Petroleum Exporting Countries (OPEC) went from a talking shop to a real force, and raised prices. Although Soviet industry was in even more trouble than the Western mass producers were, its weakness was masked by revenues from oil and other primary sector exports. This was the context in which Krasner wrote his paper on hegemonic political power and trade liberalization: the 1970s looked to him like a repeat of the 1870s, when Britain's hegemony was ending. It was also the period in which Japanese competition brought the mass production model into question. As we will see below, political changes from 1978 onward scrapped the postwar labor–capital accord in the US.

Why did the Golden Age end? There are two explanations we need to consider. One is that the slowdown was due to the diminishing possibilities for growth within the mass production system. The other is that it was due to decay in the social accord that underpinned the Golden Age. In either case, explaining the end of the Golden Age actually requires explaining two things. One is the slowdown in productivity growth; the other is the labor disputes and other social conflict which accompanied it. Most would agree that the two are connected, but there is disagreement about how.

The growth of the mass production economy may have slowed simply because the market for uniform, low cost goods became saturated. When the middle income consumers of Fordist America all had cars, washing machines, and television sets, producers had to change their product lines, offering more variety and changing products more quickly. Mass production methods are ill-suited to this, and trying to achieve greater variety and shorter product life cycles within a mass production framework may have slowed productivity growth. Declining productivity growth set the stage for social conflict – workers expected wages to rise as before, and their unions demanded as much, but if wages rise faster than productivity then profits must fall. The view that the crisis was due to such a playing-out of the mass production model is associated with Michael Piore and Charles Sabel (1984), and also to writers of the French *régulation* school, such as Michel Aglietta (2001).

The other explanation reverses this causality, attributing slow productivity growth to social conflict. One thing a social system does is to reconcile competing claims. A basic (and important) example of such claims is that workers want higher wages, while shareholders want higher dividends. Smaller conflicts can be found throughout the economic system: who pays taxes, who gets subsidies, who gets protected by trade barriers, who pays higher prices as a result of somebody else's protection, and so forth. In the absence of a framework that resolves such claims, output may be lost to work slowdowns or strikes; future productivity may suffer because a lack of agreement about distributing the gains may lead business to reduce investment.

Fordism, and notably the post-World War II labor–capital accord, provided a way of reconciling the claims of labor and capital. Consider two very different explanations of why this social accord came undone.

One has to do with the marginal workers of American Fordism – African-Americans, temporary workers from Mexico, and women generally. Members of these groups were typically not paid as well as white male Americans, and tended not to have the same job security. A "secondary labor market" of this sort reduces the cost of offering job security to the "primary" work force. It can also serve to keep the workforce divided politically. America was, and is, by no means unique in this regard. Japan, long famous for "lifetime employment," was at the same time making heavy use of low-paid temporary workers – mostly women. In many countries, immigrants fill this role. In the US in the 1960s, the various groups of marginal workers rebelled against this status. According to the *social structure of accumulation*, or SSA, school (Weisskopf et al. 1983; Kotz et al. 1994), the strength of this rebellion was due in part to the success of Fordism: a long period of steady growth and high employment engendered a sense of security, which not only emboldened the marginal workers, but made their claims less threatening to those who did have good jobs. Labor unions came to support the civil rights claims of African-Americans, and also the claims for equal treatment of both migrant agricultural laborers (mostly immigrants) and women in workplaces generally. The SSA theory applies the same logic to the workers who had stable jobs, as well: long term economic stability and high levels of employment reduced the fear of unemployment, and encouraged workers to push claims for higher wages.[9]

Mancur Olson (1982) makes a more general argument about why different nations' periods of economic ascendancy come to an end. Growth is killed off, he says, by "distributional coalitions" fighting over rents. Ongoing economic growth, according to Olson, requires that a country be controlled by an actor or set of actors with an *encompassing interest* – which is to say that the dominant decision makers benefit not from the gains of certain interest groups in the economy, but from an overall increase in productivity or wealth. Such a configuration is difficult to sustain.

SSA theory and Olson's view will both come to mind when, in future chapters, we consider how different political–economic systems today resolve (or fail to resolve) conflicting claims by different classes or interest groups. For now, let us note that what these two very different theories have in common is that they see the social and political framework which governs an economy as being unstable; indeed, more than unstable, they see social stability as something that can undermine itself, carrying as it were the seeds of its own destruction.

The *régulation* school, on the other hand, stresses the stability of institutions and the change in technology. It has much in common with the neo-Schumpterian model of techno-economic paradigms, introduced in Chapter 7. According to these theories, a particular way of organizing production and regulating the economy are built around a particular set of technologies and cheap inputs. Technologies and markets change. Instability can occur because the social relations do *not* change sufficiently, even after the growth potential of the paradigm's technologies is played out, and even though the next generation of technologies requires new social institutions.[10]

A casual reading of the neo-Schumpeterian/*régulationist* schema could leave one with the impression that it is naively functionalist. The crisis of the 1970s can be seen as a crisis of transition from one techno-economic paradigm to the next, i.e., from the fourth to the fifth Kondratief wave. If we consult Table 7.1, and imagine the transition from one paradigm to the next as a crisis, then it would appear that after each crisis we get a new paradigm, a new set of institutions tailored to the new cheap key factors and technologies. Do these institutions and business practices emerge automatically to fill the functional requirements of the new situation? A better way to read the table, and its sequence of paradigms, is that it gives a sequence of the institutions and practices prevalent in the parts of the world that were leading the development of the new industries. The entries for the first and second Kondratief waves (cotton and iron/coal) are based on Britain, those for the third and fourth (steel/electricity and petroleum/plastics/mass production/Fordism) are based on the US. In other words, these "paradigms" are a retrospective assessment of the institutions and business practices in those countries that made the most successful use of the dominant cheap inputs and new technologies of a particular period. It is the institutions of Britain and not the Austro-Hungarian Empire, of the US and not Brazil, that are the basis for the "paradigms". With the advantages of hindsight, we can say that those institutions and practices were functional, but that does not mean that they were selected *because* they were functional: it just means that the countries in question were in a leading position in part because the institutions and practices they selected *happened to be* functional. How and why those countries came to have institutions and practices which put them at the leading edge in their eras, is a different question altogether.

A country that provides the model for one paradigm does not necessarily do so for the next: the difficulty in changing institutions and practices may lead to a crisis, such as that at the end of the Fordist era. But a crisis and the subsequent adjustment are not necessarily sufficient to set a country on the road to a new set of institutions and practices that are well suited to the new technologies and inputs. Moreover, as we move on to considering differences between business systems in the world today, we will see that there is probably not a single institutional/business "paradigm" that is best for the technologies and inputs of a particular time in history. I will return to the problem of post-crisis adjustment at the end of this chapter, and of competing, cotemporaneous paradigms in Chapter 10.

Part III
Business Systems Today

10 Two Forms of Post-Fordism

After Fordism came ... post-Fordism. The latter is not a very revealing handle, but there are reasons for this. One is that we are still in the post-Fordist period, and it is always hazardous to make generalizations about one's own age; all that I need to say about that I've already said in Chapter 3, with reference there to "globalization." Another is that there is reason to believe that, in the aftermath of Fordism, the economic institutions and production systems of industrial countries in fact became more diverse; thus, there is no one post-Fordism but, in a way that would delight a postmodernist, many post-Fordisms.

The discourse(s) of post-Fordism(s) starts, however, with the study of certain production systems that overcame some important limitations of mass production. The foremost of these is Toyota-style "flexible mass production" or "lean production." This system has certain key features – the return to highly skilled production labor, the use of more flexible equipment, and the network organization of production – in common with other post-Fordist production systems, sometimes brought together under the heading "flexible specialization" (FS).

Japanese management methods, and methods associated with flexible production more generally, have been influential everywhere over the past few decades. It has not, however, proved possible simply to transplant these methods from one country to another, because their use depends on particulars of the institutional environment. For this reason, among others, the forms of post-Fordism that actually prevail in the US and other liberal market economies show only passing resemblance to FS.

10.1. Japan and flexible mass production

During the Golden Age of mass production, Japanese companies set about improving mass production methods. The approach they developed has come to be known, variously, as "Toyotaism," "lean production" (Womack et al. 1990; Womack and Jones 1994), and "flexible mass production" (Boyer and Coriat 1986). Whatever the label, the nature of their accomplishment became apparent in the early 1970s. North America's, and many of Europe's, industrial systems were mired in problems of bad quality, slow productivity growth, low profits, labor–management conflict, high unemployment, and inflation – in short, the crisis of mass production, discussed in the previous chapter. At the same time, Japanese products – automobiles, ships, office machines, consumer electronics, cameras, industrial equipment, and so on – were gaining market share.

The Japanese manufacturers were producing higher quality goods, and doing so at lower cost. They did this by modifying mass production methods. They kept mass production's focus on maintaining the flow of materials, and also on the precise specification of measurements and methods, in order to produce interchangeable parts reliably and cheaply. They made fundamental changes, however, to the inflexibility of manufacturing equipment; to quality control procedures; to the methods used to improve production processes; and to design processes for parts and sub-assemblies. In making these changes, they also changed the relationship between the company and its employees, and between the company and its suppliers. I discussed these changes briefly in Chapter 2, and will now consider them in greater detail.

Bringing flexibility to mass production was initially a method for coping with both the shortage of equipment and the small consumer market in Japan during the late 1940s and 1950s. Toyota sought to move from craft production to mass production, but it could not afford such luxuries as separate press for each sheet-metal shaping oper-ation. A press can be used for many different operations, but the die used in the press provides the shape for a particular part. To use the same press for multiple operations, they had to work out how to change the die quickly. Learning how to be quick was a gradual process. Beginning with American presses in the late 1940s, it took Toyota a day to change a die; by the late 1950s, it took three minutes. One of the things that made such quick changes possible was a change in the organization of work. The mass production practice was to have die-changing done by specialists, while the stamping operation was done by less skilled operatives. The Toyota practice was to have the press operators change the die themselves (Womack, Jones, and Roos 1990, pp. 50–2). In this way the use of multi-skilled production workers became central to flexibility.

The gradual progress toward the three-minute change of die is emblematic not only of production flexibility, but of the continuous improvement for which Toyota-style systems are known. Process improvement is about both lowering cost and improving quality, and it is convenient to discuss it together with quality control. The general approach is to involve production workers in both the identification of problems and possibilities for improvement, and in the formulation of new procedures to address these problems and opportunities. At the simplest level, this meant suggestion boxes, and the recognition of workers who had suggested improvements that the management adopted. The suggestion box was a simple idea observed by Toyota engineers on a visit to Detroit in the late 1940s; like many such ideas, it was implemented more effectively by Toyota than by those they had learned it from.

Another tool for problem identification has been the systematic collection of data on defects as they show up during the production process, and analysis of that data using simple statistical techniques. Like suggestion boxes, the principles of statistical quality control were imported to Japan from the US. The approach had been promoted by the military for American wartime production. The US Army carried on with this advocacy when it occupied Japan after the war. In the end, statistical quality control was far more enthusiastically received by Japanese manufacturers than it had been by American ones, perhaps because it worked best when implemented by skilled production workers with job security. American statisticians W. Edwards Deming and Joseph Juran first became famous in Japan, and then decades later in the US.

Compared with other large Japanese manufacturers, Toyota was a latecomer to the use of statistical quality control (Fujimoto 1998). When it did embrace the technique, however, Toyota combined it with another system the company had pioneered: just-in-time (JIT) delivery of parts. In some respects, JIT would have seemed familiar to Henry Ford: Ford's early assembly lines had been part of a lean system; one of that system's great accomplishments had been to synchronize the production cycle times for parts, so that the flow of production continued uninterrupted. But the Model T was a simple car, with far fewer parts than a modern one, and Ford made it with almost no options ("any colour you want as long as it's black"). As mass produced products had become more complex and options had proliferated, the once-lean system had become flabby. Toyota worked out how to synchronize the delivery of just the right parts for the models and options being produced. For a good standard discussion of the JIT method, see Womack et al. (1990).

It is obvious that JIT can reduce inventory holding costs, but the logic linking JIT and quality management is less well understood. In any system, production workers have schedules to keep. Noticing a defect in the parts or materials they are using, they would like to meet their schedule by setting the defective item aside and reaching into inventory for a replacement. Once set aside, tracing the origins of the defect becomes a low priority. The problem with *that* is that a defective part is usually not alone: it indicates a problem in the process for making the part. JIT makes it impossible to ignore defects.

One might object that there is as second way production workers can deal with defective parts, which is simply to use them and then try to hide the defect. This was a common problem under mass production. The system lacked good ways of identifying defects, tracing them to their source, and correcting the system that had produced them; despite large inventories, there were often no really good parts or materials available. One might expect that the problem would be even greater under JIT; with no inventory to fall back on, the pressure to accept parts as is can surely be tremendous. Yet, in practice, the lean production system has avoided this problem.

Advocates of lean production and total quality management argue that the reason this problem persisted under mass production is the Taylorist separation of conception and execution: production workers were told simply to produce, and were not enlisted in identifying and solving problems. Quality control under mass production was a matter for inspectors at the end of the production process. They would look for defects, and when these were found somebody would be blamed. For production workers, hiding defects from the inspectors became a game. Attempting to "inspect quality in" is held to be inherently inferior to the lean production approach of "building it in." The quality accomplishments of Japanese manufacturers are evidence that employee involvement in quality management can turn the pressure imposed by JIT from a motive to hide problems to a motive to identify and solve them.

But once problems have been identified, how are they solved? Here, again, the Toyota-style systems depart from Taylorist mass production in fundamental ways. A problem may be assigned to a team of employees – sometimes called a "quality circle" – who are asked to study the problem and propose a solution. Participation by production workers in this kind of problem-solving is usually devoted to making incremental improvements in the production process. Yet though the composition of a problem-solving group for a large design project will be different from one devoted to incremental improvement in production, what we see in both cases is a wider circle of collaboration than there would be under mass production. Collaboration up and down the supply chain with the system of "black box" design has been noted in Chapter 2. In addition to this, the Toyotaist approach has long been one of design-for-manufacture. In mass production systems, design and production engineering tended to be distinct stages; in the Toyota-style, systems have product designers and production engineers working together from the start.

The Toyota approach – skilled production workers solving problems – is seen by many as the antithesis of Taylorism. It is, and it isn't. The tasks of Toyota's multiskilled production workers are minutely specified, as in any mass production system. A solution to a production problem, after it has been proposed by a team of workers and accepted by their managers, serves to refine those task instructions. From an engineering standpoint, the new instructions are better than the old ones, which is why Toyota was able to produce cars with fewer defects than its mass production rivals. From the production worker's standpoint, however, the instructions left even less discretion, and less slack time, than the mass production system. For this reason, some critics of the Toyota system call it "management by stress" (Parker and Slaughter 1998). It is perhaps no coincidence that the system was developed in a country where the attachment of workers to their jobs, and the common requirement to work long hours, have given the language a single word (*karoshi*) meaning "death by over-work." The roots of this extreme devotion to the company will be considered below.

10.2. **Visions of a post-Fordist world**

10.2.1. FLEXIBLE SPECIALIZATION

Some of the things I have described as features of Toyota-style production could also be found in much different production systems that were emerging, more or less simultaneously, elsewhere in the world. The turn away from mass production and back to the use of highly skilled production labor and more versatile equipment; the turn from centralized vertical integration, toward network production; the shift from long runs of uniform, low-cost products to shorter production runs, continuous improvement, and an emphasis on quality – all of these features could be seen in clusters of small- and medium-sized companies (SMEs) in various cities in Italy, Germany, and elsewhere. The particular quality management methods of Japanese companies, discussed above, and the organization of the Japanese corporate groups, or *keiretsu*, discussed later in this chapter, both were unique to Japan. Even so, much of what was happening in Osaka was also happening in Bologna and Stuttgart.

Piore and Sabel (1984) proposed that the Japanese corporate groups and the SME clusters of Italy and Germany were both manifestations of a new, emerging production system which they called "flexible specialization."[11] Where the Japanese groups were led by large corporations, with managerial control maintained by cross-shareholding within the group, the SME clusters were usually composed of independent entrepreneurial (owner-managed) companies that specialized in particular production processes and collaborated voluntarily in production.

Let me note two features of Piore and Sabel's theory: the implications of flexible production for increasing returns, and the institutional environment needed for FS to thrive.

In the combination of skilled labor and general purpose tools, Piore and Sabel see a return to craft production. Technological advances have eroded, if not eliminated, the cost advantages enjoyed by special-purpose equipment for long production runs of uniform products; more critically, general purpose equipment allows short production runs, and thus facilitates switching from one product to another or modifying the production process to improve a product. Following a line of argument similar to that of Chandler, and of Chapter 8, Piore and Sabel saw costly special purpose equipment as the foundation of economies of scale and of the large corporation. With flexible equipment operated by skilled labor, there was no need for any company to internalize so many functions. Instead, SMEs could specialize in particular processes, working with other SMEs in what we would now call a network. Economies of scale and scope which had been internal to the corporation are now external, properties of the network.

Whatever the productive advantages of FS, it may not be appealing to employers if they have the option of using cheap, less-skilled labor; from the labor side of the bargain, if wages are too low, then workers may lack the means and motivation to acquire specialized skills. FS, in Piore and Sabel's view, therefore requires labor market institutions that support the acquisition of specialized skills and which limit downward competitive pressure on wages.

Similar considerations apply to relationships between firms under FS. Cooperation between specialized companies in a network requires a measure of trust; trust may be something personal between particular people working for the particular companies that are part of a network, but it may also be shaped by the larger social and institutional environment in which the companies are situated.

Two supposed features of FS – the prevalence of high skills and high wages, and the ability of networked SMEs to compete on a level playing field (or better) with large, vertically integrated corporations – had considerable political appeal. If the world moved to FS, the Golden Age of mass production would be succeeded by an era even more lustrous. The strength of this appeal has probably led to greater enthusiasm for FS than its empirical incidence merits.

10.2.2. DIFFICULTIES IN TRANSPLANTING JAPANESE MANAGEMENT METHODS

The export-oriented industries of postwar Japan offered one suitable environment for the development of FS; others could be found in parts of Europe, as will be seen in Chapter 11. The management and production methods of Japanese companies have been imitated more widely than that, however.

Enthusiasts such as William Ouchi (1981) and James Womack and colleagues (Womack et al. 1990; Womack and Jones 1994) have promoted the methods of Toyota and other leading Japanese companies as a set of management practices which can be adopted, pretty much intact, by companies anywhere. Yet the management system has been harder to export than the cars. As practiced in Japan, the Toyota system has made use of a strong bond between employees and companies, and also of close relations between firms along the supply chain. For most of the post-World War II period, employees of large companies in Japan have identified strongly with their employers, and have expected to stay in the same job until retirement; companies reciprocated with good wages, job security, and gradual promotion. The suppliers of a large manufacturer were typically members of the same corporate group, or *keiretsu;* companies within the group were bound not only by the ties of repeat business, but also by cross-shareholdings.

Neither the employee–employer bond nor the relationships between companies is easy to replicate outside of the particular institutional setting in which it developed. When Japanese companies establish operations abroad, the ties are weaker and adoption of the methods is incomplete (Kenney and Florida 1994, 1995); American companies have had even greater difficulty following the recipe (Helper 1991; Konzelmann and Forrant 2002). Variants of Japanese employment and work practices, on their own or combined with the older human relations tradition in management, have been promoted under a variety of labels. These include "high-involvement work practices" (HIWPs), "high-performance work practices" (HPWPs), or simply "human resource management" (HRM).[12] While these have become standard elements of management theory in most of the world, most companies in liberal market economies don't adopt the practices; do so halfheartedly; or do so and then abandon them (Huselid 1995; Delery and Doty 1996; Guest 1997; Appelbaum et al. 2000). Evidence from the US (Ramirez et al. 2007), Australia (Drago 1996), and Britain (Ramirez et al. 2007) suggests that the full package of HIWPs goes together with job security and high wages: since liberal market economies don't provide either of these as a matter of law, the practices tend to be adopted by companies where the workforce is unionized. Sandra Black and Lisa Lynch (2001) find that HIWPs adopted by American manufacturers improve productivity only when the workforce is unionized. But that, in the US and other liberal market economies, applies to a small and shrinking proportion of the manufacturing workforce.

10.3. **Explaining failures of transition: Production methods embedded in institutions**

Why has it been so difficult for companies in liberal market economies to adopt the management and production methods pioneered decades ago in Japan? Both FS theory and what we have just seen of the difficulties of transplanting suggest that the problem may be that many countries lack institutional environments suitable for the new methods. But, then, if the new production methods are so much better, why do institutions not change to suit them?

It will help us in answering this question if we consider not only the difficulties faced by American manufacturers as they were overtaken by Japanese competitors in the late twentieth century, but also the similar difficulties which had confronted British manufacturers when they were overtaken by the Americans in the late nineteenth and early twentieth centuries. In the eyes of many, the British failure to complete this transition was still hurting it a century later (Elbaum and Lazonick 1986).

William Lazonick (1991) gives a history of institutions, corporations, and industrial production systems in Britain, America, and Japan. His theoretical framework is consistent with the neo-Schumpterian/*régulation* approach: the leading countries of a particular period are those which developed institutions that match the needs of the period's cutting-edge production systems. Technology moves on, but the institutions of the once-ascendant countries may fail to do so:

Because of vested interests and the ability to compete by making adaptive responses using traditional technologies and organizations, the very business institutions that formed the foundations for the rise to industrial leadership in one era can and do persist to pose barriers to industrial transformation within the once-dominant economies. (Lazonick 1991, p. 24).

Consider, first, America's replacing Britain as the industrial leader. Britain's ascendancy was a period of factories using craft methods; its family-controlled companies, heavy on skilled labor and light on professional management, were the core of what Lazonick calls "proprietary capitalism." A shift to American methods of mass production and professional management would have threatened both the capitalist families and the skilled workers. As a younger industrial country, America lacked both the long-established companies and the pool of skilled manufacturing labor; it was a relative blank slate on which financiers and the professional managers they hired could create scalable, mass production companies, and what we know as managerial capitalism.

The growth of mass production required a financial system geared to corporate engineering. Wall Street provided this, while the City of London did not. The City's clients (the families controlling Britain's established manufacturers) didn't want it; London finance bestrode the world in the late nineteenth century, and felt no pressing need to change its practice in this way; and between the good supply of skilled labor and the poor supply of managers, it is not obvious that establishing Taylorist mass production in Britain would have been a sensible financial investment, even if both industrialists and bankers had been willing. Deidre (née Donald) McCloskey (1973) is among those arguing that the corporate decisions leading to Britain's relative decline were quite rational choices for profit-maximizing investors to make.

Neither the British education system nor the American one did much to train skilled industrial workers. In Britain, however, the existing stock of skilled workers was replenished by a system of on-the-job training: boys who had left school in their early teens joined industrial companies as apprentices. America started with a smaller supply of skilled workers. Its unskilled manufacturing workers were usually fresh arrivals from agriculture, and many were new to the US and the English language as well. The adoption of manufacturing practices that did not require many skilled manual workers came easily.

But America's emerging industrial system needed managers and clerks; these, unlike factory workers, could not be found in the ranks of poorly educated farm laborers. The American state made its contribution to the development of managerial capitalism by providing education suited to the needs of corporate administration. Although school enrollments rose in all countries as part of the process of industrialization, they rose faster in the US: in the nineteenth century, US primary school enrollments were ahead of most other countries; by 1910, the leading European countries had almost caught up with the US in primary enrollments, but local governments in the US – both cities and rural school districts – had started building high schools at a furious pace. In 1938, over 45 per cent of 17-year-olds in the US were enrolled in secondary school, compared with 4 per cent in Britain; in the late 1950s, these figures had grown to 63 per cent (US) and 9 per cent (Great Britain) (Goldin and Katz 1997). The same pattern was repeated with postsecondary (college and university) education.[13]

Limited neither by the desires, competencies, and fortunes of a founding family, nor by a need for workers with specialized skills, American companies were scalable in ways that British companies were not. Not only were they able to achieve greater economies of scale, but they were better able to organize, and make use of, industrial R&D. American managerial capitalism was therefore able to best British proprietary capitalism both in production costs and in innovation.

From the late 1960s onwards, Japanese companies showed themselves similarly able to beat their American competitors. Lazonick calls the system they developed "collective capitalism"; among its accomplishments is the production system discussed earlier in this chapter. Why did American companies not simply follow the Japanese lead? Lazonick points again to interdependencies between the system of finance and production. Although the separation of ownership and control was, in Lazonick's estimation, the key to giving American managers the liberty to build large corporations, the separation was not complete. America's corporate managers remained ultimately accountable to financial markets, and this accountability was expressed through a focus on short-term financial results. A short-term financial focus can make a company an unreliable partner, whether for other companies or for its own employees.

The teamwork within Japanese companies is built on the long-term incentives provided by the expectation of stable employment and gradual promotion together with the specter of early retirement for underperformers. The trust required for a collaborative relationship between companies in corporate groups depends on the confidence that the relationship will not be sacrificed for the pleasure of the shareholders.

This analysis may be surprising to readers accustomed to thinking that accountability to a "principal" – that is, to the shareholders or the judgment of financial markets – is essential for corporate efficiency. If financial ownership is separated from control to such an extreme extent that the CEO doesn't care about the share price, what keeps the CEO from getting lazy, or from stealing everything? To see the plausibility of the argument, consider that the Japanese companies that were held up as models were in highly competitive international markets. (Other Japanese companies, serving protected domestic markets, were – and are – far less efficient.) While executives may not have been accountable to shareholders, they were responsible for maintaining the employment and earnings of those working for their company and for other companies in their group. The objectives of stability and steady employment growth, subject to the constraints imposed by competitive product markets, discipline executives and yet allow them to focus on the needs of the community of employees in the long term.

Alternatively, we might regard managers of Japanese companies in the way Masahiko Aoki (1980, 1984) does: not so much controlling the firm, as acting as mediators in a bargaining relationship between workers and shareholders. This still leaves the Japanese firm far less responsive to shareholder and stock market pressure than its American counterpart, and so remains consistent with Lazonick's theory.

The institutional configuration that made this system possible is the one that emerged in Japan after World War II. Before World War II, Japanese industry was dominated by a few large, family-controlled corporate groups, called *zaibatsu*: Mitusi, Mitsubishi, Sumitomo, and so on. After the war, the American occupation authorities removed the families – many were implicated in war crimes – and broke up the *zaibatsu*. Yet, within a few years, the groups had reformed – but without the families in control. The reformed group – now with a new label, *keiretsu* – typically included a bank, which all companies in the group dealt with; companies bought shares in other companies within the group. New groups also arose, headed by new industrial companies – Toyota, Sony – which had not been part of the old *zaibatsu*. The new groups tend to be defined by the supply chains of their leading companies, and so are sometimes called *vertical keiretsu*. The older groups typically include companies in several unrelated lines of business, and so are called *horizontal keiretsu*.

Managerial control of the horizontal *keiretsu* has been reinforced by government policies which minimize the effective legal rights of minority shareholders. The vertical *keiretsu*, having been formed after the war, are often effectively controlled by the founding families of the lead firms. Yet even these companies are constrained by the need to compete within the rules of the Japanese labor market. Japan has a negligible social safety net; in an urban industrial economy this leaves employers with a large responsibility for social insurance, provided mainly in the forms of stable employment, out-placement in the event of early retirement, and lump-sum pensions. The long-term incentive system provided by the combination expected long-term employment and gradual promotion together with the threat of enforced early retirement for under-performers, has until recently been underpinned by a collusive understanding between employers that they will not poach employees. Thus, within the Japanese system, even a large company that is shareholder-controlled must operate under rules and norms designed for collective capitalism.

The essence of Lazonick's argument is that, however superior collective capitalism might be in terms of cost, quality, or innovation (and the last claim, in particular, is a contentious one), it is not coming to America anytime soon: American financial markets and American shareholders are powerful actors who are not about to sacrifice their interests on the alter of long-run productivity growth.

10.4. **Actually existing American post-Fordism**

In the waning years of the Soviet Union and its sphere of influence, many observers came to refer to that system as "actually existing socialism." This was to distinguish what was observed in the Soviet system from the aspirations and unfulfilled blueprints that socialist theory had inspired. Without asking whether the prison system of post-Fordist America can be in any way compared with the Soviet Gulag, we can say that the gulf between what is observed in the US and other liberal market economies today, and theories of post-Fordism along the lines of Piore and Sabel's, is great. Hence the title of this section.

There are three aspects of actually existing post-Fordism in the liberal market economies that we need to note. First, the continued importance of giant corporations; second, the polarization of the economy between the "knowledge economy" and an economy of low-wage services; and, third, the transition in the control of corporations from managerial to financial, a process sometimes called "finacialization."

10.4.1. THE LARGE CORPORATION, CONTINUED

The difficulties adopting high-participation work practices in American business have been discussed above. One might think, though, that the more basic elements of the FS model – that flexible production equipment, combined with skilled labor, could reduce the importance of internal economies of scale and usher in an era of business dominated by networks of SMEs – was somewhat closer to actual experience. SMEs are everywhere extolled as prime sources of economic growth, job creation, and innovation (Harrison 1997). Certainly, many have found the proposition both persuasive and attractive, and it has influenced both policy and business rhetoric around the world. We will return to that in some detail in Chapter 12. Yet, while networked production has advanced in many industries and many places, very large corporations are more important than ever.

Piore (1994) interviewed the top executives of several large, technology-intensive American corporations. It is plain in his account that he was looking hard for evidence that flexible production had eroded economies of scale, and that he had a hard time facing the fact that no such evidence was offered to him. His sources confirm that a switch to flexible production methods had taken place, but tell him that this had been accompanied by the development of massive corporate information systems. The flexible production systems described to him were coordinated neither by the invisible hand of the market nor by face-to-face negotiations between the owners of SMEs; production was coordinated by the visible hand of management, now embodied in special-purpose software and computer networks. These information systems, he found, provided a new foundation for internal economies of scale and scope, securing the place of the large corporation. FS was nowhere in the picture.

10.4.2. POLARIZATION: MODULARIZATION, THE KNOWLEDGE ECONOMY, AND LOW-WAGE SERVICES

Although large corporations remain powerful in the American economy, the largest do not employ as many people as they once did. Partly, this is a result of modularization – hiving off or outsourcing specialized functions, the reverse of vertical integration; partly, it is a result of low-skilled labor being displaced by computers and by advanced manufacturing equipment; and, partly, it is a result of a shift toward a "weightless" economy, with more companies specializing in the production of information products. The American economy's capabilities in advanced technology and information products should not be underestimated; for a good account of the resilience of these sectors see Michael Best (2001).

Neither automated production nor the production of information products can employ as many people as non-automated mass production; who, then, now employs those who made up the legions of semi-skilled factory workers and clerical workers? The answer is that those workers – together with a steady stream of immigrants – staff a growing sector of low-wage services: retail, food service, and household services.

This post-Fordist economy is, again, a long way from the FS vision of a manufacturing economy with large numbers of highly skilled, well-paid manual workers. Not only has manufacturing ceased to be the center of economic concern, but the distribution of both income and opportunity have polarized. Although the gap between rich and poor rose within many countries in the last quarter of the twentieth century, among the rich industrial countries this rise was particularly extreme within the US and other LMEs. Why it happened is a matter of ongoing debate. There are actually two different debates, one to do with why wages at the bottom of the distribution have not risen in line with productivity, the other with why earnings at the top of the distribution have taken off so dramatically.

Some of the stagnation of low-end earnings can be attributed to institutional changes, and some to changes in the demand for skills. A few changes in institutions – a roll-back of the bargaining power of unions and a decline in the proportion of the private sector workforce represented by unions; deregulation, which was followed by a particularly rapid decline of union power and of wages in industries such as trucking; and a prolonged decline in the real value of the minimum wage – explain about a third of the rise in inequality during the late 1970s and 1980s (DiNardo et al. 1996; DiNardo and Lemieux 1997). That, of course, still leaves us with the need to explain why the institutions changed when they did.

There were two sources for the reduction in demand for unskilled labor in the US: new technology and competition from poorer countries. The mass production technologies of previous generations had replaced skilled workers with a combination of unskilled workers and machines, while early computers took care of complex calculations but were served by armies of clerks preparing and entering data. In the late twentieth century it was the turn of these unskilled jobs to be replaced by machines (Levy and Murname 2004), or to be exported to countries with lower wages (Wood 1994).

Neither the change in labor market institutions nor the reduced demand for unskilled labor can begin to explain the rise of pay at the top end of the distribution, however.

Recall from Chapter 9, in particular Figure 9.1, that after 1980 the real incomes of the top 1 per cent of the American income distribution rose rapidly, while those of the bottom 99 per cent rose only slightly. This was part of a great U-turn in the distribution in American income: the share of total income going to those in the top 1 per cent of the distribution was returning, in the 1990s, to pre-World War II levels. Yet now the income of the rich took a different form: until the early 1940s, over half of it had been capital income, largely dividends on shares. By the 1990s, less than 20 per cent of the income of those in the top 1 per cent came from capital: most of it now came from wages (broadly construed to include salaries and bonuses), and entrepreneurial income (Figure 10.1). The new breed of fat cat is fed not on profits and bond coupons, but on big paychecks.

Why are they paid so much? Robert Frank (1997; see also Rosen 1981) attributes it to the growing importance of winner-take-all markets. In most traditional lines of manufacturing and services – furniture, shoes, chemicals, cars, banking, catering, and so forth – there are anywhere from a small handful of competitors to thousands; no company can hope to control the market, or to have average costs that are orders of magnitude below those of their competitors. With information products, these rules change. A software program can capture an entire market – or get no market share at all. A movie may become a blockbuster, or it may go straight to the DVD bargain bin. To ensure that as many of its products as possible will be winners and not losers in such competitions, companies are willing to pay very high wages to employees who they think are even slightly better than those of the competitors, in hopes of winning in such lottery-like markets.

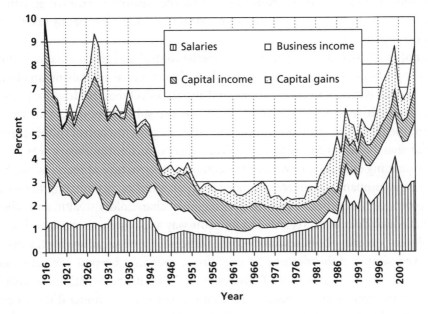

Figure 10.1. Top 0.1 per cent income share and composition: US, 1916–2005

Source: Piketty and Saez (2003), figure updated 2008. Reproduced by permission of the authors.

10.4.3. FINANCIALIZATION

Financialization refers to the growing power of financial markets and dispersed share-holders in the system of corporate governance. In raw terms, this power is exercised through hostile takeovers and leveraged restructurings of companies, and by the actions companies take to avoid either of these outcomes; it is reflected in the very high levels of pay for both top corporate officers and for the bankers and lawyers involved in mergers and other corporate control transactions; and it speaks to us through a public rhetoric of shareholder value and shareholder rights, which makes the welfare of the shareholder not merely the first, but the only, objective of the corporation. Grammatically, of course, "financialization" refers to a process, not a state. That process is a move from managerial capitalism toward a capitalism dominated by financial markets.

10.4.3.1. Managerial control comes to be seen as a problem

As the crisis of the 1970s wore on, the power of corporate managers came under attack. Berle and Means' (1967) observations on the separation of ownership and control (originally published in 1932) were revived. It was also noted that corporate executives often favored projects that were not the most financially remunerative for shareholders. This observation was hardly new, either. Both William Baumol (1959) and Robin Marris (1963, 1964) proposed that, contrary to economists' standard model of a profit-maximizing firm, a corporation controlled by its managers would maximize growth (or, in Marris' version, growth subject to the constraint of avoiding being taken over by another company).[14]

Baumol and Marris did not present managerial control and growth maximization as a particular *problem*. It was seen simply as a fact of managerial capitalism, an attempt to understand the behavior of corporations, and also the effect that the drive for growth had on the competitive structure of markets. When the subject resurfaced in the 1970s, however, the focus had shifted from the fact of management control to the question of what the shareholders can do about it. From this point on, the theory was no longer about explaining corporate growth or the competitive structure of markets, but how far the use of a company's resources deviates from an ideal of maximizing the wealth of shareholders. Some corporate growth does augment shareholder wealth, and other does not. That which does not is regarded in the same way as paying unnecessarily high wages to employees; excessive bonuses, fancy corner offices, or long vacations for the executives themselves; simple embezzlement by executives; spending beyond the minimum required by law on the reduction of environmental pollution; donations to charity; or investment in promising but highly uncertain technologies or (under different circumstances) the failure to make such an investment. This may seem a bizarre list of completely unrelated, and often quite innocent, things, but in the rhetoric of shareholder value, *any* action the executive might take knowing that it is likely to reduce the wealth of the shareholders, poses exactly the same problem. As Milton Friedman (1962) put it, "the social responsibility of business is to maximize profits".

10.4.3.2. The principal–agent problem and the market for corporate control

The problem of corporate governance, in this line of thinking, is essentially one of how the shareholders control the managers. In the formal language of the models, the shareholders are the "principal" and the manager is the "agent." The problem of control comes in two parts: information and intervention.

The information problem is that, while the shareholders want the manager to use the corporation's resources to maximize financial returns, they usually don't know what the manager ought to do to accomplish this. The manager may not know, either, but does have better information than the shareholders about the likely returns from different spending choices. (In technical terms, this is a problem of asymmetric information.) The intervention problem is that there is no straightforward way for the shareholders to ensure that the company does what they want (assuming, here, that they have overcome the information problem sufficiently to know what they want, and whether the manager needs to do something different to achieve that). Both information and intervention are enormously complicated by the fact that most large corporations in LMEs have thousands of small shareholders, and no shareholder with a controlling interest. Consequently, shareholders face a considerable collective action problem: who will spend the resources needed to monitor management (reducing the information asymmetry), or to see that the board of directors represents the shareholder interest?

A partial solution to the collective action problem in monitoring is found in disclosure requirements, imposed either by the state, or as a requirement for listing the company's shares on a particular stock exchange (by listing on a particular exchange, the management is pre-committing to the disclosure of certain information; this type of corporate disclosure is trusted more than strictly voluntary disclosure, which is expected to be selective and designed to present the management in the best light). A different sort of response is to structure the manager's compensation contract in a way that gives the manager an interest in maximizing shareholder wealth. If shareholder and manager interests can be aligned in this way, then the information asymmetry is not important. This is the normative implication of a long line of principal – agent theory, starting with Michael Jensen and William Meckling (1976; see also Jensen and Zimmerman 1985; Jensen and Murphy 1990).[15] In practice, compensation contracts like the "efficient" ones of the theory do not exist, for two reasons. One is that it is impossible to find measures of the manager's performance which reflect the long-run interests of the shareholders and which the manager cannot manipulate. This problem has been repeatedly demonstrated as corporate boards of directors have striven to formulate executive compensation packages that meet the criteria of principal–agent theory; the stubborn persistence of the problem should not be surprising, as it follows from the same information asymmetry that gives us the principal–agent problem in the first place. The second reason is that corporate boards are often not motivated to create compensation contracts such as the theory suggests, because the boards are influenced by the managers they supervise (see O'Reilly et al. 1988; Hallock 1997; Yermack 1997).

Even though the efficient principal–agent contract has proved unattainable, it has become a normative standard. And, as corporate boards have loudly proclaim their allegiance to this norm, at least one prescription of the theory has been implemented: executive pay has risen. Executives did not need the theory, of course, to tell them that they would like to be paid more, so just why executive pay has risen at the same time managerial control has been compromised is a puzzle – why didn't they take the opportunity to pay themselves more in the "managerial" era? I will return to this question below.

Who intervenes if the management of a corporation appears to be acting – either by design or simply due to incompetence – against the investors' interests? In many countries, either a lender – such as a bank – or somebody holding a large bloc of shares could be expected to fill this role. For reasons discussed in the previous chapter, banks in Britain never took up this role, and those in the US backed off from it over the course of the early twentieth century. Controlling blocs of shares became rare in large American corporations in the early twentieth century, and in British ones in the decades after World War II. Intervention in the affairs of a company in either country thereafter became a costly special project, taking the form of a hostile takeover of the company or the imposition of a highly leveraged financial structure. Henry Manne (1965) saw the takeover process as one in which competing teams of managers bid for the right to run a company, with the market awarding control of the corporation to the team of managers that offered shareholders the best value. This market, however, does not operate cheaply, a fact that enthusiasts like Manne, or Jensen (1988), tend to overlook. Marris had treated the threat of takeover as a constraint on the extent to which a manager could reduce the firm's value through growth, but not as something that altogether prevented the manager from doing so. Ajit Singh (1971) cast doubt on the relevance of this constraint: large companies are less likely to be taken over than small ones, and for UK firms Singh found that a manager who wanted to avoid being taken over was better off with a high-growth strategy than with a profit-maximizing one. As the managerial era gave way to that of financialization, financing did become available for the takeover of even very large corporations. It remained costly, though: Sanford Grossman and Oliver Hart (1980, 1981) observed that the price of a company's stock often rose by as much as 50 per cent during a takeover, implying that managers could reduce the company's market value by one-third before a takeover took place.

And after a company gets taken over? This part of the story casts further doubt on the market for corporate control as something that solves the principal–agent problem: the overwhelming evidence is that the shareholders of acquired firms do well in the transaction, while those of acquiring ones often lose out. In short, what looks like the solution to a principal–agent problem for the shareholders of the seller is often an empire-building boondoggle in the eyes of the shareholders of the buyer.

The market for corporate control does not work only through takeovers of one company by another. Often a company, or part of a company, will be taken over by a private equity firm. This includes most management buyouts – CEOs may look rich to the rest of us, but they are not billionaires, and when they "buy," somebody else signs the checks. Like all private equity deals, the action in management buyouts is in debt, not equity. Equity does play some role in that managers are given a big slice of it, to align their incentives with those of investors, just as the principal–agent models suggest. In keeping with the norms of shareholder value, the highly leveraged financial structures are intended to force the executives to pay out all "free cash flow" to investors (Jensen and Meckling 1976; Jensen 1986, 1989). Such highly leveraged financial structures are not meant for the long run, however: they render the company financially vulnerable in the course of the normal vicissitudes of business. They are normally maintained only as long as the financiers want to keep the management on a short leash while the company is restructured, assets are stripped, and the business prepared for sale.

It is through these mechanisms that executives are compelled always to keep an eye on financial markets. Whether the financialized industry of liberal market economies today is better or worse than managerial industry is not something I will try to judge here. What is clear is that it is different. It is different, too, from industry directly controlled by banks or by the owners of large blocs of shares – a common situation in many countries, to be considered in the next chapter.

10.4.3.3. The ideology of shareholder value and the growth of pension funds

The transition from managerialism to financialization in America occurred without any really big changes in the laws governing either corporations or financial markets (one exception is the reform of private sector pension funds under ERISA in 1974, see below). Companies that had been under management control since the 1920s or 1930s were suddenly subject to discipline imposed by stock markets. Some attribute this to the growing strength of neo-liberal ideology, others to volume of pension fund investment in the stock market.

After a decade of slow productivity growth and low profits, putting shareholder value to the fore was part of the social and political change that came with Margaret Thatcher and Ronald Reagan – privatization in the UK, deregulation in the US, new restrictions on the rights of trade unions in both, and the praise of profits: in the words of the fictional Wall Street takeover artist Gordon Gecko, "greed is good." On screen, Gecko is plainly an amoral monster, a cartoon villain; the ideology he gives voice to, however, is indistinguishable from that of financialization theorists such as Jensen.

Mary O'Sullivan (2001) gives some weight to ideology, but at least as much to the growth of pension fund investments in the stock market. In the US case, this followed reforms to the management of private sector pension funds under ERISA in 1974. Since then, in both the US and the UK, pension funds for both public- and private sector workers have come to be the biggest holders of corporate stock. The growth of pension funds led to some extravagant predictions: both the conservative management guru Peter Drucker (1976) and the American socialist leader Michael Harrington (1972) saw it as a way that workers might come to control the means of production, without even intending to do so. A less expansive and more influential line of reasoning identified pension funds and other institutional investors as a new class of *monitors*: outsiders who would have the motivation to keep track of the performance of managers, and the means to intervene when improvement was needed (Roe 2003). Such a monitoring role has gradually developed, with a handful of large public pension funds – notably the California Public Employees Retirement System (CALPERS) taking the lead – but it is not clear how far this actually affects the behavior of companies, beyond what can be attributed to the pension funds' participation in the market for corporate control.

A bigger change, according to Peter Gourevitch and James Shinn (2005), is that the growing dependence of pensions on stock market performance produces a political alliance between current and future pensioners, and stockholders, joined together against the interests of managers. In international comparisons, Gourevitch and Shinn show a close correlation between pension fund investments in the stock market and laws protecting the rights of minority shareholders. They argue that both of these phenomena are strongest in countries with majoritarian political systems, and where the economy's coordinating mechanisms are weakest. In the next chapter, we will see that countries with these characteristics – financialization, strong protection for minority shareholders, high levels of pension majoritarianism, weak coordination mechanisms – are also what we call *liberal market economies* (LMEs), which are essentially the English-speaking industrial economies.

10.4.3.4. Executive pay

A paradox of financialization is that the growing power of shareholders has been accompanied by a growth in the pay of top managers. If managers were really in control in the era of managerialism, why did they not pay themselves more? If shareholders are really in control now, why are managers paid so much?

During the managerial era, the pay of top executives could be seen as part of the overall pay structure of the organization. As you went up through the ranks of a company, the percentage increase in pay from one rank to the next was fairly stable (Roberts 1956; Simon 1957; Lewellen 1968). This meant that the CEOs of big companies got paid more than those of small ones, and that in companies where (or times when) the pay differences between ranks were greater, the pay of the CEO was also greater. Financialization, however, has broken this relationship, with executive pay rising out of proportion to differentials lower in the distribution (Guy 2005).

As shareholders have gained influence over corporations, both the system of account-ability and the job responsibilities of the top executives have changed.

In a managerial firm, accountability is hard to specify, but it is to some combination of one's peers on the board of directors, ones subordinates in the management team, and a sense of the corporation as an ongoing competitive entity. In the financialized era, it is clearly understood that accountability is to the shareholders. Yet, while accountability may be clearer, the actual mechanisms by which shareholders can control corporate executives are much clumsier than the mechanisms available to, say, a collegial board of directors. This we know from our discussion, above, of the principal–agent problem and the market for corporate control. To redress this problem, the basic control mechanism consists of very high pay together with the prospect of dismissal if expectations aren't met.

Top executives' responsibilities under financialization are different from what they were in the managerial era, because the corporation is treated as a portfolio of assets: every part of a corporation is always a candidate for closure, sale, or expansion; other businesses are not simply competitors, suppliers, or customers, but candidates for purchase. This state of affairs is the product, jointly, of financialization and the mod-ularization of production. What it means for the top executives' jobs is that their focus is less on fostering the gradual growth and pruning of an ongoing set of operations, and more on making a never-ending sequence of high-stakes bets as operations are added to, or dropped from, the portfolio. Transactions of this sort are highly sensitive to the judgment and probity of the executive, and are also exceedingly difficult to monitor; this shift in responsibilities has an effect on executive pay similar to that of the change in accountability.

What goes for the pay of corporate executives also goes for the pay of investment bankers, hedge fund managers, corporate lawyers – everybody who is involved in the process of corporate governance and the market for corporate control: the same sort of agency issues apply to all of them. This helps us understand why incomes in the top 1 per cent in America now come more from work than from property: much of that "work" consists of responsibility for *transactions* in property, and in today's fluid environment those transactions are at the fore.

11 Varieties of Capitalism

Kenichi Ohmae, a business strategy guru from Japan, says there are no successful countries, only successful companies. In his view, the nation-state serves mainly to get in the way of business: it taxes its successful businesses to prop up the unsuccessful ones, the prosperous regions to subsidize the less prosperous. The wealth created by Toyota and Canon is used to maintain inefficient Japanese agriculture and forestry. The world as a whole would be more prosperous, in his view, if states simply got out of the way, eliminating trade barriers, subsidies, and regulations (Ohmae 1996, 1999).

Michael Porter, a business strategy guru from the US, believes there are successful – and unsuccessful – countries. His book *Competitive Advantage* (Porter 1985) is a handbook of strategy for corporations; his next book, *The Competitive Advantage of Nations* (Porter 1990), offered a parallel set of prescriptions for states. Porter might agree with Ohmae that many of Japan's industries are inefficient, effectively subsidized by the successful ones. But he sees the success of companies like Toyota and Canon as something made possible by the particular institutional environment of Japan, an environment the Japanese state has had a large part in creating and sustaining. Japan, after all, has *clusters* of successful companies in the industries represented by Toyota and Canon, something hard to explain without reference to their environment.

Porter's view is more plausible to those of us who think that states actually do something useful. Ohmae's argument seems to imply that Somalia or Paraguay would soon foster numerous successful multinational companies if their respective states simply got out of the way; to believe this requires a truly religious faith in the power of the invisible hand. But what neither Porter nor Ohmae can explain is why Japan's successful companies are concentrated in certain industries (cars, optics, and consumer electronics, for instance) while America's are concentrated in others (general purpose software, movies, pharmaceuticals, and biotechnology, for instance).

11.1. Institutional difference as a source of comparative advantage

Porter's use of the term *competitive advantage* is in deliberate contrast to the term *comparative advantage*. Recall, from Chapter 4, that standard trade theory tells us there are usually mutual gains to be had from exchanges based on comparative advantage. The standard theory takes advantage as *given*, on the basis either of natural endowments such as climate (when Honduras and Lithuania trade, the former has a comparative advantage in bananas and the latter in rye), or of accumulated factor endowments (Switzerland has a higher capital–labor ratio than Bangladesh; hence, Switzerland exports pharmaceuticals while Bangladesh exports cheap clothing). But in fact, a county's comparative advantage in a particular industry depends on more than just natural endowments and the accumulation of generic "factors." The New Trade Theory acknowledges this through the idea of increasing returns resulting from external economies: countries (or regions or localities within countries) accumulate the knowledge and infrastructure required to do certain things well. We can call this *acquired comparative advantage*.

Increasing returns, however, still fall short of explaining *patterns* of industrial specialization. Countries do not always specialize in those industries where they have high levels of investment and experience. The US exports general purpose computer software, such as Microsoft Windows, to Japan, while Japan exports cars to the US. The US and Japan each has ample investment and experience in both the software and automotive industries, so it is hard to explain this pattern of specialization in terms of increasing returns alone.[16]

We had the beginnings to an answer to this conundrum in the previous chapter: Lazonick's progression of types of capitalism – proprietary, managerial, and collective. Each type featured a particular form of corporate organization, and a particular set of institutions – corporate governance and finance, education and training, and so on. These different types of capitalism fostered different systems of production and innovation. Lazonick is interested in these differences as a historical progression from one dominant system of production to the next. But, although this is not the direction Lazonick took the story, we can see from his account that each type of capitalism had a comparative advantage in making certain types of product. For instance, British craft methods may have been less productive on average, but they were good for relatively short production runs of specialty steel or ceramics. The post-Fordist production system of the US still can't match Japan in making automobiles or cameras, but it is very good at software, movies, pharmaceuticals, biotechnology, and advanced manufacturing (automation) systems. Instead of seeing different national systems in terms of the historical sequence of development, with some more up to date than others, we can see them as specializing in products suited to the strengths of their respective production systems. And those production systems, in turn, depend on the institutional environments in which they operate.

11.2. Two varieties of capitalism?

There are many different possible configurations of institutions, systems of production organization, and product specialization – we will see examples of several of them in the course of this chapter. But let us begin with two types, what Michel Albert calls "Anglo-Saxon capitalism" and "capitalism of the Rhine" (Albert 1993), and which Peter Hall and David Soskice have more recently labeled "liberal market economies" (LMEs) and "co-ordinated market economies" (CMEs) (Hall and Soskice 2001). The essential idea is that in the LMEs, business relationships are simple market relationships that are easily entered into and just as easily abandoned, while in CMEs business relationships are more complex, and not so simple to enter or to leave. "Business relationships" here covers a lot of things – the relationship between employer and employee, between investor and firm, between buyer and supplier in a supply chain, or between rival firms in the same industry.

Hall and Soskice go on to argue that LMEs and CMEs are good at doing different things. The ease of entering and leaving relationships means that the LMEs are good at quickly mobilizing and demobilizing resources – labor, capital, and organization – to produce radically new products or, if those products don't sell, to fold up shop. In the CMEs it is more difficult to mobilize and demobilize resources; this could be described as having less flexible markets for labor and capital, and less competitive markets between firms, but the upside is that companies have ongoing teams of workers, and the workers tend to be highly skilled. This lends itself to making products which benefit from incremental improvement of the products or the production process.

Roughly speaking, the LMEs are the English-speaking industrial countries: the US, Canada, Britain, Ireland, Australia, and New Zealand. The boundaries of the CME group are a bit fuzzier; by most definitions, it would include the German-speaking countries (Germany, Austria, and Switzerland), the Nordic countries (Denmark, Sweden, Norway, and Finland), the Benelux (Belgium, the Netherlands, and Luxembourg), and Japan. How Italy or France should be classified is subject to ongoing debate, but if they need to go in one of these two categories they would be CMEs.

The LME/CME classification is based on differences in three areas: first, labor markets, skill formation, and social insurance; second, capital markets and corporate governance; third, relations between firms, both vertically (up and down the supply chain, between buyer and supplier) and horizontally (between competitors). The broad nature of these differences will not come as a surprise to those familiar with Lazonick's description of the difference between American and Japanese capitalisms, but the understanding of their origins, strengths, and weaknesses is different.

11.3. **Labor market institutions**

11.3.1. SOCIAL PROTECTION AND INVESTMENT IN SKILLS

My office is in a university building in London. One day when I came to work, a man was busy replacing the sliding glass doors at the entrance. I asked him something about what he was doing, and what I got was a short lecture on the varieties of entry systems.

The "entry system," it seems, includes not only the door but also such things as my swipe card. So it's a complex system, with parts both mechanical and electronic, and an interface with the university's information systems. There were many such systems on the market, of which ours was apparently not the most advanced. I learned something about how this one differed from the older ones, and from the more advanced ones, all of which I have now forgotten. What I remember was that within a few minutes I had heard a concise dissertation on entry systems, and that the man who delivered this oration was a German.

Compared with LMEs, there are a lot fewer workers in CMEs who have very low levels of numeracy and literacy. CMEs have far higher participation in vocational training and smaller proportions of the population with university degrees. In other words, the distribution of skills in CMEs is more concentrated around the mean than in LMEs, with thinner tails at both the low (illiterate) and the high (advanced degree) ends.

The types of skills found in CMEs and LMEs differ as well. One of the implications of high levels of participation in vocational training is that workers in CMEs typically have higher levels of skills specific to a particular craft, profession, industry, or company.

It takes a considerable investment of time to learn as much about the installation and maintenance of entry systems as had my German informant in London. All of that industry-specific knowledge might suddenly be worth little if a shift in the market left fewer jobs in entry systems than the number of trained entry system technicians. What leads workers in CMEs to make much heavier investments in such specific skills than those in LMEs?

Margarita Estevez-Abe, Torben Iversen, and David Soskice (2001) draw a connection between the willingness to make such investments and the level of "social protection" for employees. By social protection they mean a combination of job security (employment protection), and unemployment protection.

In LMEs, private sector employment contracts are built on the principle of "employment at will," in which either the employer or the employee may unilaterally end an employment relationship. And, in an LME, if you lose your job you cannot normally expect more than modest income support from unemployment insurance, if you are lucky. So, in an LME, if you've invested in nontransferable skills and the demand for those skills suddenly shrinks, you can find yourself thoroughly out of luck.

In all CMEs there is stronger *employment protection*, or job security, than in any LME. There is a lot of variety between CMEs, however, both in the strength of employment protection and in the way it is provided. The latter includes legal constraints on the actions of the employer, the power of trade unions to protect employment, and employer policies aimed at earning commitment from employees. Some variants of these protect individuals from dismissal, while others protect groups of employees in the case of downsizing, relocation, and other forms of corporate reorganization. Legal constraints include the grounds, formal procedures, and severance payments required for dismissal of a worker. Unions may have a legally established right to consultations on dismissals or workforce reductions, and may also have the practical ability to disrupt production or otherwise impose costs on employers if jobs are cut without the union's agreement. Companies may, for strategic reasons, adopt policies which commit them to ensuring job security; for instance, they may agree to participation of the union in decisions about employment reductions, or have a practice of transferring employees within a group of affiliated companies in order to avoid layoffs.

The mix of different sources of employment protection – the state, trade unions, and employer policy – varies considerably between countries, reflecting differences in institutions. Estevez-Abe et al. boiled them all down to a single index of employment security. It is indicated on the horizontal axis of Figure 11.1.

In most CMEs, there is also stronger *unemployment protection* than in any of the LMEs. That is, if you do lose your job in most CMEs, there is more generous provision for transition to a new one: better unemployment benefits, and/or better provision of retraining. An index of unemployment protection is shown on the vertical axis of Figure 11.1.

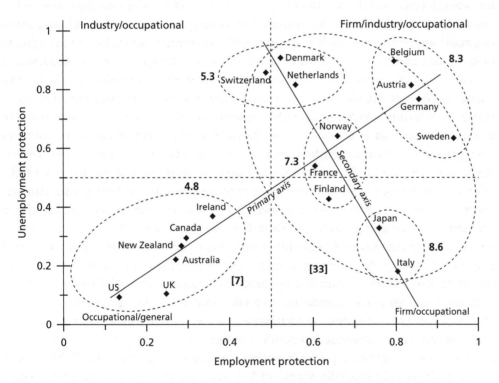

Figure 11.1. Employment security, unemployment security, and vocational training

Note: Bolded numbers are mean tenure rates for the cluster of countries circled; bracketed numbers are the percentage of the relevant age cohort going through vocational training.

Source: Estevez-Abe, Iversen, and Soskice (2001). Reproduced by permission of the authors.

We should bear in mind that creating indices of this sort invariably requires the addition of apples and oranges, and so some arbitrary choices cannot be avoided in arriving at the numbers; see Estevez-Abe et al. (2001) for details. Different ways of slicing the numbers on employment systems can result, for instance, in moving Ireland out of the LME category, and putting the Netherlands and Switzerland in an indeterminate zone (Amable 2003). With this caution in mind, the indices are helpful in cutting through the thicket of the institutional variation and creating a clearer picture.

Notice that all LMEs are clustered in the lower left-hand corner, with low levels of *both* employment and unemployment protection. Although employment protection is higher in all CMEs than in any LME, there are big differences between the CMEs. The range of unemployment protection between CMEs is even more striking: in Japan and Italy, it is fully as weak as in most LMEs. On the basis of these differences, we can identify some CME sub-types. In Japan and Italy, job security is an extremely important form of social insurance, since in both cases the state's social safety net is weak (the number next to each subcluster is the average job tenure for countries in that group: at 8.6 years, Japan and Italy are the highest of any). That worked well from the end of World War II through the 1980s, when both countries were growing fast and the systems described here were developing; in more recent years, slower growth has meant a dearth of good jobs and an accentuation of the dual labor market in both countries, with a growing secondary work force that is less well paid and has virtually no job security. Denmark, the Netherlands, and Switzerland have systems sometimes described as "flexicurity," in which it is relatively (by CME standards) easy and cheap for a company to dismiss a worker, but in which unemployment benefits and retraining are excellent. In recent years, many have regarded this system as the best of both worlds (Visser and Hemerijck 1997; Becker 2005). In Austria, Belgium, Germany, and Sweden, both types of protection are quite strong; these labor markets have often been regarded as quite inflexible, and their successful functioning depends on high levels of cooperation between unions, employers, and the state. If we were to define CME quite narrowly, it might be limited to the countries in this group; many papers in the Hall/Soskice volume deal with Germany alone. France is *sui generis*. It was the most Fordist of European countries, its economy dominated by large, hierarchically managed companies with relatively unskilled production workers. While France's employment system is plainly not that of an LME, it is difficult to classify it as a CME; we will see similar problems when we come to its financial and political systems.

The overall level of participation in vocational education and training (VET) is much higher in CMEs than in LMEs. Figure 11.1 shows the average levels of such participation, among the relevant age group, for LMEs and CMEs (with the latter broadly defined): 7 per cent in the LMEs, against 33 per cent in the CMEs.

The crux of the Estevez-Abe et al. argument is that investment in specific skills goes hand in hand with social protection. Notice how their argument parallels Williamson's transaction cost theory: industry- or firm-specific skills have transaction-specific value, just like special-purpose machines. Workers with specific skills can, in many situations, be more productive than those with only general skills, but investment in the specific skills is risky for the individual. A governance framework which insures against their sudden loss of value encourages investment in the special-purpose skills.

11.3.2. VOCATIONAL EDUCATION AND TRAINING SYSTEMS

Estevez-Abe et al. (2001) treat the acquisition of skills as an investment decision by the individual worker. This is, broadly speaking, an approach consistent with human capital theory, which is part of standard labor economics. But human capital theory predicts that employers, not workers, pay for the investment in firm-specific skills (Becker 1993). As we will see shortly, with joint action among employers, industry- and craft-specific skills can be treated in the same way as firm-specific ones. So human capital investment decisions by employers can also be important. A related issue is that Estevez-Abe et al. do not say anything about the supply side of skills: workers or employers may decide to pay for VET, but who actually provides it?

Colin Crouch, David Finegold, and Mari Sako (1999) compare the VET systems in seven industrial countries. They distinguish between five modes of provision for VET: direct provision by the state; provision based on the terms of a "corporatist bargain," which is to say agreements between employers and unions at the industry, national, or regional levels; provision agreed by networks of employers on a local basis; internal provision by large companies (institutional companies); and "free market" provision, which is to say that workers pay for training from specialist training providers. The mode of training is often different for "initial" and "further" VET. This is not surprising as the initial training is more likely to take the form of transferable basic skills, while the further training tends to have a larger company- or industry-specific component. And, not surprisingly, there is a mix of training systems within each country; Crouch et al. distinguish between "dominant" forms and "minor" forms within both initial and further VET. Their results are summarized in Table 11.1.

Notice that, of the countries in this study, free market provision of initial VET is important only in the two that are LMEs – the US and the UK. We know from Figure 11.1 that these are also countries with very low rates of *participation* in VET. The fact that the countries with low rates of participation are also those that depend on the free market, tells us something about the limitations of Estevez-Abe et al. human capital reasoning. If the only important variable were workers' willingness to invest in specific human capital, there would be no particular reason for free market training to be associated with low levels of training.

To understand the supply side for skills a bit better, we can turn to the cases in Table 11.1 in which initial VET is *not* a free market proposition. This means that it is provided by employers, by the state, or in some joint arrangement between employers

Table 11.1. Dominant forms of skills provision in eight industrial countries

Direct state	Corporatist networks	Local firm networks	Institutional companies	Free markets
Initial VET				
France			(France)	
	Germany			
Italy		Italy		
	(Japan)	(Japan)	Japan	
Sweden	(Sweden)		(Sweden)	
UK			(UK)	UK
			(US)	US
Further VET				
(France)			France	
			Germany	(Germany)
		Italy		Italy
		(Japan)	Japan	
Sweden	(Sweden)		Sweden	
			UK	UK
			US	US

Source: Crouch, Finegold, and Sako (1999), Table 1.1. Reproduced by permission of the authors.

and the state. For these systems, Crouch et al. (1999) identify the following problem. On the one hand, pure state provision has become increasingly difficult as the pace of technological change picks up, because it is hard for state providers to keep up with what employers need. On the other hand, if VET is left to employers, they will under-provide it, because with the exception of those few skills that are entirely firm-specific, VET is a public good: a firm that provides training may simply end up subsidizing other employers, because its employees can leave after they have been trained.

Two very different solutions to the public goods problem with skills are the German apprenticeship system and the training provided by large Japanese firms. I described the Japanese system in the previous chapter: the core (male) workforce of large companies receives systematic training on an ongoing basis; workers are expected to be multiskilled, and are also rotated through departments to become familiar with the company's whole operation. The public goods problem is limited because employee tenure in Japan is extremely high: employees stay with the same employer, so the employer can realize the benefits of the training it provides. Tenure is high both because employees have job security and because large employers accept the norm of not poaching employees; the second of these two reasons may be understood as the employers' collective solution to the public goods problem in training. (Local firm networks are shown in Table 11.1 as a secondary source of initial VET in Japan. The companies in question are smaller ones, outside of the *keiretsu*. See Crouch et al. 1999, pp. 165–6, 178–83.)

In the German system, initial VET comes through apprenticeships. This is sometimes called a "dual" system because apprenticeships are provided jointly by the public centered on firms and, secondarily, on national political constitutions, Hall and Soskice treat wage bargaining systems almost as epiphenomena. This may be, or they may prove to have been an important part of the glue that held CMEs together. Time will tell.

11.4. Varieties of finance and corporate governance

We turn now from the labor market to the relationship between the corporation and that other factor of production, capital. In the previous chapters, we have traced changes in the American system of corporate governance and finance: in the late nineteenth and early twentieth centuries, large American corporations were formed, and initially controlled, by the guiding hand of investment banks; they emerged gradually from bank control until, during the Fordist era, they were essentially controlled by their managers; since the late 1970s, they have existed under the constant scrutiny of financial markets.

11.4.1. CONTROL BY OUTSIDERS, OR QUASI-INSIDERS?

America's system today is the archetypal LME financial system. In most large companies, shareholding is widely dispersed so that shareholders cannot exercise direct control. Shareholders do, however, assert the *right* to control. This assertion is evidenced in the rhetoric of shareholder value; in institutions such as the market for corporate control, disclosure requirements, and other legal protections for the rights of minority shareholders; and in very high levels of executive pay.

Outside of the LMEs (i.e., both in CMEs and also in a host of countries that don't really fall in either category), most companies are effectively controlled by some combination of insiders (managers) and what I will call quasi-insiders: founding families, shareholders who have bought large blocs for strategic reasons, banks with which the companies do business. The Japanese *keiretsu* system described in Chapter 10 is one example of this, but should not be regarded as typical – quasi-insider control looks very different in different countries. Germany lacks *keiretsu*-like groups, but does have widespread cross-shareholding between companies. In Germany, banks may also own shares in their customers; this, together with their role as trustees managing (and voting) the shares of others, can give them considerable influence *as shareholders*; on their influence as lenders, more in a moment. In some countries – Sweden, South Korea, and South Africa, for instance – a large share of industry is grouped into a handful of corporate pyramids, which are controlled (often by one family) from the top (LaPorta, López-de-Silanaes, and Shleifer 1999); another example of such pyramids, of course, is the old *zaibatsu* system in Japan, abolished by the US occupation authorities after World

education system and employers: certain days at school, other days at work. The terms for employer participation in the program are worked out state by state (the states, or *länder*, being the sub-national unit in the German federal system) and industry by industry, by agreement of the employers' associations, trade unions, and school system. The label "corporatist" refers to the fact that the system is governed by rules negotiated between associations representing major stakeholders. This system depends on the successful enforcement of participation by the major employers. German employees have considerable job security but, unlike Japanese employees, they do expect to be able to change employers; if broad participation were not enforced, the employers participating in training would end up subsidizing their competitors involuntarily.

The "German" system is actually that of the former West Germany (Austria, Switzerland, and parts of Belgium have similar systems). The delicacy of its solution to the collective action problem among employers can be seen in the difficulty (and, in most cases, failure) met by efforts to establish the system in the former East Germany, and also by the longer standing efforts by the French government to change from pure state provision to a German-style dual system. In the absence of powerful employers' associations and unions, it appears that free riding prevails and a high-skill equilibrium is not achieved. Yet, the employers' associations and unions in the former West Germany are powerful in part *because* of their ongoing management of the apprenticeship programs. There does not seem to be a good recipe for switching to such a system. Pepper Culpepper (2001) provides a good discussion of this problem.

11.3.3. LABOR RELATIONS

Two decades ago, international comparison of employment systems would not have focused on skills, training, or choices by individual employees. Rather, it would have focused on the collective power of workers, as represented by their unions. Questions would have been asked, first, about wage bargaining and, second, about the ability of unions to influence company plans regarding employment levels, production systems... and also skills. Most of the current varieties of capitalism literature downplays the importance of unions. This is both because, in most countries, unions are less powerful now than they were a few decades ago, and because the leading VOC authors seek to differentiate their product as "firm-centered" (Hall and Soskice 2001, p. 4. For a critique of Hall and Soskice on this point, see Howell 2003). Yet, as we look closely at the VOC accounts of how CMEs are actually coordinated, we find that even in these accounts the power of organized labor is still treated as an important variable.

11.3.3.1. Wage bargaining: Centralized, individual, and points between

Abstract models of perfectly competitive labor markets treat wage determination as a simple market bargain between individual workers and employers. It is tempting to treat LMEs as if they operate that way. There is good reason to believe, however, that even in markets without unions, wages don't rise and fall with supply and demand in quite the way that, say, the price of apples would. In Chapter 9 we saw how, according to efficiency wage theory, wages for most jobs have to be too high to allow a standard supply-and-demand equilibrium, in order to encourage greater effort and reliability on the part of workers. In addition to this, employers can face serious problems if they are seen to be treating employees unfairly; good sources of the implications of *that* problem include Akerlof (1982), Frank (1985), and Bewley (1999). Moreover, both the US and the UK set legal minimum wage levels for most jobs; contrary to the predictions of standard competitive models, there is little evidence that such a wage floor decreases employment (Blanchflower and Oswald 1994; Card and Krueger 1994), even though it can achieve a substantial reduction in the inequality of earnings within a country (DiNardo, Fortin, and Lemieux 1996). Finally, a moment's reflection will tell you that competition in labor markets is asymmetric: there are many fewer employers than employees; in a particular industry and in a particular locale, there may be many workers with a particular skill set and only a few employers (maybe just one) they might work for. For this reason *monopsony*, or buyer's power, is pervasive in labor markets, placing workers at a distinct disadvantage when bargaining is individual (Manning 2003). So when we call the labor markets in LMEs "competitive," we should not imagine that we are talking about the simple supply-and-demand model of textbooks.

One way of understanding unions is that they are a way in which workers achieve some degree of countervailing seller's power (in the extreme, monopoly) in part of the labor market. A monopsonist (the employer) and a monopolist (the union) then sit down and agree a price (the wage). This immediately raises the question, however, of how far the market power of either party reaches. In some settings unions are limited to narrowly defined groups of workers with particular skills (butchers, medical doctors), credentials (medical doctors again), or workers who happen to occupy certain strategic sites in the production process (recall the discussion in Chapter 9 on the bargaining power of assembly line workers and others who were in a position to disrupt the production chains of mass production). If, however, a union can extend its monopoly to a larger group, it may be able to enhance its bargaining power. Recall, again, the discussion in Chapter 9 on the growth of *industrial* unions in America in the 1930s, which sought to represent all workers in particular industries (steel, autos, retail trades, and so forth). During the Golden Age of mass production, it was common in the US for uniform contracts to be agreed between a union and most of the major employers in a particular industry, either on a national or a regional basis. In the US case, a union

would pick one company with which to bargain, with the aim of using the contract with that company as a model for the industry. Contracts in one industry then often formed a model for subsequent negotiations in another. This was called "pattern bargaining," and during the Golden Age it produced a sort of coordination in American labor markets.

In CMEs, this process of centralization went further, and continued after the American system had faded away. In Germany, for instance, unions in a particular industry would negotiate the main points, not with individual companies, but with an association representing all companies in that industry (the same association that was responsible, together with the union and state, for managing the apprenticeship program). In some relatively small European countries, such as Sweden and Austria, the national union confederation and the national association of employers would bargain over the basic wage increase at the national level.

During the crisis of mass production, strong unions in some countries were blamed for inflation. With productivity growing at a snail's pace, expectations of wage increases outstripped the resources available; countries such as Britain, France, Italy, and to a lesser extent the US. Countries with the highly centralized wage bargaining, such as Austria and Sweden, managed to maintain a combination of high employment and low inflation. Lars Calmfors and John Driffill (1988; see also Rowthorn 1977, 1992) argued that wage–price spirals could be kept under control either with very weak unions or with centralized bargaining; they became a problem when unions were strong enough to demand wage increases, but bargaining separately so that there was no way to agree to keep demands at a sustainable level. In this discussion, the reasons for Japan's combination of high employment and low inflation received different interpretations. Japanese unions are usually regarded as weak "company" unions, and the annual wage bargaining *shunto* appeared to be more ritual than bargaining, and in any case the *shunto* bargaining seemed to take place at the company and industry level. More recent interpretations see serious negotiations behind the ritual: one large industry – always one that is exposed to international competition – is picked to set the pattern for wage increases, and employers and unions in that industry negotiate with each other, all the while consulting with their counterparts in other industries and the government. After a settlement is reached in the selected industry, the others soon reach similar settlements. See Mari Sako (1997).

From the 1980s onward, the most centralized wage bargaining systems in Europe broke down. In Sweden, for instance, unions representing different groups of employees – white collar versus blue collar, large firms versus small – were no longer able to agree. The functional centralization of Japan's system, however, strengthened during the same period.

In sum, we can say that LME labor markets are liberal, this does not mean they act like textbook markets for widgets. Nor are CME labor markets always as centralized as supposed. The general trend in both for the past few decades has been one of decentralization – and sometimes individualization – of bargaining. In adopting an approach

War II. While these mechanisms differ, what they have in common is that the influential shareholders are *strategic* shareholders, who tend to hold their shares for very long periods, and who typically own them not as a passive portfolio investment but as part of a more complicated business relationship with the firm.

Banks in LMEs play a relatively passive role in the affairs of their customers. In many other countries they are inclined to take a far more active role, and should be regarded as a second category of quasi-insider, along with strategic shareholders (in Germany, as just noted, the two can be the same). Indeed, before Hall and Soskice's the LME/CME distinction became current, a common way of classifying capitalist economies was in terms of whether their financial systems were "bank centered" or "stock-market centered" (Franks and Mayer 1990). It turns out that all the CMEs fall into the former category, and the LMEs into the latter. Today, more attention is focused on the role of block-holders than of banks, but the banks in CMEs play a role which parallels, and complements, that of strategic shareholders.

11.4.2. PROTECTION OF MINORITY SHAREHOLDERS AND MINORITY CREDITORS

Why do quasi-insiders exercise such influence in most countries and not in LMEs? One answer is that in most countries it is more common for a single shareholder to hold a controlling interest in a large company (this is not so in Japan, where in statistical terms shareholding is fully as dispersed as in the US, but in Japan effective control resides with banks and cross-shareholding networks, so we have control by strategic investors even if they don't own large blocs). That answer just pushes the question back: *why,* outside the LMEs, are controlling interests likely to be held by a few strategic investors? We also need to understand *how* quasi-insiders are able to exercise control.

LMEs tend to have strong provisions for minority shareholder protection (MSP). MSP is any application of the principle that all holders of common shares in a company should be treated equally. This principle can be reflected in a number of different legal or regulatory requirements, and in corporate practice. Gourevitch and Shinn (2005, p. 48) prepared an index of MSP for different countries; this included the provision for getting information about the company (both through company disclosure and through independent audits), oversight (which they treat as a function of the proportion of independent members on the board of directors), control (the extent to which insiders and strategic investors are prevented from interfering with the market for corporate control), and incentives (the extent to which executive compensation is structured to align executives' interests with those of shareholders). With the same caveat about adding apples-and-oranges that I gave for Estevez-Abe et al. (2001) indices of

Table 11.2. Minority shareholder protection index for selected countries

US	97
Canada	84
UK	74
Australia	71
Ireland	70
France	52
Spain	50
Sweden	43
Finland	41
India	38
Japan	37
South Korea	36
Denmark	36
Netherlands	35
Taiwan	34
Germany	33
Brazil	30
Italy	23
China	11

Source: Gourevitch and Shinn (2005), Table 3.1.

employment and unemployment protection, an extract from Gourevitch and Shinn's index is reported in Table 11.2. Notice that countries with the strongest MSPs are former British colonies: legal traditions have an effect. The two former British colonies that come in relatively low on this list – India and South Africa – had vigorous post-independence regimes of import substitution industrialization (ISI), and their corporate governance was reshaped in that period.

Countries with strong MSP also tend to be countries where it is uncommon for a single shareholder to have a controlling interest (Gourevitch and Shinn 2005, Figure 3.3). One way of explaining this empirical relationship is that shares are more valuable to those with controlling blocks when MSPs are weak, because with weak MSPs large blockholders can use the company's resources to help themselves at the expense of minority shareholders. Another interpretation is that in return for the privileges they enjoy when MSPs are weak, large block-holders provide a service: monitoring the performance of the firm's managers, and step in to sort things out if the company is doing badly. An investor does not want to hold a large, undiversified block of a company's shares unless she *can* monitor and intervene in this way, but since it is costly to play this role she would not be willing to do so if she had to share the benefits equally to a lot of free riding minority shareholders.

The difference in the role played by banks has a similar explanation: small *creditor* protection (SCP). We don't have information about such a wide range of countries as in the case of MSP, but Frankel and Montgomery (1991) provide a comparison of the US, Britain, Germany, and Japan – two LMEs and two CMEs. We saw in Chapter 9 that American and education system and employers: certain days at school, other days at work. The terms for employer participation in the program are worked out state by state (the states, or *länder*, being the sub-national unit in the German federal system) and industry by industry, by agreement of the employers' associations, trade unions, and school system. The label "corporatist" refers to the fact that the system is governed by rules negotiated between associations representing major stakeholders. This system depends on the successful enforcement of participation by the major employers. German employees have considerable job security but, unlike Japanese employees, they do expect to be able to change employers; if broad participation were not enforced, the employers participating in training would end up subsidizing their competitors involuntarily.

The "German" system is actually that of the former West Germany (Austria, Switzerland, and parts of Belgium have similar systems). The delicacy of its solution to the collective action problem among employers can be seen in the difficulty (and, in most cases, failure) met by efforts to establish the system in the former East Germany, and also by the longer standing efforts by the French government to change from pure state provision to a German-style dual system. In the absence of powerful employers' associations and unions, it appears that free riding prevails and a high-skill equilibrium is not achieved. Yet, the employers' associations and unions in the former West Germany are powerful in part *because* of their ongoing management of the apprenticeship programs. There does not seem to be a good recipe for switching to such a system. Pepper Culpepper (2001) provides a good discussion of this problem.

11.3.3. LABOR RELATIONS

Two decades ago, international comparison of employment systems would not have focused on skills, training, or choices by individual employees. Rather, it would have focused on the collective power of workers, as represented by their unions. Questions would have been asked, first, about wage bargaining and, second, about the ability of unions to influence company plans regarding employment levels, production systems... and also skills. Most of the current varieties of capitalism literature downplays the importance of unions. This is both because, in most countries, unions are less powerful now than they were a few decades ago, and because the leading VOC authors seek to differentiate their product as "firm-centered" (Hall and Soskice 2001, p. 4. For a critique of Hall and Soskice on this point, see Howell 2003). Yet, as we look closely at the VOC accounts of how CMEs are actually coordinated, we find that even in these accounts the power of organized labor is still treated as an important variable.

11.3.3.1. Wage bargaining: Centralized, individual, and points between

Abstract models of perfectly competitive labor markets treat wage determination as a simple market bargain between individual workers and employers. It is tempting to treat LMEs as if they operate that way. There is good reason to believe, however, that even in markets without unions, wages don't rise and fall with supply and demand in quite the way that, say, the price of apples would. In Chapter 9 we saw how, according to efficiency wage theory, wages for most jobs have to be too high to allow a standard supply-and-demand equilibrium, in order to encourage greater effort and reliability on the part of workers. In addition to this, employers can face serious problems if they are seen to be treating employees unfairly; good sources of the implications of *that* problem include Akerlof (1982), Frank (1985), and Bewley (1999). Moreover, both the US and the UK set legal minimum wage levels for most jobs; contrary to the predictions of standard competitive models, there is little evidence that such a wage floor decreases employment (Blanchflower and Oswald 1994; Card and Krueger 1994), even though it can achieve a substantial reduction in the inequality of earnings within a country (DiNardo, Fortin, and Lemieux 1996). Finally, a moment's reflection will tell you that competition in labor markets is asymmetric: there are many fewer employers than employees; in a particular industry and in a particular locale, there may be many workers with a particular skill set and only a few employers (maybe just one) they might work for. For this reason *monopsony*, or buyer's power, is pervasive in labor markets, placing workers at a distinct disadvantage when bargaining is individual (Manning 2003). So when we call the labor markets in LMEs "competitive," we should not imagine that we are talking about the simple supply-and-demand model of textbooks.

One way of understanding unions is that they are a way in which workers achieve some degree of countervailing seller's power (in the extreme, monopoly) in part of the labor market. A monopsonist (the employer) and a monopolist (the union) then sit down and agree a price (the wage). This immediately raises the question, however, of how far the market power of either party reaches. In some settings unions are limited to narrowly defined groups of workers with particular skills (butchers, medical doctors), credentials (medical doctors again), or workers who happen to occupy certain strategic sites in the production process (recall the discussion in Chapter 9 on the bargaining power of assembly line workers and others who were in a position to disrupt the production chains of mass production). If, however, a union can extend its monopoly to a larger group, it may be able to enhance its bargaining power. Recall, again, the discussion in Chapter 9 on the growth of *industrial* unions in America in the 1930s, which sought to represent all workers in particular industries (steel, autos, retail trades, and so forth). During the Golden Age of mass production, it was common in the US for uniform contracts to be agreed between a union and most of the major employers in a particular industry, either on a national or a regional basis. In the US case, a union

would pick one company with which to bargain, with the aim of using the contract with that company as a model for the industry. Contracts in one industry then often formed a model for subsequent negotiations in another. This was called "pattern bargaining," and during the Golden Age it produced a sort of coordination in American labor markets.

In CMEs, this process of centralization went further, and continued after the American system had faded away. In Germany, for instance, unions in a particular industry would negotiate the main points, not with individual companies, but with an association representing all companies in that industry (the same association that was responsible, together with the union and state, for managing the apprenticeship program). In some relatively small European countries, such as Sweden and Austria, the national union confederation and the national association of employers would bargain over the basic wage increase at the national level.

During the crisis of mass production, strong unions in some countries were blamed for inflation. With productivity growing at a snail's pace, expectations of wage increases outstripped the resources available; countries such as Britain, France, Italy, and to a lesser extent the US. Countries with the highly centralized wage bargaining, such as Austria and Sweden, managed to maintain a combination of high employment and low inflation. Lars Calmfors and John Driffill (1988; see also Rowthorn 1977, 1992) argued that wage–price spirals could be kept under control either with very weak unions or with centralized bargaining; they became a problem when unions were strong enough to demand wage increases, but bargaining separately so that there was no way to agree to keep demands at a sustainable level. In this discussion, the reasons for Japan's combination of high employment and low inflation received different interpretations. Japanese unions are usually regarded as weak "company" unions, and the annual wage bargaining *shunto* appeared to be more ritual than bargaining, and in any case the *shunto* bargaining seemed to take place at the company and industry level. More recent interpretations see serious negotiations behind the ritual: one large industry – always one that is exposed to international competition – is picked to set the pattern for wage increases, and employers and unions in that industry negotiate with each other, all the while consulting with their counterparts in other industries and the government. After a settlement is reached in the selected industry, the others soon reach similar settlements. See Mari Sako (1997).

From the 1980s onward, the most centralized wage bargaining systems in Europe broke down. In Sweden, for instance, unions representing different groups of employees – white collar versus blue collar, large firms versus small – were no longer able to agree. The functional centralization of Japan's system, however, strengthened during the same period.

In sum, we can say that LME labor markets are liberal, this does not mean they act like textbook markets for widgets. Nor are CME labor markets always as centralized as supposed. The general trend in both for the past few decades has been one of decentralization – and sometimes individualization – of bargaining. In adopting an approach

centered on firms and, secondarily, on national political constitutions, Hall and Soskice treat wage bargaining systems almost as epiphenomena. This may be, or they may prove to have been an important part of the glue that held CMEs together. Time will tell.

11.4. **Varieties of finance and corporate governance**

We turn now from the labor market to the relationship between the corporation and that other factor of production, capital. In the previous chapters, we have traced changes in the American system of corporate governance and finance: in the late nineteenth and early twentieth centuries, large American corporations were formed, and initially controlled, by the guiding hand of investment banks; they emerged gradually from bank control until, during the Fordist era, they were essentially controlled by their managers; since the late 1970s, they have existed under the constant scrutiny of financial markets.

11.4.1. CONTROL BY OUTSIDERS, OR QUASI-INSIDERS?

America's system today is the archetypal LME financial system. In most large companies, shareholding is widely dispersed so that shareholders cannot exercise direct control. Shareholders do, however, assert the *right* to control. This assertion is evidenced in the rhetoric of shareholder value; in institutions such as the market for corporate control, disclosure requirements, and other legal protections for the rights of minority shareholders; and in very high levels of executive pay.

Outside of the LMEs (i.e., both in CMEs and also in a host of countries that don't really fall in either category), most companies are effectively controlled by some combination of insiders (managers) and what I will call quasi-insiders: founding families, shareholders who have bought large blocs for strategic reasons, banks with which the companies do business. The Japanese *keiretsu* system described in Chapter 10 is one example of this, but should not be regarded as typical – quasi-insider control looks very different in different countries. Germany lacks *keiretsu*-like groups, but does have widespread cross-shareholding between companies. In Germany, banks may also own shares in their customers; this, together with their role as trustees managing (and voting) the shares of others, can give them considerable influence *as shareholders*; on their influence as lenders, more in a moment. In some countries – Sweden, South Korea, and South Africa, for instance – a large share of industry is grouped into a handful of corporate pyramids, which are controlled (often by one family) from the top (LaPorta, López-de-Silanaes, and Shleifer 1999); another example of such pyramids, of course, is the old *zaibatsu* system in Japan, abolished by the US occupation authorities after World

War II. While these mechanisms differ, what they have in common is that the influential shareholders are *strategic* shareholders, who tend to hold their shares for very long periods, and who typically own them not as a passive portfolio investment but as part of a more complicated business relationship with the firm.

Banks in LMEs play a relatively passive role in the affairs of their customers. In many other countries they are inclined to take a far more active role, and should be regarded as a second category of quasi-insider, along with strategic shareholders (in Germany, as just noted, the two can be the same). Indeed, before Hall and Soskice's the LME/CME distinction became current, a common way of classifying capitalist economies was in terms of whether their financial systems were "bank centered" or "stock-market centered" (Franks and Mayer 1990). It turns out that all the CMEs fall into the former category, and the LMEs into the latter. Today, more attention is focused on the role of block-holders than of banks, but the banks in CMEs play a role which parallels, and complements, that of strategic shareholders.

11.4.2. PROTECTION OF MINORITY SHAREHOLDERS AND MINORITY CREDITORS

Why do quasi-insiders exercise such influence in most countries and not in LMEs? One answer is that in most countries it is more common for a single shareholder to hold a controlling interest in a large company (this is not so in Japan, where in statistical terms shareholding is fully as dispersed as in the US, but in Japan effective control resides with banks and cross-shareholding networks, so we have control by strategic investors even if they don't own large blocs). That answer just pushes the question back: *why*, outside the LMEs, are controlling interests likely to be held by a few strategic investors? We also need to understand *how* quasi-insiders are able to exercise control.

LMEs tend to have strong provisions for minority shareholder protection (MSP). MSP is any application of the principle that all holders of common shares in a company should be treated equally. This principle can be reflected in a number of different legal or regulatory requirements, and in corporate practice. Gourevitch and Shinn (2005, p. 48) prepared an index of MSP for different countries; this included the provision for getting information about the company (both through company disclosure and through independent audits), oversight (which they treat as a function of the proportion of independent members on the board of directors), control (the extent to which insiders and strategic investors are prevented from interfering with the market for corporate control), and incentives (the extent to which executive compensation is structured to align executives' interests with those of shareholders). With the same caveat about adding apples-and-oranges that I gave for Estevez-Abe et al. (2001) indices of

Table 11.2. Minority shareholder protection index for selected countries

US	97
Canada	84
UK	74
Australia	71
Ireland	70
France	52
Spain	50
Sweden	43
Finland	41
India	38
Japan	37
South Korea	36
Denmark	36
Netherlands	35
Taiwan	34
Germany	33
Brazil	30
Italy	23
China	11

Source: Gourevitch and Shinn (2005), Table 3.1.

employment and unemployment protection, an extract from Gourevitch and Shinn's index is reported in Table 11.2. Notice that countries with the strongest MSPs are former British colonies: legal traditions have an effect. The two former British colonies that come in relatively low on this list – India and South Africa – had vigorous post-independence regimes of import substitution industrialization (ISI), and their corporate governance was reshaped in that period.

Countries with strong MSP also tend to be countries where it is uncommon for a single shareholder to have a controlling interest (Gourevitch and Shinn 2005, Figure 3.3). One way of explaining this empirical relationship is that shares are more valuable to those with controlling blocks when MSPs are weak, because with weak MSPs large blockholders can use the company's resources to help themselves at the expense of minority shareholders. Another interpretation is that in return for the privileges they enjoy when MSPs are weak, large block-holders provide a service: monitoring the performance of the firm's managers, and step in to sort things out if the company is doing badly. An investor does not want to hold a large, undiversified block of a company's shares unless she *can* monitor and intervene in this way, but since it is costly to play this role she would not be willing to do so if she had to share the benefits equally to a lot of free riding minority shareholders.

The difference in the role played by banks has a similar explanation: small *creditor* protection (SCP). We don't have information about such a wide range of countries as in the case of MSP, but Frankel and Montgomery (1991) provide a comparison of the US, Britain, Germany, and Japan – two LMEs and two CMEs. We saw in Chapter 9 that American and

British banks take care not to be seen as managing a company, because if they did and if the company subsequently went bankrupt, a court would treat them as an owner, not a lender: all other creditors – suppliers, for instance – would be repaid before the bank. Therefore, whatever information the bank might have about the way the company is managed, and whatever worries it may have about being repaid, it maintains a strictly arm's length relationship with the company. The bank's only real sanctions are to refuse further credit or to call in loans outstanding. It will have larded the loan agreement with covenants detailing circumstances – most commonly, balance sheet benchmarks – which would place the borrower in default, giving bank the option of calling in the loan. The German or Japanese bank has a wider range of intervention options because minority creditor protections are weaker. Because they *can* intervene, they also have an incentive to monitor the company more closely – the information is more useful to them.

Our story so far, then, is that quasi-insiders take strong roles in companies, except in the LMEs. They do so because, except in LMEs, MSP and SCP are weak. But (at the risk of sounding like a broken record here), *why* are MSP and (as far as we know from a few important cases) SCP weak in so many countries?

Mark Roe (2003) offers a functional explanation: the countries that have weak MSP are those that need weak MSP, and they need it because employment protection is strong. They have strong employment protection not for functional reasons, but from the vagaries of politics. He assumes that quasi-insider monitoring is more costly, overall, than monitoring conducted through financial markets. He also assumes that it is more effective. Strong employment protection accentuates the principal-agent problem between shareholders and managers, since managers not looking out for the shareholders' interests can easily allow the firm to get locked into a high-cost workforce. Therefore, countries with strong employment protection need strong quasi-insiders. Weak MSP is an institutional solution to this problem. Comparing Table 11.2 and Figure 11.1, we do indeed see that, of the countries included in both, those with the strongest employment protection (Austria, Belgium, Germany, Italy, and Japan) are also those with the weakest MSP. Those with the weakest employment protection and the strongest MSP are, of course, the LMEs. Gourevitch and Shinn (2005) noted this relationship and a similar strong correlation between employment protection and the prevalence of controlling blockholders (see Gourevitch and Shinn 2005, Table A.13).

Roe assumes that market governance is less costly than quasi-insider governance and will be more efficient when agency costs are lower; that employment security raises agency costs; and that governments will act to adopt efficient systems of corporate governance. It is possible that all of these are true, but Roe does not demonstrate them: they are assumptions he uses to explain some empirical correlation. Gourevitch and Shinn have a different explanation for the same correlations, based on the constitutional structures of the countries in question. I will return to that below. First, let us consider some of the practical implications that quasi-insider control has for corporate governance.

11.4.3. WHAT DO QUASI-INSIDERS DO?

The effects of quasi-insider governance are in the eye of the beholder: it has its fans, and its detractors. Let us consider two aspects – the governance function (monitoring and intervention), and the effect on the character of investment.

Quasi-insiders can keep a close eye on a company, can intervene early if things are going badly, and have a broad range of intervention tools rather than a few crude clubs. If we assume that the intervention is an efficacious response to problems that are causing avoidable losses, then earlier, gentler intervention seems better than waiting for the company to lose much of its value before it is reorganized via the market for corporate control. Of course, some part of our assumption might be incorrect.

There are at least three reasons why quasi-insider control is likely to produce different investment choices than market control: information, time horizon, and attitude toward risk. Quasi-insiders get information from close monitoring; markets don't have a visible monitoring mechanism, but market prices are based on some information – including, plausibly, things the inside monitors might have missed. Takeo Hoshi, Anil Kashyap, and David Scharfstein (1991) test the effects by comparing the investment behavior of Japanese companies that are part of a keiretsu, and those which are independent. They find that the investment behavior of firms which are independent is influenced by their cash position, while that of the keiretsu members is influenced by the firm's profitability. This is evidence that a keiretsu – a network of companies controlled by quasi-insiders – does a better job of channelling its members' investable funds to profitable uses, than Japanese financial markets do for independent firms. Depending on your perspective, that says something good about quasi-insider control, or something bad about Japanese financial markets.

Quasi-insider systems are often said to have, *patient capital*, on the grounds that strategic investors take a long view, while stock markets look at the most recent financial report. This is as much about information as patience: minority shareholders often have no information about a company other than what is in its financial reports, while quasi-insiders can know quite a bit more about the company's plans and prospects. Patience can also reflect a lack of liquidity in large-block investments.

Quasi-insiders are likely to be more risk averse than outsiders. In the case of large block shareholders, this is because their portfolios are undiversified. Banks will be risk averse because part, if not all, of their financial interest in the company is in the form of loans earning fixed rates of interest, giving the bank little to gain from its client's spectacular profits and much to lose from the firm's insolvency.

Much of what is written on this topic takes the form of advocacy of one system of the other. The VOC analysis has striven to tone down the discussion, by making the argument that quasi-insider control and market control are good for different things. Patient capital fits well with highly skilled teams of workers with good job security, who work together to make incremental improvements in complex products. Automobiles are one example, manufacturing equipment is another. (In the Hall–Soskice world, patient capital and secure workers are complementary inputs – a world apart from Roe's story that quasi-insider control is a costly but necessary response to politically driven job security). Similarly, liberal financial markets are seen as fitting well with flexible labor markets – capital and labor are complements, and it does no good to be able to scale capital quickly up or down if labor can't be treated in the same way. Again, the system of governance is suited to particular products and particular approaches to production. A Hollywood movie, a new software product, an oil field – investments and workforces put together for the occasion.

11.5. **Relationships between companies and systems of innovation**

Two other distinctive features of national business systems are the character of relationships between companies, and the systems of innovation. There is not the space here to deal with either in detail, but let me take a moment to situate them in the rest of the discussion.

We can think of relationships between companies in two dimensions: horizontal (between competing firms) and vertical (up and down the supply chain or, more generally, between firms that bring different specializations to a particular production system). We saw the question of horizontal cooperation in Chapter 8, with regard to the stabilization of markets in since the early days of the large corporation. In this chapter, we have seen how industry associations are key to organizing Germany's apprenticeship system, and its wage negotiations.

An example of how vertical relationships can differ between LMEs and CMEs was seen in Chapter 10, with the comparison of supply chains in Detroit-style and Toyota-style production systems. We will see more on such vertical relationships in the case of localized industrial clusters, in the next chapter.

If we may generalize about both the horizontal and the vertical in both LMEs and CMEs – and that covers quite a lot of territory, so take this with appropriate caution – LMEs favor simple arms' length relationships between companies, while CMEs favor more complex, less formalized, and longer lasting relationships. Mari Sako (1992), comparing supply chain relationships in Britain and Japan, calls it a difference between adversarial and obligational contracting. See also the papers in Lane and Bachmann (1998).

Approaches to innovation differ between countries in ways that will probably not be surprising in light of the discussion in this chapter and the one before: patient capital and incremental improvement by stable teams of skilled workers leads to a different approach to innovation than a facility for rapid mobilization of resources for a promising and radical new product. The connection between corporate governance and innovation is explored in depth by Mary O'Sullivan (2001).

11.6. **Political systems: Consensus and CMEs, majoritarianism and LMEs**

We saw above that one reason workers in CMEs make bigger investments in specific skills is that their investment is insured by stronger employment protection and, in most CMEs, unemployment protection. If you are a young worker making such an investment choice, however, how do you know that the social protection that exists today will still be around in twenty or thirty years when you actually need it? The government might decide to change laws and opt for "labor market flexibility," reducing social protection. Political pressure to do so might, in fact, come from members of your own generation, since you contribute to the costs of social insurance through higher taxes or lower wages, while the benefits are collected by older people whose vocational training choices turned out to be bad ones. If a country goes through a spell of major industrial adjustment – coal mines closing, or manufacturing jobs moving to low-wage countries – a country will be paying out heavily on this insurance, and younger workers (and voters) may want out of the deal.

Social insurance, then, is a form of *intergenerational bargain.* The particularly difficulty with such bargains is that if today's younger generation enters into the bargain, they're depending on people not yet born to sign on to the bargain a few decades later.

A similar problem applies to pensions. Pension systems in CMEs tend to be pay-as-you-go, with the contributions of those working today paying the pensions of the retired. A young voter or worker might ask, "Why am I paying the pensions of retired people? Will the younger taxpayers a few decades from now vote to pay me as a good a pension?" Pay-as-you-go pensions, then, also depend on an intergenerational bargain. Pension systems in LMEs tend not to be pay-as-you-go. Instead, most of them are *funded*: funds for the pensions of a particular worker or cohort of workers are set aside and invested, whether in individual accounts or in company or industry plans. Funded pension systems face the problem of where to invest so much money, and how to manage those investments; much of it goes into the stock market.

We saw in Chapter 10 that a major force in the financialization of the US economy has been the growth of pension fund investment in stock markets. Other LMEs have followed a similar pattern. Gourevitch and Shinn (2005) argue that political support for minority shareholder protection (MSP) is directly linked to pension fund investment in stock markets: if your pension money is invested in a company, you tend to feel strongly about insiders feathering their nests. For the reasons discussed above, MSP is incompatible with governance by insiders or quasi-insiders. So the type of pension system a country has is closely linked with its system of corporate governance.

Two key features of CMEs – investment in specific skills which depends on job-related insurance (employment protection, unemployment protection), and insider control free of the depredations of institutional investors – thus depend on bargains between different generations of workers. What makes these bargains credible? Iversen (2005), in the case of investment in skills, and Gourevitch and Shinn (2005), in the case of pensions and corporate governance, argue that the intergenerational bargains which make CMEs possible are underpinned by "consensual" systems of government; LMEs, in contrast, tend to have "majoritarian" systems of government. The distinction between consensual and majoritarian systems is analyzed in detail by Arend Lijphart (1999).

Majoritarian systems get their name from the fact that their elections usually result in a clear majority for one party or another, leaving that party free to implement its program. Majoritarian systems are therefore prone to decisive shifts in direction, and one would not bet heavily on such a government's keeping any promise for the next several decades. In consensual systems, it is usually the case that no one party is in a position to push through its program without securing the agreement of others. This may be because the legislature is elected by proportional representation, which tends to lead to coalition governments; it may be because of supermajority requirements, bicameral legislatures, or a separation of powers between branches of government give different actors the ability to veto changes. Westminster-style parliamentary systems – the model for most LMEs – are decisively majoritarian; US voting systems are majoritarian, but a consensual element is introduced through the constitutional separation of powers; most CMEs have proportional representation systems.

Japan is an odd case, in that one party has had outright control almost continuously for over half a century. For several decades, from the 1950s through the 1980s, the Italian story was similar. It is noteworthy that these are unusual among CMEs in the weakness of their public social safety nets: they have high employment protection and very weak unemployment protection.

11.7. Continuity and change in national business systems

11.7.1. POST-FORDIST DIVERGENCE

In the 1960s, the industrial systems of the LMEs and CMEs were both more self-contained, and more alike, than they are today. Mass production went further in some countries than in others, but it was the dominant model for all. Social insurance was weaker in CMEs than it is today, while in LMEs labor unions were far more powerful than they are now (Iversen 2005). In the LMEs, insider (managerial) and quasi-insider (bloc-holder) control had not yet given way to financialization.

In the 1980s, Piore and Sabel (1984) were arguing that the world stood at a "second industrial divide." The first divide had been in the late nineteenth century, when the decisions had been made that led to mass production as the hegemonic model; the second divide now required choices about what the post-mass production world would look like. American post-Fordism turned out nothing like Piore and Sabel expected, while the emerging post-Fordism of the CMEs was the basis for Piore and Sabel's flexible specialization model. So the second divide saw not only a break from the mass production model of the past, but also a divergence between different types of post-mass-production economy.

11.7.2. POSTWAR RECONSTRUCTION PLUS CONSENSUAL GOVERNMENT

What led some countries to become CMEs, and others LMEs? For the most part, we can explain this as a deepening of differences that already existed during the Fordist era, and which made one path or the other easier. One critical dimension, we have seen above, is the nature of the political system: consensual systems had an easier time making the intergenerational deals that are a big part of the coordination for which CMEs are known. Barry Eichengreen and Torben Iversen (1999; see also Iversen 2005; Eichengreen 2007) argue that a second critical factor was the amount of damage the country suffered during World War II.

The functioning of a CME requires solving certain collective action problems that can be ignored in an LME. It is not easy or costless to set up the institutions required to solve these problems: wage bargaining systems that minimize the costs of the conflict in dividing the gains from growth; employers' associations to channel competition into constructive rivalry, and to provide shared services for rival firms. If these problems have been solved, there can be a big bonus in terms of productivity growth. The Eichengreen–Iversen argument is essentially that if the potential productivity bonus is big enough, it can provide the motivation the various actors need to bury their differences and solve the problems. For countries whose industries have been devastated by war, the potential productivity bonus is huge, so the potential for reaching agreement is strong.

A related argument, from Wolfgang Streeck and Kozo Yamamura (2001), focuses particularly on postwar (West) Germany and Japan, as rare examples of what they call "non-liberal capitalism." Both Eichengreen–Iversen and Streeck–Yamamura see the institutions facilitating CMEs as postwar accidents. Where the Hall–Soskice argument presents CME institutions as underpinning comparative advantage and for that reason being self-sustaining, these arguments see their unique features as unlikely to survive as the growth bonus from postwar reconstruction fades into history.

11.7.3. LATE DEVELOPMENT

Countries do change direction, and catastrophic wars are likely turning points, both offering as they do both the aforementioned benefits from reconstruction, and the opportunity to change political institutions. We could, then, stop at World War II and dig no further for the origins of today's varieties of capitalism. It is useful, though, to look just a bit further back, to a set of theories which places the origins of difference in a country's initial industrialization.

Alexander Gerschenkron (1952) argued that late industrialization requires different institutions than early industrialization. Britain could industrialize with liberal economic institutions for two reasons: one is that companies were smaller and capital requirements for industrialization were less; the other was that international industrial competition was less. Later industrialization required greater concentration of resources: it came at a time when industry was more capital intensive, when the technological change required to move from being an agrarian society to being an industrial one was greater, and when the large corporation was coming into being. International competition had become tougher. The countries that succeeded in getting on the industrial ladder later – the US, then Germany, then Japan, then Russia – did so with the aid of progressively greater centralization of control. In the US, this centralization was manifest in the role of Wall Street banks in assembling the large corporations; in Germany, the role of banks persisted after it had faded in the US; in Japan, the prewar *zaibatsu* and, after the war, the *keiretsu* along with the guiding hand of the state; in Soviet Russia, fully centralized state planning.

John Zysman (1983) used a late development framework to explain differences among capitalist economies in the late twentieth century. Comparing the US, UK, (West) Germany, France, and Japan, he offers a classification which follows the market versus bank scheme discussed above, but with a twist: Germany, France, and Japan are all credit (i.e., bank) centered, but France and Japan differ from Germany in that the state (at the time) guided the investment priorities of the banks.

A related line of reasoning locates the origins of modern institutions in the particular political settlement that makes those who have power in an agrarian country willing to make the investments, and to countenance the social changes needed for the transformation to a modern commercial and industrial society. Here we see the problem not so much in terms of the requirements of competitive catch-up, as the problems of overcoming domestic resistance to change. This argument is developed by Gerschenkron (1966), Barrington Moore (1966), Charles Tilly (1992), and others. Gøsta Esping-Andersen (1990) uses it in explaining why different parts of Europe developed different kinds of welfare state – a story that feeds into the VOC analysis. We will see, in Chapters 13 and 14, that the same issues come up today in the newly industrialized countries.

11.7.4. CONVERGENCE?

Does the liberalization of international markets make us all more alike, or does it promote further differentiation? The VOC story suggests the latter: increased trade makes comparative advantage more important, and institutional differences are sources of comparative advantage. On the other hand, capital mobility could force countries to converge toward a single model. Systems with quasi-insider control of companies can be efficient competitors and, at the same time, offer a worse deal for portfolio investors – that is to say, for minority shareholders. Portfolio investment can have greater international mobility than either labor or quasi-insider investment. Liberalization of international financial markets makes it easier for portfolio investors to shop around, and they seem likely to favor countries with strong MSP protection.

Michel Goyer (2006) shows that, among American institutions investing in continental Europe, public employee pension funds prefer Germany with its strong job security and consensual management, while hedge funds prefer France with its somewhat weaker job security and extremely hierarchical management. If that sounds like public employee pension funds make investment decisions based on a sentimental attachment to workers' rights, consider what Lily Qiu (2006) finds: that in the US, firms in which those same public pension funds invest are much less likely to make bad acquisition decisions, while other institutional investors have either no effect or an adverse effect on the quality of acquisition decisions. German institutions may not, in the end, be a bar to increased returns for minority shareholders. Ronald Gilson (2000) argues that a great deal of functional convergence can happen without institutional change, or formal convergence. He argues that international capital mobility simply results in higher payouts to shareholders and closer attention to the preferences of minority shareholders, in countries like Germany.

11.7.4.1. Convergence as illusion

In considering this and other convergence narratives, let me offer the following caution: in my memory, there have been three important convergence narratives regarding national business systems. Each promised an entirely different kind of convergence.

The first was convergence of bureaucratic capitalism and bureaucratic communism into one form of "industrial society." In the 1950s and 1960s, business corporations in all industrial countries seemed to be getting larger and more bureaucratic; they were particularly large and bureaucratic in the leading capitalist economy, the US, and in its big communist rival, the Soviet Union. It was, of course, the age of mass production and managerialism (Gordon 1945; Berle and Means 1967). Large industrial companies could be viewed as miniature planned economies, or planned economies as gigantic industrial enterprises, so the differences between industrial capitalism and industrial communism could be viewed as matters of degree, not fundamental differences in character (Galbraith 1967). There also appeared to be a trend, within the capitalist economies, for the state to take on an increasing economic role, whether as an owner or as a regulator of enterprise (Harrington 1972). To the extent that capitalist firms were controlled by shareholders, rather than managers, the former were now likely to be workers, through their pension funds (Drucker 1976). The Soviet bloc would eventually liberalize somewhat, and we would have similar bureaucratic industrialisms, a Weberian dream or a Kafka-esque nightmare, depending on your predilections, on both sides of what had been the Iron Curtain.

It didn't happen. By the late 1970s, it was apparent that mass production was a spent force. The leading actors in the first convergence drama were struggling, and while some of the supporting players – Japan, West Germany, Sweden, and Italy – were thriving, their departures from the model of bureaucratic mass production were suddenly more interesting than anything they shared with that model. This led, for the convergence-minded, to various stories of Japanization, flexible specialization, and lean production, all discussed in the previous chapter. This set of narratives was persuasive because Japan had so quickly emerged from the rubble of war to best the US at what it seemed to do best – the mass production of cars, televisions, and other consumer goods. And many of the techniques pioneered by Japanese companies, in quality management, inventory management, continuous improvement, teamwork, multiskilling, contracting practices, and so forth, were eagerly adopted by companies around the world.

Yet, Japanization didn't happen, either. In the 1990s, Japan was in crisis. Germany had its own crisis, as the West absorbed the East at considerable expense. Centralized wage bargaining retreated in Scandinavia, Italy stopped growing. Did this dissuade many from believing in convergence? No, instead, a new type of convergence, a new focus for the convergence narrative, was identified. While Japan and the economies of continental Europe were slowing down, their Anglo-Saxon counterparts were picking up. So the future became American again: not the America of bureaucratic mass production, but a neoliberal model, deregulated, flexible, entrepreneurial, financialized, globalized.

Each of these convergence stories starts with a very big element of truth: bureaucratic mass production, flexible production, and neoliberalism are all real; for a time, each of them was ascendant, affecting the path of development everywhere in the world. In each case, I would suggest, the result was a sort of optical illusion. Framing our understanding of the world by looking at a particular important trend, other changes that are happening at the same time fade into the background. In particular, processes of differentiation fade into the background, because they are harder to encapsulate in a trend. But different places remain different, and there will be new and different universal trends in the future: that much we can predict with confidence.

12 Clusters

Who makes your computer, and where is it made? There is probably no simple answer to that question. The laptop I'm working on right now is branded by RM, a British company that sells to schools and universities. Reading the fine print on the back I'm not surprised to find it's made in Taiwan by ASUS. ASUS also sells computers under its own brand, but here it is playing the role of OEM, or original equipment manufacturer. OEMs put products together to the specifications of the company that brands them and sells them to consumers. In some industries, such as clothing or footwear, the term "full package supplier" might be used instead of OEM.

Part of this OEM's work takes place in its factory in Taiwan, but before it makes the machine ASUS must source the parts: specify the components needed, select the suppliers, negotiate terms, and secure delivery. These activities, which we summarize as "coordinating the supply chain" (also known, in different contexts, as the value chain, the commodity chain, or the supply network), are one of the basic roles of the OEM – sometimes the *only* role, as the final assembly may itself be outsourced.

Where do the parts come from? Taiwan is the world's leading manufacturer not only of notebook computers but also of their components, so many of the parts are sourced there, and more specifically in the fifty mile stretch between Taipei and Hsinchu, at the northern end of the island. Others will have come from China, Singapore, Korea, Japan, Malaysia, or the US.

We shouldn't ignore the software, though most of that will have been added later, by RM, by the systems support people where I work, or by me; most of it comes from the US – the inevitable contributions from Microsoft (Redmond, near Seattle, in Washington State), Adobe, Mozilla (both in California's Silicon Valley), and so on. All of those companies will have incorporated code produced by individual companies, or programmers, scattered around the world.

So where is the computer from, and who makes it? It would be tempting, and easy, to say that it is the product of a global network: hundreds of companies are involved, in many different countries. That, however, would be a cop-out: notebook computers come not just from anywhere in the globe but from particular places and particular organizations. Two of those places, Taipei-Hsinchu and the Silicon Valley, are each the home to clusters of hundreds of microelectronics, computer systems, and software companies. Some of the organizations that contributed to the computer are small companies, many of them located in these clusters. Others are multinational corporations (MNCs). Of those MNCs some, including ASUS, and the chip-maker Intel, are based in those clusters; others, such as the beloved Microsoft, are based elsewhere.

Notebook computers are also produced elsewhere, of course. South Korea and mainland China both produce a lot of them, although some of the suppliers (Intel or its lone rival AMD; and, inevitably, Microsoft) are the same no matter where the machine is put together. Overall, the number of places in the world where this kind of work gets done is not very large, nor is the number of companies capable of contributing certain components, or playing certain roles in putting in together.

Taipei-Hsinchu and the Silicon Valley are examples of specialized industrial clusters. In our world of nearly instant long-distance communication and overnight airfreight across oceans, it turns out that many companies still find it advantageous to locate near to their customers, their suppliers, even their competitors. These two clusters are particularly interesting both because they are high technology clusters which others have tried hard to imitate (usually without much success); and because they are closely linked, by both business and personal relationships, in spite of the Pacific Ocean and what might seem to be large linguistic and cultural differences.

12.1. **The industrial district narrative**

Geographically concentrated clusters of companies in the same, or related, industries have always have existed as long as industry. There has been particular new interest in clusters since the 1980s, however. Giacomo Becattini (1979), studying SME clusters in Italy, saw in them the reflection of English industrial districts described by the Victorian economist Alfred Marshall (1925) almost a hundred years earlier.

Marshall had studied several districts in Britain, including the cutlery and specialty steel district in Sheffield. A century ago, Sheffield was facing stiff competition from abroad, particularly from the US and Germany. The British companies tended to be smaller than their overseas competitors. Marshall argued that the clusters of small companies he observed were able to match big companies with regard both to production efficiency and to product and process development. Being located in the same city, the companies could draw on the same pool of skilled labor, and use the same specialist suppliers and service companies. In this context, different companies specializing in different stages of production could each achieve scale economies in their own activities and, between them, match the performance of a vertically integrated producer.

But as innovators, how can a bunch of small companies hope to match the performance of a big business with its technical staff and its research and development laboratories? Sheffield, despite the small size of its companies, remained at the cutting edge of steel technology (and bear in mind that steel was the silicon of the day). Knowledge, Marshall argued, was "in the air" of the steel district: in place of formal research labs were a large number of expert artisans who knew each other, talked, and did business:

new discoveries and techniques did not stay secret long, were quickly adopted through-out the district.

Mass production industries were in trouble during the 1970s and 1980s, in Italy as anywhere else. What Becattini and numerous others observed was that SME clusters were growing, and were succeeding in competitive international markets. Many of these clusters specialized in high-quality, design-led products in such industries as clothing, textiles, leather goods, ceramics, or furniture; others in applications of mechanical engineering, such as food processing equipment, motor scooters, machine tools, and household appliances; still others in food processing.

A particularly striking feature of these districts is the extreme segmentation of the supply chain. We saw in Chapter 3 how the vertically integrated system of Ford gradually gave way to that of Toyota, outsourcing both production and design of components. To do so required a cooperative working relationship with suppliers along the chain, including the sharing of information which, in the Ford system, had been kept secret within companies.

Now consider the following: in Prato, a town near Florence, there were once vertically integrated mass producers of cloth. In the late 1940s, these companies found themselves in difficulty because their major overseas markets – India, South Africa, and some countries in the Middle East – had at about the same time adopted ISI policies: they had placed high tariffs on textile imports, with the aim of developing their own textile industries. The industry in Prato might simply have collapsed. The big companies did cut back production, lay off employees, and sell off much of their equipment. But they offered the equipment for sale to their employees: individual employees bought indi-vidual pieces of equipment, and set up their own workshops. Within a few years, employment in the district was growing rapidly. In place of cheap, mass-produced cloth for export to the Third World, it came to specialize in high quality wool fabrics, as might go into making a good Italian suit. Production was no longer organized by vertically integrated companies, but by hundreds of independent *impannatori*.

An *impannatore* buys raw materials and contracts with a series of workshops to carry out different phases of production. This is sometimes called stage production. This has something in common with the putting-out system, the way textiles were produced in Britain before the existence of factories (Chapter 7). The difference is that the workshops to which the putting out is done now are equipped with modern, high-speed equipment, and typically have several employees. Notice, too, that there is a visible hand here – the path from fibre to finished fabric is *planned*, each operation done not on a speculative basis but with the next stage already scheduled, the aim being a product of a particular design – but rather than the hand of Chandler's managerial hierarchy, it is that of the *impannatore*, one person with a desk and a telephone. In the 1980s and 1990s, people were writing about virtual companies, which the word "virtual" might lead us to associate with networked computing: the idea, however, came from cases such as this, *circa* 1952.

What is the purpose, and what are the effects, of carrying supply chain segmentation so far? Less extreme forms of stage production have often been used as a way to cut wages. Along the US–Mexican border, for instance, it has been common for the higher skill (and better paid) stages in clothing production to be carried out on the US side, the lower paid stages in Maquiladora plants on the Mexican side: for instance, cutting fabric in the US, sewing in Mexico; on the same border, a similar cross-border division of labor is found in the electronics industry (Kenney and Florida 1994). The Italian industrial districts are not located on a border; wages for many jobs are negotiated nationally in Italy, and the industrial districts are located in areas which, at the time of their development, had not only strong unions but in many cases Communist-led municipal and regional governments (it once seemed a great irony that Communist governments had fostered such entrepreneurial cultures, but China and Vietnam have since left Italy's little local ironies in the dust). Although the variance of wages was higher in the industrial districts than in Italian mass production companies, and that the average wage was slightly lower, the jobs were generally regarded as good (Brusco 1990). Moreover, the big role for very small, specialized companies meant that ambitious skilled workers had a good chance of setting up their own businesses. The improbable mix of working class organization and entrepreneurship, of good wages, high quality and high export growth, was appealing to many.

How did the Italian industrial districts produce these results? The explanation developed by Becattini (1979), Brusco (1982), Piore and Sabel (1984), among others, is what Piore and Sabel called *flexible specialization*. As we saw in Chapter 10, that term has been applied to situations other than SME clusters; moreover, similar analyses of the Italian industrial districts have used different terms. Here's how Piore and Sabel described flexible specialization in this context:

It is seen in the networks of technologically sophisticated, highly flexible manufacturing firms in central and north-western Italy. Flexible specialization is a strategy of permanent innovation: accommodation to ceaseless change, rather than an effort to control it. This strategy is based on flexible – multiuse – equipment; skilled workers; and the creation, through politics, of an industrial community that restricts the forms of competition to those favoring innovation. (1984, p. 17)

So we have a system of production which is also a strategy of innovation. The production process stands Chandler's theory on its head, so that the economies of speed lie with small firms rather than large ones. Chandler wrote of a world in which companies with special purpose equipment produced uniform products. In that world, economies of speed, or flow, were about moving the materials and the product through the production chain, minimizing costs and inventories, eliminating bottlenecks. Not only were the products uniform within a given production run, but they did not change much from month to month, or even year to year.

In a world of flexible machines, Chandler's imperative for vertical integration disappears. The story here is much the same as with the progression from mass to lean production in automobile manufacturing, discussed in Chapter 10. In the classic industrial district, however, the extent of vertical disintegration is much greater than in Toyota's flexible mass production.

What do Piore and Sabel mean by "the creation, through politics, of an industrial community that restricts the forms of competition to those favoring innovation"? Essentially, that price and wage competition are curtailed within a district, so that competition is in the form of offering improved products, improved processes, and new designs. How are price and wage competition curtailed? Standard measures in districts of the Third Italy aren't so different from those between firms, or between firms and unions, in an oligopolistic mass production economy, albeit on the scale of a small city rather than a national market: published price lists for particular or manufacturing services; a wage floor provided by national union agreements; a wage ceiling provided by anti-poaching agreements among employers in the district.

Gabi Dei Ottati (2003) tells how such agreements came into force in the Prato textile district. When the big companies first started selling equipment to individual artisans in 1948, savage price-cutting ensued: the big companies were cutting back, after all, because they had excess capacity. So, on a very small scale, they re-created the problem that had faced early big business in the 1880s and 1890s: with lots of producers with high fixed costs, a fall in demand led to a situation in which no producers made a profit. It took a few years to sort out the institutions of cooperation – or, if you will, price fixing – but by 1952 that was accomplished and the district was set on its course of flexible, design-oriented, high quality manufacture. Competition is thus channeled into what Michael Porter (1990) calls rivalry, an ongoing contest to create the better new design or improved product, a competition which raises the game of the whole district and maintains its competitive position in wider markets.

Cooperation figures in the classic industrial district model in many ways beyond the price-and-wage fixing noted above. These include cooperation between pairs of buyers and sellers along the supply chain (vertical cooperation); horizontal cooperation between pairs of competitors; and collective action by groups of firms, particularly horizontal, to secure common services or favorable actions by the state. We might also list (though it is not clear whether to call it cooperation) what Marshall called an "industrial atmosphere," in which the secrets of the trade were not very secret at all.

The problem of vertical cooperation I will leave to the next section, where I deal with the problem of interfirm trust in some detail. Explicit horizontal cooperation between pairs of competitors is found in most studies to be of marginal importance.

Small differences in the sharing of information, however, may make big differences in the industrial atmosphere – the quality of information in the air. Michael Best (1990) compares the conduct of the owners of small furniture factories in a district in Emilia-Romagna, and in the (now largely defunct) furniture manufacturing district of north

London. The factory owners in Emila-Romagna were, according to Best, in and out of each others establishments on a casual basis; those in London were loath to have competitors visit, for fear that their designs would be stolen. Ironically, the London manufacturers produced mostly reproduction Edwardian furniture, while their Italian counterparts produced new designs. Best did his study in the early 1980s, when flat-packing of furniture together with the reduction of trade barriers within Europe had made the European furniture market fiercely competitive. The Italians thrived, the secretive Londoners closed their doors – first to each other, then to business altogether.

I should note that evidence from other studies suggests that producers in design-led districts in Italy do, in fact, try to keep their new designs secret; apparently, that doesn't always mean keeping their factories off limits. Why would it matter if competitors saw one another's factories? For a start, factory visits can be a simple method of disseminating new techniques. The firms in the district are competing not only with one another, but also with manufacturers elsewhere. For each, then, there is some small cost to letting local rivals see how they've gone about solving production problems, but for the district as a whole such sharing is beneficial. This presents a simple collective action problem. In Best's account, the district in Emilia-Romagna appears to have solved this problem informally. He also relates a different furniture manufacturing district in which the same problem was solved formally. The office furniture manufacturers of Grand Rapids, Michigan tour one member's factory every time their trade association meets. The proud owner shows off the latest equipment and at least some of its uses.

Khalid Nadvi (1999) offers an example of collective action among manufacturers of surgical instruments in Sialkot, Pakistan. The Sialkot cluster makes Pakistan the world's second largest producer of surgical instruments, after Germany. Stainless steel, produced by recyclers in a nearby town, is transformed into scalpels and other instruments by about 300 SMEs in Sialakot. Each firm engages in one or more stages of instrument production: forging, milling and grinding, filing, polishing, and heat treatment. In 1994, the cluster faced a crisis, when the US Food and Drug Administration (FDA) banned Sialkot instruments on the grounds of inadequate quality assurance procedures. Getting back into its largest market required training in, and implementation of, procedures which require tests and written records at each stage of production. This was a particular problem for the smaller companies, which tended to operate in a paperless world and many of whose owners were illiterate. The larger producers were better equipped to make the changes; they also had better contacts with foreign customers, who could help with training. In the absence of collective action by the smaller companies, it is likely that only the larger companies would have succeeded in implementing the required quality assurance procedures; that could have led to a major shakeout of smaller producers, transforming the district from an SME cluster into the home of a handful of large companies. The smaller companies, in alliance with some of the larger ones, worked through the local manufacturers association to put a training program in place.

There we have the picture of a cluster of networked SMEs replacing large companies with something more flexible; more innovative; providing good jobs generally, and opportunity for the creative and the ambitious; a place where cooperation and community replace the nastier aspects of competition. Utopian though this may sound, it has been a powerful and persuasive narrative. It has shaped UNIDO's program for industrial development in poor countries. At the other end of the scale, in terms of both technology and wealth, it gives us Annalee Saxenian's (1990, 1994) influential interpretation of the success of California's Silicon Valley. It is worth our while, then, to ask two questions. First, do these districts really work as advertised? Second, in whatever way they do work, why do we see them in some places and not in others?

I will unpack those questions in the following way. In the next section I will consider the basis for cooperation and trust between companies in clusters. In the following, and last, section of this chapter, I will examine the idea that SME networks replace large firms, that they are a great source of innovation, and that they create good jobs.

12.2. **What makes firms cluster?**

There are many specialized business clusters in the world. The industrial district narrative concerns only some of those clusters in which cooperation between firms becomes an important aspect of the production, innovation, and market regulation processes. Before examining this narrative more closely, let's clarify some basic concepts about clusters, and about cooperation between firms.

12.2.1. DEFINITIONS

A *cluster*, as I've used the term here, is a geographical agglomeration of business establishments in the same industry, or in related industries along a supply chain or related supply chains. Since property usually costs more in an agglomeration than it does outside of one, we assume that there is some benefit to the business from locating in the agglomeration. We call these benefits *agglomeration economies*. Hoover (1948) divided agglomeration economies into two types: *urbanization* economies are benefits derived from locating in a diversified agglomeration, while *localization* economies are derived from locating close to businesses in the same industry, or along the same supply chain. Clusters, then, are taken as evidence of localization economies. I won't deal with urbanization economies here; if you're interested in cities in the context of international business, good places to start are Saskia Sassen's *Cities in a World Economy* (2000), or the same author's *The Global City: New York, London, Tokyo* (1991).

Michael Porter has done a lot to promote the concept of business clusters. Unfortunately, he hasn't used the term in a consistent way. In *The Competitive Advantage of Nations* (1990), he said they were concentrations of interconnected companies, specialized suppliers and service providers, firms in related industries, and associated institutions. *Sometimes*, he said, these clusters were also geographically concentrated, but he made a clear distinction between his concept of the cluster (which was not, then, a geographical concept), and the possibility that such a cluster might look like a cluster when plotted on a map. More recently he specifies that clusters are

"... *geographic* concentrations of interconnected companies, specialized suppliers and service providers, firms in related industries, and associated institutions..." (Porter 2000, p. 253; emphasis added)

Even then, for Porter, "geographic concentration" is a very flexible concept: a concentration might be confined to a small city, or spread out over quite a large region. Ron Martin and Peter Sunley (2005) give him a lot of grief for this, but don't propose any alternative.

Also, for Porter, "cluster" always means *interconnected* companies, so a bunch of companies clustered together geographically and which happen to be in the same industry is not, for Porter, necessarily a cluster. The interconnections which Porter requires to call something a cluster are similar to what others might require to call a spatial cluster an industrial district. For our purposes here, a geographical concentration of firms in the same or related lines of industry is a cluster, whether or not they do business with each other or have any other connections.

12.2.2. CLUSTERS EVEN WITHOUT TRUST: SIMPLE LOCALIZATION ECONOMIES

The reason for splitting this particular hair is that there are plenty of clusters in which the firms hardly relate to each other at all. Firms may cluster because there is some advantage to a particular location; in the city of Lampang, in northern Thailand, there are over a hundred ceramics manufacturers – largely as the result of natural deposits of clay. Of somewhat more interest are what we can call passive agglomeration economies: benefits from locating near to other companies in the same business. Recall, from Chapter 4, that this is a form of external economy. External economies in Marshall's analysis of clusters included access to a pool of skilled labor and specialized suppliers; the shared use of non-traded inputs, such as public infrastructure or services; and access to information or ideas – "knowledge in the air," or what we might today call knowledge spillovers. Although these factors were not present when the first ceramics factories were established in Lampang fifty years ago, they now offer additional reasons for ceramics manufacturers to locate there (Kamnungwut 2009).

Notice that there may also be external *diseconomies* to agglomeration: traffic congestion and air pollution are obvious examples, but there are also diseconomies that weigh directly against the purported benefits of clustering: the flip side of a pool of labor skilled specialized is the poaching of skilled staff by nearby competitors; knowledge in the air may be a benefit to you, or it may be your trade secrets going out the window. These issues are examined in detail by Ian Gordon and Philip McCann (2000).

12.2.3. COOPERATION AND TRUST

The neo-Marshallian industrial district model applies where firms benefit not only from being close to each other, but from working together. But, actually, we find firms benefiting from working together within specialized agglomerations that are not neo-Marshallian districts, as well as those that are. A neo-Marshallian district is distinguished by cooperation among SMEs, in the manner described in the previous section. In many clusters we have firms working together, but coordinated by one leading firm – the network of suppliers around Toyota or Boeing, for example; variants of this are referred to as the "solar" or "industrial complex" model. I'll come back to issues growing out of the presence of one or two powerful companies within a cluster in Section 12.3. For now, I want to focus on the neo-Marshallian cluster, in which SMEs cooperate.

The purported benefits of cooperation have been described in Section 12.1. Briefly, we can classify them as the provision of public goods (e.g., common services in areas such as training; price- and wage-fixing; political and regulatory advocacy on behalf of firms in the cluster), the creation of collective capacities (for instance, Marshall's "industrial atmosphere" and "knowledge in the air" may not follow automatically from agglomeration, but may depend on the willingness of firms to share knowledge), and the reduction of transaction costs (if the conditions in the cluster somehow reduce the likelihood that firms will treat each other opportunistically, then greater use can be made of a division of labor between specialized firms). Sometimes, firms in clusters cooperate, sometimes they don't. What leads to cooperation?

One source of mutual gains from repeated business is the fact that "flexible" manufacturers are never perfectly flexible: there is often some transaction-specific investment. Mark Lazerson and Gianni Lorenzoni (2005) offer an example of garment makers, who may require that the fabric for a particular line of clothing have a consistent appearance; having started the line with one fabric supplier, they then cannot change to another without a small but unacceptable change in appearance. Moreover, Lazerson and Lorenzoni argue, the equipment in industrial districts is not always flexible, contrary to the picture presented by Piore and Sabel. Sometimes this is because old equipment remains in use, but at other times it is because, even within the range of output experienced by industrial district SMEs, the flexible equipment has higher unit production costs than special-purpose equipment.

So, even within flexible networks of SMEs, Williamson-type lock-ins exist, and with them the need to find a governance mechanism for the transaction.

12.2.3.1. Repeated games

One way of approaching a problem is to think of the firms – a supplier and a customer, perhaps – as engaged in a repeated game. The prisoner's dilemma game provides an abstract version of the problem. In this game, two players have a choice between cooperating and cheating. If the game is played just once, each of the two players will do better by cheating the other, with the perverse result that the potential mutual gains are thrown away. One solution to the problem is to bring in some form of third party enforcement – a contract that can be enforced in court, for instance. Yet this may not be necessary: if the two players think they are likely to do business again, cooperative behavior may emerge. Robert Axelrod's *The Evolution of Cooperation* (1984) offers an excellent introduction to this question.

The repeated game model obviously applies in a relatively small community of specialist SMEs: you are likely to meet the same player again, and will take this possibility into account. Moreover, there are factors at work in most such clusters that can strengthen the results of the repeated prisoner's dilemma model. The model starts with the assumption that all you know about the other player is from your own previous meetings with that player; within a cluster, you are likely to know the player by reputation, even before you do business with her. In such settings, personal reputation becomes a form of capital. Dei Ottati (1994) argues for the importance of such reputational capital in the case of Prato. Moreover, the simple repeated game models typically assume that doing business again (or not) is a chance event; in practice, mutually beneficial transactions lead to more business between the same partners: Lorenz (1988) finds this in metalworking districts in both France and Britain, Uzzi (1997) and in garment manufacturing in New York.

The repeated game model also provides a useful way of thinking about cases in which cooperation does *not* occur. Mark Lazerson and Gianni Lorenzoni (2005) cite a study by Passaro (1994), of a leather tanning district in southern Italy in which much less interfirm contracting occurs than in districts in the same industry in Tuscany. Most of the firms in the southern district are vertically integrated – they take care of all of the relevant stages of production on their own, so they seldom *need* the help of other firms in the industry. This leaves little room for repeated games to develop.

12.2.3.2. Embeddedness and civic engagement

The standard game-theoretic approach treats each firm as a self-interested rational actor. A different approach is to see the choices made by each actor affected by their social environment. Some older traditions in sociology take this to extremes, and treat our actions as fully structurally determined – that is, they do away with "actors" altogether. More recent work tries to get away from this, and to achieve some understanding of the interplay between the actor and the environment. Such an approach may help us to understand why cooperation emerges in some clusters and not in others.

Mark Granovetter (1985) sees us all as embedded in networks of social ties. These ties don't strictly determine who we are or what we do, but they do shape us and constrain us. In some cases, they might even constrain us from cheating business partners. Robert Putnam (1993) uses Granovetter's framework to help explain differences in economic performance (and, as part of this, the presence or absence of industrial districts) in different parts of Italy.

Italian industrial districts are concentrated in north central and northwest Italy, and particularly in the regions of Emila-Romagna, Tuscany, and Veneto. Why there, in particular? For as long as the districts have been studied, there have been efforts made to trace their origins to the political and social characteristics of this region. Bagnasco (1977) dubbed this area "the third Italy," on the grounds that its industrial structure was distinct from both the northwest and the south. The name has stuck.

As a nation-state, Italy has existed only since 1860, and its different regions bear the marks of their different histories before the *risorgimento*. The Third Italy happens to coincide with the area which had the longest history of independent city-republics: Florence, Pisa, Bologna, Venice, and suchlike. The northwestern areas of Piedmont and Lombardy had an early history of city-republican rule, but by 1300 were monarchies and later were absorbed for long periods by various foreign kingdoms, notably France, and Austria-Hungary. Areas to the south and east of Rome, including Naples and Sicily, were long ruled by Spain. Some areas near to Rome were ruled by the Pope, though the strength of papal authority varied.

These different histories provide a good map of Italy's socioeconomic system today. The Third Italy is home to the greatest concentration of industrial districts; in the 1970s and 1980s, as flexible production eclipsed mass production, these regions grew rapidly and surpassed the northwest in per capita income. The northwest is also home to some industrial districts, but is far better known as the centre for business services (Milan) and mass production (Turin). The areas once ruled by Spain are by far the poorest, and their few clusters of industry generally do not share the characteristics of industrial districts.

Putnam found that political participation, involvement in voluntary civic organizations, attitudes toward government, and attitudes toward cooperation with political rivals were, generally, higher in the parts of Italy which had a long civic republican history, which is to say also those with prosperous industrial districts today; lack of participation, political polarization, and distrust, all were more prevalent in the south. Putnam's contention is that the political and social variables he studied are measures of something he calls *social capital*, and that social capital contributes to economic performance. In this, he is drawing explicitly on Granovetter: businesspeople in the Third Italy are, he says, embedded in "networks of civic engagement," which can help to replace opportunism with trust. In the south of Italy, there are also social networks and embeddedness, but those networks are different and the effects are not so benign. For a concise account of the effects of Spanish rule on that area, see Anthony Pagden (1988); for a discussion of the role of the Sicilian Mafia and its mainland counterparts, see Diego Gambetta (1988).

There are two readings of the implications of Putnam's work, assuming that he is correct. One is that the only road to building thriving local SME networks is an accident of medieval history. This is not good news: try as we might, it is hard to choose our parents wisely. The other is that the route to economic prosperity (and, because this is Putnam's real concern, democracy) is through a thriving civil society.

12.2.3.3. Trust and power

Henry Farrell and Jack Knight (2003) dispute Putnam's conclusions. They argue that trust and cooperation among firms is possible where there is a parity of power between the firms. For a variety of historical reasons, such parity prevailed in many Italian industrial districts for a few decades in the second half of the twentieth century. Farrell and Knight study the packaging machine industry in the province of Bologna. In the 1980s and 1990s, the large food, pharmaceutical, tobacco, and consumer product companies that buy the machines have themselves outsourced engineering functions, and came to prefer larger, full-service suppliers of packaging equipment. Within the district, this contributed to the growth of a few large "final" firms; these both do the final assembly of the machine, and deal with customers outside the district. As a consequence, vertical relationships based on trust are increasingly replaced by arm's length agreements with written contracts.

It is possible that Putnam's argument, and Farrell and Knight's, are both right. Farrell and Knight are bringing us back to the land of game theory, and reminding us that if one big company controls the access to markets and technology, not even the most deeply rooted networks of civic engagement will produce trusting relationships among firms. Yet when we look back to the example of the leather-tanning districts of southern and northern Italy, Putnam seems plausible: game theory might help us understand why each keeps doing business the way it does, but to understand how they came to do business in those ways it helps to understand the structures of their respective civil societies.

12.3. **The classic industrial district model versus actually existing clusters**

The flexible specialization vision of clusters is one in which networked SMEs can replace large companies, both as a system of production and as a system of innovation; it is also one where the workforce is highly skilled and paid good wages, and where workers and owners can easily change places. The wheels of both production and innovation are greased by trust and cooperation between companies.

When we look closely at clusters, however, we never find these characteristics in quite their ideal forms. On the one hand, SME networks may not behave as advertised; on the other, pure local SME networks are hard to find, as SMEs and clusters are almost always interdependent with large companies and distant companies in the areas of marketing, new technology, and even production itself.

In this section, I will first examine more closely the interaction of SME networks with large companies and with international production networks; second, the question of whether SME clusters can be counted on to provide good jobs.

12.3.1. LARGE COMPANIES, INTERNATIONAL NETWORKS, AND SME CLUSTERS

12.3.1.1. The continued presence of mass production

Hubert Schmitz (1995), reporting on a large shoemaking cluster in Brazil, tells us that it deviates from the received industrial district model in that it includes both small specialized manufacturers, and large vertically integrated ones. He also tells us that the large ones started out small. What is interesting here is not so much the fact that the Sinos Valley of Brazil is home to both large and small shoemaking companies, but that Schmitz, a perceptive student of such clusters, and *World Development,* which has published quite a bit of good research on the subject, found this fact worth reporting as one of the main findings of the study. The SME story had been so internalized that the coexistence of large and small producers had become news.

What Schmitz found particularly interesting about the mass production companies within the Sinos Valley district is that they were not relics of a distant Fordist past, but of a very recent Fordist past. In the 1960s, there was a significant shoe cluster in the Sinos Valley, but craft production dominated. In the 1970s, exports and mass production grew up together. The cluster that exists now includes both mass producers and specialized, or stage, producers; the latter incline to something like flexible specialization, but they must coexist with their larger neighbors.

12.3.1.2. Retailers, brands, and international commodity chains

Even where there are no economies of scale to be had in manufacturing, however, large size may aid the marketing of consumer products. Schmitz emphasizes the problem small companies face in marketing, and argues that cooperation in that area is a key to their success: hence the small shoe companies of Brazil's Sinos Valley organized trade fairs (Schmitz 1995), and aspired to develop an international brand (Humphrey and Schmitz 2002).

Often, however, marketing is in the hands of large companies. These companies may be from within the cluster, or outside of it. An example of the former is Benetton. Bennett Harrison (1997) notes its growth from a small clothing designer to a dominant force within the Treviso clothing and textile cluster. Benetton gained fame in the 1990s for its innovative supply chain management, using point-of-sale data from its retail stores around the world to adjust the color mix of its product line, and in general achieving economies of speed at which Chandler's nineteenth century pioneers would marvel. Although the supply chain coordinated by Benetton involves many flexible SMEs, the visible hand is that of a large company. The Spanish retailer Zara has more recently gained fame for its own version of this approach.

Benetton is unusual in that it built an international retail network from a base in a clothing, and textile design and manufacturing district. More often, access to international consumer markets goes either through retail chains based outside of the manufacturing districts or through brands controlled by companies based outside of the districts. In most consumer markets, the market share and hence the buying power of large retailers has been increasing for many decades now (think Wal-mart, Ikea); brands, too, have become fewer and far more powerful (think Nike). Small manufacturers can deal directly with smaller retail and wholesale dealers; in Italy, home of so many industrial districts, it is easier to do this than in most industrial countries, because the Italian government has favored small business in retail as well as in manufacturing. To meet the requirements of large retailers or branders in the rest of the world, however, it is often necessary to be large. That doesn't mean that every company in the supply network will be large, but the smaller ones may find themselves dealing through a large OEM, sometimes called a "lead firm" in the industrial district literature.

Within the literature on international trade and development, the building of large and powerful OEMs has come to be seen as an important objective for countries with SMEs producing goods for export (see, for instance, Gereffi 1999; Gereffi et al. 2005). This may be seen as an end in itself, or as a step toward the development of international brands (some successful OEMs move on to branding while continuing their OEM role: the Taiwanese computer maker ASUS is one example of this; the Turkish blue jean manufacturer Mavi (Tokatli and Kızılgün 2004) is another). But the importance attached to such OEMs casts doubt on the pure SME model of flexible specialization.

This problem of access to international distribution channels says nothing about the productive or innovative capabilities of local SME networks. Nor does it mean that such networks are inherently inferior in their ability to reach international markets. The power of huge retail chains is contingent on government policy; the difference between Italy and other countries shows this, as does the varied experience of community campaigns to block Walmart's expansion in the US. In a world with fewer huge chains and brands, SME networks might have a much stronger role in the provision of consumer products. That is not, however, the world industrial districts are in today.

The problem of marketing the products of industrial districts, however, brings to light other blind spots in the flexible specialization model. The model asserts the importance of locality and community, and it focuses on – one might say, makes a fetish of – manufacturing. Even within the manufacturing supply network, locality and community have their limits: manufacturers in industrial districts outsource; while the small size of the companies involved and the proximity to subcontractors keep much of the outsourcing local, some of it can also go quite far afield. But even supposing the manufacturing work were kept within the district, the companies in the district may be part of a dense business network that covers a much larger territory, far beyond the bounds of any civic community. Michael Dunford (2006) shows that the textile and clothing industry (TCI) districts of small Italian cities depend on a range of specialized services available in Milan. "The district model," says Dunford,

underplays the interdependence of districts with the areas in which these services are found (and with each other). In the Italian case, Milan is at the center of the TCI system. Milan is important for several reasons. First, it occupies a dominant position in international networks. Second, it has a major concentration of services that are connected with the immaterial/knowledge-related aspects of the fashion system. Third, it has a high share of headquarters. As a result, it also has a high share of the higher-paid jobs. (p. 51)

The irony, of course, is that the Third Italy was seen by many as an alternative to the big-business decadence of Milan and Turin. It turns out, much of the Third Italy works for Milan.

12.3.1.3. Hollywood: Filmmaking versus financing and distribution

SME networks are not restricted to manufacturing. Nor is the role of large companies in securing – and controlling – the path to market of SMEs' products. Consider the case of movie production. Hollywood can be understood as an industrial district, with flexible specialization in production, but with a few large companies controlling both finance and the distribution and marketing of the product. This was not always so. Its transformation has been charted by Michael Storper (1989), and more recently by Allen Scott (2002), on both of whose work I draw here.

Like weaving in Prato, moviemaking in Hollywood used to be a mass production process. Under the studio system, which prevailed from the 1910s (when the US movie industry was still concentrated in New York) to the 1970s, one company took charge of a movie from conception to theatrical distribution. Most movies were made at the company's production facility (the studio, or lot); performers, directors, writers, and others were often on long-term contracts, placed in whatever project the studio chose. The system first began to break down after the US courts required, in 1948, that the studios sell off their chains of theaters (cinemas), to further competition. Television then created demand for a large number of short films. Finally, production technology became more portable and, eventually, less expensive, allowing different stages of production to be parceled out to specialists in many different locations. The production of a movie now typically involves bringing together a collection of companies and individuals for the project; those involved may, or may not, work together again. A low budget movie can be shot on handheld digital camera and edited on a MacIntosh computer.

The studio's role now is not production, but financing, marketing, and distribution. Financing is not a trivial consideration, since some movies are very expensive to make, and because many movies (both expensive ones and cheap ones) flop: somebody with deep pockets is needed to take on this risk. But the motivation to place bets on big budget movies, potential blockbusters but also potential budget busters, is in the structure of the distribution system. In theatrical (i.e., cinema) distribution, only a small number of movies can achieve widespread screening in a particular city in a particular week. Huge production budgets, for stars and special effects, along with huge marketing budgets, are ways of bidding for that space. So, just as the structures of manufacturing clusters for clothing and shoes are shaped by the power of large retailers and brands, the kind of movies made and the control of the product are shaped by the mode of distribution.

12.3.2. TECHNOLOGY AND INNOVATION

12.3.2.1. Large firms and innovation in the classic industrial districts

Although networked SMEs can, as per the flexible specialization narrative, be quite innovative, we need to understand the limits of that innovative capacity and, again, the role of large companies. There are two issues to be considered here. One is the limits of innovation in SME networks. The other is the way in which technological dependence on large companies affects relationships among SMEs.

Keith Pavitt (1984) classifies companies according to the technological innovation processes they use. His basic categories are supplier dominated (i.e., technological innovation comes mostly from the company's suppliers, not from the company itself), production intensive (technological innovation occurs in the process of solving production problems), and science based. Pavitt further subdivides production intensive companies into scale intensive ones and specialized suppliers. This gives a total of four categories.

Most of the companies we find in the industrial district literature fit into two of Pavitt's four categories: they are either supplier dominated when it comes to technology (textiles, ceramics, furniture, for example) or they are specialized suppliers. Note, though, that Pavitt's categories deal with technological innovation only. Many of the companies that are supplier dominated, in terms of technology, are constantly innovating in terms of design, whether in furniture, in fabrics, or in ceramics.

The effect of large suppliers dominating the provision of technology is illustrated in Lazerson and Lorenzoni's (2005) study of the women's stocking district in Castel Goffredo. The synthetic materials for stockings are, of course, one of the technological inputs that stocking manufacturers obtain from large companies outside the district. Filadoro, one of the larger companies in the district had been an early user of Lycra, and had a close relationship with the multinational chemical giant DuPont; this relationship allegedly resulted in a more reliable supply of Lycra, at lower prices.

As in many other Italian industrial districts, poaching of skilled workers was discouraged in Castel Goffredo, and a ceiling kept on wages, by an agreement among employers not to offer pay increases to get workers to change companies. Filadoro was a growing company using new materials, and needed additional skilled workers; it violated the agreement. The owners of Filadoro and the other companies had been members of the same social networks since childhood, and the owners of the other companies ostracized the owners of Filadoro. All in keeping with the social network model of industrial districts: Robert Putnam could have written the script. Except that, Filadoro didn't change its behavior, and continued to thrive. Lazerson and Lorenzoni conclude that Filadoro's external network had become more important than its local one. That situation was a consequence of the company's reliance on an external supplier of new technology. Lazerson and Lorenzoni also report that in 1992 Filadoro was sold to Sara Lee, a US-based multinational; from that point on, I suppose, we can say that its owners' local social network means nothing at all. The district continues to thrive, albeit with fewer and larger companies.

Lazerson and Lorenzoni also provide us with a good illustration of the relationship between a producer of food packaging equipment – itself a specialized supplier – and *its* specialized suppliers. Tetra-Pak, a Swedish multinational which is a leading manufacturer of food packaging equipment, makes that equipment in Modena, Italy. It also does much of its research and development there. An executive of the company gave this explanation to a reporter:

In Emilia-Romanga [the region in which Modena is located] there is a web of small- and medium-sized firms and artisanal workshops in the mechanical engineering sector capable of supplying all of the necessary components to optimize the performance of our equipment. This combination of technical knowledge, craft skills, and innovation represents a winning card that is difficult to find anywhere else. (Bonicelli 1993, quoted in Lazerson and Lorenzoni 2005, p. 178)

The executive's statement could well be a testimonial for flexible specialization – indeed, one suspects that he or she studied it somewhere – but for the conspicuous presence of a large multinational in the picture. But the presence of the multinational is not fortuitous: there is good reason to believe that the cluster of flexible and innovative SMEs and the multinational are complementary, and that the former is kept on its game through interaction with the latter. To remain a state-of-the-art solver of technical problems, a small company needs sophisticated customers (Carlsson and Eliasson 1991). Sophisticated customers know what they need from suppliers, what technical problems to set them to solve. Knowing this requires that they have a good technical staff of their own, and also exposure to what is happening in other markets. Large companies, and especially multi-national companies, have such exposure, while smaller local ones tend not to.

Tetra-Pak is not the only large, sophisticated customer of Emilia-Romagna's packaging equipment cluster. Another company based there is SASIB – a multinational specializing in cigarette packaging machinery, and itself owned by another Italian multinational, Olivetti. Yet another Bologna packaging machine company, ACMA, used to be owned by the American multinational, American Machine and Foundry. Nor are such relationships limited to the mechanical engineering sector; nearby Truciolo is home to Magneti-Marelli, a fairly large manufacturer of automotive electrical components and a supplier to sophis-ticated customers such as Fiat. Magneti-Marelli is, in turn, the relatively sophisticated customer of many smaller suppliers in its district.

The relationship between large final firms in these districts and even larger customers from elsewhere is, of course, exactly what Farrell and Knight say undermines trust and cooperation within the district itself.

12.3.2.2. High technology districts

Other specialized clusters fall in Pavitt's fourth category, that of science based innov-ation. Some science based clusters bear considerable resemblance to the classic indus-trial district model; just how close a resemblance, is in dispute. Simona Iammarino and Philip McCann (2006) label the classic districts "old social networks," and some of the science-based ones "new social networks."

In the US, there are three large clusters of firms – some very large, but most of them SMEs – engaged in high-tech activity. One is on the east coast, near Boston; the other two are on the west coast, one around San Diego and the other centered in Santa Clara County. The Boston cluster is also known as Route 128, after the highway that traces a semicircle around the western perimeter of the city. The Santa Clara County cluster is known as the Silicon Valley, an informal rechristening of the Santa Clara Valley. All three agglomerations include companies dealing in microelectronics, computer software, and biotechnology and, to lesser extents, other advanced technologies. The Silicon Valley and Route 128 were once major centres for manufacturing in the same industries, but over the years their roles have shifted increasingly to research, development, and administration.

The Silicon Valley is the largest of the three. Fifteen years ago, the San Diego cluster was small and Route 128 was going through hard times. Annalee Saxenian (1994) wrote a book contrasting the success of the Silicon Valley with what appeared, at the time, to be the decline of Route 128. In many respects, the two seemed quite similar. Both had grown as technology districts in the 1950s, 1960s, and 1970s with a combination of spillovers and spin-offs from nearby universities (MIT and Harvard for Route 128, Stanford and later Berkeley for the Silicon Valley) and fat contracts from the Pentagon. Why had the Silicon Valley done well, while Route 128 had not?

Saxenian attributed the Silicon Valley's success to its operating like a classic industrial district. Although many of the companies based there are large information technology companies (Hewlett Packard, Apple, Cisco, Intel, AMD, and such), their usual approach has not been to build an entire computer system: instead, firms specialize in particular components or in systems integration. With this approach, subcontracting relationships proliferated. Saxenian maintained that these relationships were cemented with high levels of trust. And knowledge was in the air; it circulated in Stanford's seminars for industry, in bars, and with the movement of employees between companies. The flow of knowledge was facilitated both by the relatively open walls of the companies – with so much subcontracting, many things needed to be shared with outsiders – and a culture which held that knowledge *should* be shared.

Saxenian portrays Route 128 as stuck in a world of vertical integration. At the time she was writing, it was dominated by several companies which specialized in what were known as minicomputers. These were the growth area for the computer industry in the 1970s and 1980s, in a window between mainframes and PCs. The leading minicomputer company, Digital, was, like its bigger rival IBM, a vertically integrated technology company. These companies designed not only the computers, but the processors (logic chips), wrote much of the software, manufactured the computers, and serviced them. Like mass production auto makers, they strove to keep tight control over research and development, and to design the whole machine. The companies were obsessed with secrecy; few attended the seminars for industry offered at MIT. Refusing to share information, and lacking the organizational flexibility to apply their considerable technological expertise to new products, Route 128 lost out.

I should also note the role of finance, as it is something I'll return to below. The Silicon Valley is the home of several venture capital companies which specialize in financing small technology companies. The principals of these companies are, in many cases, people who made fortunes in technology themselves, and so have a good understanding of technology and technology-driven businesses. This background not only put them in a position to evaluate proposed ventures, but was helpful when – as was often the case – the company's founders turned out not to be up to the task of making it grow, and the venture capitalists had to install new management. Route 128 companies dealt more with investment bankers of Boston and Wall Street, ill-equipped to fill these roles.

Saxenian's account has been roundly criticized in terms that will seem familiar if you've just read the material on Italian industrial districts, above. Trust and free flow of information seem to be in the eye of the beholder. But where the absence of trust in Bologna means some relatively simple contracts and the replacement of old social ties with arm's length business relationships, in the Silicon Valley we see armies of lawyers, an obsession with intellectual property rights (IPRs), and of course lawsuits (Kenney and Seely-Brown 2000). The focus on IPRs is not surprising, given that the Silicon Valley is engaged in transforming new scientific discoveries and the tacit knowledge of scientists and engineers into new products. Given the importance of technical standards and network economies in the ICT field, this process produces big winners and big losers. In a manner which parallels the Hollywood process discussed above, the possibility of a big win invites large investors to place big bets.

The Silicon Valley model has proven extremely difficult to replicate, and not for want of trying. Hans Joachim Braczyk and Martin Heidenreich (1998), summing up the findings of numerous studies of different "regional systems of innovation" (Braczyk et al. 1998) conclude, not very helpfully, that for a technology-oriented region to thrive it had to be at the cutting edge. That may seem a chicken-and-egg proposition, but their studies, and studies they cite, do suggest an answer. First, many commercially successful technology districts are not based on SME clusters, but on multinational technology firms; the SMEs in these clusters serve the needs of the MNCs. These would include, for instance, the large pharmaceutical cluster in the Philadelphia region; the aerospace cluster around Toulouse; and the "Research Triangle" of North Carolina, where large companies like IBM locate facilities in order to get away from the free flow of knowledge, and poaching of skilled workers, rather than to be in the thick of it.

Another answer is suggested by the studies on the Silicon Valley and its imitators, summarized by Timothy Bresnahan et al. (2005). They found several technology districts – in India, Ireland, Israel, Scotland, England, and Taiwan – which have managed to become part of production networks which also include the Silicon Valley. All of them found niches which complemented the products of the Silicon Valley, rather than competing head-on. That much sounds like standard advice on strategic positioning – not easy to do, but you know what needs to be done. They all had two other characteristics which are not at all easy to replicate, however. One was that all of them had, for a variety of reasons, a surplus of high quality human capital – Russian émigrés in Israel; a successful higher education system not matched by demand from domestic industry in Ireland and India; returning American PhDs in both India and Taiwan, and so on. The other was that they had close ties to the US generally, and the Silicon Valley in particular, in terms of language, culture, and/or networks of returning PhDs.

12.4. **Good jobs?**

The classic industrial district narrative began with a concern about the quality of jobs: quality in terms of wages and working conditions, and also in terms of dignity, opportunity, and respect for skill. Do actual industrial districts deliver?

Criticism of the narrative on these grounds extends back to examination of the paradigmatic cases: even in the prosperous Italian districts of Tuscany and Emila-Romagna, unregistered home-workers have long worked for very little; the more routine stages of production have often been outsourced to workshops in the south of the country, far from the districts and their regulatory umbrella (Harrison 1997). In recent years, many of the workshops of Tuscany have themselves been filled by Chinese immigrants, working under the regulatory radar and far under the nationally bargained wage. These, however, are but blemishes: on the whole, industrial districts in places like Italy and Germany do provide jobs not so far from those envisioned in the classic narrative.

If we move on to industrial districts in poor countries, it is easy to find ones in which there is no evidence of the networked SMEs doing anything for the quality of jobs. Schmitz (1995) reports that, as the giant Sinos Valley shoe cluster grew and its companies thrived in world markets, wages fell sharply. Nadvi (1999) tells us that child labor remains a problem in the surgical instrument cluster of Sialkot – as it does, more notoriously, in that city's sporting goods cluster.

Experience is likewise mixed in the clusters that dot the hierarchical supply chains of multinational corporations. Consider the automobile chains: Shaiken (1994) found that wages remained low in the Maquiladora plants of northern Mexico, even though quality standards had come up to match North American and European levels; the same appears to be the case for the local companies supplying the assembly plants. The workers making auto parts in the Mondragon cooperatives of Spain's Basque country, on the other hand, receive good wages and a share of the profit.

The picture that emerges is that industrial districts themselves probably do little to level up the wages or working conditions of ordinary workers. Districts in Italy and Germany succeed in this area to the extent that their national institutions of industrial relations, workplace regulation, and vocational training succeed in setting wages, enforcing standards, and providing skilled labor; when they fail, it is because those institutions fail. Such institutions are much weaker in Brazil and Mexico, and far,

far weaker in Pakistan, so the jobs are not good jobs. The Mondragon workers are less dependent on national institutions because they own the company.

12.5. Conclusion

We may conclude simply that, while the classical industrial district has characteristics which are much sought after by policy makers, entrepreneurs, trades unions, and some customers, it remains an elusive package.

13 Newly Industrialized Countries

Before the late 1970s, the industrialized countries of the world were essentially those which had already been industrialized in 1940. The industrial world roughly corresponded to the membership of the OECD, plus the Soviet Union and its allies in central and eastern Europe. Those were the First and Second Worlds. The Third World consisted of all other countries; the same countries are also known as "less developed countries," or sometimes "underdeveloped" or "developing" countries.

There were, of course, industries in Third World countries, but we refer to them as nonindustrial because few of their exports were manufactured – their comparative advantage and international specialization were in the primary sector, the products of farms, mines, and oil wells. Most imports to Third World countries were manufactured products from the First or Second World. This broad pattern of specialization defined the international division of labor.

Most of the countries of the Third World pursued policies of import substitution industrialization (ISI) from the 1950s into the 1980s. ISI manufacturing was carried out within protected national markets; the policy was often founded in the aspiration of nurturing infant industries that would eventually become competitive exporters, but in most cases this didn't work out and ISI industry stuck with serving domestic markets.

Then, from the 1970s onward, many countries in the Third World became significant exporters of manufactured goods. Third World countries tend to specialize in manufacturing which is relatively labor-intensive (more precisely, relatively unskilled manual labor-intensive), or which has relatively high environmental costs, or which has relatively modest infrastructure and supply network requirements, or some combination of these three. This pattern of specialization is called the new international division of labor (NIDL).

Some Third World countries have had more success than others, however, in developing more integrated and diversified industrial sectors; in moving on from export processing to higher-wage, higher-skill processes; and in becoming the home of new MNCs. The exemplary cases here are the Tigers of East Asia: South Korea, Taiwan, Hong Kong, and Singapore.

The success of the Tigers raises two questions. One is why they grew so fast while other Third World countries that had built considerable industry – countries like Brazil and Mexico – did not. The other is about countries that are industrializing now – China, India, and others: can they follow the Tigers' path, or have institutions, markets, and production systems changed in such a way that another path must be found? These two questions will be addressed in the first and second sections of this chapter, respectively.

13.1. **The Tigers: Overcoming the limits of ISI**

A contrast is often drawn between the "outward" or "market" orientation of the Tigers, and the "inward" and "dirigiste" orientation of countries pursuing ISI. Yet, as we will see, protected markets and state-led industrial strategy are an integral part of the South Korean and Taiwanese stories. To understand the difference between what happened in these countries and the much less impressive growth performance in Latin America and most of the rest of the Third World, we need to understand two things: first, the standard analysis of the ills of ISI; second, the important differences in how ISI was carried out in South Korea and Taiwan, which enabled those countries to overcome the usual problems.

13.1.1. PROTECTED MARKETS AND DEVELOPMENT

We've seen reference to ISI before, in Chapter 2 and in passing elsewhere. In Chapter 2, I argued that ISI had run into problems from the late 1970s onward at least in part because of increasingly rapid technological change, and the modularization and internationalization of value chains. We'll come back to these points, but many of the arguments for and against ISI have little to do with either the pace of technological change or the organization of production. They focus instead on the political economy of trade barriers. For a good review, see Bruton (1998). Another interesting perspective is provided by Waterbury (1999).

ISI is a strategy for national industrialization behind trade barriers. The basic logic is that of "infant industry" protection: it is impossible to become internationally competitive in a particular industry (or in manufacturing generally), overnight. There are various reasons for this, but all can be classified as forms of increasing returns, as discussed in Chapter 4; external economies and learning-by-doing are of particular importance.

Historical precedents for ISI go back to the industrial revolution. Alexander Hamilton, the first US Treasury Secretary, was an advocate for the policy; in the mid-nineteenth century, the philosopher and economist John Stuart Mill allowed the infant industry argument as an exception to his cherished principle of free trade; a central plank in the platform of the Republican Party of Abraham Lincoln was in favor of protective tariffs for manufacturing. Such endorsements were more than matched by actions: every country which has become a major exporter of manufactured goods went through a period in which its industries were protected from import competition.

In Chapter 5 we saw that the renewed colonial empires of the late nineteenth century served as protected markets for their respective metropolitan powers. In this sense, they facilitated ISI for the late-industrializing countries trying to catch up with Britain. At the same time, these empires *prevented* the adoption of ISI strategies by their colonies.

If the decades after World War II are particularly well known as the era of ISI, it is for three reasons. One is that the dismantling of European overseas empires created many new candidates for ISI; while independent countries like Argentina, Brazil, Japan, and the US had been engaging in ISI for decades, dozens of other countries in Africa, Asia, the Pacific and the Caribbean, had been attached to colonial empires and, as such, required to be "open" to exports from their respective metropolitan powers. As they gained independence, most adopted ISI policies of their own.

Second, during this period the ISI strategy was broadly supported by international institutions and the policy establishment in Western capitals.

Third, this is when the term "ISI" came into use.

13.1.2. DIAGNOSING THE ILLS OF ISI: THE NEOLIBERAL CRITIQUE

Since ISI is, by definition, directed at goods which are traded internationally, it is a natural ambition to make these goods not only for the protected domestic market but also, eventually, for export. By the late 1970s, however, ISI in the Third World had a reputation as an inward-looking, seldom leading to significant exports by the ISI industries. Not only did it fail to produce export revenue, but it also came to be associated with more widespread economic and political malaise (Krueger 1974, 1980).

The standard critique of ISI begins with the proposition that protected markets are inefficient both because they abandon the fruits of comparative advantage and because they are prone to domination by monopolies. One reason that ISI got into difficulties is that the trade barriers were protecting small markets. The markets were small either because the countries had small populations, or because most of their citizens were poor and had little purchasing power, or both. Because the markets were small, the companies protected were often monopolies, and were also often producing on a relatively small scale. This was a recipe for inefficiency, for several reasons. In standard, static, economic theory, monopolies misallocate resources because they can maximize profits by restricting production and raising prices. Moreover, we expect monopolies to be inefficient for other reasons: because monopolists can afford to be lazy, and enjoy the quiet life; because they have little incentive to innovate. Yet, if a market is too small to support multiple producers operating at the minimum efficient scale, domestic competition is not a viable option.

A second problem with ISI was introduced in Chapter 2. To manufacture complex, capital-intensive or advanced technology products often requires a flow of costly inputs – machines, materials, parts, licenses for the use of patents – from abroad. The smaller or less developed the market, the greater the proportion of inputs that will need to be imported. Buying all of these inputs and using them on a small scale was often more costly than just buying the finished product. Over time, this problem tended to get worse, for two reasons. One is that countries often started with the "easy ISI" targets – clothing, kitchen implements, small tools, and furniture: things that are not complex, capital-intensive, or needing advanced technology – and then moved on to the harder projects. The other is that each industry was a moving target, with technologies getting more sophisticated over time.

The consequence was that ISI led to foreign exchange problems. When exchange rates were fixed (as under the Bretton Woods system between 1948 and 1971), ISI led to an excess demand for foreign currency; when exchange rates floated, the ISI-driven demand for inputs could lead to a fall in the value of the country's currency, raising the costs of *all* imported goods. In either case, a common policy response was foreign exchange controls. Such controls regulate the exchange of a country's money for the money of other countries, and by so doing regulate trade. The controls might cover particular categories of foreign transaction – depending on the country and period, that might be travel, investment abroad, the repatriation of profits from foreign investment, the import of luxury goods, of capital goods, of materials and parts, or some combination of those or other things. If a transaction is covered by the controls, then it can't be done without permission from the government.

Foreign exchange controls contributed to the third big problem with ISI, which was rent-seeking. If trade barriers create and protect monopolies, then the creation and maintenance of trade barriers is worth something to monopolists. If foreign exchange is controlled, then permission to change money is valuable. ISI therefore gave government officials something valuable to sell to businesspeople, and led to particularly corrupt relationships between government and business. There is some corruption everywhere, of course, and it does not help our understanding of the world to be shocked every time we notice any. We can say, however, that the corruption associated with ISI had two bad consequences. One was, again, that resources were misallocated: not, this time due to monopoly pricing or inefficient scale (although those were still in the picture), but because the valuable efforts of skilled and powerful people were applied to *seeking rents*: businesspeople applied their energies to getting their markets protected; civil servants and politician to getting into the right position to extract a bribe. The second was that the proliferation of this sort of activity contaminated public life generally: it set a standard, and a low one, for behavior in business and in government. As a result, other government functions became less efficient, the costs of contract enforcement rose, and so on.

Finally, it needs to be noted that although ISI policies could be justified with sound economic arguments, it appears that there was little rational economic planning connected with them (Bruton 1998). Trade barriers were seldom established in a systematic way to achieve particular ends, but in response either to political pressure or to the untested belief that protecting this or that product was important. One reason for this was simply that the governments of poor countries did not have the information – the statistics and the economic models – that would have been needed to design more rational ISI policies. All of the problems previously noted therefore became greater than they would have been had such information been available and put to use.

13.1.3. THE TIGERS VERSUS LATIN AMERICA

The problems identified in the neoliberal critique of ISI are real. Yet they cannot be the whole story: we know that development behind trade barriers has historically been the rule, not the exception; and we know that, in the post-World War II period on whose experience the critique focused, some of the exemplary cases of economic growth made systematic use of ISI. What we really need to understand, then, is how the ISI strategies and outcomes differed between the Tigers and some other equally ambitious, but less successful, ISI programmes.

At the Tiger end of the comparison, I will focus on South Korea and Taiwan. It is more difficult to generalize from the experience of the other two Tigers, Singapore and Hong Kong, because they are cities without countryside (we would call them city-states, were it not for the fact that Hong Kong has never quite been a state, but a semiautonomous subject first of Britain and now of China). For reasons that will become clear in the course of this chapter and the two following, the relationship between city and countryside, between industry and services on the one hand and the primary sector on the other, is central to the problem of economic development. It is a question that city-states side-step, by virtue of historical accidents which have made them politically independent of their countrysides.[17]

For examples of less successful ISI, we are spoiled for choice. I will focus on the comparison with two large Latin American countries, Brazil, and Mexico. In this I follow the comparison of these countries with South Korea and Taiwan developed in the various essays in the volume edited by Gary Gereffi and Donald Wyman (1990); and between South Korea and Brazil in both Peter Evans (1995) and Atul Kohli (2004). We should bear in mind that the Latin American countries considered here are not total failures in matters of industrialization and development: along with numerous other countries such as South Africa, India, and Turkey, their role in today's more open international markets is built to a significant degree on the legacy of ISI. The issue here is that, despite ambitious industrialization policies, these countries have not done as well as the Tigers; they have not grown as fast, they have not exported as much, and a great many of their citizens remain poor. But this is a *relative* failure: if we wanted examples of

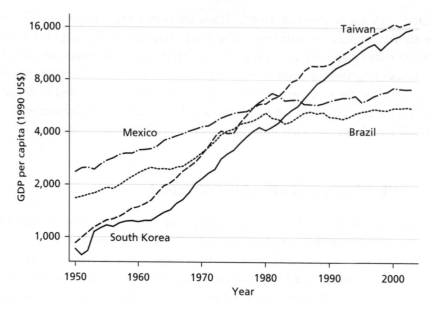

Figure 13.1. NIC and not

Source: Maddison (2007).

really failed ISI we would look elsewhere: the Philippines, Nigeria, Venezuela . . . again, we would have plenty of choices, and we will return to such cases in Chapter 14. The relative growth performances of South Korea, Taiwan, Brazil, and Mexico are compared in Figure 13.1.

In the 1970s, when ISI was getting a bad name, the Tigers were growing fast, and were winning sales in export markets. Their "outward orientation" and "export-led growth" have been heralded as alternatives to the inward-looking practice of ISI, and to slow growth in the Third World. Moreover, both South Korea and Taiwan developed successful, domestically owned companies, largely in the private sector. In Brazil and Mexico, the largest companies have typically been either state-owned enterprises (SOEs), or subsidiaries of foreign multinationals.

It would be easy, from this comparison, to attribute the growth of South Korea and Taiwan to free trade and free enterprise. It would also be a mistake. While both countries pushed their industries into export markets, they also protected home markets, and used a mix of export promotion and ISI. In both countries, some sizeable and important companies were SOEs during the period of rapid growth, and in both the state took a strategic role in planning the direction of industrial development; in the South Korean case, the state was a hands-on manager of the economy, through its control of the banking system.

Facing these facts, however, just leaves us with a deeper puzzle. In many respects, the intended policies of Brazil, Mexico, and many other countries were not so different;

what did South Korea and Taiwan have that others lacked? Or, considering the problem from the neoliberal perspective, if these two countries kept protection and state ownership in their policy mix, how were they able to avoid all the ills associated with ISI, and also those generally attributed to state-owned enterprise?

13.1.3.1. Managed trade: Picking winners and backing them

The governments of South Korea and Taiwan *managed* their trade. Exports were promoted not simply by lowering trade barriers, but through subsidies. Trade barriers were reduced in some areas, but stayed in place in others; in some sectors, South Korea and Taiwan have maintained ISI policies into the twenty-first century. The adoption of new technologies and the development of R&D capabilities were actively promoted by these governments, with the objective of moving their countries up the technological ladder.

The ways in which the two governments did these things were quite different. In South Korea, the government seized control of the banking system, and between 1961 and the late 1980s controlled private industry through its control of credit. It made access to low-cost financing conditional on investing in technologies and industries favored by the government, and on meeting export targets. This method of control was biased in favor of a handful of favored borrowers, who became the big *chaebol*, family-controlled corporate groups similar to the *zaibatsu* of prewar Japan. The Taiwanese government also promoted particular technologies and industries, but through strategic public investment: in several instances it nationalized an industry, invested heavily in capital and technology, and after several years eased the industry back into the private sector. It also subsidized exports, but unlike the South Korean government it did not channel its subsidies to a handful of large companies. Both governments welcomed investment by foreign multinationals, and engaged in low-wage export processing, but required foreign investors to share technologies with domestic companies.

By subsidizing exports and reducing trade barriers in a calculated way, these governments pushed companies out of their protected domestic nests and into the rough and tumble of world markets. The companies still had protected domestic markets as a foundation, but the pressure to export required them to raise their game in terms of technology, quality, and cost reduction. The process began with relatively low tech, labor-intensive products – shoes, clothing, electronic assembly – and moved steadily up the technology and value-added ladders, to microchips, automobiles, and branding. At the same time, ISI advanced into heavy industry sectors producing materials for infrastructure, and for the supply of the export industries.

One way of understanding this process is that the governments *used* international markets to discipline their industries. The problems of rent-seeking and monopoly associated with ISI did not go away altogether, but they were mitigated by the fact that, to succeed in the Tiger economies, an industrial company needed to export.

All of this might tempt us to say that the reason the Latin American countries did not grow as far or fast as the Tigers is that the Latin American states did not provide the necessary incentives for exports, or make strategic choices to guide their economies. Yet many less successful ISI economies enjoyed (if that is the word) state guidance. During the second half of the twentieth century, many states throughout the Third World took a strong hand in directing industrial investment, whether public or private.

States may, of course, have chosen the wrong industries. Or, having chosen, they may have failed to provide a structure of incentives that led those industries to export and grow, in the manner of the Tigers. In the Latin American cases, both were true, and they had a common cause. While the Tigers' early ISI focused on simple consumer goods, the Latin American countries went also for more complicated and expensive ones, notably automobiles. South Korea and Taiwan in the 1970s could compete internationally in international markets for clothing, textiles, shoes, kitchen implements, bicycle parts, or consumer electronics assembled from imported parts; neither they nor the Latin American countries could compete internationally in automobiles. So, the Tiger economies started their ISI path with goods that served both domestic and foreign markets, and then subsidized exports. In the Latin American cases, many more ISI industries were effectively restricted to domestic markets. Differences in the two strategies are illustrated in Figure 13.2.

The problems created by a focus on complicated, costly consumer goods go further than that. Recall that these were poor countries. Costly goods had a limited market. The Latin American countries had (and have) far more unequal distributions of income than either South Korea or Taiwan, so the market for automobiles was restricted to a relatively small minority of the population. The small domestic market and lack of export competitiveness reinforced one another. The fact that the products of some of the

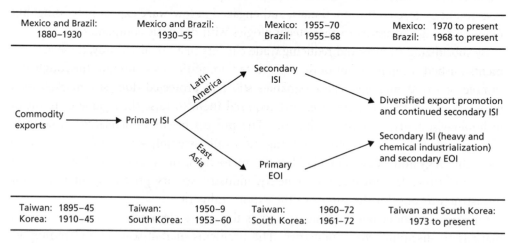

Figure 13.2. ISI and EOI in Latin America and East Asia

Source: Gereffi (1990).

Latin American countries' most important consumer goods industries were far beyond the budgets of most of the working class in Brazil and Mexico also eliminated the possibility of a Fordist accommodation (recall Chapter 10). In South Korea and Taiwan, rising wages meant rising costs but also rising demand for locally manufactured goods, somewhat ameliorating (though by no means eliminating – see Hart-Landsberg 1993) social conflict over wages. Moreover, a strong domestic market is often an important complement to export business: competition in world markets may make a good cost/quality package necessary, but demanding local consumers are often necessary to make it *possible* (Carlsson and Eliasson 1991).

The Tigers' policies were not rocket science. Export subsidies, selective use of trade barriers, and subsidizing industry through public spending on education, science and R&D, are all familiar policies in many countries. In particular, South Korea and Taiwan can be seen to have followed the path blazed by Japan a decade or two earlier. The Ministry of International Trade and Industry (MITI) had helped guide the investment strategies of Japan's *keiretsu*, with the aim of moving toward higher technology, more knowledge intensive, and higher value-added products; Japan's huge export growth had likewise taken place from behind significant barriers to imports – tariffs, import licenses, and a considerable practical difficulty faced by foreign firms attempting to get retail distribution for their products. The Japanese model was well known and well understood, and in these important respects South Korea and Taiwan followed the model. The puzzle is why more poor and middle-income countries have not done this.

The Latin American focus on goods that were not competitive internationally and were, in the local context, luxury goods aimed at a privileged minority of the population, was bad policy. It was not, however, a simple blunder that better policy-makers could have avoided. It was itself a *product* of the preexisting inequality of income, and the political and economic power of that privileged minority.

In short, the solutions to the puzzle of Korean and Taiwanese success are deceptively easy: we can point to the policies they followed, and realize that they were quite simple. The big problems are not in finding the right policies but in a distribution of political power that is conducive to adopting those policies, and in institutions that can see through their implementation. For this reason, later in the chapter, I will return to the political economy of the Tigers: understanding it is important in understanding problems of economic development in other countries as well. Before doing that, however, we should take a look at some of the important differences between the business systems of South Korea and Taiwan, and between them and Japan, the former colonial master in whose footsteps they followed.

13.1.3.2. Investment and education

In the 1980s, the rich countries started to notice the Tigers as industrial competitors. This coincided with the apogee of interest in Japanese management and production

Table 13.1. Firm structure and state–business relationships in three East Asian countries

Country	State–business relationships	Principal corporate actors	Management control	Market strategies
Japan	Negotiated	• *Keiretsu* • Local networks of small firms	Identification with company norms, "clan control"	High R&D; keep market edge with new products and high quality
South Korea	State-directed	*Chaebol*	Hierarchical management	Well-capitalized entry into established markets
Taiwan	Separation of spheres	• Family ownership • Networks of SMEs	Personal management	Lower capital, lower R&D, search for market niches

Sources: Hamilton and Biggart (1988), Table 6; also Ouchi (1980) and Whitely (1991).

systems. Was the Tigers' rise perhaps due to the adoption of superior management and production techniques? A few years later, several studies were published which argued that the rapid growth of East Asia could be accounted for by the growth of capital, employment, and education (human capital) (Kim and Lau 1994; Krugman 1994; Young 1995. For a critical view of these studies, see Sarel 1996).

As we will see in section 13.3 below, these studies were right that East Asian growth could not be attributed to a unique new way of organizing production and industry: Japan, South Korea, and Taiwan have very different forms of business organization, and different strengths and weaknesses in production (Table 13.1).

Should we also take them as a refutation of the managed trade story told above? Perhaps the real secret of the Tigers was to get everybody to go to school, save, and invest. That, however, gets the causation wrong. *Why* did people in those countries go to school and invest? Consider two parts of the economic calculation behind sending children to school, and also behind children's motivation to apply themselves to schooling: can the parents afford it, and is education a good investment? Affordability is affected by the cost of schooling, the cost of taking children out of paid employment, and the distribution of income and wealth. Whether it is a good investment depends on how an education improves a young person's job opportunities. Without going into the details of the supply of education – school systems and education policies – we can see that the *demand* for education depends on modernization of the economy and a reduction of poverty, just as those things depend on an educated workforce. A very similar story can be told about investment in business assets: it occurs in response to profitable business opportunities. The industrial policies of the Tigers, like Japan before them, created profitable business opportunities; growing business, a government-promoted emphasis on lines of business requiring increasingly educated and skilled workers, and a relatively equitable distribution of income and wealth, all contributed to a demand for education. In short, this set of policies brought about the rapid accumulation of business assets and human capital, and so "explain" the growth of the East Asian economies. But how can we explain the policies themselves?

13.2. **The political economy of the developmental state**

13.2.1. WHAT CAN A STATE DO? THE QUESTION OF CAPACITIES

We've seen states doing a lot of things in this book: establishing trade policy (Chapters 2 and 5), creating empires (Chapter 6), and stabilizing demand in a mass production economy (Chapter 9), to take just three examples. Sometimes we've assumed that a state's objectives are given, based on an understanding of "the national interest"; at other times, its objectives have been understood as the result of a domestic political process, a deal carved out between classes or interest groups, perhaps with some added input from multinational corporations. In none of those cases, however, have we questioned the state's capacity to make policy and to implement it.

State capacity did show its face, just barely, in our discussion of the varieties of capitalism in rich countries (Chapter 11). We saw both employment and unemployment security, and pensions, as dependent on a sort of intergenerational bargain, with the credibility of that bargain depending on the state's electoral system. States whose constitutions made them majoritarian were unable to sustain certain kinds of bargain, while those with consensual systems were able to. To simplify the story a bit, from a relative state's *capacity* to sustain an intergenerational bargain flowed a certain skill profile for the workforce, a system of finance and corporate governance, and many other aspects of economy that would lead us to classify it as "liberal" or "coordinated." In that story, the state's capacity turns out to have huge ramifications, but it is an extremely limited notion of "capacity"; the state is seen not as an *actor,* but as a *mechanism,* consisting of a set of rules – a constitution – which determine whether or not the voters will trust an intergenerational deal. The state simply carries out the bargain that is reached and, as with our earlier models of the state, it has no difficulties doing so. I'm being a bit harsh here: it is possible to find richer treatments of the state in the VOC literature, even if much of that literature does reduce the state to the set of rules by which the voters make choices. Moreover, when we're comparing the rich industrial countries, this isn't such a problem: we can understand a great deal about these countries without going beyond this simple model. That is because the rich industrial countries have relatively effective states, and their politics is carried out within stable constitutional frameworks.

In the developing world, the same simplifying assumption would not be harmless – it would be the end of analysis. The path of development is littered with policies that couldn't be implemented, with states that tried and failed. That is a major reason (if not *the* major reason) why poor countries remain poor. So the question is how effective states get established, and maintained.

How did the Japan, South Korea, and Taiwan avoid being brought to a standstill by rent-seeking and corruption, as many projects of state-led industrialization have? Part of the answer is that the emphasis on exports imposed a market discipline on both state- and non-state actors, constraining their rent-seeking or, at least, channelling it to more productive ends. That answer, however, only brings us back to the question. Exporting manufactured goods is hard, and moving up the ladder to higher levels of technology and value-added is even harder. Sliding back into a cosy world of protected markets must have been, on thousands of occasions, the easy option. What gave the states the strength and resolve to make their leading corporations do the difficult thing?

Sometimes, states like these are called "strong," for reasons that should be self-evident. Controversial labels, with more analytical potential, are "autonomous," and "relatively autonomous."

We have seen the concept of state autonomy before, in Chapter 9. Weir and Skocpol argued that one reason policy responses to the depression of the 1930s were different in different countries is that the decision-making processes *within* the governments differ-ered, and favored different theories and different solutions. They claimed that govern-ments of the US, Britain, and Sweden – the states they studied – all had a degree of *autonomy* from the representatives of business interests, political parties, labor unions, and other non-state actors (Weir and Skocpol 1985. For more general discussions of state autonomy, see Evans 1995, and Ruschemeyer and Evans 1985). That autonomy was employed differently in each of the three cases, because each state had different capacities, and because the organs of state formulating policy had different ideologies.

When we try to transfer this reasoning to the developing world, however, we must make some adjustments. The US, Britain, and Sweden all have stable constitutional orders, a fairly reliable rule of law, and well established Weberian bureaucracies with certain professional standards, an ideology of public service, and pay sufficient that non-corrup-tion is at least an option for a public servant with a family to support. Moreover, business in these countries has long since adapted to the production of goods and services in competitive markets. This is not to say that rent-seeking and corruption have been abolished in any country – business and politics both would be unrecognizable without it – but only that countries that have grown rich (and have done so by means other than sitting atop vast oil deposits) are by and large those that have managed to contain rent-seeking and corruption so that they are not threats to prosperity or growth.

When we try to apply this thinking to developing countries, we run into two problems. One is that states often lack the capacity to make and carry out policies.

The other is that there are often powerful non-state interests within poor countries that have reason to oppose policies that would make the country richer.

Part of the answer for Japan, South Korea, and Taiwan has been that all have powerful and highly professional state bureaucracies, with well-paid public servants drawn from the countries' elite universities. It is worth noting that the top bureaucrats in these countries tend to have studied the same subjects as the leaders of industry. This common background supports social networks between government and industry, and also dual government/industry careers for many. Compare this with the civil service of India, which also has a long tradition of professionalism and of elite recruitment, but which has tended to recruit graduates in humanities: study of the humanities is just as good a screening device for selecting competent civil servants as the study of science and engineering, but it doesn't foster the social network and career crossovers that would make for bonds with industry. This difference in recruitment practice can be put down to accidents of foreign influence, with India inheriting Britain's model, South Korea and Taiwan inheriting Japan's, which in turn was influenced by Germany's.

Social and career bonds, of course, can hurt as well as help; they can provide the nexus for corrupt relationships, adding to the state's capacities but at the same time compromising its autonomy. If the right balance is struck, we have what Peter Evans (1995) calls "embedded autonomy": a relatively autonomous state embedded in the commercial and industrial milieu it seeks to regulate. Others looking at the same situation do not see an autonomous state, but a state reflecting the interests of the country's capitalists as a class – Atul Kohli calls it a "cohesive capitalist state" (Kohli 2004; on pp. 385–6 he contrasts the "cohesive class state" and Evans' concept of "embedded autonomy.") Kohli's vision comes close to the classical Marxian understanding of the state as the executive committee of the ruling class, but for Kohli as for Evans (and contrary to classical Marxism) the key point is that this outcome is anything but inevitable. We may see it in South Korea and Taiwan, but in India and Brazil we observe what Kohli calls "fragmented multi-class" states; these states are pulled this way and that, accommodating rent-seekers from various classes and industries, and consequently unable to formulate and implement a coherent development strategy.

The meritocratic state bureaucracy has a long history in northeast Asia, in both China and Korea. Japan came to this only after the Meiji restoration, influenced more by Germany than China. As their colonial ruler until 1945, Japan itself had influence on both Korea and Taiwan. The extent of this influence is fiercely disputed, at least in part for reasons of nationalism; on this dispute in the Korean case, see Cumings (1984), Kohli (1994, 1997), and Haggard et al. (1997). Whatever its extent, we should consider the *nature* of the colonial legacy in light of recent research on the way in which ex-colonies institutions are shaped both by the institutions of the colonizing power and by the function of the colony. I will have more to say about that research in Chapter 14, but the cases of Korea and Taiwan call for this observation. With regard to colonial function, Acemoglu et al. (2001) find that ex-colonies offer better security for investment today if they were established to accommodate settlers, rather than simply to extract resources. Korea and Taiwan were extremely unusual colonies, in that Japan actually promoted industry in both of them. By an extension of the Acemoglu et al. argument, we would expect an institutional legacy more friendly to industrialization than in other colonies.

13.2.2. LAND REFORM

In the late 1940s and early 1950s, both South Korea and Taiwan adopted major land reforms. Landlords who rented farms to tenants were forced to break their land up and sell it to the individual tenants (many sold in anticipation of the reforms, hoping to get a better deal). The reforms helped raise agricultural productivity. That should not be surprising: owners have better incentives than either tenants or employees, both to work hard and to take a long-term view in caring for the land. In some situations, this incentive effect would have to be weighed against illiteracy – which makes it hard for farmers to make good use of modern agricultural techniques – or lack of credit, either of which can put the average small landowner at a disadvantage to large ones. In these two countries, the literacy rates were already high, and rising; the two states established institutions which provided credit to small farmers, both to encourage investment and to maintain control of the rural population.

Both states used the rising agricultural productivity to help finance industrial growth. The ex-landlords became an important source of investment and entrepreneurialism – they had been compensated for their land, and needed a new place to invest. The new owners of the land were less powerful politically than the landlords had been: they were numerous, and so had collective action problems; they lacked the personal networks within their country's elite; and, as these were not functioning democracies, their voting power made little difference. So, it became politically feasible to squeeze surplus from agriculture through taxation and other means. The Taiwanese government, for instance, had a monopoly on chemical fertilizer. It would advance fertilizer to farmers in exchange for a promised delivery of sugarcane or rice. The rate of exchange between fertilizer and crops was set by the government, to its own advantage. It then sold the crops on in the market, at a considerable profit.

This may sound simple, and in one sense it is: as we will see in Chapter 14, the economic benefits of an equitable distribution of agricultural land are well understood. Yet, it is not at all easy to carry out. In a largely agrarian society, agricultural landlords usually form a powerful political class. It is, moreover, a class which will be hurt by policies favoring industrialization. Imagine that you owned a sugar cane plantation in Taiwan in 1949. Your gross income would be determined largely in the export markets for sugar. From that, you would deduct expenses – mostly wages and taxes. You cannot affect the price in export markets, and there is little prospect of differentiating your product. To make more profit, there are two things to do: increase the productivity of labor, and keep wages and taxes as low as possible. If the government wants to invest in infrastructure and education and industry, that will mean higher taxes. Demand for labor in construction and manufacturing will raise wages. None of the steps toward industrialization is likely, on its own, to boost agricultural productivity. So you, as a landlord, have a strong motive to block the policies that would create an effective developmental state.

The difficulties of overcoming this opposition from the landlord class can be very great indeed, and the circumstances that made effective land reform possible in South Korea and Taiwan give some idea of why it is so seldom achieved.

In both countries, changes began under Japanese occupation in the 1920s and 1930s. In South Korea, various changes in the collection of taxes and the handling of contractual disputes between landlord and tenant, had the result of encouraging tenants to join together in disputes with their landlords. Gi-Wook Shin (1998) argues that this made rural landlords receptive to moving out of agriculture. In Taiwan, there were often two levels of landlord – large absentee landlords, renting to smaller local ones, who in turn rented to tenants – and the Japanese authorities removed the top level (Amsden 1985).

In both countries, a significant amount of land was owned by Japanese nationals. In Korea, this was redistributed to tenants by the American occupation authorities after World War II (Kohli 2004); in Taiwan, it was redistributed by the Koumintang (KMT or Nationalist) government, newly arrived from the mainland.

The KMT was in an unusual position, in that it consisted of the former government and army of China, which had retreated to Taiwan after defeat in a civil war. It owed nothing in particular to the local power structure on Taiwan. While governing China, it had long espoused a policy of land reform – "land to the tiller" – but this had proved an empty promise, its implementation blocked by the political power of rural landlords. The Communists, who had won the civil war, had made land reform an effective political tool in areas they controlled. Not about to make the same mistake twice, and no longer dependent on landlords for political support, the KMT redistributed the holdings of Taiwanese landlords in the early 1950s.

The course of land reform in South Korea was more difficult. In 1948, when the American authorities had redistributed the land which had been owned by Japanese nationals, they urged the government of Syngman Rhee to redistribute the holdings of Korean landlords as well. Rhee, whose network of supporters included many landlords, refused. Then North Korea invaded. In the areas they controlled, the North Koreans quickly redistributed farmland. After the North retreated, the South Korean government (now more dependent than ever on American support) decided to leave this redistribution in place.

Thus, in both South Korea and Taiwan, the beginnings of a restructuring of land tenure came from the Japanese colonial authorities, seeking to improve agricultural productivity and tax revenue; in both, large scale reforms were carried out under the direction of a new set of occupying armies – in Taiwan the KMT, and in South Korea the unlikely combination of the US and North Korea. This is an unusual set of conditions, to say the least. We can say, however, that both land reforms were carried out by decision makers who enjoyed political autonomy from the landlord class; once it had been accomplished, the new agrarian system helped solidify the autonomy (or "embedded autonomy") of the state.

13.2.3. AUTHORITARIANISM

One awkward fact about the East Asian models is that none of the three countries had democratically accountable governments during their periods of rapid growth. Japan's pre-World War II government had been an authoritarian nationalist one; in Europe it would have been called fascist. Japan's postwar government is democratic in principle, but has been controlled almost continuously by the same party since the 1950s; that party is kept in office by a combination of an electoral system that gives vastly disproportionate weight to rural votes, and its deep intertwining with the business, agricultural, and criminal interests that support it.

Taiwan was under martial law from 1948 to 1987. It was ruled by the same political party from 1945 until 2000: that party, the Kuomintang (KMT) was that of the Chinese Nationalist government, which after defeat on the mainland by Mao's Communists, retreated to Taiwan in 1948. The Taiwanese government in those years held to the fiction that it was the government of all of China; consequently, the legislature was dominated by aging "representatives" of the various mainland provinces, providing the KMT with a legislative majority that no election could dent. South Korea had a rather ineffective elected government in the 1950s. Its effective developmental state arrived together with the dictator Park Chung Hee, the leader of a coup in which the elected government was overthrown in 1961. South Korea was then a dictatorship until 1987. During this period, both South Korea and Taiwan were police states: state control of their populations was aided by extensive networks of spies and informers, and by an unaccountable police and judicial system. And we should note that Hong Kong and Singapore – the other two Tigers – likewise had notably unaccountable governments. Singapore is nominally democratic, but has been governed by the same rather authoritarian party since independence in 1965. Hong Kong was a British colony until 1997; now it is a democracy so long as it doesn't upset Beijing.

If we add to these examples the fact that, since about 1980, the world's great growth story has been China, we might easily believe that authoritarianism is necessary for rapid economic growth. Kohli picks up this argument, noting (in addition to the South Korean and Taiwanese cases) that one of Brazil's periods of rapid industrial growth came under the military dictatorship of 1964–85. Brazilian industry also grew rapidly under the elected government of Kubitschek (1956–61), but Kohli puts this down to it being a "more elitist democracy" than those before or after it, "shar[ing] some characteristics of cohesive capitalist states" (Kohli 2004, p. 372); he makes the same claim about India's spurt of industrial growth in the Nehru period (1947–64). Even so, Brazilian and Indian growth in those periods wasn't as impressive as South Korean and Taiwanese growth under their dictatorships, and the elitist democracies gave way to less elitist ones.

It is easy to see how a state that is not democratically accountable might be more "autonomous" than one which is, and might be better able to override the objections of particular interests in pursuit of what it sees as the national interests. This does not, however, make dictatorship a good recipe for economic growth. The trouble is that an unaccountable state could choose to do any number of things – and, as they are unaccountable, who's to stop them? The country now known as the Democratic Republic of the Congo (for a few decades it was Zaire) endured over a century of completely unaccountable government, first as a property of the King of Belgium and then as an independent country, and all its rulers ever did was to steal as much as possible and send the proceeds to banks in Europe: no growth, lots of poverty. This is not an isolated example. Raaj Sah (1991) argues that a centralized system of government is akin to an undiversified investment portfolio: you can win big and you can lose big. This speculation is confirmed in a recent paper by Timothy Besley and Masayuki Kudamatsu (2007), which finds that among countries with autocratic governments there is higher variance in the rates of growth, life expectancy (controlling for GDP), and school enrolment than among countries with democratic ones. The modal rate of economic growth is higher for democratic states, but the cases of extremely high (and, though not so dramatically, extremely low) growth are all from autocracies. In short, no country with a democratic government has grown as fast as South Korea and Taiwan, but the typical dictatorship grows more slowly than the typical democracy.

13.3. **Varieties of Tiger: Differing institutions, production systems, and products**

So far, we have been considering South Korea and Taiwan as part of an East Asian model: export promotion combined with ISI; high rates of saving, investment, and literacy; land reform and relative economic equality; lack of democratic accountability. Not only did the two countries look similar in these respects, but they seemed to be following in the footsteps of their erstwhile colonial master, Japan. Yet, when we look closely at the business systems of Japan and its former colonies, we see that they are very different indeed.

13.3.1. INSTITUTIONS AND BUSINESS ORGANIZATION

Gary Hamilton and Nicole Biggart (1988), and Richard Whitely (1991, 1992) delineate differences between the three countries in state/business relations, the nature of the principal corporate actors, and typical management strategies with reference to both organization structure and markets (Table 13.1).

We have encountered the postwar Japanese model in previous chapters. It features *keiretsu*, corporate groups which are ongoing alliances of companies, usually management-controlled, which have cross-shareholdings with each other. A large manufacturer or bank may play a leading role within a *keiretsu*, but the groups are not centrally owned or managed, so the individual firms retain a significant degree of responsibility and initiative. Long-term employment relationships and the absence of a controlling external block-holder allow for high levels of employee commitment and participation. The system has been excellent at both the rapid development of new products and the refinement of products and processes to ensure quality. The state, through organs such as the Ministry of International Trade and Industry (MITI) provided "administrative guidance" to encourage the leading firms in these groups to invest in particular industries or technologies.

Where the *keiretsu* are management-controlled inter-company alliances, South Korea's *chaebol* are hierarchical; each is typically controlled by a family which owns large blocs of shares. In this regard, the *chaebol* are similar to corporate pyramids found in many countries today (and to the *zaibatsu* of pre-World War II Japan). Relations both with employees and with allied firms tend to be less cooperative than in the Japanese case, and as a result the Korean firms have trailed the Japanese in the areas of quality management and continuous improvement.

Taiwan's industry is dominated by smaller firms. These tend to be independently owned, rather than gathering together in pyramids or through cross-shareholdings. Being smaller they are often specialized, and their networked production relations have been compared to those of the Third Italy (Guerrieri et al. 2001).

Hamilton and Biggart attribute these differences in the ownership structure of industry to differences in the three states' approaches to managing the economy. Japan's state has taken what is, by the standards not only of LMEs but also of most European CMEs, a highly directive role, steering companies toward investment in particular industries. One lever it had for this was the ability to persuade Japan's major banks; the banks, in turn, had influence in their respective *keiretsu*. Zysman (1983) compares this with state-directed investment in France, at a time when the French government actually owned some of the major banks. A closer analogue to the France of the 1970s and 1980s would be South Korea, where the state owned the banks and used this ownership to compel, rather than persuade. Taiwan's government preferred to set up a framework that provided incentives for investment in certain areas – demand from strategic SOEs, subsidies for research, protection from imports – and then let firms compete.

Why did the governments of South Korea and Taiwan choose such different paths? One explanation is that Taiwan's government, having transplanted itself from the mainland, was less well connected with the business class of its country; this outsider status was a reason to set up rules and stand back, rather than trying to micromanage. Another explanation is that, despite (or perhaps because of) its outsider status, Taiwan's government was much stronger than South Korea's: that the latter stepped in close because it was the only way of staying in charge. When Park Chung Hee seized control in 1961, deposing a rather ineffective elected government, one of his first actions was to arrest the major business leaders of the country; after what one imagines must have been a short tutorial in the new rules of the game, they were released, and some of them became fabulously rich under Park's rule.

An alternative explanation for the differences in the business systems of the three countries – dismissed by Hamilton and Biggart but given more credit by Whitely – is that it is a reflection of their different cultures. As a general explanation, this is hard to credit: as noted previously, the industrial structure that emerged in South Korea under Park was not dissimilar to that of Japan before World War II; the postwar modifications of Japan's system were due to the actions of the American authorities, not a change in Japanese culture. On the other hand, family-centred networks of small- and medium-sized companies are typical of Chinese business communities, both at home and abroad.

13.3.2. PRODUCTION SYSTEMS AND PRODUCT SPECIALIZATION

Whatever the sources of difference, it does not stop with the ownership and organization of corporations: it extends to product specialization as well. Biggart and Mauro Guillén trace the progress of exports of cars and car parts from South Korea and Taiwan (their study also covers Spain and Argentina), between 1970 and 1995 (Biggart and Guillén 1999). Both countries make car parts, and both assemble cars; Taiwan exports lots of parts and virtually no assembled cars, while for South Korea the reverse is true.

Biggart and Guillén attribute the differences in export specialization to differences in business organization. The small-firm orientation of the Taiwan's economy does not lend itself to the scale of organization required to make cars competitively for world markets. Taiwanese parts manufacturers have done very well, however, and supply multinational auto companies based in Japan and elsewhere. The weakness of South Korea's parts exports is attributed to the hierarchical or adversarial relationships which the *chaebol*-controlled car companies have with their suppliers. Korean suppliers, they argue, are efficient mass producers of low-cost parts, but they are not good partners for the Japanese car companies, or for other multinationals trying to emulate the Japanese companies' practices of collaborative product development and quality assurance.

13.3.3. EAST ASIA AND THE "VARIETIES OF CAPITALISM" FRAMEWORK

In terms of the Varieties of Capitalism categories from Chapter 11, we would include both South Korea and Taiwan among the coordinated market economies: high rates of participation in vocational training, weak protection for minority shareholders, firms controlled by large block-holders. They follow Japan – and depart from the European CMEs – in having very weak public social safety nets. In Japan, social insurance is provided mostly by employers in the form of job security and pensions; in Taiwan and South Korea, it is primarily a family function.

The differences between the business systems of the three countries, discussed above, have parallels within Europe. We can call both Japan and Germany examples of alliance capitalism. "Alliance" here can refer both to the ubiquity of relational contracting and cross-shareholding among firms, and to the two countries' penchant for centrally negotiated settlements on wages and industrial policy issues. In its *dirigiste,* or state-led capitalism, South Korea is much like France. These two countries depart from the idealized CME model in their attachments to hierarchical control and mass production methods; and, in both countries, the state has controlled industry both through control of the banking system and through extremely tight-knit elite networks (Lee and Yoo 2006).

13.4. **Later waves of new: NICs in the age of international production**

13.4.1. HAS THE LADDER BEEN PULLED AWAY?

Having learned these lessons, can the current wave of NICs follow in the footsteps of Japan and the Tigers? Will they, too, be able to move up the ladder from their current position on the lower rungs, assembling parts made by others to produce products designed by others and carrying the brands of others? Maybe, maybe not. Let us consider how their situation differs from that of the Tigers.

Figure 13.3 compares the growth performances of China, India, and the ex-USSR with that of South Korea.

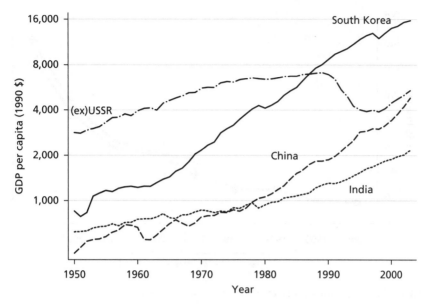

Figure 13.3. NIC and BRIC

Source: Maddison (2007).

We saw above that South Korea and Taiwan began their export drives with low-wage assembly work. In this they were like today's NICs, and unlike Japan. But the Tigers had more control over production and product than today's NICs do. One reason for this is that the modularization of value chains is now more extreme. The spatial separation of stages of production, and the management of value chains by multinationals, both have become routine. This makes it easier to get on the bottom rung of the ladder, but harder to move up: there are few advantages to doing other functions close to the assembly work, and with plenty of assembly sites for multinationals to choose from.

Critics of international economic liberalization, such as Robert Wade (2003) and Ha-Joon Chang (2002), argue that development strategies such as those followed by Japan, South Korea, and Taiwan are now impossible under WTO rules: with low barriers to international trade and foreign investment, it will be impossible for poorer countries to build their own corporations and deepen their industrial competencies.

Lee Branstetter and Nicholas Lardy (2008) would dissent on the matter of liberalization, at least in the case of China. The Chinese government, they claim, accepted more stringent liberalization conditions from the WTO than was necessary to gain membership; the government did this, they argue, in order to commit itself to liberalization of China's internal markets. China, of course, is a unique case: its old economy was illiberal in the extreme, and its potential gains from internal trade may be larger than those from foreign trade.

Branstetter and Lardy do, however, believe that even China faces a more difficult task climbing the value-added ladder today than South Korea and Taiwan did just a couple

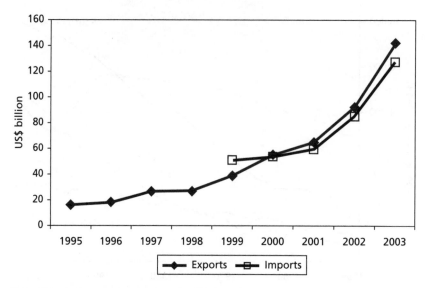

Figure 13.4. China's imports and exports of high-tech products

Source: Branstetter and Lardy (2008). Reprinted by permission of the publisher.

of decades earlier. China looms large in the consciousness of people around the world as the place where more and more manufactured goods come from. Yet, when it comes to high-technology products – and here we mean mostly electronics – what gets done in China is usually just the final assembly. Figure 13.4 shows Chinese imports and exports of goods classified as "high technology." There is a reason the two curves track so closely: most of the imports are parts, from which to assemble the exports.

To many countries, China looks like the new workshop of the world, making seemingly everything: a source of cheap goods and, to other NICs, low cost competition that cannot be beaten. But with some countries, China runs a significant trade deficit. The high-tech imports shown in Figure 13.3 are coming, largely, from its richer neighbors in East Asia – Japan and the Tigers. For these countries, China is both a big market and a source of low-wage labor for their companies' simple manufacturing operations. The question for China, of course, is whether they can upgrade to control more of the value chain – and more of the high value-added, high skill processes.

The same question arises in all of the new (i.e., post-Tiger) NICs. Martin Kenney and Richard Florida (1994) studied electronics assembly plants operated by Japanese MNCs in Mexico, mostly near the US border and to serve the US market. These companies had not brought their high-involvement, high-skill practices with them to Mexico: if a stage of production required those functions, it was left in Japan. Similar considerations applied to US companies.

Beyond the question of skill development is one of technology transfer. In another study of electronics manufacturing in Mexico, Simona Iammarino, Ramon Padilla-

Pérez, and Nick von Tunzelmann (2008) compare two states, Baja California and Jalisco. Baja California, hard on the US border, has only become a manufacturing centre in recent decades. This began with the Maquiladora laws, which from 1965 allowed the tariff-free import of parts, assembly, and reexport between Mexico and the US, and then got a big push in 1994 with the North American Free Trade Agreement (Canada, Mexico, US). Jalisco, much further south, was a location for earlier generations of ISI industry. Iammarino et al. find that there is little knowledge transfer between MNC subsidiaries in Baja and their local suppliers, while there is considerable knowledge transfer in Jalisco.

The problem extends into R&D as well. MNCs, as we saw in Chapter 2, are important agents of technology transfer (Patel and Pavitt 1991). This is now commonly understood to be a two-way transfer. An important factor in MNCs' choices when they locate facilities is the local knowledge base, because while MNCs bring knowledge from their home countries, they also pick up what they can from abroad (Cantwell 1989; Cantwell and Iammarino 2003). This two-way transfer has been studied mostly in cases involving the "triad" of large, technologically advanced rich countries – North America, the EU, and Japan. With China and India making concerted efforts to expand their own science bases and their science-industry links, the question arises of how these countries figure in the MNCs technology transfer pictures.

MNCs do an increasing amount of research with partners in both China and India. Cantwell's theory predicts that such research should complement the technological capabilities of the MNCs involved. Recent research by Suma Athreye and Martha Prevezer (2007) finds that, on the contrary, most of this research is in areas where the MNCs are already strong: they are using China and India for low-cost research labor, to solve routine problems, just as they use them for low-cost assembly labor. Athreye and Prevezer argue that the MNC partnerships are actually diverting research resources in China and India away from areas in which their domestic industries are strong (pharmaceutical manufacturing processes in India, for example). They also cite evidence that it has become difficult for Indian universities to hire science and engineering faculty, thus undermining future science and technology development.

China and India both have better prospects than most NICs of overcoming these problems, and climbing the value-added ladder. Both countries are huge, each with a greater population than North America and the EU *combined*. Their large internal markets and their geopolitical importance can help them overcome the obstacles posed by the global production system. Both countries historically have fairly closed economies, and domestic industries are meeting much of the growing demand that comes from higher consumer spending, and from rising public and private investment. Moreover, the economic restructuring associated with export growth is also integrating the domestic market of each country. Many Chinese companies are owned by local or regional governments, and though national markets exist these authorities have often discouraged competition.

The national government has been breaking down internal trade barriers, however, and investing heavily in transportation infrastructure. Branstetter and Lardy mention these developments as beneficial to foreign investors, which they are – but they are also helping to create the world's most populous barrier-free market.

Similarly, Indian consumers and businesses have long had to deal with regional quasi-monopolies in many industries – in this case, mostly private sector – because of a bad national transportation and communications infrastructure. (Notice that India's most prominent export industries – phone centres and computer software – require little in the way of local infrastructure: with satellite links and back-up generators, they can serve overseas customers regardless of local conditions.) Recent economic growth has funded infrastructure improvements, so that the national market is becoming more integrated, and more competitive.

The size and rapid growth of the Chinese and Indian markets gives their governments leverage. China has famously exploited this in its dealings with such companies as General Electric (to obtain access to turbine technologies for electric power plants), and Boeing (for technology transfer and the associated subcontracting work on aircraft).

Moreover, China and India both are nuclear powers, with large armies and significant armaments industries. Military research and production has often been an avenue for governments to fund and organize the growth of a country's technology and production capacities. In America, this has been clear from the federal armories that persevered in the development of interchangeable parts (recall Chapter 8), to the Pentagon's hand in the growth of the Silicon Valley (Castells 1996). In principle, governments could fund such capabilities for purposes other than making bombs, and the money might be better spent. Research with applications to weapons, however, has powerful military and nationalist constituencies, and so can sometimes get funding when other research cannot. Hence, Brazil's great symbol of technologically advanced industry is Embraer, a company that has a good world market share in small- and mid-sized jet planes; the company would not have come into existence without military backing.

An additional problem for today's NICs is that serving as an assembly platform does not depend on domestic demand; nor does it require a good national infrastructure or a high level of education among the population as a whole. Assembly operations can operate as enclaves. That can put the owner of an assembly plant in a position similar to the owner of a sugar plantation: with an eye on low labor costs, low taxes, and international markets, this industrialist can easily become a political foe of the policies required for further development. While falling inequality was part of the Tigers' growth package, sharp rises in inequality are common within the new NICs of recent decades.

13.4.2. CHINA: MARKET-SUSTAINING FEDERALISM

The Chinese government set out to create a market economy in 1978, but for the time being it kept most business in state ownership. It also maintained an autocratic system of government, controlled by the Communist Party. Domestic investment has boomed, and FDI has flowed in from abroad. This presents a puzzle. Standard liberal theory predicts that the high level of state ownership, the lack of an independent judiciary, and an unaccountable government with the ability to reverse its pro-market policies at any time, potential investors – whether foreign or domestic – would not regard their investments as secure and so would not invest. Yet China has had no problem securing the huge investment required for its astonishing growth.

Gabriella Montinola, Yingyi Qian, and Barry Weingast (1995) offer a solution to the puzzle with what they call "market sustaining federalism." Federalism is of course a multilayered system of government, in which the central government and the smaller units have distinct roles, rights and spheres of authority that cannot be easily changed. Montinola et al. argue that despite the lack of clarity about property rights in China, the security of investments is ensured by the relationship between the national government and the various provinces, cities, and so forth.

Even before the reforms, most SOEs in China were not owned by the national government, but by various subnational units of government – provinces, regions, cities, townships, and villages. As the reforms progressed, the national government's ownership position was further reduced. Investors who do business with Chinese SOEs, then, are usually not dealing with the national government. The national government, however, has set up the rules of the game.

Montinola et al. identify the following characteristics of market sustaining federalism:

1. A *hierarchy* of governments with a *delineated scope of authority* (e.g., between the national and subnational governments) exists so that each government is autonomous within its own sphere of authority.
2. The subnational governments have primary *authority over the economy* within their jurisdictions.
3. The national government has the authority to police the *common market* and to ensure the mobility of goods and factors across subgovernment jurisdictions.
4. Revenue sharing among governments is limited and borrowing by governments is constrained so that all governments face *hard budget constraints.*
5. The allocation of authority and responsibility has an *institutionalized degree of durability* so that it cannot be altered by the national government either unilaterally or under the pressures from subnational governments." (1995, p. 55)

Subnational governments often have a strong motive to resist point 3 on this list, since they are the owners of many industries that would, in the absence of a common market, be local or regional monopolies. MQW report that enforcement of this point has been difficult. More recently, Branstetter and Lardy (2006) report considerable progress on in this area.

The key feature of China's post-reform revenue system has been point 4. The arrangements for revenue sharing have varied. Some poorer provinces receive subsidies, but the more prosperous, fast-growing regions contribute revenue to the center. As per point 4, the national government commits in advance to certain revenue sharing terms with government units the next level down; those units do the same with the units below them. These agreements ensure the more prosperous subnational units of government that they will be allowed to keep a known, and large, share of the profit and tax revenues coming out of businesses within their borders. There has also been growth in certain subnational government revenue screens that are not even included in the national fiscal calculations.

Subnational governments thus have a strong incentive to provide a favorable climate for investment, because they get to keep part of the revenue, not only from businesses they own but from the next level of government down. The national government works to ensure a common market. The remaining question, however, is Montinola et al.'s (1995) point 5. What ensures that the national government will not reverse its policy of market reform? There have been times, such as the aftermath of Tiananmen Square (1989–91), when there was a powerful movement at high levels in the government for the restoration of central control of the economy. Montinola et al. argue that two things have occurred which thwarted that effort, and would likewise thwart any such effort in the future. One is that the reforms have made local officials in the richer regions much more powerful in the political process. The other is that the central government's revenue now depends on a thriving market economy. If it were to reassert central control, much of this revenue would probably dry up; in the place of thriving businesses, the government would be stuck with the cost of providing a social safety net for those losing their jobs.

The association of growth with increased inequality is, as noted in the previous chapter, something which distinguishes industrialization today with the earlier East Asian model of the Tigers and Japan. We should note here, as Montinola et al. do, that in China market-sustaining federalism increases the inequality between rich and poor regions in China. This is in marked contrast to many federal systems, whether national or (in the case of the EU) supranational, which take it as an important obligation to reduce such inequalities.

14 Poverty Traps

The previous chapter dealt with newly industrialized countries – countries which had, in the space of a few decades, joined the industrial world. Reading about those countries, one could be forgiven for getting the impression that the whole world is fast becoming part of the modern industrial and service economy. Many countries, we know, are quite poor and not growing very fast. Figure 14.1 provides some comparisons.

We've all heard that about half of the world's population lives on incomes of less than US$2 per day, whether in backward countryside or urban slums. Most readers of this book will never have had to live that way, nor has the author; for this reason, attempting to understand the situation of the poorer half of humanity requires, for most of us, greater efforts of imagination and sympathy than do the topics discussed in previous chapters. And yet here, for half of the world, is just one chapter. We have space to deal with only a few aspects of the big question: why is it so hard for so many people to join the rich world?

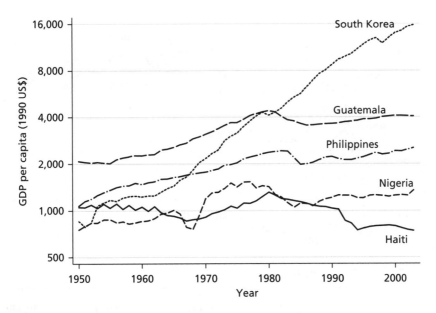

Figure 14.1. Stuck in neutral: Some countries don't grow much

Source: Maddison (2007).

14.1. **Life and death**

The ins and outs of measuring poverty are many, and are beyond the scope of this book. To get an approximation of how poverty is distributed around the globe, we'll make do with the Preston Curve shown in Figure 14.2. This gives us the life expectancies in different countries, plotted against GDP per capita. Each circle represents a country, with the area of the circle proportional to the country's population. Only a few of the more populous countries are named on the graph. Notice that life expectancy rises steeply with small increases in income per capita, up to a turning point. That turning point is where very basic public health, maternity care, and child nutrition needs have been met for most of the population – after that, extra income doesn't save many lives. Most of the countries lower down on the almost vertical portion of the curve – the poor portion where infant mortality is high – are in Africa. Near the top of the vertical portion we find countries such as India, Pakistan, and Indonesia – countries now often numbered among the newly industrializing, but in which large parts of the population remain very poor. (The extreme outliers, with very low life expectancies for their level of income, are countries with high HIV infection rates, such as South Africa.)

Each axis of the Preston Curve tells us something about poverty. GDP per capita tells us whether a country as a whole can be considered rich or poor; it does not tell us what

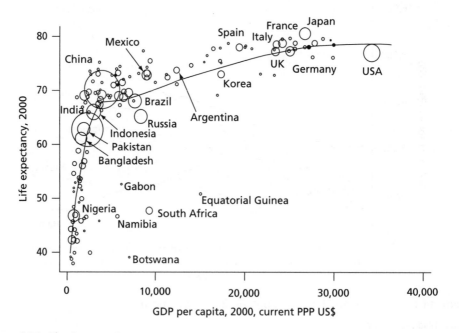

Figure 14.2. The Preston Curve

Source: Deaton (2003). Reproduced by permission of the American Economic Association.

proportion of a country's people subsists on very low incomes, since that is also affected by the distribution of income within the country. Life expectancy gives a crude but useful indicator of how much serious poverty there is in a country. It is affected by any number of things. For the poorest, the critical questions are clean water and other basic public sanitation measures, adequacy of nutrition, and access to basic medical care. The likelihood of an early death for want of such things is a good practical indicator of poverty.

What messages can we take home from the Preston Curve? One is that, using life expectancy as a rough and ready measure of poverty, poverty tends to fall as a nation's per capita income rises. This might not be so, if growth is accompanied by a sufficiently large increase in inequality. Sometimes, but not always, growth is accompanied by substantial increases in inequality. Yet on the whole, absolute poverty has fallen (and life expectancy has risen) with rising per capita incomes.

A second is that, in the small matter of life and death, the crucial difference is not between rich and poor, but between moderately poor and very poor.

A third is that, for any given level of per capita income, there are appreciable differences in life expectancy. If we exclude countries where HIV is a big factor, these differences are not nearly as big as the differences between the very poor and the rest; they are, however, big enough to worry about.

14.2. **Life, death, and institutions**

In Chapter 13 we considered, briefly, whether there was a difference in the growth performance of autocratic states and democratic ones. The answer turned out to be complicated, since both the high- and low-growth extremes of the distribution were dominated by autocratic states. Let us look at the same question again, through the lens of life expectancy. Again, the answer will turn out to be complicated.

Jean Dreze and Amartya Sen (1989, 2002) compare life expectancy in India and China from 1950 to 2000 (Figure 14.2). Their comparison also breaks out one Indian state, Kerela, for reasons that will become clear shortly. In 1949, just before the comparison begins, both countries got new systems of government: India because it gained independence from Britain, China because the Communists defeated the Nationalists in China's civil war. The Chinese Communist state was (and is) an authoritarian. Among other things, this meant that all communications media were controlled by the state and subject to political censorship; criticism of the government was not tolerated. It was also a state of the Left, committed in principle to economic equality, and drawing its political support from the poor.

India's early independence governments have been what Kohli calls a "fragmented, multi-class" type. Although committed, in principle, to economic equality and poverty reduction, their ability to act has been curtailed by the conflicting claims of various classes and interest groups. Life expectancy in India has risen steadily, but slowly; through the 1960s and 1970s, China's lead actually increased, even through the chaos of the Cultural Revolution from 1966 to 1976. In most years, China's autocratic system was simply more effective at delivering the basics, bettering the life of the poor.

But what about the collapse of Chinese life expectancy, from 1958 to 1961? This was caused by a famine: between 15 and 30 *million* people died of starvation and of the various illnesses to which hunger makes people vulnerable (Dreze and Sen 2002, p. 132). We might say that the famine was caused by a misguided set of economic policies called the Great Leap Forward, and might put this down as another example of the extremes of economic performance, both low and high, that are common in autocratic systems: in this case, extremely low economic performance meant not enough food. Dreze and Sen, however, say that it's not as simple as that. Famines are rarely caused by absolute shortages of food. A famine happens when a large number of people lose their *access* to food. This may start with a failure of crops or a loss of income, but such things do not on their own cause famine; a famine results only if nobody steps in to provide food before people starve (Sen 1981). Dreze and Sen argue that this *never* happens where there is a free press: the publication of pictures of mass starvation would bring down the government, so even the most cynical government will not allow mass starvation in its own country if it faces an independent press. There were mass famines in India under British rule, but there have been none since independence. In China from 1958–61, millions starved in certain regions of the country, but political control of communications was so complete that it could be, and was, covered up. The government did not fall: Chairman Mao remained at the helm until he died of old age, and the party that was in power then remains in power today.

The irony is that, despite this catastrophic famine in China, for the period 1950–2000 as a whole, the rate of death from malnutrition and related causes has probably been higher in India than in China. Democracy and a free press would not tolerate famine, but they did (and do) tolerate shockingly high ongoing rates of early death from a variety of causes related to poverty and poor public services.

Figure 14.3 provides additional information that requires comment. Notice that the rate at which China improved life expectancy slows down after 1980. One contributing factor is that the market-based reforms, which began in 1979–80, included the elimination of free public medical care.

Notice too, the Indian state of Kerela. In terms of life expectancy, Kerela is like China without the famine, and without the post-1980 drop-off in the rate of improvement. We find a similar picture if we compare literacy rates: China generally does better than India, but Kerela's rate far exceeds that of all other Indian states, standing with the most literate provinces of China (Dreze and Sen 2002, p. 119). It is perhaps not surprising, then, that Kerela, like China, has a government run by a Communist party, obsessed

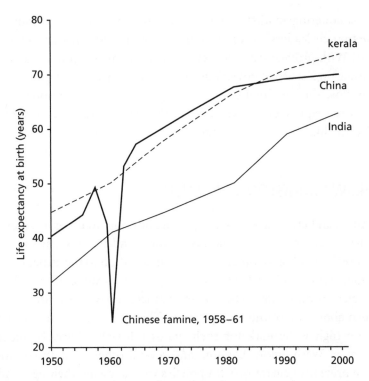

Figure 14.3. Life expectancy in China, India, and Kerela

Source: Dreze and Sen (2002).

with improvements to public health, medical care, and education. Being a state of India, however, Kerela's government must live with elections and a free press. If success is measured in vital statistics, it seems to have the best of both worlds. Is Kerela then a model for economic development? Sadly, no. For all its accomplishments, it is not a centre of India's booming high tech, industrial, and service economies; its prosperity today comes from remittances, sent by its well-educated citizens who go to find work abroad (Dreze and Sen 2002, pp. 97–101).

14.3. **Institutions or policies?**

When we tell a story of success or failure, be it of an individual, a company, or a country, it is easiest to speak in terms of clear, simple (if not easy) choices. Not only easiest, but most satisfying: narratives of tragedy, redemption, salvation, love or loss, wealth or poverty; of businesses adopting strategies which lead to the development of new products, to conquering markets, or to failure; of countries overcoming some great problem due to their leaders' vision, or blundering into decline due to their avarice or incompetence. With protagonists, clear choices, and clear outcomes, we have satisfying stories. We also gain a sense of power ourselves, just from *knowing what should be done.* Yet, if we look closely at the situation of anybody who has the ambition of helping make a poor country more prosperous, we find that the choices available to them are seldom clear, and that the likelihood of clear-cut success is very small.

14.3.1. THE WASHINGTON CONSENSUS

Simple narratives and clear choices are appealing not only to observers like us, but also to aid agencies, international financial institutions, and the governments of powerful countries that seek to influence other countries. In addition to the esthetic of intellectual tidiness, a simple set of policies has the advantage that it can be proposed by people in Washington, New York, or Brussels to a government anywhere in the world, without knowing much about the country in question. The final two decades of the twentieth century were a high watermark for such one-size-fits-all advice. Neoliberalism had swept to power in Washington, London, and several other capitals; communism was collapsing; the previous generation's ISI policies were showing their age; and, crucially, many countries of both the Third World and the former Soviet bloc found themselves with debts they could not repay.

The arguments of neoliberalism have persuaded many, but most thoroughgoing adoptions of neoliberal policies in developing and transition economies were due to financial need rather than conviction. The debts in question resulted from heavy borrowing in the late 1970s and early 1980s. In those years, the international banking system had been awash with deposits from oil exporters, and the rich countries themselves were growing slowly and borrowing little. The banks needed customers, and for many poor and middle income countries borrowing was an easy way to relieve financial pressures. Many of them were exporters of oil, or of other commodities whose prices were high at the time. The obligations taken on were in foreign currencies – mostly American dollars – and this left the borrowers at the mercy of changes in exchange and interest rates. In the case of the transition economies, the problem of this debt burden had been magnified by collapse of centrally planed industry.

When countries get into financial difficulty, they often turn to the International Monetary Fund (IMF) for assistance, and assistance is conditional on following policy advice. Financially troubled "transition" (former Communist) and other poor or middle income (i.e., Third World) countries were faced by a common set of neoliberal policy prescriptions. Proponents of these prescriptions included the World Bank, IMF (both based in Washington, DC), leading figures on Wall Street, and most Western governments. The label "Washington Consensus" (WC) was applied to it retrospectively by one of its framers, John Williamson (1990), who wrote down this list:

1. Fiscal discipline, i.e., restrain public spending
2. Reorientation of public expenditures
3. Tax reform, meaning in this context lowering marginal tax rates on income, and shifting taxes toward consumption
4. Financial liberalization
5. Unified and competitive exchange rates. (Many countries had dual exchange rates, with preferential rates for inputs required for favored industries, either ISI or export-oriented.)
6. Trade liberalization
7. Openness to FDI
8. Privatization of SOEs
9. Deregulation
10. Secure property rights

WC did have institutional implications; in particular, as we shall see shortly, "secure property rights" is not as simple as it sounds. Still, it was regarded largely as advice to simply let markets rule: countries were asked to let markets determine interest rates (financial liberalization), exchange rates, investment (openness to FDI, privatization), market entry and rates of profit (privatization again, and deregulation). The application of WC policies to countries in financial difficulty contributed to compromises in its free market character. On the one hand, it sought market-determined exchange rates, which typically required a sharp devaluation of the nation's currency. Another objective was controlling inflation, but devaluation contributed to inflation. One response to inflation was the distinctly non-free-market restriction of wage increases, to break the inflationary spiral. With wages controlled and other prices continuing to climb, real incomes of wage earners usually fell. The prescription also sought fiscal discipline – the reduction or elimination of government budget deficits – which meant reduced government spending. There were three different reasons for prescribing this course of action. One was the expectation that certain parties favored by the WC promoters would benefit; these include, in particular, banks to which debts were owed, and multinationals expecting to make a profit on the sudden privatization of public utilities. A second was market fundamentalism – the belief that unregulated markets are simply the best system, and that such markets can be created simply by policy choices which remove certain barriers to their operation. A third was a belief in the need for "shock therapy" (in the former Communist countries) or "structural adjustment" (elsewhere in the world), meaning in either case the abrupt introduction of free markets as a means of sweeping away the old regime of planners, protectionists, and such; shock therapy proponents were not all market fundamentalists, but came to the same policy prescription on the grounds that more gradual change and case-by-case policy development would allow rent-seekers to capture the process.

During the heyday of WC, the average rate of growth among poor- and middle-income countries was fairly high, and the rules of international trade and investment both did become more liberal. Yet it would be difficult to say that, as a policy prescription, WC was a great success. The liberalization of trade and investment was due primarily to multilateral trade negotiations and the growing role of global production networks. Countries that made big changes in their domestic policies in keeping with WC – notably, those of sub-Saharan Africa, Latin America, and the former Soviet bloc – on the whole continued to grow more slowly than those of East Asia and India, which kept control of their own policies (Rodrik 2006). There is, of course, a selection bias here: the countries that adopted consensus policies could be made to do so because they were in a bad way already, so their subsequent relatively poor performance was not necessarily due to these polices. On the other hand, it was clear that superior economic performance could be had without adopting these policies; moreover, in many cases, structural adjustment policies required by the IMF or World Bank appear to have made things much worse. Russia and Mexico are two cases of this.

Russia lacked any recent heritage of private property or commercial law; most business assets and real estate were owned by the state. Shock therapy policies called for the rapid privatization of the state's assets. Without an experienced and trustworthy legal system in place, this opened the way for an alternative vehicle of private contract enforcement – organized crime, or the Russian mafia. Organized crime is itself a sort of institution, and not easy to remove – as long experience in southern Italy and elsewhere shows. Hasty policy changes therefore contributed to an undesired institutional change. (On the transition in Russia, see Amsden, Kochanowicz, and Taylor 1998; and Glenny 2008).

In Mexico, a neoliberal effort to stamp out inflation through liberalization and privatization began in 1982, and succeeded only in producing negative economic growth for five years after that. The foreign banks got paid, and the rich of Mexico got richer despite the decline in GDP; real wages of industrial workers fell by 47 per cent between 1982 and 1988, and the real value of the minimum wage fell by 40 per cent. (For details, see Ray 1998, pp. 696–9).

Advocates of the neoliberal position often spoke of "getting prices right." Their argument was that free, competitive markets would allocate resources efficiently and solve many of the problems of the developing world. The prices that would be determined by free and competitive markets were seen as the "right" prices; policies or market structures which led to other prices were creating "distortions." Alice Amsden retorted that the Tigers had, on the contrary, deliberately got prices "wrong." Export subsidies and the selective use of trade barriers had created incentives for investment in particular sectors and for penetrating international markets. These incentives would not have existed if the prices were "right" (Amsden 1989).

14.3.2. INSTITUTIONS AGAIN

Disillusionment with the quick policy fix of WC has led to a new focus on institutions (World Bank 2005). Institutions may, like policies, result from choices made by governments. One difference is that policies are choices that can be made – and changed – within a relatively short time frame, while changing institutions generally takes longer. Another difference is that, while policies don't make policies, institutions do make institutions: institutional change requires changing the rules of the game, while you are playing it. So changing institutions is more difficult than changing policies.

Some widely cited studies during the heyday of WC had attributed economic growth to openness to trade and investment, and other measures of liberalization (e.g., Dollar 1992). A representative work of more recent institutional tilt is that of William Easterly and Ross Levine (2003). They run regressions similar to Dollar's, but include a variable meant to measure the strength of economic institutions. This variable is an index which reflects, in one number, data from various sources on the following institutional variables:

1. Voice and accountability – the extent to which citizens can choose their government, political rights, civil liberties, and an independent press. 2. Political stability and absence of violence – a low likelihood that the government will be overthrown by unconstitutional or violent means. 3. Government effectiveness – quality of public service delivery, competence of civil servants, and the degree of politicization of the civil service. 4. Light regulatory burden – relative absence of government controls on goods markets, government interference in the banking system, excessive bureaucratic controls on starting new businesses, or excessive regulation of private business and international trade. 5. Rule of law – protection of persons and property against violence or theft, independent and effective judges, contract enforcement. 6. Freedom from graft – absence of the use of public power for private gain, corruption. (Easterly and Levine 2003, p. 18)

To compile such an index obviously requires adding apples, oranges, and a few other kinds of fruit. The arithmetic of that exercise aside, it doesn't allow us to pick out the effects of one type of institution on economic growth. It also assumes a remarkable consensus on what "good" institutions are, while I know from today's newspaper that one economist's government interference in the banking system is another's prudential regulation. Dani Rodrik (2006) contends that many have replaced the market fundamentalism of WC with a sort of institutional fundamentalism, a belief in a unique set of "good" institutions; Easterly and Levine's index could be seen as an example of this. Yet, crude instrument though it is, it does the job: with this index of institutions in the regression, policy variables lose any statistical significance.

14.3.3. LAW AND PROPERTY RIGHTS

One important aspect of a country's institutions is its legal system – its laws, and the framework within which laws are made, interpreted, and enforced. A country's development may be affected by the legal system it has inherited. Easterly and Levine's paper is in fact just one entry in ongoing debates about how a country's legal institutions come to be, and what effect they have on economic outcomes. We need to be aware of two distinct positions here.

What Levine (2005) calls the "law view" holds that the economic effects of a country's legal system depend primarily on the legal tradition to which it belongs. Most countries of the world have a legal system that derives from that of one of three countries – England, France, or Germany – and the argument is that these legal traditions produce different economic outcomes. The "endowments view," on the other hand, holds that a country's legal system is shaped by its function, so that countries whose legal system was established by a colonial government bent on extracting resources at minimal cost to the colonizing power would be different from one established by a colonial power that wanted to encourage settlement by entrepreneurial immigrants.

Levine's nomenclature reflects the fact that the first attributes greater causative power to the formal aspects of the legal system, as embodied in a particular tradition, while the second sees the implementation of the legal system as shaped by function, with function determined by endowments (e.g., natural resources and climate). Notice the parallel, in the formal/functional distinction, with Gilson's discussion of convergence of corporate governance systems, mentioned in Chapter 11. We encountered the endowment view toward the end of Chapter 6, when reflecting on the legal heritage of resource-extracting empire.

The Law View, as represented here, is a subset of the American Law and Economics school. Not to put too fine a point on it, the Law and Economics school holds that the English legal tradition is more conducive to economic efficiency than the continental systems, and that the French tradition is the worst. (Caution is required here, however: "law and economics" can also refer to any economic analysis of the law, whether or not it is from the Law and Economics school.) This school shares much, intellectually and in terms of personnel, with the New Institutionalist school of economics; Ronald Coase, in particular, is treated as a founding father of both schools. We have encountered the New Institutionalist school in two settings: in Chapter 7, we considered the argument of North, Thomas, and Jones that a thousand years of interstate competition led to the evolution of efficient institutional forms in western Europe; in various places throughout the book we have encountered Oliver Williamson's transactions cost theory, which deals *inter alia* with the consequences of incomplete contracts. We find reflections of both in the law and economics tradition.

In the English tradition – which applies in all the former British colonies, including the US – law is made not only by the legislature, but also by judges: judges interpret the law, and a considerable body of law within the English tradition consists of precedents established in the courts, on the basis of a combination of written law, prior precedents, and broad principles of justice. Law emerging from accumulated precedents in this way is known as "common law," and the English system is also called the common law system. More broadly, it is a system that relies on *jurisprudence* – the (prudential) decisions or jurists. Although American law appears to differ considerably from that of Britain in that the former grows out of a written constitution while the latter does not, the US Constitution is in many places either vague or archaic, and its interpretation has given American judges at least as much latitude as their British counterparts.

In contrast, the French system, since Napoleon, is one in which the law as determined by the legislature and the executive is expected to be very clear (*bright lines* in legal jargon), and judges are expected to simply enforce it. The *Code Napoleon* took the written civil law of the late Roman Empire as its model. The French system is thus called a civil law system; versions of the French system are found in former French colonies, and in Belgium, the Netherlands, Spain, Portugal, Italy, and most of the former colonies of these countries. A different civil law system developed in Germany, with a somewhat stronger role for judges than in France; the German system has been influential in both central Europe and East Asia. Some of the studies discussed below also make reference to a Scandinavian legal tradition, which falls somewhere between the German and the English with respect to the role accorded judges.

Why should systems with powerful judges produce more efficient law? There are two distinct arguments. Both of them take as given that judges are typically fair people, and independent both of the government and of any private parties to lawsuits that come before them.

Given that, the first and simplest argument is that governments, left to their own devices, will often take actions – regulation, taxation, or simple confiscation – which unexpectedly reduce the value of the property of certain people. The risk of such government action discourages investment, and also biases investment toward assets that are less likely to be subject to adverse action by the state. Where judges can act on the basis of broad principles of fairness, they will tend to protect private property from arbitrary state action, and thereby create an environment conducive to investment.

The second argument is the evolutionary one. To understand it, it is first useful to think of the law in the same way that transaction cost theory thinks of incomplete contracts. The world is a complicated and uncertain place; business conditions and technologies change. Those who write the law cannot begin to anticipate every circumstance that might arise. For a system of law to be efficient, therefore, it must be adaptable. The law and economics school holds that the English legal tradition produces more efficient law than the French one because it has a better mechanism for adapting to changing circumstances: the parties to lawsuits make arguments before judges, and judges make decisions; decisions get appealed, and the conflicting decisions of different judges get compared in higher courts.

The Law View studies begin with Rafael La Porta, Florencio Lopez-de-Silanes, Andrei Shleifer, and Robert Vishny (1998). Their question is how the rights of investors – both shareholders and creditors – are defined and enforced in different legal traditions. They find that investor protections are strongest in countries of English legal origin and weakest in countries of French legal origin, with countries of German and Scandinavian legal origin somewhere in between. Their prediction is that investor protection will result in more and better allocated investment, and thus better economic performance.

A more recent study by Daron Acemoglu, Simon Johnson, and James Robinson (2001) uses institutional differences to explain the GDP per capita of former colonies today. Like La Porta et al., they accord central importance to investor protection, and in particular whether the government can take arbitrary actions which reduce (or wipe out) the value of an investment. They, too, argue that the institutions governing investment in the developing world today are a colonial legacy. Acemoglu et al., however, find that the most important features of that legacy lie not in the particulars of the legal tradition of the colonizing power, but in what the colonists used the colony for. Settler colonies, like Canada or New Zealand, got institutions that protected investors from arbitrary action by the state. Other colonies had virtually no European settlers, and were organized simply to extract resources as cheaply as possible. In all colonies, the colonizing state engaged in arbitrary seizure of property belonging to indigenous peoples, so the imported legal systems had in any case to be adapted to accommodate these acts. In colonies like the Belgian Congo or the Gold Coast (now Ghana), there was little hope of attracting entrepreneurial immigrants, and the basic business of the colonial state was to facilitate the ongoing seizure of local property and to leave indigenous people with no choice but to contribute their labor to the extraction of resources. Investment in these countries was not in conflict with the arbitrary seizure of property by the state: it was entirely *dependent* on such seizure. Other colonies – South Africa, Brazil, and India – fell somewhere between.

Lacking consistent comparative statistics on settlement, Acemoglu et al. assume that settlement is inversely related to settler's death rates from disease. Comparative figures on European soldiers' death rates from disease are available. These death rates, from the nineteenth century, turn out to be a good predictor of the risk of expropriation in the late twentieth century. Risk of expropriation has a large negative impact on GDP. After taking death rates into account, the effects of legal origin or the particular colonizing power are small, and ex-British colonies actually do slightly worse than others.

14.4. **Two obstacles to institutional change**

All of this talk of historical factors can leave us with the impression that there is no hope. But things do change, and the relative position of countries changes. For a reminder of

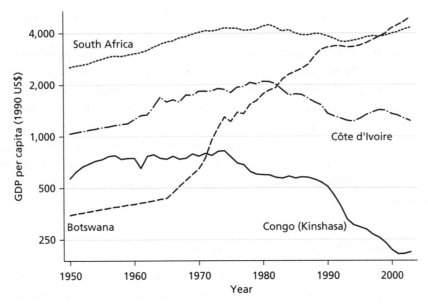

Figure 14.4. Different Africas

Source: Maddison (2007).

this, and before we continue, consider the path of per capita incomes, over time, in four African countries (Figure 14.4).

There are many, many obstacles to institutional change. Here I have space to deal only with two: the distribution of ownership of agricultural land and the role of the economy of extractive resources.

14.4.1. THE LAND PROBLEM

In the previous chapter, I said the land reform was an important pre-condition for rapid industrial growth in South Korea and Taiwan. If that is so, why has land reform not been carried out more widely?

14.4.1.1. Agriculture in economic development

The transition from a society in which most people are employed in agriculture, to one in which most are employed in manufacturing or services, is not accomplished by abandoning agriculture. It requires changes in agriculture.

First, since the society will still need just as much food and fiber (and will probably use even more), this step in development requires a large increase in agricultural productivity – each person working on a farm must now be able to feed more who are not.

Second, if a primarily agricultural economy is to finance rapid industrialization out of domestic savings, the principal source of funds for investment must be surplus from the agricultural sector – the other sectors are, by assumption, small. Yet most farmers are not industrialists, so the problem of how to move savings out of agriculture and into industry is not a simple one.

Third, it requires political acquiescence. The shift from an agricultural to an industrial/service economy may threaten the interests of many involved in the former. Overcoming opposition from the agricultural sector can be critical in the creation of a developmental state.

14.4.1.2. Land reform: Logic and evidence

The distribution of land to the families that farm it can, if handled properly, contribute significantly to the first and third of these requirements. The productivity question is simply one of incentives. Large landholdings worked by tenants or by hired labor are beset by huge agency problems (see Stiglitz 1974. This classic paper deals with sharecropping, but the insight extends easily to hired labor.) We endure such agency problems in other lines of work because the economies of scale and scope and the advantages of visible hand coordination, can compensate for the cost of agency, and then some. In agriculture, however, there are seldom economies of scale beyond what can be achieved on an owner-operated farm. Large agricultural landholdings exist, not for efficiency reasons, but because of inequalities of the distribution of wealth.

The issue of political support for, or at least acquiescence in, development is this: In agrarian societies landowners, whether large or small, are politically powerful. For reasons discussed in Chapter 14, large landowners producing crops for export have a strong interest in keeping both wages and taxes as low as possible: their profit margin is simply the wedge between these basic costs and market prices for their crops. Large landowners will be interested in public investment to the extent that it increases the productivity of large landholdings, and after that their interest in public spending tends to end abruptly. Development requires public investment (which means taxes), and it leads to rising wages. Small landowners may not pose the same obstacle to development policy because they are less powerful than large ones: recall the Taiwanese government's political control of farmers' organizations. At least as important, however, is the fact that small farmers have an interest in economic development that large landowners do not. When most of the labor on a farm is done by the family that owns it, these farmers have no particular interest in keeping wages low; not being wealthy, small farmers tend to support public investment in education, as a way for their children to advance. These differing political inclinations of small and large landowners have been noted in connection with political coalitions in nineteenth century Germany (Gourevitch 1977) as we saw in Chapter 5. In the US, it is reflected in the much higher levels of public investment in education and infrastructure in the Midwestern states (where the federal government had used the Homestead Act to establish family owned and operated farms) compared with the South (where, after the civil war, the plantations once worked by slaves were instead worked either by sharecroppers or by hired labor).

The economic and political advantages of land redistribution have long been well understood. In addition to the South Korean and Taiwanese examples, we can note that land reform was a cornerstone of the Chinese Communists' victory on the mainland, and at the same time a standard policy prescription issued by Washington, DC during the Cold War. Even allowing that, when the large landowners were American corporations, US support for land reform was honored more emphatically in its breach than in its execution – recall, from Chapter 6, Guatemala's fate – this suggests a fairly broad consensus in favor of the approach. And it has been attempted, and remains the law of the land – more on this in a moment – in a great many countries, from Mexico to India. Yet in most places (including those), its success has been patchy.

Evidence for the benefits of equitable land distribution continues to accumulate. Land reform in India, after independence in 1949, was made a matter for its twenty-eight states to decide for themselves. The nature and timing of land reform therefore differed from one part of the country to another, creating a sort of natural experiment. In general, the Indian states did not redistribute land in the way South Korea or Taiwan did, but many took steps to make tenancies more secure, or to outlaw the activity of intermediaries acting on behalf of absentee landlords. Tim Besley and Robin Burgess (2000) find that even such modest measures reduced poverty by as much as would have been achieved with a 10 per cent increase in GDP per capita. That would be impressive even if a more equal distribution did not improve agricultural productivity or economic growth, but there is reason to believe that it does both: see Dietrich Vollrath (2007) on productivity, and Alberto Alesina and Dani Rodrik (1994) on economic growth. Vollrath and Lennart Erickson (2006) find that reduced land inequality of land ownership is associated with better development of a country's financial system.

14.4.1.3. Political and institutional obstacles, again

If the equitable distribution of land is such a wonderful idea, why doesn't it happen more often? Let us try to understand the political and institutional obstacles.

The first obstacle is that large landowners are likely to oppose land redistribution, and to have the political muscle to block it. This is a fairly common outcome. In countries such as Pakistan and the Philippines, the political power of agricultural landlords is immense. In many parts of the world, large landowners remain a deeply conservative force in much of the countryside, opposing anything that would empower the poor, with every instrument at their disposal, including armed force.

Assuming that this first obstacle can be overcome, there remain two obstacles to the continued success of the program. The first of these is that, while owner-operated farms have the potential to be more efficient, this outcome is not automatic. Former farm laborers or tenants may lack the education and technical knowledge necessary to make the best use of their land. The systems for supplying inputs or marketing produce may not be geared to the needs of small farmers, or may be controlled by monopolists. The small farmers may also lack access to credit. The second is that, between the uncertainties involved in farming – weather and prices both are unpredictable – and the limited financial resources of most small farmers, it is easy for an equitable distribution of land to decay: some farmers get into debt, and eventually lose their farms, while others accumulate large holdings again. Even if the indebted farmers do manage to keep title to their land, what they once paid in rents may now be going in interest to extortionate creditors. All of these problems can be overcome, but doing so requires an institutional framework for education, technical support, finance, marketing, and supply. Some parts of this framework may be provided by the state, others by farmers' cooperatives, and still others by commercial suppliers. All of this is possible; if we are starting from a situation in which the best land is concentrated in a few hands, however, none of it is likely to be in place, and establishing it is not a simple task.

14.4.1.4. Top–down, or bottom–up?

The question, then, is not whether land redistribution can reduce poverty and increase economic growth, but how it can get such a program past the political power of the landlords in the first place, and then how to preserve it. South Korea and Taiwan are among the rare twentieth century land reforms that were decisively successful, and we see in both cases a vital role for the relative autonomy of the state. It would be a mistake, however, to think of these cases as arguments for the imposition of land reform from above by an authoritarian government. To begin with, it oversimplifies what happened to the Tigers. Gi-Wook Shin (1998) argues that the ground for the Korean land reform was prepared by the growing organization and militancy of tenant farmers (peasants) during the Japanese occupation. Shin's analysis follows in the tradition "agrarian conflict theory." This is the tradition of Barrington Moore (1966) who traced the role of conflict between lord and peasant in facilitating the shift of both labor and capital from agriculture to industry. Dreze and Sen paint a similar picture, albeit in less adversarial language: the success of initiatives to improve the lot of the rural poor depends on their political and social participation – which, they note, is often blocked by powerful landowners. So, while the state's ability to resist the influence of landowners is important, we should not imagine that this happens in a vacuum. Evans and Kohli, in their different ways, emphasize the mutual dependence of the developmental state in the capitalist elite. Yet, early in the process of industrialization, the capitalist elite is weak and most people depend on agriculture. The role of small farmers in a developmental coalition has been alluded to above. Even Taiwan, where the outcomes of World War II and the Chinese civil war had left the government with an unusually high degree of autonomy and the framework for development was established in a top–down manner, the state used land reform to establish an important political base in the countryside. But, for reasons previously discussed, trusting economic development to an autocratic state is like trusting your fortune to a lottery ticket: you can win big, but you are more likely to lose.

14.4.2. ARE RESOURCES A CURSE?

Nigeria earns huge revenues from its oil, yet its people remain poor. The Tigers of East Asia have scant natural resource endowments, yet they have become rich. Can we generalize from this experience?

There is a school of thought that says we can. Jeffery Sachs and Andrew Warner (2001) argue that countries with high initial exports of natural resources also tend to have lower rates of growth in industrial exports. In a simple univariate regression, primary sector exports as a proportion of GDP in 1970 account for 26 per cent of the international variation in the *growth* of manufacturing exports from 1970 to 1989. More complex models, controlling for initial per capita income, openness to trade, and other factors, and using overall economic growth as the dependent variable, continue to find a large negative effect from a high initial dependence on natural resource exports.

Yet if this is so today, it is clear that it has not always been the case. Britain's industrial revolution was fuelled by British coal; the US, Canada, and Australia are all big natural resource producers, and were big exporters of raw materials before they were exporters of manufactures.

Even as a generalization about recent times, the sweeping resource curse hypothesis of Sachs and Warner does not withstand scrutiny. Sachs and Warner treat dependence on resource exports as a measure of "resource abundance." Gavin Wright and Jesse Czelusta (2004) point out that it is really a measure of comparative advantage: Somalia exports cattle, not because it has abundant well-watered pastures, but because it produces little else that can be sold. In one study, the resource curse vanishes when resource abundance is defined in terms of the value of reserves or resource exports per worker, rather than resource exports as a proportion of GDP (Maloney 2002). Another study explores the possibility that the slow growth of primary sector exporters during the 1970–89 period was due to the cost of a heavy debt overhang, the result of loans taken out during the commodity price booms of the 1970s; again, when this is taken into account, the effect of resources on growth goes away (Manzano and Rigobon 2001).

Yet, even if these resource curse skeptics are correct, what they show is that resource abundance has no effect on growth. Many had expected countries generously endowed with oil or some other resource to grow *faster*. These optimists included both Walt Rostow (1961) in the 1960s, and proponents of the neoliberal WC in the 1980s (Balassa 1980; Krueger 1980). There seemed to be good reasons for this optimism. A windfall from, say, oil, can provide capital for development, a "big push" that catapults a poor country into the global middle class; rather than specializing in simply selling its resources, the country can build up the specialized services, technologies, and manufactured inputs required for resource extraction and processing.

Sachs and Warner (1999), and Francisco Rodriguez and Sachs (1999) see the big push as self-defeating. Prices rise, and the country adopts over-ambitious spending habits, oblivious to the fact that ore and oil – extractive resources – are exhaustible, that the supply will diminish and the cost of extraction will rise. Paul David and Gavin Wright (1997), and Wright and Czelusta (2004) argue that such arguments are based on a faulty understanding of natural resource industries. Supplies of ore and oil diminish, they say, only if technology and geological knowledge don't progress. In the early twentieth century, the US became the world's leading producer, and exporter, of copper, despite the fact that its copper ore was inferior to that of Chile. The same applied to many other minerals. This happened, in their estimation, both because the US made mining rights available to big mining companies (often not as a result of stated policies, but of clearly corrupt deals); because of the US Geological Survey, a government agency dedicated to mapping geological formations and mineral resources throughout the country, and to making this information available to the public; and because many of the country's major research universities took to training mining engineers and to researching both mining technology and geology. Similar stories about the development of technical competencies in resource extraction can be told about Australia, Norway, Venezuela, and South Africa, among others. Mines and oil wells are not simple holes in the ground, but technically sophisticated operations. The technical competencies that extend the life of "exhaustible" resources become a product themselves. We still associate Texas with oil, although it is now only a minor oil producer, because it is a big exporter of oil exploration and production equipment, oil field services, and petroleum-related financing.

It is clear, then, that abundant natural resources are not necessarily a brake on the growth of per capita income, or even on the growth of technologically dynamic manufacturing and services. At the same time, it is undeniable that many countries that have stumbled on huge resource windfalls are no better – and perhaps worse – off than they would have been without them; Nigeria, Angola, and Congo are clear cases of this. Moreover, as we study the political economy of these resource-rich but nonetheless poor countries, we can see pathologies that are present even in much richer resource exporters, such as Saudi Arabia and Russia.

How can a resource endowment hinder growth? Albert Hirschman (1958) argued that natural resource industries tend to be enclave activities, with weak backward (upstream) and forward (downstream) linkages. Inputs other than labor are often sophisticated capital goods, which are imported. Processing raw materials before exporting them is often discouraged by the structure of tariffs in importing countries, which protect industries by charging lower tariffs on raw materials than on processed ones. In today's terms, that makes mines and oil wells a lot like low-skill assembly operations: it's easy to get that part of the business, but once you have it, how do you build your technological and organizational capabilities, and gain control of more of the value chain?

Then we have the "Dutch disease" – named for the slow growth and high unemployment experienced by the Netherlands in the late 1970s and early 1980s, just after it began exploiting natural gas fields in the North Sea. The standard explanation for the Dutch disease is that a high exchange rate, brought about by the sudden addition of natural gas to the Netherlands' other exports, raised the prices of its other exports and hurt sales. Since the marginal cost of extracting additional natural gas was very low, gas production and exports were unaffected by the change in exchange rates, while other exports – manufactures, services, and foodstuffs – were hurt (Bruno and Sachs 1982; Corden and Neary 1982). In this way a natural resource boom can kill growth in other industries, rather than kick-starting it as the optimists had anticipated. When Norway began exploiting North Sea oil, it dealt with this problem by setting aside much of the oil revenue in a public trust fund invested in foreign assets, as well as systematically developing its technical capacities in offshore oil exploration and production.

14.4.2.1. The political economy of oil wells

While both the enclave economy and the Dutch disease are problems, they are fairly well understood, and it is not clear why they should lead to the wide range of outcomes – compare Australia and Nigeria – that we observe in resource rich countries. To understand this, we must turn, again, to our old friends, institutions, and rent-seeking.

Consider oil, and ignore for the moment both the technological dynamism of the oil industry and the fact that we will eventually burn it all up if we don't cook the planet first. Consider a country with a large, high quality (which is to say, cheaply extracted) reserve of oil. Once the oil has been discovered, the difference between the (rather small) marginal cost of pumping the oil out of the ground and its market price is pure rent. It is easy for the politics and business of the whole nation to become organized around the question of who gets how much of that rent.

Occasionally, we read of some poor people in Nigeria dying in an explosion or fire, along an oil pipeline they were tapping into. We can read this as a particular tragedy of some citizens of an oil-rich country who are nonetheless so poor that they risk their lives draining cans of oil from a hole in a pipe. We can also read it as a metaphor for the entire economy of that country: everybody is working to tap into that pipe somehow. In villages in the Niger delta, where most of the oil is produced, oil companies pay young men *not* to tap or sabotage the pipelines – their implicit *opportunity* to tap into the pipe becomes the source of a no-show job. The generals at the top of the government have often tapped in for billions, which find their way to Swiss banks. The country's best entrepreneurial energies are directed to getting a share of the oil revenue.

Income from rent generates a different set of ethics, different codes of social behavior, than other kinds of market income. Within limits, the division of revenues from an oil well does not affect the output. In the short run, it is a zero-sum game: there is a fixed pie to be divided, so one person's gain must be another person's loss. Contrast this with other situations we have considered in previous chapters, where cooperation or market exchange offers the possibility of mutual gains, of win-win solutions. Not surprisingly, greater dependence on resources is associated with greater corruption (Leite and Weidmann 1999).

Win–win scenarios for oil-rich countries do exist. If only nobody stole the money, and it was wisely invested, the country as a whole could be better off in the long run. Individual decision makers, however, will be better off if they can take the money now. Without sufficiently strong institutions, the win–win outcomes are unlikely, and the zero-sum short run dominates decisions. If we want to understand the difference between the Norwegian experience and that of less fortunate oil-exporting countries, we need only to observe that before it had oil, Norway already had very strong, CME-type institutions, within which it was possible to establish an intergenerational bargain about the use of the windfall. Few countries' institutions are that strong.

The political economy of oil wells helps us understand the different trajectories of China and the former Soviet Union. The opportunity to profit from natural resource rents in the Soviet Union helps explain why the Soviet institutions broke, while those in China bent and adapted. In the 1980s, these two Communist giants both faced up to the fact that their centrally planned economies were inefficient and very slow to incorporate new technologies. The Soviet Union was by far the richer and more industrial of the two, but the process of reform saw its industry collapse; China's industry boomed, and it has never looked back. A key reason for this difference is that while the Soviet Union was an industrial country, its great wealth was in mineral resources, particularly oil and gas. Mikhail Gorbachov sought to reform the old system, but its institutions had grown weak and its future was uncertain; under those circumstances, many well-connected members of the elite reckoned they had better prospects supporting the abrupt privatization of state assets. In this process, well-connected individuals became billionaires overnight by gaining control of oil, gas, aluminium, and so forth. Since then, Russian politics and business both have focused more on fighting for control of these assets than on creating new wealth. In China, without such mineral wealth, the elite saw its interests to be in keeping the Communist party in power while fostering the growth of competitive markets and manufacturing.

Just as the opportunities provided by natural resource rents can break institutions, institutions designed to facilitate the appropriation of natural resource rents can be a barrier to the development of other lines of business. Recall Acemoglu et al.'s (2001) argument that colonial institutions designed to facilitate simple resource extraction have left behind, many decades and sometimes centuries later, a business environment not conducive to investment.

Mick Moore (2004) offers a somewhat different way of understanding this situation based on Joseph Schumpeter's concept of fiscal sociology. Governing, in this view, cannot be separated from taxation. The state serves society as part of a bargain with taxpayers, who expect something from the government in return for their taxes. The early modern British state had a famously effective revenue system (see Brewer 1990; and Macdonald 2003); it also delivered the goods to the landowners and merchants who paid the taxes, by creating business opportunities at home and (via empire and control of the seas) abroad. Contemporary developmental states deliver goods to their taxpayers in the form of education, infrastructure, research, and export promotion. All of this service provision is hard work for the state, but necessary both as part of the political bargain under which taxes are collected, and to maintain and develop the economy on which tax revenues are based. In an economy where the revenues come out of a few oil wells, the state can continue operating without delivering the governmental goods.

14.4.3. EMPIRE'S NEW CLOTHES?

So far in this chapter, I have treated problems of development mostly as a domestic problem within each country. Developing countries, however, obviously do not develop in isolation. Most of the economics professionals would not blame the rich countries for the plight of the poor ones, but many of them are quite happy (as we have seen above) to pin responsibility on colonial administration a hundred years ago or more. In the heyday of the WC, many more were happy to design experiments in neoliberal economic management, carried out by poor countries under duress. There is little question that the gradual negotiated reduction of trade barriers since World War II has not taken a fair path toward freer trade, but instead has often favored the rich countries, protecting those industries most vulnerable to less developed country (LDC) competition – various categories of manufactured goods such as textiles and steel and, in particular, agriculture. Things change, but do they change for the better? It remains to be seen whether upgrading to higher value-added processes is more or less difficult in the new international division of labor – with highly modular production and easy entry to low-wage manufacturing – than it was in the old. The WTO's intellectual property regime,

TRIPS, can be seen as encouraging the dissemination of ideas and technology, or as cementing rich country control of rents from software, pharmaceuticals, and seeds. All of these issues are well understood; some have been addressed in previous chapters, others will have to wait for another occasion.

In keeping with this chapter's focus on institutions and the appropriation of rents, however, there is an issue that needs to be addressed. This is the hazard of treating a country as having a unified interest, a single identity, when dealing with the rest of the world. When officials in Nigeria skim off rents from oil concessions, or landlords in the Philippines favor governments that keep wages and taxes low at the expense of services and infrastructure, or the owners of garment factories in Honduras depend on low wages as a source of comparative advantage, we cannot understand the situation without understanding two facts about the country's relationship with the rest of the world. One is how the interests of that country's elite have been shaped by the overwhelming importance of export markets and the relative underdevelopment of domestic markets, for their products. The other is the role of the international banking system in sustaining their position.

In the previous chapter, we saw that the Asian Tigers – the great success stories of export-led growth – had the advantage of healthier *domestic* markets for their products than did countries practicing "inward-looking" ISI. This was the result both of the more equal distribution of income and wealth in the Tigers – in part a product of land redistribution, in part a product of investment in education – and also in the types of products they produced. In this regard, South Korea and Taiwan were following the same path as today's rich countries, which were always significant consumers of their own products in the course of their industrialization. When the income of a country's elite depends neither on domestic demand nor on a large pool of skilled domestic workers, then the interests of the elite become divorced from those of their compatriots. This is not to say that their interests would ever be identical – there are always conflicts over who gets what – but that the divorce eliminates the basis for a constructive resolution of those conflicts.

Some attribute the problems of the poorest countries to official corruption. Official corruption is certainly a problem, but it is easy to exaggerate its importance. There is plenty of corruption in many countries that are rich, and also in those that are growing fast. In the richest country, the US, the bulk of official corruption is not even regarded as such; it takes the form of campaign contributions which have no other purpose but to win legislation or regulations favorable to a particular company, industry, or professional group. Corruption does not stop a country in its tracks.

In some countries, however, the personal appropriation of funds becomes the principal business of government. Kohli (2004) calls this the "neo-patrimonial state," meaning that the rulers treat the state as if it were their patrimony, their personal inheritance. Others have called them "kleptocracies" – countries governed by thieves. These are usually LDCs that are resource rich, and the domestic politics of these countries is as discussed above. But consider the international aspect of it. Mobuto

Sese Seko, who ruled Congo (which he renamed Zaire) from 1960 to 1997, took billions from that poor country's revenues (mostly mining and forestry, some plantation crops – all simple resource extraction) as his personal fortune. It was too much to spend – where did he put it? Not under his mattress. Certainly not in a bank in Zaire. Some of it went into real estate in France. Some of it found its way, as such money usually does, to banks abroad. You cannot steal billions without the use of the international banking system. That banking system is concentrated in two kinds of places: the financial centers in certain rich countries – New York, London, Frankfurt, Zurich, Tokyo – and "offshore" locations. The latter are most often in small island countries – hence the name – or mini-states in Europe (Lichtenstein, Monaco). There is, however, a close dependence between the larger rich countries and the offshore centres, in three respects. The first is that most of the offshore centres are politically dependent on a larger rich country: crown dependencies of the UK; overseas territories of the US; countries such as Panama, over which the US has occasionally asserted political or military control; mini-states in Europe that enjoy most of the benefits of location within the European Union without any of the responsibilities. The second is that the offshore banks are often closely linked to those onshore: money deposited in secretive tax havens of the Channel Islands or the Isle of Mann is managed by banks in London. The third is that the offshore banks are used by companies and wealthy individuals in the rich countries, usually for the purpose of avoiding taxes. All of these connections give the offshore banks political protection, without which they would not be regarded as safe places to keep money.

Banks, of course, like the business brought to them by the elites of neo-patrimonial states. The political shield which makes it possible for banks to keep taking this business, however, is that the same willingness to keep secrets and to not ask questions in the first place, also benefits wealthy individuals, corporations, and banks in rich countries. By providing this shield, the governments of rich countries make a large contribution to kleptocracy in a number of poor countries.

Part IV
Prospect

15 The Future: Regional Rivalries, Environmental Limits, and the Likely Retreat of the Global Corporation

I have tried, in this book, to share with you an understanding of the world in which we make our livings. It is a short and foolish step from thinking that you understand something to trying to predict its future. Will both coordinated and liberal market economies survive in a world of global competition, or will they converge to a single model? Will the newly industrialized countries (NICs) overcome their dependence on low-wage assembly and high levels of inequality, and join the ranks of the world's rich countries? I don't know the answers to such questions, and I don't believe that anybody does.

In studying the international business system, however, we frequently encounter an implicit prediction. That prediction is often found couched in such phrases as "the forces of globalization." When the various aspects of international economic integration are regarded as a single package called globalization, use of that term often entails a tacit assumption that the phenomena it encompasses will all continue unabated. Specifically, that would mean that the trend toward ever more widely dispersed value chains and ever more globalized and powerful MNCs will continue; and that this will happen because both natural and political barriers to international trade, international investment, and other aspects of the operation of MNCs on a global stage will continue to fall.

It is possible that this will happen, but I think that the stronger likelihood is that it will not, and that a more localized economy, regulated at the level of mega-regions, will emerge instead. There are four reasons for believing this. The first, and simplest, is that much of what we think of as "global" is regional already. We often think in just two levels, the national economy and the international, and when we think that way, "international" easily becomes "global." But, as we have seen, a disproportionate share of the growth of international economic activity has actually taken place within well-defined mega-regions: regional blocs such as the EU, and also regions without blocs but with particularly intense international economic activity such as Northeast Asia.

In addition, there are three reasons to expect that this pattern of regional concentration will intensify. First, much of the current advantage of intercontinental value chains – what we might call "long-haul" value chains – and of MNCs with *global* aspirations will vanish if a substantial proportion of the newly industrializing world manages to upgrade its position in the global division of labor. Second, the political and economic logic favors the strengthening of mega-regional blocs. Third, rising incomes in LDCs, together with the need to reduce greenhouse gas (GHG) emissions, will probably combine to raise fuel prices for aviation and shipping, and that would raise the relative costs of long-haul value chains and global business operations. None of these outcomes is certain, but all are likely. Let us consider each of these in turn.

15.1. Upgrading, diversification, and absorptive capacity

As we have seen in earlier chapters, many countries in the world now specialize in the ill-paid assembly of imported parts. We can safely say that most people in these countries would be happy to follow the path of Taiwan and South Korea, upgrading from low-wage assembly to higher paid, higher-skill parts of the value chain. Even if countries such as China and India do manage to grasp the higher rungs of the ladder, they will still have their feet in assembly operations: somebody will have to do that work, and if the countries doing it today were taken out of the picture not much of the world would be left. Successful upgrading in the future, then, is likely to be accompanied by some degree of increased co-location of different stages of production.

Moreover, upgrading implies an increase in the absorptive capacity of a country's companies and research institutions. Much of what MNCs do can be described as managing knowledge between countries and over long distances: the know-how of organization, of production, and of technology integration, and the protection of the intellectual property associated with all of these. When a country's own companies and institutions have sufficient absorptive capacity, their relationship to these processes changes. The companies have the option of turning much of that knowledge into a commodity that can be licensed, and bought and sold, between countries. There is no reason to expect that this would entirely displace MNC activity; indeed, as a country develops its own science and technology base, MNCs are drawn to take advantage of that. But the *option* of making knowledge a commodity is an important consideration in the following sections, as we consider both the politics of regionalization and the rising costs of global operations.

15.2. **The economic and political logic of regions**

When we speak of lowering trade barriers, opening national economies to international competition, and liberalization of international financial markets, are we talking about the creation of a completely free, unregulated market?

If we are, we're fooling ourselves. Markets are always regulated. Today, as throughout the twentieth century, most market regulation takes place at the level of the nation-state: macroeconomic stabilization, banking supervision, consumer and workplace health and safety protection, the legal framework for employment relations and trade unions, various forms of social insurance, environmental regulation, competition policy, and so on. The nation-state is the unit of regulation in large part because it is the unit that defines the barrier-free market. Markets and regulation go hand in hand.

Karl Polanyi (1957) described the development of markets and regulation as a sort of a seesaw process: markets reach into more and more areas of our lives; this creates instability (mass unemployment, financial panics, inflation) and society responds by creating new institutions to control the market. This doesn't happen just once – both the extension of the market and the evolution of regulation are ongoing. Polanyi's account is mostly about developments *within* nation-states, but the same logic applies to the spread of markets between them. Liberalization is the simple part; building institutions to deal with the consequences is the hard part.

Today's trade is not just about an exchange of goods between countries: the growth of trade today is in the growth of cross-border production networks, which means that trade is coupled with the movement of capital and of people. So, lowering barriers to trade between two countries today can mean creating very deep connections between their economies, and that raises demand for regulation.

Some of the demand for regulation is met at the global level. We have the WTO for agreeing and enforcing global rules about trade, intellectual property rights, and investment. The IMF, the Bank of International Settlements, and consultations among the finance ministers of leading countries, together provide a system for ensuring financial stability. In addition, there is a large body of treaties on a wide range of issues, from the law of the sea to restrictions on landmines; for the most part, however, these treaties lack any serious enforcement mechanism and depend on voluntary compliance by national governments. Altogether, this global regulatory framework is minimalist.

Will the demand for market regulation be met by global institutions? Some have seen signs of this. Deborah Cass (2001), for instance, argues that the way in which the WTO's appeals panel has handled a number of trade disputes has contributed to a process of "constitutionalization," the gradual transformation of voluntary agreements into a body of substantive and procedural law that will become binding on the parties. This may be so, but by even the most generous interpretation it is quite feeble compared with the process of constitutionalization that is occurring within the EU.

While we should not expect any other regional trade bloc to become as closely integrated as the EU in the near future, there is good reason to expect that the institutions of economic regulation will develop more on the mega-regional scale than on the global scale. The large number of sovereign states involved in any global agreement means that it is usually more difficult to arrive at an agreement, whether on objectives, or rules, enforcement mechanisms. There are problems of accountability: to whom does a global institution answer? Is it answerable to the 195 sovereign states or do a few big states dominate the process?

Mega-regional governance is not easy, but it is generally easier than global governance. Moreover, for most of the tricky problems of regulating a market economy, it is enough. Most of the functions of most production networks occur within a single mega-region just as most of the functions of most production systems occurred within a single nation-state fifty years ago. This is true even where the mega-region is not defined by a bloc (as in Northeast Asia), meaning that transportation and communications considerations were the only constraints on the production networks.

Consider that in most industries, regional production networks are a phenomenon of the past few decades; the process of integrating markets within regions is ongoing and far from complete. Where blocs do exist, the accretion of regulatory responsibilities by the blocs and the continuing integration of production in regions run in parallel and reinforce each other. The combination of political and economic integration will raise the likelihood that these blocs will act in a protectionist manner.

It is useful, in thinking about blocs, to remember that China and India could each be regarded as a mega-regional bloc on its own. Not only does each have a population larger than any of the (international) mega-regional trade blocs, but both have been undergoing internal processes of market integration that parallel the processes of breaking down trade barriers within international blocs. In both countries, improved internal transport and communications infrastructures have contributed to this. In China's case, the change has been bigger because it had further to go: the central government has struggled to create a single market by requiring provinces and other subnational units of government to allow competition in markets that had been the preserve of provincial or local state monopolies. China's government used the WTO accession process as a lever to force through aspects of this internal liberalization, making "concessions" that were clearly unnecessary (Branstetter and Lardy 2008): the negotiations looked like globalization at work, but deeper regionalization was the result. China, of course, is itself part of the larger Northeast Asian mega-region, which is not defined by a bloc.

China, India, and the EU between them account for 45 per cent of the world's population. The prospects for the development of other blocs with even quasi-governmental characteristics are decidedly mixed. We can, however, expect both the production networks and the blocs' regulatory functions to strengthen.

15.3. **Economic growth, global warming, and energy prices**

For reasons detailed in Chapter 2, managing production networks over distances requires speed not only in communication, but also in the transport of goods and people. Production networks are built on timely delivery of components and face-to-face meetings. It is likely that in the next few years rising fuel prices will raise the costs both of high-speed transport of goods and air travel by people. This would raise costs for far-flung supply chains and travel-intensive business organization, relative to more localized, transport-stingy production systems.

Rising energy costs will affect all aspects of our lives. The situation with long-distance transportation is unusual, however, in the lack of alternatives to fossil fuels. Aviation and ocean shipping are powered entirely by fossil fuels, and there are no promising substitutes on the horizon; the prospects for large increases in efficiency are similarly dim.

Fuel costs have risen in recent years because demand has been rising, largely as a result of economic growth in NICs. If economic growth continues, demand will continue to grow as well. Higher prices will encourage some conservation, but not enough to offset the effects of growth: this is the straightforward logic of supply and demand.

Rising consumption has two effects on the supply of oil or any mineral resource: it drains the known reserves, but higher prices provide an incentive for exploration and for the improvement of exploration, drilling, and processing technology. It is possible that this effect will lower production costs and increase supplies so much that growth would not push up prices, but this is unlikely. For years now, the growth of oil reserves has been slower than the growth of consumption despite high and rising prices.

However high energy prices are driven by increasing demand, they are likely to be driven still higher by some system of carbon pricing.

This is not the place for a technical discussion on climate change, or for an assessment of the plausible range of consequences of such a change. If you think that there is some doubt as to whether the phenomenon is real, that human activity plays a big part in it, or that the consequences for humanity could well be quite serious, then I respectfully suggest that you've been listening to industry-funded propaganda and manufactured "controversy" rather than science (Oreskes 2004; Oreskes et al. 2008). What I am interested in here is the effect of GHG reduction policies on the structure of the international business system. I will take as given the following: keeping climate change to a manageable and safe level will require, among other steps, a substantial reduction in the release of carbon dioxide and other GHGs into the atmosphere; with current technologies, this cannot be done without reducing the consumption of fossil fuels; even if carbon capture technologies were to be developed, it would remain to be seen whether they were practicable for moving vessels such as ships and (especially) planes; to bring about a substantial reduction in fossil fuel consumption in these modes of transport, it would be necessary to adopt some sort of carbon pricing system. Carbon pricing could be implemented through taxation, cap-and-trade, or the auction of carbon rights – there are considerable practical differences between these approaches, but for the purposes of this discussion those differences don't matter.

In his report to the UK Treasury, the World Bank's former chief economist Nicholas Stern recommended that carbon dioxide emissions be taxed at a rate of US\$77 per ton (Stern 2007). That would make it more costly to generate electricity with coal or oil than with nuclear or wind, and so would lead to a swift reduction in GHG emissions in that sector. It would have only a marginal effect on emissions from aviation, ocean shipping, and trucking, however, because alternative technologies are not currently available. A more recent report by the International Energy Agency (2008) has concluded that, for this reason, with CO_2 priced at US\$77 per ton, reduction in GHG emissions would not be sufficient to meet the 450 ppm target recommended by the Intergovernmental Panel on Climate Change; they recommend a taxation rate of US\$200 instead.

Such a taxation rate would add something over US\$500 to the cost of a round trip (economy) between San Francisco and Taipei, which would raise costs for the employers of Taiwan's "astronauts." More generally, a stiff tax on carbon is a tax on *speed*. Weber and Matthews (2008) estimate that the carbon dioxide cost of shipping a ton by air is over forty-eight times that of shipping it by ocean container (Table 15.1). (Their estimate of CO_2 equivalents for air travel includes the warming effect of high altitude water vapor emissions, omitted from some studies.) Yet ocean shipping, despite its apparent efficiency per ton kilometer, is also coming to be seen as a problem because of the huge and growing volumes that are shipped very large distances, and also because increasing speeds are raising fuel consumption; it now produces about 5 per cent of global CO_2 emissions. The problem of reducing GHGs from shipping is summarized in

Table 15.1. Greenhouse gasses from different forms of freight transport

Mode	Tons CO_2 equivalent per million ton kilometers
Inland water	21
Rail	18
Truck	180
Air	680
Ocean container	14
Ocean bulk	11
Ocean tanker	17

Source: Weber and Matthews (2008).

a study for the International Maritime Organization by Roar Frode Henningsen (2000), who finds that reducing a ship's speed by 10 per cent brings about a 23 per cent reduction in CO_2; reviewing the technologies in prospect, he finds that reductions in speed are likely to be the most viable means of achieving such reductions for years to come. Yet, "The main innovation in ship design during the recent years has been towards increased ship size and increased transportation speed." In early 2008, shipping companies were reported to be reducing speeds in response to higher fuel costs; airline schedules were being cut back for the same reason (BBC 2008; Kirschbaum 2008).

It is possible, of course, that there will be unexpected technological breakthroughs that sharply reduce the carbon cost of high-speed, long-distance transport; it is also possible that carbon pricing will be applied in an uneven manner, focusing on other sources and continuing the special treatment historically accorded to shipping and aviation fuel; and, finally, it is possible that no effective action will be taken to control GHGs. In any of these circumstances, relatively cheap international transport would continue.

The most likely scenario, however, is that the price of fuel will keep going up, due both to rising demand and to carbon pricing. That means that either the price of transport goes up or that the vessels slow down. Either of those options would have a big effect on supply chains, corporations, and business alliances that are closely coordinated and also operate over great distances. The relative gainers would be more localized production systems and old-fashioned trade in raw materials, finished products, and technology licenses.

15.4. **Upgrading, regionalism, and high energy prices: Completing the picture**

The present system of international business was formed in circumstances that can be described as follows: numerous countries with little recent history of internationally competitive industry were industrializing rapidly – not least, China and India; national markets were being opened, creating opportunities for the growth of international production systems and markets, both mega-regional and global; and, a failure to internalize the environmental costs of transport had produced a regime of unsustainably low prices and high speeds for transport. All of these circumstances – the blossoming of the NIDL, the internationalization of production and markets, and the underpricing of transportation – have favored relatively long-distance supply chains and the aspiration of corporations to global status.

Companies and governments of today's NICs will continue to strive to deepen their technological and managerial capabilities. If they succeed in this, they will increase their absorptive capacities for technology and for management and productive methods; this will change the nature of their interaction with MNCs. The governance mechanisms for many of the mega-regional markets will probably continue to develop, and this will make the renewed protection of these markets an increasingly likely option. Higher fuel prices will raise the relative cost of doing business over long distances; it will favor a tilt back toward trade of the old-fashioned type, with more localized production systems and trade in raw materials and complete products.

None of this is certain. Upgrading within the international division of labor is also problematic for reasons that have been made clear in previous chapters. It does seem likely, however, that China, India, and probably some other countries will move up this ladder, improving their capabilities and at the same time strengthening their domestic markets. The politics of regional consolidation are also problematic. Finally, while some sort of carbon pricing – whether taxation or cap-and-trade – is probably a necessary part of an effective effort to control GHG emissions, there are many uncertainties between that statement and the reality of carbon pricing scheme that actually alters the cost calculations of international business. On balance, however, my best guess is that in twenty years we will be in a regionalized world, looking back at today as the golden age of the global corporation and international production.

NOTES

1 This account is taken from (Pomeranz 2000, especially pp. 159–62, 189–91). Pomeranz, in turn, gets his information on the silver trade from Frank (1998), Flynn and Giraldez (1996), and Von Glahn (1996).

2 Again, the account here follows Pomeranz, *op cit*. A good standard account of the first industrial revolution in Britain can be obtained from Landes (1969, pp. 1–123).

3 Paul Samuelson and Ronald Jones each developed a different version of this model, long after both David Ricardo and Jacob Viner were dead. Ricardo appears in the name because, in his theory, there were three factors of production: land, labor, and capital.

4 In technical economics, "economies of scale" has a narrower definition. In that context, an increase in scale means a proportional increase in *all* inputs. So it means a larger factory (more capital), but assumes a proportional increase in labor. If a 10 per cent (say) increase in all inputs results in more than a 10 per cent rise in output, we have economies of scale. The more casual definition I have used differs from this in two ways. One is that it isn't bothered about the mix of inputs: the larger factory may be more (or less) capital intensive. The other is that it measures inputs in terms of money – as costs, not as physical inputs; by keeping input proportions constant, the technical definition makes it possible to talk about rising or falling costs without making any assumptions about input prices. These differences don't matter in most contexts.

5 A good account of the Soviet economy up to the 1960s is Nove (1969). A good recent biography of Stalin is Service (2004). The weakness of the Soviet system in turning science into technology and technology into useful products or processes has been addressed by several authors in ways relevant to themes developed elsewhere in this book: Graham (1993) is a brief and incisive analysis of what was wrong with the Soviet science and engineering systems, despite heavy spending in these areas and very large number of trained scientists and engineers; Freeman (1995) compares the Soviet innovation system with that of Japan, a country that was spending a similar amount but with more success; Castells (2000) has an excellent chapter on the Soviet Union, interpreting its collapse in terms of its inability to keep up in the information age; Weitzman (1970) is an early demonstration that Soviet growth was driven by increased resource and labor inputs, not by innovation.

6 Good summaries on the interwar economies of the industrial economies include Frieden (2006: pp. 127–250) and Findlay and O'Rourke (2007: pp. 429–72). For more detailed analysis, see Galbraith (1954); Polanyi (1957, pp. 201–58); Kindleberger (1973); and Temin (1976).

7 Note, though, that "Fordism" has sometimes been used to mean, not a system for regulating a mass production economy, but mass production itself – see Edward Filene (1925).

8 David Fairris (1997) addresses similar issues in his study of the rise and decline of union power in the US. Kelly sees the coming and going of union power as a long wave process; Fairris doesn't push that point as hard, but his story is a long wave story (albeit of just one wave – Fairris is not asking us to believe that history comes in fifty-year segments). Both provide explanations for long waves in industrial relations which do not seem to rely on the existence of the Kondratief waves or techno-economic paradigms that I discussed in Chapter 7; yet the timing of the waves described by Kelly and Fairris matches the standard (if rather imprecise) Kondratief timing, and their analysis fits easily with the "social structures of accumulation" (SSA) version of long wave theory, discussed later in this chapter.

9 SSA theory has its roots in a Marxian analysis of class conflict, and in particular in Michael Kalecki's (1971) contention that full employment is politically unsustainable in a capitalist economy because it makes workers so powerful. A combination of successful macroeconomic stabilization and demand from the war in Vietnam kept US employment high during the 1960s; according to this theory, profit rates fell in later years of the decade due to a "full employment profit squeeze." One interpretation of efficiency wage models, discussed above in connection with Ford's five dollar day, is that they provide the microeconomic underpinning for Kalecki's theory and SSA theory. See Bowles (1985); Gintis and Ishikawa (1987).

10 Those familiar with Marx's theory of history will notice the influence on these theories of the idea of *modes of production*. A mode of production consists of certain *forces of production* (technology, capital stock) and *social relations of production* (institutions and so forth). The forces of production improve (technological progress, accumulation of capital), and eventually the social relations of production come to hinder further development of the forces of production. This, the theory holds, leads to revolution: the bourgeoisie overthrowing feudalism, for instance (Marx and Engels 1848; Cohen 1978). Douglass North and Robert Thomas (1973), coming from different political and methodological tradition and adding a demographic variable to the mix, propose a similar theory of institutional evolution, though there the selection mechanism is not revolution but competition among states. Among historians today, both classical Marxism and the early New Institutional Economics represented by North and Thomas are regarded as hopelessly mechanistic. Yet, the idea of complementarity of institutions and technologies and methods of production, together with the resistance of institutions to change, is a useful one.

11 See also Sabel and Jonathan Zeitlin (1985). The comparison between SME clusters and Japanese corporate groups is also developed by Michael Best (1990). Some writers define flexible specialization more narrowly, covering only SME networks. See, for instance, Robert Boyer and Benjamin Coriat (1986), Wolfgang Streeck (1991), and the typology of "social systems of production" offered by J. Rogers Hollingsworth and Boyer (1997). The more encompassing use of the term employed in this book is in keeping with that of Piore and Sabel (1984: especially pp. 265–8), and Hirst and Zeitlin (1991).

12 The HRM label can be confusing because most large organizations, regardless of their work practices, have an HR department. HR departments were once called personnel departments, before the idea took hold that they should be facilitating skill development, teamwork, and other features of the approach discussed here. The eternal frustration of the HR profession is that they don't often get to do this. See Guest (1997).

13 Education is not primarily a function of the national (i.e., "federal") government in the US, but of the state and local governments. Educational provision varied widely, with the extreme highs and lows both found in rural areas: it was typically strongest where the farms were owner-operated, and weakest in the areas where land ownership was concentrated and hired farm labor, tenant farming, or sharecropping predominated. We will see parallels of these outcomes in Chapters 13 and 14, when we consider the role of land reform in the path to industrialization.

14 These models should be distinguished from Penrose's (1959) theory of corporate growth. Penrose argued that a company that is growing develops a *capacity* for growth; that capacity is a sort of non-tradable asset, which is worth something as long as the company grows and worthless otherwise. Growth motivated in the way Penrose describes is not necessarily in conflict with profit maximization, while Baumol and Marris are plainly modeling growth that occurs at the expense of profit.

15 The theory can also be understood in a positive, or predictive, sense: it implies that when the executive's contract is closer to the "efficient" one of the theory, the stock market will value the company's shares more highly. Testing this theory is a major theme in corporate governance research.

16 Both American and Japanese investment and experience in automobiles, and America's in software, are obvious. Japan's software expertise is less well known. Michael Cusumano published a study of the Japanese auto industry (Cusumano 1989), and followed it up with one arguing that Japanese companies were successfully applying the same principles of production organization to software (Cusumano 1991). While the software factories he describes are real, his prediction that this poses a competitive threat to the US has proved unfounded; Cusumano's subsequent work on software has focussed on the US.

17 Milton and Rose Friedman seized on the success of Hong Kong as evidence for the great virtues of the free market (Friedman and Friedman 1980); the late urbanist Jane Jacobs relayed, with approval, the view of an unnamed economist that if Mumbai were independent from India, it would be like Singapore (Jacobs 1984: p. 144). We can enjoy the irony of the libertarian Friedmans' making such an example of a city whose prosperity owed so much to its place as an entrepot for communist China, and also of Jacobs – the most influential exponent of the virtues of "organic" city growth against those of planning – viewing the tightly planned and controlled Singapore as an example of anything good. But for our purposes these examples are less useful simply because in most of the world's cities come with hinterlands attached, and cannot be ordered *á la carte*.

REFERENCES

Acemoglu, Daron, Simon Johnson, and James A. Robinson. 2001. The Colonial Origins of Comparative Development: An Empirical Investigation. *American Economic Review* 91 (5):1369–401.

Adams, Douglas. 1979. *The Hitchhiker's Guide to the Galaxy*. London: Pan.

Aglietta, Michel. 2001. *A Theory of Capitalist Regulation: The US Experience*. Translated by D. Fernbach. London: Verso. Original edn. 1979.

Akerlof, George A. 1970. The Market for "Lemons": Quality Uncertainty and the Market Mechanism. *Quarterly Journal of Economics* 84 (3):488–500.

—— 1982. Labor Contracts as Partial Gift Exchange. *Quarterly Journal of Economics* 97:543–69.

—— and Janet L. Yellen. 1986. *Efficiency Wage Models of the Labor Market*. Cambridge: Cambridge University Press.

Albert, Michel. 1993. *Capitalism Vs Capitalism: How America's Obsession with Individual Achievement and Short-Term Profit Has Led It to the Brink of Collapse*. New York: Four Walls Eight Windows.

Alchian, Armen A. 1950. Uncertainty, Evolution and Economic Theory. *Journal of Political Economy* 57:211–21.

—— 1953. Biological Analogies in the Theory of the Firm: Comment. *American Economic Review* 43 (4, Part 1):600–3.

Alesina, Alberto and Dani Rodrik. 1994. Distributive Policies and Economic Growth. *Quarterly Journal of Economics* 109 (2):465–90.

Amable, Bruno. 2003. *The Diversity of Modern Capitalism*. Oxford: Oxford University Press.

Amsden, Alice H. 1985. The State and Taiwan's Economic Development. In *Bringing the State Back In*, edited by P. B. Evans, D. Rueschemeyer, and T. Skocpol. Cambridge: Cambridge University Press.

—— 1989. *Asia's Next Giant: South Korea and Late Industrialization*. Oxford: Oxford University Press.

—— Jacek Kochanowicz, and Lance Taylor. 1998. *The Market Meets Its Match: Restructuring the Economies of Eastern Europe*. Cambridge, Mass.: Harvard University Press. New edn.

Aoki, Masahiko. 1980. A Model of the Firm as a Stockholder–Employee Cooperative Game. *American Economic Review* 70:600–10.

—— 1984. *The Cooperative Game Theory of the Firm*. Oxford: Oxford University Press.

Appelbaum, Eileen, Thomas Bailey, Peter Berg, and Arne L. Kalleberg. 2000. *Manufacturing Advantage: Why High-Performance Work Systems Pay Off*. Ithaca: ILR Press.

Arita, Tomokazu and Philip McCann. 2000. Industrial Alliances and Firm Location Behaviour: Some Evidence from the US Semiconductor Industry. *Applied Economics* 32:1391–403.

Athreye, Suma and Martha Prevezer. 2007. R&D Offshoring and the Domestic Science Base in India and China. Brunel University: CGR Working Paper No. 26.

Axelrod, Robert. 1984. *The Evolution of Cooperation*. New York: Basic Books.

Bagnasco, A. 1977. *Tre Italie: La Problematica Territoriale Dello Sviluppo Italiano*. Bologna: Il Mulino.

Baier, Scott and Jeffrey Bergstrand. 1998. The Growth of World Trade: Tariffs, Transportation Costs, and Intermediate Goods: University of Notre Dame.

Balassa, B. 1980. The Process of Industrial Development and Alternative Development Strategies. In *Princeton University Essays in International Finance*. Princeton: Princeton University, International Finance Section.

Baumol, William J. 1959. *Business Behavior, Value and Growth*. New York: Harcourt, Brace and World. Revised edn. 1967. BBC. 2008. Airlines Cut Costs as Fuel Rises, June 13.

Becattini, Giacomo. 1979. Dal Settore Industriale Al Distretto Industriale: Alcune Considerazioni Sull'unità Di Indagine Dell'economia Industriale. *Rivista di economia e politica industriale* 1:7–21.

Becker, Gary. 1993. *Human Capital: A Theoretical and Empirical Analysis, with Special Reference to Education*. 3rd edn. Chicago: University of Chicago Press. Original edn. 1964.

Becker, Uwe. 2005. *Employment "Miracles": A Critical Comparison of the Dutch, Scandinavian, Swiss, Australian and Irish Cases Versus Germany and the US*. Amsterdam: Amsterdam University Press.

Beniger, James R. 1986. *The Control Revolution: Technological and Economic Origins of the Information Society*. Cambridge, Mass.: Harvard University Press.

Berle, Adolph A. and Gardiner C. Means. 1967. *The Modern Corporation and Private Property*. New York: Harcourt, Brace Inc. Revised edn. Original edn. 1932.

Besley, Timothy, and Robin Burgess. 2000. Land Reform, Poverty Reduction, and Growth: Evidence from India. *Quarterly Journal of Economics* 115 (2):389–430.

Besley, Timothy, and Masayuki Kudamatsu. 2007. *Making Autocracy Work*. London: London School of Economics.

Best, Michael H. 1990. *The New Competition: Institutions of Industrial Restructuring*. Cambridge, Mass.: Harvard University Press.

—— 2001. *The New Competitive Advantage: The Renewal of American Industry*. Oxford: Oxford University Press.

Bewley, Truman F. 1999. *Why Wages Don't Fall During a Recession*. Cambridge, Mass.: Harvard University Press.

Bhagwati, Jagdish. 2002. *Free Trade Today*. Princeton: Princeton University Press.

Biggart, Nicole Woolsey and Mauro F. Guillén. 1999. Developing Differences: Social Organization and the Rise of the Auto Industries of South Korea, Taiwan, Spain, and Argentina. *American Sociological Review* 64 (5):722–47.

Black, Sandra E. and Lisa M. Lynch. 2001. How to Compete: The Impact of Workplace Practices and Information Technology on Productivity. *Review of Economics and Statistics* 83 (3):434–45.

Blanchflower, David G., and Andrew J. Oswald. 1994. *The Wage Curve*. Cambridge, Mass.: MIT Press.

Bonicelli, E. 1993. La Svedese Tetra Pak Crede Nell'italia E Sposta a Modena Il Centro Di Ricerca. *Il Sole-24 Ore*, June 1, 18.

Bowles, Samuel. 1985. The Production Process in a Competitive Economy: Walrasian, Neo-Hobbesian and Marxian Models. *American Economic Review* 75:16–36.

Boyer, Robert and Benjamin Coriat. 1986. Technical Flexibility and Macro Stabilization. *Ricerche Economiche* 40:771–835.

Braczyk, Hans-Joachim, Philip Cooke, and Martin Heidenreich, eds. 1998. *Regional Innovation Systems*. London: UCL Press.

—— and Martin Heidenreich. 1998. Regional Governance Structures in a Globalized World. In *Regional Innovation Systems*, edited by H. J. Braczyk, P. Cooke, and M. Heidenreich. London: UCL.

Branstetter, Lee and Nicholas Lardy. 2008. *China's Embrace of Globalization*. In *China's Great Economic Transformation*, edited by Loren Brandt and Thomas G. Rawski. Cambridge: Cambridge University Press, pp. 633–82.

Braudel, Fernand. 1981. *The Structures of Everyday Life*. Translated by S. Reynolds. New York: Harper and Row.

Braverman, Harry. 1974. *Labor and Monopoly Capital*. New York: Monthly Review Press.

Bresnahan, Timothy, Alfonso Gambardella, and AnnaLee Saxenian. 2005. "Old Economy" Inputs for "New Economy" Outcomes: Cluster Formation in the New Silicon Valleys. In *Clusters, Networks, and Innovation*, edited by S. Breschi and F. Malerba. Oxford: Oxford University Press.

Brewer, John. 1990. *The Sinews of Power: War, Money and the English State, 1688–1783*. Cambridge, Mass.: Harvard University Press.

Brown, Peter. 1971. *The World of Late Antiquity*. London: Thames and Hudson.

Bruno, M. and Jeffery Sachs. 1982. Energy and Resource Allocation: A Dynamic Model of the "Dutch Disease". *Review of Economic Studies* 44:845–59.

Brusco, Sebastiano. 1982. The Emilian Model – Productive Decentralization and Social Integration. *Cambridge Journal of Economics* 6 (2):167–84.

—— 1990. The Idea of the Industrial District: Its Genesis. In *Industrial Districts and Inter-Firm Cooperation in Italy*, edited by F. Pyke, G. Becattini, and W. Sengenberger. Geneva: International Institute for Labour Studies.

Bruton, Henry J. 1998. A Reconsideration of Import Substitution Industrialization. *Journal of Economic Literature* 36 (2):903–36.

Buckley, Peter J. and Mark C. Casson. 1976. A Long-Run Theory of the Multinatioinal Enterprise. In *The Future of Multinational Enterprise*, edited by P. J. Buckley and M. C. Casson. London: Macmillan.

Calmfors, Lars and John Driffill. 1988. Bargaining Structure, Corporatism, and Macroeconomic Performance. *Economic Policy* 6:12–61.

Cantwell, John. 1989. *Technological Innovation and Multinational Corporations*. Oxford: Basil Blackwell.

—— and Simona Iammarino. 2003. *Multinational Corporations and European Regional Systems of Innovation*. London: Routledge.

Card, David and Alan Krueger. 1994. Minimum Wages and Employment: A Case Study of the Fast Food Industry in New Jersey and Pennsylvania. *American Economic Review* 84:772–93.

Carlsson, Bo and Gunnar Eliasson. 1991. The Nature and Importance of Economic Competence. Case Western Reserve University: mimeo.

Cass, Deborah Z. 2001. The "Constitutionalization" of International Trade Law: Judicial Norm-Generation as the Engine of Constitutional Development in International Trade. *European Journal of International Law* 12 (1):39–75.

Castells, Manuel. 1996. *The Rise of the Network Society, The Information Age: Economy, Society and Culture*. Oxford: Blackwell.

—— 2000. *End of Millenium. The Information Age: Economy, Society and Culture*. Vol. 3. Oxford: Blackwell. 2nd edn.

Chandler, Alfred D. Jr. 1962. *Strategy and Structure: Chapters in the History of the American Industrial Enterprise*. Cambridge, Mass.: MIT Press.

—— 1977. *The Visible Hand: The Managerial Revolution in American Business*. Cambridge, Mass.: Harvard University Press.

Chandler, Alfred D. Jr. 1990. *Scale and Scope: The Dynamics of Industrial Capitalism*. Cambridge, Mass.: Harvard University Press.

Chandler, Alfred D. Jr., and Herman Daems. 1980. *Managerial Hierarchies: Comparative Perspectives on the Rise of Modern Industrial Enterprise*. Cambridge, Mass.: Harvard University Press.

Chang, Ha-Joon. 2002. *Kicking Away the Ladder: Development Strategy in Historical Perspective*. London: Anthem Press.

Clark, Gregory. 1994. Factory Discipline. *Journal of Economic History* 54 (1):128–63.

Coase, R. H. 1937. The Nature of the Firm. *Economica* 4:386–405.

Cohen, G. A. 1978. *Karl Marx's Theory of History: A Defense*. Princeton: Princeton University Press.

Cohen, Wesley M. and Daniel A. Levinthal. 1990. Absorptive Capacity: A New Perspective on Learning and Innovation. *Administrative Science Quarterly* 35:128–52.

Corden, W. and J. Neary. 1982. Booming Sector and De-Industrialisation in a Small Open Economy. *Economic Journal* 92:825–48.

Cortada, James W. 1993. *Before the Computer: IBM, NCR, Burroughs, and Remington Rand and the Industry They Created, 1865–1956*. Princeton: Princeton University Press.

Crouch, Colin, David Finegold, and Mari Sako. 1999. *Are Skills the Answer? The Political Economy of Skill Creation in Advanced Industrial Countries*. Oxford: Oxford University Press.

Culpepper, Pepper. 2001. Employers, Public Policy, and the Politics of Decentralized Cooperation in France and Germany. In *Varieties of Capitalism: The Institutional Foundations of Comparative Advantage*, edited by P. A. Hall and D. Soskice. Oxford: Oxford University Press.

Cumings, Bruce. 1984. The Origins and Development of the Northeast Asian Political Economy: Industrial Sectors, Product Cycles, and Political Consequences. *International Organization* 38 (1):1–40.

Cusumano, Michael A. 1989. *The Japanese Automobile Industry: Technology and Management at Nissan and Toyota*. Cambridge, Mass.: Harvard University Asia Center.

—— 1991. *Japan's Software Factories: A Challenge to US Management*. New York: Oxford University Press.

Cyert, Richard M. and James G. March. 1963. *A Behavioral Theory of the Firm*. Engelwood Cliffs, NJ: Prentice Hall.

David, Paul A. and Gavin Wright. 1997. Increasing Returns and the Genesis of American Resource Abundance. *Industrial and Corporate Change* 6 (2):203–45.

Davis, Mike. 2001. *Late Victorian Holocausts: El Niño Famines and the Making of the Third World*. London: Verso.

Deaton, Angus. 2003. Health, Inequality, and Economic Development. *Journal of Economic Literature* 41 (1):113–58.

Dei Ottati, Gabi. 1994. Trust, Interlinking Transactions, and Credit in Industrial Districts. *Cambridge Journal of Economics* 18:529–46.

—— 2003. Exit, Voice and the Evolution of Industrial Districts: The Case of the Post-World War II Economic Development of Prato. *Cambridge Journal of Economics* 27 (4):501–22.

Delery, John E. and D. Harold Doty. 1996. Modes of Theorizing in Strategic Human Resource Management: Tests of Universalistic, Contingency, and Configurational Performance Predictions. *Academy of Management Journal* 39 (4):802–35.

Dicken, Peter. 2007. *Global Shift: Mapping the Changing Contours of the World Economy*. London: Sage. 5th edn.

DiNardo, John, Nicole M. Fortin, and Thomas Lemieux. 1996. Labor Market Institutions and the Distribution of Wages, 1973–1992: A Semiparametric Approach. *Econometrica* 64 (5):1001–44.

—— and Thomas Lemieux. 1997. Diverging Male Wage Inequality in the United States and Canada, 1981–1988: Do Institutions Explain the Difference? *Industrial and Labor Relations Review* 50 (4):629–51.

Dollar, David. 1992. Outward-Oriented Developing Economies Really Do Grow More Rapidly: Evidence from 95 LDCs, 1976–1985. *Economic Development and Cultural Change* 40:523–44.

Drago, Robert. 1996. Workplace Transformation and the Disposable Workplace: Employee Involvement in Australia. *Industrial Relations* 35 (4):526–43.

Dreze, Jean and Amartya Sen. 1989. *Hunger and Public Action.* Oxford: Oxford University Press.

—— —— 2002. *India: Development and Participation.* Oxford: Oxford University Press. 2nd edn.

Drucker, Peter F. 1976. *The Unseen Revolution: How Pension Fund Socialism Came to America.* New York: Harper & Row.

Dunford, Michael. 2006. Industrial Districts, Magic Circles, and the Restructuring of the Italian Textiles and Clothing Chain. *Economic Geography* 82 (1):27–59.

—— and Grigorio Kafkalas. 1992. The Global–Local Interplay, Corporate Geographies, and Spatial Development Strategies in Europe. In *Cities and Regions in the New Europe: The Global–Local Interplay and Spatial Development Strategies,* edited by M. Dunford and G. Kafkalas. London: Belhaven.

Easterly, William and Ross Levine. 2003. Tropics, Germs, and Crops: How Endowments Influence Economic Development. *Journal of Monetary Economics* 50 (3):3–39.

Edwards, Richard. 1979. *Contested Terrain: The Transformation of the Workplace in the Twentieth Century.* New York: Basic Books.

Eichengreen, Barry. 2007. *The European Economy since World War II.* Princeton: Princeton University Press.

—— and Torben Iversen. 1999. Institutions and Economic Performance in the 20th Century: Evidence from the Labour Market. *Oxford Review of Economic Policy* 15 (4):121–38.

Elbaum, Bernard and William Lazonick. 1986. *The Decline of the British Economy.* Oxford: Oxford University Press.

Esping-Andersen, Gøsta. 1990. *The Three Worlds of Welfare Capitalism.* Princeton: Princeton University Press.

Estevez-Abe, Margarita, Torben Iversen, and David Soskice. 2001. Social Protection and the Formation of Skills: A Reinterpretation of the Welfare State. In *Varieties of Capitalism: The Institutional Foundations of Comparative Advantage,* edited by P. A. Hall and D. Soskice. Oxford: Oxford University Press.

Evans, Peter. 1995. *Embedded Autonomy: States and Industrial Transformation.* Princeton: Princeton University Press.

Evenett, Simon, Simeon Djankov, and Bernard Yeung. 1998. The Willingness to Pay for Tariff Liberalization. University of Michigan: mimeo.

Fairris, David. 1997. *Shopfloor Matters: Labor–Management Relations in Twentieth-Century American Manufacturing.* London: Routledge.

Fama, Eugene F. 1980. Agency Problems and the Theory of the Firm. *Journal of Political Economy* 88 (2):288–307.

Farrell, Henry and Jack Knight. 2003. Trust, Institutions, and Institutional Change: Industrial Districts and the Social Capital Hypothesis. *Politics and Society* 31 (4):537–66.

Filene, Edward A. 1925. *The Way Out: A Forecast of Coming Changes in American Business and Industry.* Garden City, NY: Doubleday, Page.

Findlay, Ronald and Kevin H. O'Rourke. 2007. *Power and Plenty: Trade, War, and the World Economy in the Second Millenium*. Princeton: Princeton University Press.

Flynn, Dennis and Arturo Giraldez. 1996. China and the Spanish Empire. *Revista de Historia Economica* 14 (2):309–38.

Frank, Andre Gunder. 1998. *Reorient: The Silver Age in Asia and the World Economy*. Berkeley: University of California Press.

Frank, Robert. 1985. *Choosing the Right Pond*. New York: Oxford University Press.

Frankel, Allen B. and John D. Montgomery. 1991. Financial Structure: An International Perspective. *Brookings Papers on Economic Activity* 22 (1):257–97.

Frank, Robert H. and Philip J. Cook. 1995. *The Winner-Takes-All Society*. New York: Free Press.

Franks, Julian and Colin Mayer. 1990. Capital Markets and Corporate Control: A Study of France, Germany and the UK. *Economic Policy* 5 (1):231.

Freeman, Chris. 1995. The National System of Innovation in Historical Perspective. *Cambridge Journal of Economics* 19 (1):5–24.

Freeman, Christopher and Carlota Perez. 1988. Structural Crises of Adjustment: Business Cycles and Investment Behaviour. In *Technical Change and Economic Theory*, edited by G. Dosi, C. Freeman, R. Nelson, G. Silverberg, and L. Soete. London: Pinter.

—— and Luc Soete. 1997. *The Economics of Industrial Innovation*. London: Pinter.

Frieden, Jeffry A. 1994. International Investment and Colonial Control: A New Interpretation. *International Organization* 48 (4):559–93.

—— 2006. *Global Capitalism: Its Fall and Rise in the Twentieth Century*. New York: Norton.

Friedman, Milton. 1962. *Capitalism and Freedom*. Chicago: University of Chicago Press.

—— and Rose D. Friedman. 1980. *Free to Choose*. New York: Harcourt.

Fujimoto, Takahiro. 1998. Reinterpreting the Resource-Capability View of the Firm: A Case of the Development-Production Systems of the Japanese Auto Makers. In *The Dynamic Firm: The Role of Technology, Strategy, Organization, and Regions*, edited by A. D. J. Chandler, P. Hagström, and Ö. Sölvell. Oxford: Oxford University Press.

Galbraith, John Kenneth. 1954. *The Great Crash: 1929*. Boston: Houghton Mifflin.

—— 1967. *The New Industrial State*. Boston: Houghton Mifflin.

Gambetta, Diego. 1988. *Trust: Making and Breaking Cooperative Relations*. Oxford: Blackwell.

Gereffi, Gary. 1990. Paths of Industrialization: An Overview. In *Manufacturing Miracles: Paths of Industrialization in Latin America and East Asia*, edited by G. Gereffi and D. L. Wyman. Princeton, NJ: Princeton University Press.

—— 1999. International Trade and Industrial Upgrading in the Apparel Commodity Chain. *Journal of International Economics* 40 (1):37–70.

—— John Humphrey, and Timothy Sturgeon. 2005. The Governance of Global Value Chains. *Review of International Political Economy* 12 (1):78–104.

—— and Donald L. Wyman, eds. 1990. *Manufacturing Miracles: Paths of Industrialization in Latin America and East Asia*. Princeton: Princeton University Press.

Gerschenkron, Alexander. 1952. Economic Backwardness in Historical Perspective. In *The Progress of Underdeveloped Countries*, edited by E. B. Hoselitz. Chicago: University of Chicago Press.

—— 1966. *Bread and Democracy in Germany*. New York: H. Fertig.

Giddens, Anthony. 1999. *Runaway World: How Globalisation Is Reshaping Our Lives.* London: Profile.

—— and Will Hutton. 2000. Anthony Giddens and Will Hutton in Conversation. In *Global Capitalism*, edited by W. Hutton and A. Giddens. New York: New Press.

Gilson, Ronald J. 2000. Globalizing Corporate Governance: Convergence of Form or Function: Stanford Law and Economics Olin Working Paper No. 192, and Columbia Law and Economics Working Paper No. 174.

Gintis, Herbert and Tsuneo Ishikawa. 1987. Wages, Work Intensity, and Unemployment. *Journal of the Japanese and International Economies* 1:195–228.

Glenny, Misha. 2008. *McMafia: Crime without Frontiers.* London: Bodley Head.

Goldin, Claudia and Lawrence F. Katz. 1997. Why the United States Led in Education: Lessons from Secondary School Expansion, 1910 to 1940. NBER Working Paper No. 5889.

Gomory, Ralph E. and William J. Baumol. 2000. *Global Trade and Conflicting National Interest.* Cambridge, Massa.: MIT Press.

Gordon, Ian R. and Philip McCann. 2000. Industrial Clusters: Complexes, Agglomeration and/or Social Networks? *Urban Studies* 37 (3):513–32.

Gordon, Robert Aaron. 1945. *Business Leadership in the Large Corporation.* Berkeley: University of California Press.

Gourevitch, Peter A. 1977. International Trade, Domestic Coalitions, and Liberty: Comparative Responses to the Crisis of 1873–1896. *Journal of Interdisciplinary History* 8 (2):281–313.

—— and James Shinn. 2005. *Political Power and Corporate Control: The New Global Politics of Corporate Governance.* Princeton, N.J.: Princeton University Press.

Goyer, Michel. 2006. Varieties of Institutional Investors and National Models of Capitalism: The Transformation of Corporate Governance in France and Germany. *Politics and Society* 34 (3):399–430.

Graham, Loren R. 1993. *The Ghost of the Executed Engineer: Technology and the Fall of the Soviet Union.* Cambridge, Mass.: Harvard University Press.

Granovetter, Mark. 1985. Economic Action and Social Structure: The Problem of Embeddedness. *American Journal of Sociology* 91 (3):481–510.

Grossman, Sanford J. and Oliver D. Hart. 1980. Takeover Bids, the Free-Rider Problem, and the Theory of the Corporation. *Bell Journal of Economics* 11:42–64.

—— ——. 1981. The Allocational Role of Takeover Bids in Situations of Asymmetric Information. *Journal of Finance* 36 (2):253–70.

Guerrieri, Paolo, Simona Iammarino, and Carlo Pietrobelli, eds. 2001. *The Global Challenge to Industrial Districts: Small and Medium-Sized Enterprises in Italy and Taiwan.* Cheltenham: Edward Elgar.

Guest, David. 1997. Human Resource Management and Performance: A Review and Research Agenda. *International Journal of Human Resource Management* 8 (3):263–76.

Guillen, Mauro F. 2003. *The Limits of Convergence: Globalization and Organizational Change in Argentina, South Korea, and Spain.* Princeton: Princeton University Press.

Guy, Frederick. 2005. Earnings Distribution, Corporate Governance and CEO Pay. *International Review of Applied Economics* 19 (1):51–65.

——. 2007. Strategic Bundling: Information Products, Market Power, and the Future of Globalization. *Review of International Political Economy* 14 (1):26–48.

—— and Peter Skott. 2009. Communications Technology and the Distribution of Income. *Journal of Income Distribution* (forthcoming).

Haggard, Stephan, David Kang, and Chung-In Moon. 1997. Japanese Colonialism and Korean Development: A Critique. *World Development* 25 (6):867–81.

Hall, Peter A. and Daniel W. Gingerich. 2004. Varieties of Capitalism and Institutional Compelementarities in the Macroeconomy: An Empirical Analysis. In *MPIfG Discussion Paper*. Köln: Max Planck-Institut für Gesellschaftsforschung.

——. eds. 2001. *Varieties of Capitalism: The Institutional Foundations of Comparative Advantage*. Oxford: Oxford University Press.

Hallock, Kevin F. 1997. Reciprocally Interlocking Boards of Directors and Executive Compensation. *Journal of Financial and Quantitative Analysis* 32 (3):331–44.

Hamilton, Gary G. and Nicole Woolsey Biggart. 1988. Market, Culture and Authority: A Comparative Analysis of Management and Organization in the Far East. *American Journal of Sociology* 94 (Supplement):S52–S94.

Harrington, Michael. 1972. *Socialism*. New York.

Harrison, Bennett. 1997. *Lean and Mean: Why Large Corporations Will Continue to Dominate the Global Economy*. New York: Guilford. 2nd edn.

Hart-Landsberg, Martin. 1993. *The Rush to Development: Economic Change and Political Struggle in South Korea*. New York: Monthly Review Press.

Hayek, Friedrich A. von. 1945. The Use of Knowledge in Society. *American Economic Review* 35:519–30.

Helper, Susan. 1991. How Much Has Really Changed between United-States Automakers and Their Suppliers. *Sloan Management Review* 32 (4):15–28.

Helpman, Elhanan and Paul Krugman. 1985. *Market Structure and Foreign Trade*. Cambridge, Mass.: MIT Press.

Henningsen, Roar Frode. 2000. Study of Greenhouse Gas Emissions from Ships: International Maritime Organization.

Herman, Edward S. 1981. *Corporate Control, Corporate Power*. New York: Cambridge University Press.

Hirschman, Albert O. 1958. *The Strategy of Economic Development*. New Haven: Yale University Press.

Hirst, Paul Q. and Jonathan Zeitlin. 1991. Flexible Specialization Vs. Post-Fordism: Theory, Evidence, and Political Implications. *Economy and Society* 20 (1):1–55.

Hirst, Paul and Grahame Thompson. 1999. *Globalization in Question*. Cambridge: Polity. 2nd edn.

Hobsbawm, Eric J. 1995. *The Age of Extremes: The Short Twentieth Century, 1914–1991*. London: Abacus.

Hollingsworth, J. Rogers and Robert Boyer. 1997. Coordination of Economic Actors and Social Systems of Production. In *Contemporary Capitalism: The Embeddedness of Institutions*, edited by J. R. Hollingsworth and R. Boyer. Cambridge: Cambridge University Press.

Hoover, E. M. 1948. *The Location of Economic Activity*. New York: McGraw-Hill.

Hoshi, Takeo, Anil Kashyap, and David Scharfstein. 1991. Corporate Structure, Liquidity & Investment: Evidence from Japanese Industrial Groups. *Quarterly Journal of Economics* 106 (1):33–60.

Hounshell, David A. 1984. *From the American System to Mass Production, 1800–1932*. Baltimore: Johns Hopkins University Press.

Howell, Chris. 2003. Varieties of Capitalism – and Then There Was One? *Comparative Politics* 36 (1):103–24.

Hummels, David. 2006. Transportation Costs and International Trade in the Second Era of Globalization. *Journal of Economic Perspectives* 21 (3):131–54.

Humphrey, John and Hubert Schmitz. 2002. How Does Insertion in Global Value Chains Affect Upgrading in Industrial Clusters? *Regional Studies* 36 (9):1017–27.

Huselid, Mark A. 1995. The Impact of Human Resource Management Practices on Turnover, Productivity, and Corporate Financial Performance. *Academy of Management Journal* 38 (3):635–72.

Hymer, Stephen H. 1971. The Multinational Corporation and the Law of Uneven Development. In *Economics and World Order*, edited by J. W. Bhagwati. London: Macmillan.

—— 1976. *The International Operation of National Firms: A Study of Direct Foreign Investment.* Cambridge, Mass.: MIT Press.

Iammarino, Simona and Philip McCann. 2006. The Structure and Evolution of Industrial Clusters: Transactions, Technology, and Knowledge Spillovers. *Research Policy* 35 (7):1018–36.

—— Ramon Padilla-Pérez, and Nick von Tunzelmann. 2008. Technological Capabilities and Global–Local Interactions. The Electronics Industry in Two Mexican Regions. *World Development.*

Ietto-Gillies, Grazia. 2005. *Transnational Corporations and International Production.* Edward Elgar.

International Energy Agency. 2008. *Energy Technology Perspectives.* Paris: International Energy Agency.

Iversen, Torben. 2005. *Capitalism, Democracy, and Welfare.* New York: Cambridge University Press.

Jacobs, Jane. 1984. *Cities and the Wealth of Nations.* New York: Random House.

Jensen, Michael C. 1986. Agency Costs of Free Cash Flow, Corporate Finance, and Takeovers. *American Economic Review* 76:323–29.

—— 1988. Takeovers: Their Causes and Consequences. *Journal of Economic Perspectives* 2 (1):21–48.

—— 1989. Eclipse of the Public Corporation. *Harvard Business Review* 67 (5):61–74.

—— and William H. Meckling. 1976. Theory of the Firm: Managerial Behavior, Agency Costs and Ownership Structure. *Journal of Financial Economics* 3:305–60.

—— and Kevin J. Murphy. 1990. Performance Pay and Top Management Incentives. *Journal of Political Economy* 98 (2):225–64.

—— and Jerold L. Zimmerman. 1985. Managerial Compensation and the Managerial Labor Market. *Journal of Accounting and Economics* 7:3–9.

Jessop, Bob. 1994. Post-Fordism and the State. In *Post-Fordism: A Reader*, edited by A. Amin. Oxford: Blackwell.

Jones, Eric L. 1981. *The European Miracle: Environments, Economies and Geopolitics in the History of Europe and Asia.* Cambridge: Cambridge University Press.

—— 1988. *Growth Recurring: Economic Change in World History.* Oxford: Oxford University Press.

Jonscher, Charles. 1994. An Economic Study of the Information Technology Revolution. In *Information Technology and the Corporation of the 1990s: Research Studies*, edited by T. J. Allen and M. S. Scott Morton. New York: Oxford University Press.

Kalecki, Michal. 1968. The Marxian Equation of Reproduction and Modern Economics. *Social Science Information* 7:73–9.

—— 1971. *Selected Essays on the Dynamics of the Capitalist Economy, 1933–1970.* Cambridge: Cambridge University Press.

Kamnungwut, Weeranan. 2009. Varieties of Cooperation in a Developing Country: The Ceramics Cluster of Lampang, Thailand, Management, Birkbeck College, University of London, London.

Kanigel, Robert. 1997. *The One Best Way: Frederick Winslow Taylor and the Enigma of Efficiency.* New York: Viking.

Kelly, John. 1998. *Rethinking Industrial Relations: Mobilization, Collectivism and Long Waves.* London: Routledge.

Kenney, Martin and Richard Florida. 1994. Japanese Maquilddoras – Production Organization and Global Commodity Chains. *World Development* 22 (1):27–44.

―― ―― 1995. The Transfer of Japanese Management Styles in Two US Transplant Industries – Autos and Electronics. *Journal of Management Studies* 32 (6):789–802.

Kenney, Martin and John Seely-Brown, eds. 2000. *Understanding the Silicon Valley: The Anatomy of an Entrepreneurial Region.* Palo Alto: Stanford University Press.

Keynes, John Maynard. 1920. *The Economic Consequences of the Peace.* New York: Harcourt Brace Jovanovich.

Kim, Jong Il and Lawrence J Lau. 1994. The Sources of Economic Growth in the East Asian Newly Industrialized Economies. *Journal of the Japanese and International Economies* 8:235–71.

Kindleberger, Charles P. 1973. *The World in Depression, 1929–1939.* Berkeley and Los Angeles: University of California Press.

―― 1975. The Rise of Free Trade in Western Europe. *Journal of Economic History* 35 (1):20–55.

―― 1981. Dominance and Leadership in the International Economy: Exploitation, Public Goods, and Free Rides. *International Studies Quarterly* 25:242–54.

Kindleberger, Charles P. 1986. Hierarchy Vs. Inertial Cooperation. *International Organization* 40:841–47.

Kinzer, Stephen. 2006. *Overthrow: America's Century of Regime Change from Hawaii to Iraq.* New York: Times Books.

Kirschbaum, Erik. 2008. Slower Boats to China as Ship Owners Save Fuel. *Reuters* January 20.

Knickerbocker, F. T. 1973. Oligopolistic Reaction and Multinational Enterprise: Division of Research, Graduate School of Business Administration, Harvard University, Cambridge, Massachusetts.

Kogut, Bruce and Udo Zander. 1993. Knowledge of the Firm and the Evolutionary Theory of the Multi-National Corporation. *Journal of International Business Studies* (4):625–45.

Kohli, Atul. 1994. Where Do High Growth Political Economies Come From? The Japanese Lineage of Korea's "Developmental State". *World Development* 22 (9):1269–93.

―― 1997. Japanese Colonialism and Korean Development: A Reply. *World Development* 25 (6):838–88.

―― 2004. *State-Directed Development: Political Power and Industrialization in the Global Periphery.* New York: Cambridge University Press.

Konzelmann, Suzanne and Robert Forrant. 2002. Creative Work Systems in Destructive Markets. In *Systems of Production: Markets, Organisations and Performance*, edited by B. Burchell, S. Deakin, J. Michie, and J. Rubery. London: Routledge.

Kotz, David M., Terrence McDonough, and Michael R. Reich. 1994. *Social Structures of Accumulation: The Political Economy of Growth and Crisis.* Cambridge: Cambridge University Press.

Krasner, Stephen D. 1976. State Power and the Structure of International Trade. *World Politics* 28 (3):317–47.

Krueger, Anne O. 1974. The Political Economy of the Rent-Seeking Society. *American Economic Review* 64 (3):291–303.

―― 1980. Trade Policy as an Input to Development. *American Economic Review* 70 (2):288–92.

Krugman, Paul. 1994. The Myth of Asia's Miracle. *Foreign Affairs* 73 (2):28–44.

―― 1995. Growing World Trade: Causes and Consequences. *Brookings Papers on Economic Activity.*

Kuhn, Thomas. 1962. *The Structure of Scientific Revolutions*. Chicago: University of Chicago Press.

La Porta, Rafael, Florencio Lopez-de-Silanes, Andrei Shleifer, and Robert W Vishny. 1998. Law and Finance. *Journal of Political Economy* 106 (6):13–55.

Lamoreaux, Naomi R. 1985. *The Great Merger Movement in American Business, 1895–1904*. Cambridge: Cambridge University Press.

—— and Daniel M. G. Raff, eds. 1995. *Coordination and Information: Historical Perspectives on the Organization of Enterprise*. Chicago: University of Chicago Press.

Landes, David S. 1969. *The Unbound Prometheus: Technological Change and Industrial Development in Western Europe from 1750 to Present*. Cambridge: Cambridge University Press.

—— 1986. What Do Bosses Really Do? *Journal of Economic History* 46 (3):585–623.

Lane, Christel and Reinhard Bachmann, eds. 1998. *Trust within and between Organizations: Conceptual Issues and Empirical Applications*. Oxford: Oxford University Press.

LaPorta, Rafael, Florencio López-de-Silanaes, and Andrei Shleifer. 1999. Corporate Ownership around the World. *Journal of Finance* 54:471–517.

Lazerson, Mark H. and Gianni Lorenzoni. 2005. The Firms That Feed Industrial Districts: A Return to the Italian Source. In *Clusters, Networks, and Innovation*, edited by S. Breschi and F. Malerba. Oxford: Oxford University Press.

Lazonick, William. 1991. *Business Organization and the Myth of the Market Economy*. Cambridge: Cambridge University Press.

Leamer, Edward E. 1996. Wage Inequality from International Competition and Technological Change: Theory and Country Experience. *American Economic Review* 86 (2):309–14.

Lee, Soo Hee and Taeyoung Yoo. 2006. A Dirigiste Form of Social Capital and Varieties of Capitalism: Elite Networks and Innovation Systems in France and Korea: Birkbeck, University of London.

Leite, C. and J. Weidmann. 1999. Does Mother Nature Corrupt? Natural Resources, Corruption, and, Economic Growth. Washington, DC: International Monetary Fund.

Leontief, Wassily. 1953. Domestic Production and Foreign Trade: The American Capital Position Re-Examined. *Proceedings of the American Philosophical Society* 97:331–49.

Levine, Ross. 2005. Law, Endowments, and Property Rights. *Journal of Economic Perspectives* 19 (3):61–88.

Levy, Frank and Richard J. Murname. 2004. *The New Division of Labor: How Computers Are Creating the Next Job Market*. Princeton: Princeton University Press.

Lewellen, Wilbur G. 1968. *Executive Compensation in Large Industrial Corporations*. New York: National Bureau of Economic Research.

Lijphart, Arend. 1999. *Patterns of Democracy: Government Forms and Performance in Thirty-Six Countries*. New Haven: Yale University Press.

List, Friedrich. 1856. *National System of Political Economy*. Translated by G. A. Matile. Philadelphia: Lippincott.

Lorenz, Edward H. 1988. Neither Friends nor Strangers: Informal Networks of Subcontracting in French Industry. In *Trust: Making and Breaking Cooperative Relations*, edited by D. Gambetta. Oxford: Blackwell.

Macdonald, James. 2003. *A Free Nation Deep in Debt: The Financial Roots of Democracy*. New York: Farar, Straus and Giroux.

Machlup, Fritz. 1962. *Knowledge: Its Location, Distribution and Economic Significance*. Princeton: Princeton University Press.

Maddison, Angus. 2007. World Population, GDP and Per Capita GDP, 1–2003 AD.

Maloney, William F. 2002. Missed Opportunities: Innovation and Resource-Based Growth in Latin America. *Economia* 3:111–50.

Malthus, Thomas Robert. 1986. *An Essay on the Principle of Population.* Hammondsworth: Penguin. Original edn. 1798.

Manne, Henry. 1965. Mergers and the Market for Corporate Control. *Journal of Political Economy* 73:110–20.

Manning, Alan. 2003. *Monopsony in Motion: Imperfect Competition in Labor Markets.* Princeton: Princeton University Press.

Mansfield, Edward E. and Helen V. Milner. 1999. The New Wave of Regionalism. *International Organization* 53 (3):589–627.

Manzano, Osmel and Roberto Rigobon. 2001. Resource Curse or Debt Overhang? NBER Working Paper No. 8390.

Marglin, Stephen A. 1974. What Do Bosses Do? *Review of Radical Political Economics* 6 (2):60–112.

—— and Juliet B. Schor, eds. 1990. *The Golden Age of Capitalism.* Oxford: Oxford University Press.

Marris, Robin L. 1963. A Model of the "Managerial Enterprise". *Quarterly Journal of Economics* 77 (2):185–209.

—— 1964. *The Economic Theory of Managerial Capitalism.* New York: Basic Books.

Marshall, Alfred. 1925. *Principles of Economics.* London: Macmillan. 8th edn.

Martin, Ron and Peter Sunley. 2005. Deconstructing Clusters: Chaotic Concept or Policy Panacea? In *Clusters, Networks, and Innovation,* edited by S. Breschi and F. Malerba. Oxford: Oxford University Press.

Marx, Karl and Frederick Engels. 1848. *Manifesto of the Communist Party.* London: Penguin. Republished 2002.

McCloskey, Donald N. 1973. *Economic Maturity and Entrepreneurial Decline: British Iron and Steel, 1870–1913.* Cambridge, Mass.: Harvard University Press.

McKeown, Timothy J. 1991. A Liberal Trade Order? The Long-Run Pattern of Imports to the Advanced Capitalist States. *International Studies Quarterly* 35:151–72.

Mintz, Sidney W. 1985. *Sweetness and Power: The Place of Sugar in Modern History.* New York: Penguin.

Miozzo, Marcela. 2000. Transnational Corporations, Industrial Policy and the "War of Incentives": The Case of the Argentine Automobile Industry. *Development and Change* 31 (3):651–80.

Mittelman, James H. 2000. *The Globalization Syndrome.* Princeton, NJ: Princeton University Press.

Montinola, Gabriella, Yingyi Qian, and Barry R. Weingast. 1995. Federalism, Chinese Style – the Political Basis for Economic Success in China. *World Politics* 48 (1):50–81.

Moore, Barrington. 1966. *Social Origins of Dictatorship and Democracy: Lord and Peasant in the Making of the Modern World.* Boston: Beacon Press.

Myrdal, Gunnar. 1968. *Asian Drama: An Inquiry into the Poverty of Nations.* Hammondsworth: Penguin.

Nadvi, Khalid. 1999. Collective Efficiency and Collective Failure: The Response of the Sialkot Surgical Instrument Cluster to Global Quality Pressures. *World Development* 27 (9):1605–26.

North, Douglass C. and Robert P. Thomas. 1973. *The Rise of the Western World: A New Economic History.* Cambridge: Cambridge University Press.

Nove, Alec. 1969. *An Economic History of the USSR*. London: Allen Lane.

O'Reilly, Charles A. III, Brian G. Main, and Graef S. Crystal. 1988. CEO Compensation as Tournament and Social Comparison: A Tale of Two Theories. *Administrative Science Quarterly* 33:257–74.

O'Sullivan, Mary. 2001. *Contests for Corporate Control: Corporate Governance and Economic Performance in the United States and Germany*. Oxford: Oxford University Press.

Ohmae, Kenichi. 1993. The Rise of the Region State. *Foreign Affairs* 72 (2):78–87.

—— 1996. *The End of the Nation State: The Rise of Regional Economies*. London: HarperCollins. Revised edn.

—— 1999. *The Borderless World: Power and Strategy in the Interlinked Economy*. London: Harper Business. Revised edn.

Olson, Mancur. 1965. *The Logic of Collective Action: Public Goods and the Theory of Groups*. Cambridge, Mass.: Harvard University Press.

—— 1982. *The Rise and Decline of Nations: Economic Growth, Stagflation, and Social Rigidities*. New Haven: Yale University Press.

Oreskes, Naomi. 2004. The Scientific Consensus on Climate Change. *Science* 306:1686.

—— Erik M. Conway, and Matthew Shindell. 2008. From Chicken Little to Dr. Pangloss: William Nierenberg, Global Warming, and the Social Deconstruction of Scientific Knowledge. Centre for Philosophy of Natural and Social Science, Contingency and Dissent in Science. Technical Report 02/08, London School of Economics and Political Science.

Ouchi, William G. 1980. Markets, Bureaucracies and Clans. *Administrative Science Quarterly* 25:129–41.

—— 1981. *Theory Z: How American Business Can Meet the Japanese Challenge*. New York: Avon.

Pagden, Anthony. 1988. The Destruction of Trust and Its Economic Consequences in the Case of 18th Century Naples. In *Trust: Making and Breaking Cooperative Relations*, edited by D. Gambetta. Oxford: Blackwell.

Parker, Mike and Jane Slaughter. 1998. Management by Stress. *Technology Review* 91 (7):37–44.

Passaro, R. 1994. Le Strategie Competitive Delle Piccole Impress Di Una Area Interna Del Mezzogirono. *Piccola Impresa/Small Business* 3:85–112.

Patel, Pari and Keith Pavitt. 1991. Large Firms in the Production of the World's Technology: An Important Case of Non-Globalization. *Journal of International Business Studies* 22 (1):1–21.

Pavitt, Keith. 1984. Sectoral Patterns of Technological Change: Towards a Taxonomy and a Theory. *Research Policy* 13:343–73.

Penrose, Edith T. 1952. Biological Analogies in the Theory of the Firm. *American Economic Review* 42:804–19.

—— 1953. Biological Analogies in the Theory of the Firm: Rejoinder. *American Economic Review* 43 (4, Part 1):603–09.

—— 1959. *The Theory of the Growth of the Firm*. New York: Wiley.

Perez, Carlota. 1983. Structural Change and the Assimilation of New Technologies in Economic Systems. *Futures* 15 (5):357–75.

—— 1985. Microelectronics, Long Waves and World Structural Change. *World Development* 13 (3):441–63.

Piketty, Thomas and Emmanuel Saez. 2003. Income Inequality in the United States, 1913–2002. *Quarterly Journal of Economics* 118 (1):1–39.

Pincus, Jonathan. 1972. A Positive Theory of Tariff Formation Applied to the Nineteenth Century United States: Stanford University.

Piore, Michael J. 1994. Corporate Reform in American Manufacturing and the Challenge to Economic Theory. In *Information Technology and the Corporation of the 1990s: Research Studies*, edited by T. J. Allen and M. S. Scott Morton. New York: Oxford University Press.

—— and Charles Sabel. 1984. *The Second Industrial Divide: Possibilities for Prosperity*. New York: Basic Books.

Polanyi, Karl. 1957. *The Great Transformation*. Boston: Beacon Press. Original edn. 1944.

Pomeranz, Kenneth. 2000. *The Great Divergence: China, Europe, and the Making of the Modern World Economy*. Princeton: Princeton University Press.

Porter, Michael E. 1985. *Competitive Advantage: Creating and Sustaining Superior Performance*. New York: Academic Press.

—— 1990. *The Competitive Advantage of Nations*. New York: Free Press.

—— 2000. Location, Clusters, and Company Strategy. In *The Oxford Handbook of Economic Geography*, edited by G. L. Clark, M. P. Feldman, and M. S. Gertler. Oxford: Oxford University Press.

Prahalad, C. K. and Gary Hamel. 1990. The Core Competence of the Corporation. *Harvard Business Review* 68:79–91.

Prichett, Lant. 1997. Divergence, Big Time. *Journal of Economic Perspectives* 11 (3):3–18.

Putnam, Robert D. 1993. *Making Democracy Work: Civic Traditions in Modern Italy*. Princeton: Princeton University Press.

Qiu, Lily. 2006. Which Institutional Investors Monitor? Evidence from Acquisition Activity: Department of Economics, Brown University.

Quadagno, Jill S. 1984. Welfare Capitalism and the Social Security Act of 1935. *American Sociological Review* 49:632–47.

Raff, Daniel M. G. and Lawrence H. Summers. 1987. Did Henry Ford Pay Efficiency Wages? *Journal of Labor Economics* 5:S57–S86.

Ramirez, Matias, Frederick Guy, and David Beale. 2007. Contested Resources: Unions, Employers, and the Adoption of New Work Practices in US and UK Telecommunications. *British Journal of Industrial Relations* 45 (3):495–517.

Ray, Debraj. 1998. *Development Economics*. Princeton: Princeton University Press.

Ricardo, David. 1817. *On the Principles of Political Economy and Taxation*. Cambridge: Cambridge University Press. Republished 1951.

Roberts, David R. 1956. A General Theory of Executive Compensation Based on Statistically Tested Propositions. *Quarterly Journal of Economics* 70:270–94.

Rodriguez, Francisco and Jeffrey Sachs. 1999. Why Do Resource-Abundant Countries Grow More Slowly? *Journal of Economic Growth* 4 (3):277–303.

Rodrik, Dani. 2006. Goodbye Washington Consensus, Hello Washington Confusion? *Journal of Economic Literature* 44 (4):973–87.

Roe, Mark. 2003. *Political Determinants of Corporate Governance: Political Context, Corporate Impact*. New York: Oxford University Press.

Rose, Andrew. 1991. Why Has Trade Grown Faster Than Income? *Canadian Journal of Economics* 24 (2):417–27.

Rosen, Sherwin. 1981. The Economics of Superstars. *American Economic Review* 71:845–58.

Rostow, Walt W. 1961. *The Stages of Economic Growth: A Non-Communist Manifesto*. Cambridge: Cambridge University Press.

Rowthorn, Robert E. 1977. Conflict, Inflation and Money. *Cambridge Journal of Economics* 1 (3):215–39.

—— 1992. Corporatism and Labour Market Performance. In *Social Corporatism: A Superior Economic System?* edited by J. Pekkarinen, M. Pohjola, and R. Rowthorn. Oxford: Oxford University Press.

Ruschemeyer, Dietrich and Peter B. Evans. 1985. The State and Economic Transformation: Toward an Analysis of the Conditions Underlying Effective Intervention. In *Bringing the State Back In*, edited by P. B. Evans, D. Rueschemeyer, and T. Skocpol. Cambridge: Cambridge University Press.

Sabbagh, Kark. 1995. *21st Century Jet: The Making and Marketing of the Boeing 777*. New York: Scribner.

Sabel, Charles and Jonathan Zeitlin. 1985. Historical Alternatives to Mass Production: Politics, Markets and Technology in Nineteenth-Century Industrialization. *Past and Present* 108:133–76.

Sachs, Jeffrey D. and Andrew M. Warner. 1999. The Big Push, Natural Resource Booms, and Growth. *Journal of Development Economics* 59:43–76.

—— —— 2001. The Curse of Natural Resources. *European Economic Review* 45:827–38.

Sah, Raaj K. 1991. Fallibility in Human Organizations and Political Systems. *Journal of Economic Perspectives* 5 (2):67–88.

Sako, Mari. 1992. *Prices, Quality, and Trust: Inter-Firm Relations in Britain and Japan*. Cambridge: Cambridge University Press.

—— 1997. Wage Bargaining in Japan: Why Employers and Unions Value Industry-Level Coordination. Centre for Economic Performance, LSE, Discussion Paper.

Sala-i-Martin, Xavier. 2002. The Disturbing "Rise" of Global Income Inequality. NBER Working Paper No. 8904.

Sarel, Michael. 1996. Growth in East Asia: What We Can and Cannot Infer. In *Economic Issues*. Washington: International Monetary Fund.

Sassen, Saskia. 1991. *The Global City: New York, London, Tokyo*. Princeton, N.J.: Princeton University Press.

—— 2000. *Cities in a World Economy*. London: Pine Forge Press. 2nd edn.

Saxenian, Annalee. 1990. Regional Networks and the Resurgence of Silicon Valley. *California Management Review* 33 (1):89–112.

—— 1994. *Regional Advantage: Culture and Competition in Silicon Valley and Route 128*. Cambridge, Mass.: Harvard University Press.

—— 1999. Silicon Valley's New Immigrant Entrepreneurs: Public Policy Institute of California.

Schelling, Thomas. 1960. *The Strategy of Conflict*. Cambridge, Mass.: Harvard University Press.

Schmitz, Hubert. 1995. Small Shoemakers and Fordist Giants: Tale of a Supercluster. *World Development* 23 (1):9–28.

Schor, Juliet B. 1998. *The Overspent American*. New York: Basic Books.

Scott, Allen J. 2002. A New Map of Hollywood: The Production and Distribution of American Motion Pictures. *Regional Studies* 36 (9):957–75.

Sell, Susan and Christopher May. 2001. Moments in Law: Contestation and Settlement in the History of Intellectual Property. *Review of International Political Economy* 8 (3):467–500.

Sen, Amartya. 1981. *Poverty and Famines: An Essay in Entitlement and Deprivation*. Oxford: Oxford University Press.

Service, Robert. 2004. *Stalin: A Biography*. Cambridge, Mass.: Harvard University Press.

Shaiken, Harley. 1994. Advanced Manufacturing and Mexico: A New International Division of Labor? *Latin American Research Review* 29 (2):39–71.

Shapiro, Carl and Joseph Stiglitz. 1984. Equilibrium Unemployment as a Worker Discipline Device. *American Economic Review* 74 (3):433–44.

Shin, Gi-Wook. 1998. Agrarian Conflict and the Origins of Korean Capitalism. *American Journal of Sociology* 103 (5):1309–51.

Simon, Herbert A. 1957a. The Compensation of Executives. *Sociometry* 20:32–35.

—— 1957b. *Models of Man*. New York: Wiley.

—— 1991. Organizations and Markets. *Journal of Economic Perspectives* 5 (2):25–44.

Singh, Ajit. 1971. *Take-Overs: Their Relevance to the Stock Market and the Theory of the Firm*. Cambridge: Cambridge University Press.

Skocpol, Theda and Kenneth Finegold. 1982. State Capacity and Economic Intervention in the Early New Deal. *Political Science Quarterly* 97:255–78.

—— and John Ikenberry. 1983. The Political Formation of the American Welfare State in Historical and Comparative Perspective. *Comparative Social Research* 6:87–148.

Smith, Adam. 1991. *The Wealth of Nations*. New York: Everyman's Library. Original edition, 1776.

Stern, Nicolas. 2007. *Stern Review on the Economics of Climate Change*. London: HM Treasury.

Stiglitz, Joseph E. 1974. Incentives and Risks in Sharecropping. *Review of Economic Studies* 41:219–55.

Stolper, Wolfgang, and Paul Samuelson. 1941. Protection and Real Wages. *Review of Economic Studies* 9:58–73.

Storck, John and Walter Dorwin Teague. 1952. *Flour for Man's Bread: A History of Milling*. Minneapolis: University of Minnesota Press.

Storper, Michael. 1989. The Transition to Flexible Specialization in the US Film Industry: External Economies, the Division of Labor, and the Crossing of Industrial Divides. *Cambridge Journal of Economics* 13:273–305.

Strange, Susan. 1992. States, Firms and Diplomacy. *International Affairs* 68 (1):1–15.

Streeck, Wolfgang. 1991. On the Institutional Conditions of Diversified Quality Production. In *Beyond Keynesianism: The Socio-Economics of Production and Full Employment*, edited by E. Matzner and W. Streeck. Aldershot, Hants, England: Edward Elgar.

—— and Kozo Yamamura, eds. 2001. *The Origins of Non-Liberal Capitalism: Germany and Japan in Comparison*. Ithaca, New York: Cornell University Press.

Sward, Keith. 1972. *The Legend of Henry Ford*. New York: Antheneum.

Taylor, Frederick Winslow. 1967. *The Principles of Scientific Management*. New York: Norton. Original edn. 1911.

Temin, Peter. 1976. *Did Monetary Forces Cause the Great Depression?* New York: Norton.

Thompson, William R. 1990. Long Waves, Technological Innovation, and Relative Decline. *International Organization* 44 (2):201–33.

—— and Lawrence Vescera. 1992. Growth Waves, Systemic Openness, and Protectionism. *International Organization* 46 (2):493–532.

Tilly, Charles. 1992. *Coercion, Capital and European States, AD 990–1992*. Cambridge, Mass.: Blackwell.

Todd, Emmanuel. 1976. *The Final Fall: An Essay on the Decomposition of the Soviet Sphere*. New York: Karz.

Tokatli, N and Ö Kızılgün. 2004. Upgrading in the Global Clothing Industry: Mavi Jeans and the Transformation of a Turkish Firm from Full-Package to Brand Name Manufacturing and Retailing. *Economic Geography* 80:221–40.

Uzzi, B. 1997. Social Structure and Competition in Interfirm Networks: The Paradox of Embeddedness. *Administrative Science Quarterly* 42 (1):35–67.

Van Alstyne, Richard W. 1960. *The Rising American Empire.* New York: Oxford University Press.

Visser, Jelle and Anton Hemerijck. 1997. *"A Dutch Miracle": Job Growth, Welfare Reform and Corporatism in the Netherlands.* Amsterdam: Amsterdam University Press.

Vollrath, Dietrich. 2007. Land Distribution and International Agricultural Productivity. *American Journal of Agricultural Economics* 89:202–16.

—— and Lennart Erickson. 2006. Land Distribution and Financial System Development. International Monetary Fund Working Paper.

Von Glahn, Richard. 1996. *Fountain of Fortune: Money and Monetary Policy in China, 1000–1700.* Berkeley: University of California Press.

Wade, Robert. 2003. What Strategies Are Viable for Developing Countries Today? The World Trade Organization and the Shrinking of "Development Space". *Review of International Political Economy* 10 (4):621–44.

Wallerstein, Immanuel. 1983. The Three Instances of Hegemony in the History of the Capitalist World-Economy. *International Journal of Comparative Sociology* 24 (1–2):100–108.

Waterbury, John. 1999. The Long Gestation and Brief Triumph of Import-Substituting Industrialization. *World Development* 27 (2):323–41.

Weber, Christopher L. and H. Scott Matthews. 2008. Food Miles and Relative Climate Impacts of Food Choices in the United States. *Environmental Science and Technology* 42:3508–13.

Weir, Margaret and Theda Skocpol. 1985. State Structures and the Possibilities for "Keynesian" Responses to the Great Depression in Sweden, Britain, and the United States. In *Bringing the State Back In,* edited by P. B. Evans, D. Rueschemeyer, and T. Skocpol. Cambridge: Cambridge University Press.

Weisskopf, Thomas E., Samuel Bowles, and David M. Gordon. 1983. Hearts and Minds: A Social Model of United States Productivity Growth. *Brookings Papers on Economic Activity* (2):381–450.

Weitzman, Martin L. 1970. Soviet Postwar Economic Growth and Capital-Labor Substitution. *American Economic Review* 60 (4):676–92.

Whitley, Richard. 1991. The Social Construction of Business Systems in East Asia. *Organization Studies* 12 (1):1–28.

—— 1992. *Business Systems in East Asia: Firms, Markets and Societies.* London: Sage.

Williamson, John, ed. 1990. *Latin American Adjustment: How Much Has Happened?* Washington, DC: Institute for International Economics.

Williamson, Oliver E. 1979. Transaction Cost Economics: The Governance of Contractual Relations. *Journal of Law and Economics* 22 (2):233–61.

Womack, James P. and Daniel T. Jones. 1994. From Lean Production to Lean Enterprise. *Harvard Business Review.*

—— —— and Daniel Roos. 1990. *The Machine That Changed the World.* New York: Macmillan.

Wood, Adrian. 1994. *North–South Trade, Employment and Inequality: Changing Fortunes in a Skill-Driven World.* Oxford: Oxford University Press.

World Bank. 2005a. *Economic Growth in the 1990s: Learning from a Decade of Reform*. Washington, DC: World Bank.

—— 2005b. *Equity and Development: World Development Report 2006*. Washington: World Bank and Oxford University Press.

Wright, Gavin and Jesse Czelusta. 2004. The Myth of the Resource Curse. *Challenge* 47 (2):6–38.

Yates, JoAnne. 1989. *Control through Communication: The Rise of System in American Management*. Baltimore: Johns Hopkins University Press.

Yermack, David. 1997. Good Timing: CEO Stock Option Awards and Company News Announcements. *Journal of Finance* 52 (2):449–76.

Yeung, Henry Wai-Chung and F.-C. Lo. 1996. Global Restructuring and Emerging Urban Corridors in Pacific Asia. In *Emerging World Cities in Pacific Asia*, edited by H. W.-C. Yeung and F.-C. Lo. Tokyo: United Nations University Press.

Young, Alwyn. 1995. The Tyranny of Numbers: Confronting the Statistical Reality of the East Asian Growth Experience. *Quarterly Journal of Economics* 110 (3):641–80.

Zysman, John. 1983. *Governments, Markets and Growth*. Ithaca, NY: Cornell University Press.

INDEX